THE AGE OF QUESTIONS

The Age of Questions

OR, A FIRST ATTEMPT AT AN
AGGREGATE HISTORY OF THE
EASTERN, SOCIAL, WOMAN,
AMERICAN, JEWISH, POLISH,
BULLION, TUBERCULOSIS,
AND MANY OTHER QUESTIONS
OVER THE NINETEENTH
CENTURY, AND BEYOND

HOLLY CASE

PRINCETON UNIVERSITY PRESS
PRINCETON & OXFORD

Published by Princeton University Press,
41 William Street, Princeton, New Jersey 08540

In the United Kingdom: Princeton University Press,
6 Oxford Street, Woodstock, Oxfordshire OX20 1TR

press.princeton.edu

ISBN 978-0-691-13115-3
Library of Congress Control Number: 2018938059

British Library Cataloging-in-Publication Data is available

This book has been composed in Arno Pro

Printed on acid-free paper. ∞

Printed in the United States of America

10 9 8 7 6 5 4 3 2 1

For the sui generis:
Itsie, Gene, and Sis
And for Tenure,
sine qua non

We don't labor under the illusion that it's possible to express everything at once, for truly not everything can be made sense of in a word. But with a little patience and attention, everything that can be known, even the most difficult mathematical questions, can be simplified and solved.

—SÁNDOR RŐNYI, WRITING ON THE HUNGARIAN QUESTION IN 1865, (MIS)QUOTES THE FOREWORD TO NEWTON'S *PHILOSOPHIÆ NATURALIS PRINCIPIA MATHEMATICA*

Why does one question impinge upon the other? Why does one evoke the other when there is no obvious connection between them? ... [A]ll the most important questions of Europe and humankind in our day are forever being raised simultaneously. And it's this simultaneity that is so remarkable. The necessary condition for these questions to appear simultaneously is what constitutes the riddle!

—FYODOR DOSTOEVSKY, *A WRITER'S DIARY* (1877)

Countless questions are on the agenda nowadays. [W]e speak and write so much about "questions," like the social or societal question, the woman question, the suffrage question, the Eastern question, the currency question, and also the religious question. Why?

—SLOVENE THEOLOGIAN DR. FRANČIŠEK LAMPE IN AN ARTICLE TITLED "QUESTION UPON QUESTION!" (1895)

[O]ne was always endeavoring to find *the solution* to *the question*, rather than accepting that many questioners will have many answers, that a philosophical question is merely a thinly veiled desire to receive a particular answer that is already implied in the question itself.

—OSWALD SPENGLER, *THE DECLINE OF THE WEST: FORM AND ACTUALITY* (1918)

CONTENTS

PREFACE

ζήτημα (Greek for "question")—"that which is sought" or "a thing not easy to find, of Pentheus' mutilated limbs" (Euripides, *The Bacchae*— They succumb to "the dementia and the delirium of a new god")[1]

—A GREEK-ENGLISH LEXICON

THIS BOOK WAS BORN of a question I could not answer. At a conference in 2008, I presented material from my first book, *Between States: The Transylvanian Question and the European Idea during World War II*. Paul Hanebrink, a great intellect and old friend, asked how the Transylvanian question related to others of the time, like the woman or the worker question. I was at a loss. Although I—like so many others—had written about questions myself,[2] I had never considered whether there was a family resemblance between the mass of geopolitical, social, economic/material, and scholarly questions that proliferated during the nineteenth and early twentieth centuries. What *were* they? And why were there so many of them? When were they first framed as "questions," and why did they beg a solution rather than an answer?

So I began to seek out scholars and thinkers who had taken this path before me. With the partial exception of Fyodor Dostoevsky, I found no one who had contemplated questions as an aggregate phenomenon with a history of its own. There are many good reasons why this is the case. One is that scholars who work on a particular historical problem or within a particular region or methodology might only concern themselves with one or two questions. International historians might encounter the Eastern or the Polish, but not the woman or the tuberculosis question. Jewish historians will have thought extensively about the Jewish question. Regional historians will know their regional questions: Kansas, Transylvanian, Macedonian, Irish, et cetera. Marxist historians will know about the social and the worker questions; historians of nationalism about the nationality question; historians of slavery about the (anti-)slavery question, and so on. Occasionally someone will show, as I did in a chapter of my first book and Wendy Brown did much better in an article, the relationship between two questions.[3] Rarely someone will wonder when it was that a particular question was formulated as such.[4]

On the whole, however, questions have been treated singly. The result is that historians—myself included—have viewed them very much as our protagonists did: defining them in accordance with our own criteria, assigning origins and a trajectory to them based on those criteria, and occasionally even offering "solutions" to them.

And yet there are many reasons why we may wish to take a broader view, especially in thinking about the extremely long nineteenth century (1770–1970). For one, questions were everywhere. From a spattering of references to the American and the Catholic questions in the mid-to-late eighteenth century, there followed a deluge in the nineteenth century. Thomas Malthus was among the pamphleteers to weigh in on the bullion question of the 1810s, and the Polish question was discussed at the Vienna Congress in 1814–1815, where Napoleonic Europe was dismantled, as were the Turkish and Spanish questions at the subsequent congress in Verona in 1822.[5] Before long, a full-blown press brawl was underway over the best solutions to the Eastern, Belgian, woman, labour [worker], agrarian, and Jewish questions. These were folded into "larger" ones, like the European, nationality, and social questions, even as they competed for attention with countless "smaller" ones, like the Kansas, Macedonian, Schleswig-Holstein, and cotton questions.[6]

The nineteenth-century drive to *settle* or *solve* questions reveals something essential about them: they were construed as problems.

The "question" had become an instrument of thought with special potency, structuring ideas about society, politics, and states, and influencing the range of actions considered possible and desirable. This potency is evident in another familiar formulation, one which nineteenth-century commentators arrived at quite early: the "definitive" or "final solution."

One effect of *the* Final Solution was that it appeared to break the ubiquity of the question idiom. In the decades that followed World War II, growing awareness of the Holocaust seemed to put an end to the heyday of questions. The formulation itself was presumed tainted. A few questions survived, emerged, or were periodically invoked: the Algerian, German, black, nuclear, gay, Israel-Palestine, and environmental questions, for example; in Turkey one can still speak of a Kurdish question, and even call it "the Eastern question." But for the most part questions have become the stuff of historical monographs or other forms of retrospective analysis. Nowadays we speak of "resolving issues" or "crises" in the international and domestic political spheres, or engage in scholarly or public "debates" on matters of culture, as opposed to "solving questions."

Perhaps this is why Vladimir Putin's reference to the Ukrainian question in 2014 did not arouse much interest: we no longer live in an age of questions.[7] And yet the *New York Times* has recently reported on the "French question";[8] the Scottish referendum and Brexit have reintroduced the "English," "Irish," and "Catalonian" questions;[9] and the "migrant (refugee) question" now regularly haunts European headlines.[10] Could it be that we are now on the cusp of another age of questions? If so, we might do well to consider what the first one wrought.

A Quest

The deepest roots of the word for "question" in Latin and Greek both contain the interrogative sense of question, and the question as problem. Yet they also conceal within them another meaning.

In Greek ζήτημα also means "that which is sought," and in Latin, *quæro* means not only "to ask" but also "to seek"; we find the word *quest* built into *question*.[11]

Writing a history of the age of questions is appropriately a quest. It is a quest to find their origins and burial spots. An honest history of the age must reckon with the unlikelihood of definitively locating either. But sometimes when we go looking for one thing, we come upon something else. In my search for the origins and burial spots of questions, I came to see the structure of nineteenth- and twentieth-century social and political thought very differently. The chapters that follow seek to replicate the myriad ways of seeing that are individually inadequate, but in aggregate indispensable to attaining this curious vantage.

Finally, since a quest to find origins and endings is partly a quest to better fathom the world we inhabit, each chapter poses anew the question of relevance to our time: how forcefully or subtly has the age of questions left its mark on our thinking and our condition? What of that age has disappeared, survived, or transmutated? Is it indeed part of the past, or are we still living in it? My intention is to make evident through historical inquiry something that generally requires a deft literary or artistic sensibility, namely, what Keats called "Negative Capability" ("that is when man is capable of being in uncertainties, Mysteries, doubts"), what Thomas Mann called *Ästhetizismus* (aestheticism), and why the writer Christa Wolf envied painters for their ability to show everything at once.[12] The arguments exist simultaneously, and the tension between them binds them together into a single whole, like the planks of a suspension bridge.

ACKNOWLEDGMENTS

A BOOK SUCH AS THIS, and for better or worse there are not many of them, owes a great deal to an international scholarly community—a republic of letters, if you will—and to institutions that place faith in scholars to push the boundaries of the thinkable, even if it means allowing them to bolt lemming-like into the abyss. It is not for me to judge whether my own trajectory tracks that of the lemming, but if it does, the fall has felt a great deal like flight thanks to a handful of people who have made writing it seem an especially worthwhile endeavor. I would like to acknowledge them first. Michael Gordin, Bahareh Rashidi, John Palattella, Ondřej Slačálek, Mary Gluck, Norman Naimark, Pavel Barša, and Joachim von Puttkamer all read the manuscript in its entirety (in some cases more than once) and offered their advice and encouragement. I owe a special debt of gratitude to Joachim von Puttkamer, who has offered feedback on everything from how to translate *Geistesartung* to the relation my analysis bears to Emmanuel Kant's idea of "universal history." Thanks to him and the others aforementioned, the project has steadily come into sharper focus. The work's remaining flaws are solely my own responsibility.

I have also benefitted from the encouragement, questions, and suggestions of a number of other scholars and friends, among them Martina Baleva, Samuel Moyn, Marci Shore, Tom Meaney, James Ward, Jan-Werner Müller, Erika Kiss, Danilo Scholz, Birthe Mühlhoff, Charly Coleman, Tamara Scheer, Dessy Gavrilova, Ivan Krastev, Corey Robin, Deborah Coen, Florian Bieber, Dietmar Müller, Natasha Wheatley, Balázs Apor, Lutz Niethammer,

Agnieszka Pasieka, Stefan Troebst, Robert Schneider, Evan Goldstein, Gábor Egry, Zsolt Nagy, Brett Whalen, George Giannakopoulos, Larry Wolff, Stephen Gross, Stefanos Geroulanos, Leslie Peirce, Dimiter Kenarov, Catherine Evtuhov, Vladimir Solonari, Leslie Butler, Bruce Pauley, Edin Hajdarpašić, Miloš Vojinović, Franziska Davies, Martin Schulze Wessel, Konrad Clewing, Edvin Pezo, Ulf Brunnbauer, Sabine Rutar, Natali Stegmann, Jan Goldstein, Bilyana Kourtasheva, Georgi Gospodinov, Jessica Reinisch, Susan Pedersen, the "Wiener Kreis," and the late and dearly missed Vangelis Kechriotis.

Most of this book was researched and written while I was teaching at Cornell, and I owe a considerable institutional and a truly outsized personal debt for those years spent among such extraordinary people. Among those who have offered substantive feedback, support, intellectual community, and/or comic relief while I worked on this project are Claudia Verhoeven, Isabel Hull, Jonathan Boyarin, Matt Evangelista, Robert Travers, Vicki Caron, Trevor Pinch, Leslie Adelson, Suman Seth, Camille Robcis, Enzo Traverso, Durba Ghosh, Duane Corpis, Oren Falk, Dominick Lacapra, Maria Cristina Garcia, Sherman Cochran, Valerie Bunce, Peter Katzenstein, J. Robert Lennon, Larry Glickman, Brian Hall, Richard Swedburg, the "Iron Circle" (most prominently Máté Rigó, Aaron Law, Chris Szabla, and Fritz Bartel), "231A-B" (Otto Godwin, Dara Canchester, and Niall Chithelen), and the people of Telluride House (to name just a few: Celina, Chinello, Albert, Stephen, Conor, Karl, Ehab, Alex, and Kevin), as well as Giorgi Tsintsadze, Sohyeon Hwang, Anton Cebalo, Alejandra Carriazo, Michael Mintz, Mwangi Thuita, the late Ann Wilde, and the many, many students over the years who have awed and inspired me with their incredible minds. To the staff of the History Department at Cornell, my friends Katie Kristof, Barb Donnell, Kay Stickane, Judy Yonkin, and Maggie Edwards, I am indebted for my (remaining) sanity.

I would also like to thank my new colleagues and friends at Brown University for thinking enough of the project to hire me, especially Omer Bartov, Ethan Pollock, Amy Remensnyder, Cynthia Brokaw, Mary Gluck, and Kevin McLaughlin.

As I was researching and writing the book, I benefitted greatly from a number of grants and visiting fellowships, including at the Imre Kertész Kolleg in Jena, the Center for European and Mediterranean Studies at NYU, the Institute for Human Sciences (IWM-Institut für Wissenschaften vom Menschen) in Vienna, and Birkbeck College in London. A Mellon New Directions Fellowship was the greatest honor and most inspiring series of opportunities one could wish for.

Some of my earlier thoughts on the "age of questions" have been published in *Modern Intellectual History* and the *Chronicle Review*, and I have given invited lectures on the project and received valuable feedback at several universities and institutions in the United States and abroad, among them the GWZO-Ringvorlesung at the University of Leipzig; the Modern Europe Colloquium at Yale; the Institut für Osteuropäische Geschichte "New approaches to Polish and East European History" series at the University of Vienna; the European University Institute (EUI) in Florence; two classes at Charles University in Prague; the Oberseminar zur Osteuropäischen Geschichte at the LMU in Munich; the conference "The Allure of Totalitarianism: The Roots, Meanings, and Political Cycles of a Concept in Central and Eastern Europe" at the Imre Kertész Kolleg in Jena; the lecture series of the Institut für die Wissenschaften vom Menschen (IWM) in Vienna; the opening of the the Centre for the Study of Internationalism at Birkbeck College in London; the Pauley Annual Lecture at the University of Central Florida in Orlando; the NYC History of Science Group; the annual convention of the Association for Slavic, East European & Eurasian Studies; the annual European Studies student conference at the College of William & Mary; the Cornell Jewish Studies Program Event Series; the Cornell Comparative History Colloquium; the Department of Science and Technology Studies colloquium series at Cornell; Cornell Adult University; the Chicago Transnational Approaches to Modern Europe Work-

shop at the University of Chicago; the "Visions of European Unity
Across the Twentieth Century" conference at NYU's Remarque
Institute; the Eastern Europe Workshop and European History
Workshop at NYU; the Ottoman Studies Lecture Series at NYU;
the New York Area Seminar in Intellectual and Cultural History;
the European History Workshop at Columbia University; the in-
terdisciplinary "Nineteenth-Century Group" at Dartmouth; the
lecture series "Eastern Europe in the World" at the University of
Pittsburgh; the WWI Symposium at the University of Wisconsin
in Madison; the International History Seminar at Georgetown
University; the conference on borderlands research sponsored by
the Harry Frank Guggenheim Foundation in Vilnius; the Zentrum
für Südosteuropastudien at the University of Graz; the Centre for
South-East European Studies at Queen's College in Belfast; Trinity College in Dublin; the Imre Kertész Kolleg colloquium in Jena;
the research colloquium "New Perspectives in Southeastern and
Eastern European History" at the Südost-Institut in Regensburg;
and a graduate course on nationalism in the Balkans at Boğaziçi
University in Istanbul.

A number of staff and friends in various countries and institutions have shown me great kindness, support, and forebearance,
without which this project would have been a great deal more difficult and less thrilling, among them Szilveszter Dékány, Diana
Joseph, Daniela Gruber, Raphael Utz, Stavroula Papagianni, An-
astasia Bolovinou, Róbert Pölcz, Ágnes Matuska, Kerim Erdoğan
(no relation), Müge Sökmen, Scott Sherman, Musa Güneş, Ana
Mohoric, Mary Kemle-Gussnig, Florian Rainer, and Maxence.

I am especially grateful to my various editors at Princeton University Press for their good nature and patience, and for letting me
keep the subtitle. Sincerest thanks to Brigitta van Rheinberg,
Amanda Peery, Kathleen Cioffi, the wonderful Plaegian (Play)
Alexander, and that god among indexers, Steven Moore. The feedback of the two anonymous readers was invaluable, and especially
that of Michael Gordin—no longer anonymous—who entered

into the soul of the project and saw an ingenious way to make it better.

For asking the Ur-question about questions, I thank Paul Hanebrink. And for everything else, my family—Linda, Tom (Sr.), and Tom (Jr.) Case, Christianne Hess, and Fergus Ryan—and *Canim*.

THE AGE OF QUESTIONS

Introduction

frage, *das worauf es ankommt, das wesentliche, der schwerpunct*: das ist die
frage, *darum handelt es sich, das musz entschieden warden.*
[*question*, that which matters, the gist, the focal point: *that is the question,*
that's what it's about, that must be decided.]

—SECOND ENTRY UNDER "FRAGE" IN THE
DEUTSCHES WÖRTERBUCH (GERMAN DICTIONARY)
OF THE BROTHERS GRIMM (1854)[1]

THIS BOOK IS STRUCTURED as an argument, not in the sense of
a claim or contention but in the sense of a dispute. Following an
introductory chapter with background on the peculiarities and
emergence of questions, I put forward seven distinct arguments
regarding the essence of the age of questions. Every chapter advances an argument of its own, but also engages in an argument
(dispute) with the others. Readers are invited not only to consider
the relative merits of the arguments but above all to gain a more
complete perspective on the age by viewing it from different van-
tages, like a town as viewed from a nearby hillside, from its sewers
and prisons, through the eyes of a child or a dandy, from a nearby
village, and from stories and songs about it. In the final chapter,
the analysis seeks to integrate all the arguments regarding the essence of the age into a single, higher-order one.

The chapters and their arguments are as follows:

The national argument is that the age of questions had a British imperial origin, but developed distinctly *national* attributes. It concludes with a case study on Hungary, which possessed both imperial and national status and ambitions, to illustrate the trajectory of the age.

The progressive argument views *emancipation* as the watchword of a fundamentally reformist and sometimes revolutionary age.

The argument about force is that *universal war* and *genocide*, the Final Solution, represent the fullest realization of the age of questions.

The federative argument proposes that the *erasure of boundaries* was the shared ideal of the age, elaborated through some of the same queristic tendencies that gave rise to genocide and emancipation.

In *the argument about farce*, the age of questions appears as a mischievous and often malicious *pretense*.

The temporal argument proposes that time was the *éminence grise* of the age of questions, for which *timing* was everything. Questions came and went, rose and fell, raised hell, mutated, and disappeared, but above all they were self-consciously *of their time* while straining to become timeless.

The suspension-bridge argument unites all opposites into one, mimicking an age that sought to do just that. Querists wanted to *span contradictions* between reality and an ideal, between timeliness and timelessness, between the universal and the particular. Their questions were a way of being in two places at once.

By design, certain pieces of evidence appear in different chapters to support divergent claims. The chapters also contain arguments that recur and are strengthened across the book. These overarching patterns can be summarized as follows:

The formulation "the x question" emerged slowly over the end of the eighteenth century and gathered momentum in the first decades of the nineteenth. Instead of being understood as questions to be answered, these were treated as problems to be solved. Some of the earliest questions were born in clusters during and after the Napoleonic Wars and were defined in opposition to their scholastic predecessors. Whereas scholastic questions were timeless, the "x question" was to be very much *of its time*. The formulation appeared in treaty negotiations, parliamentary debates, and related pamphlets, and Great Britain was very likely its birthplace. Querists soon emerged in France, the German states, the Habsburg Empire, and North America. By the second half of the nineteenth century, questions were being discussed and debated in nearly every language of Europe and beyond: into Tsarist Russia, the Ottoman Empire, Asia, Latin America, and Africa.

What I call the "age of questions" began in the 1820s and 1830s as a result of the expansion and politicization of press distribution, the enlargement of the voting franchise (in Britain), and a tight series of international events. These three developments gave rise to an international public sphere, the habitat in which questions thrived and proliferated. The attendant international events included: the Greek uprising in the Ottoman Empire (1821–1832), ultimately resulting in the independence of Greece; debates in the British parliament around the Bill for Removal of Jewish Disabilities (1830) and the reform act for the expansion of the voting franchise (1832); the Polish November uprising in tsarist Russia (1830–1831), crushed by tsarist troops; the Belgian Revolution (1830–1839), resulting in Belgium's independence; the French invasion and conquest of Ottoman Algiers (1830); the Mehmet Ali crisis in the Ottoman Empire (1831–1833), which resulted in the Great Powers coming together to prevent Ottoman collapse; and the July Revolution (1830) and the June rebellion (1832), which codified popular sovereignty in France.

Since questions were irritants that begged a timely solution, the age of questions had an allergy to the present. The many individuals who weighed in on questions—I call them *querists*—wanted change.[2] Being allergic to the present suggests movement *forward*, so the fundamental impulse of the age often *appears* progressive. But moving away from the present is not *inherently* progressive, nor were querists themselves.

Early on, querists had a fairly mathematical understanding of questions: they viewed them like math problems that could have only one solution, like $2 \times 2 = 4$. One-solution thinking implied that a question/problem could be solved once and for all, so querists sought a definitive or final solution. But not everyone agreed on whether something was a question/problem or not, and oftentimes querists created or wielded questions to serve a political purpose or personal gain, or accused each other of doing so. Certainly when querists made their interventions, they generally had a particular solution in mind, so they defined a question so as to make their preferred solution seem the more attractive or obvious. Part of defintion was assigning a date of origin. Birthdates were often chosen strategically to point to a particular definition, and hence solution, of a question.

The realm of questions was highly contentious and competitive: querists sought to raise the profile of their questions in order to draw attention to preferred solutions. Because querists generally worked backward from favored solutions, there were often as many different formulations and definitions of a question as there were solutions (or querists). The question: "What *was* the Eastern question?" might seem a simple one, and many seemingly straightforward answers have been offered, such as that the Eastern question was the matter of how to manage the decline of the Ottoman Empire. But since the "Eastern question" was defined by individual querists in accordance with their desired future, some defined the question/problem as the presence of Muslim Turks in Europe, for others it was Russian expansion, or Poland's right to exist, and for still others it was about the looming Apocalypse and the Second Coming of Christ. Querists deployed questions to stake out the terrain of the future. While there was overlap between some of their plots, such overlap was not common but rather disputed terrain. Assigning a singular definition to any given question belies one of querism's essential features; its competitive spirit.

Not everyone could create or weigh in on questions, but by the end of the nineteenth century, the number of querists swelled considerably, representing different professions, ages, genders, nationalities, and walks of life. Their interventions came mostly in the publicistic realm of newspapers and pamphlets but could also be found in government correspondence and parliamentary debate; there were even some periodic leaks of questions into poetry, fiction, philosophy, and scientific works. When this happened the publicistic boundary was often policed by other querists.

The publicistic habitat of questions was a function of their deliberate timeliness and urgency. As some lingered over decades and even a century, however, querists began to lose faith in final solutions and started to see questions as chronic or recurring. During the second half of the nineteenth century, the mathematical model was yielding to a medical one: the driving metaphor was no longer the mathematical problem or equation to be solved, but instead one of an illness to be cured or a biological condition, such as hunger, that could recur. This meant that a question periodically had to be addressed anew.

It was mostly around wars and periods of social and political upheaval that questions were most hotly debated and discussed, and when querists hoped for expedient solutions. At other times, a question might seem to recede or even disappear. The fickleness of questions resulted in a series of common strategies among querists: To gain attention or promote a particular solution, they tied their questions to larger ones and to ones that had been solved the way querists wanted theirs to be solved. Size mattered for querists, who often declared their questions to be of *Europe-* or *worldwide* significance and therefore "everyone's" problem. They also regularly cast questions as vital, a matter of life and death. In the words of Fyodor Dostoevsky, "a question like 'to be or not to be.'"[3] Querists also inserted urgency into these discussions by outlining what would happen if a given question were *not* solved in accordance with their wishes: common threats were violence, civic unrest, and war.

These strategies had four significant implications. First, insofar as questions were cast as vital, they were presumed to penetrate into multiple realms of human existence (science, religion, politics, metaphysics, economics, etc.). This meant that a solution had to be *fundamental* enough to penetrate into all those realms. Some querists argued, for example, that a solution to the social question would necessarily entail the creation of a whole new man, or that a solution to the Polish question would require the total reinvention of international diplomacy.

Second, insofar as querists bundled questions together and implied that one could not be solved without addressing or at least affecting the other(s), both questions and querists' wished-for solutions grew larger and more wide ranging, such that solving them was also presumed to require international cooperation.

Thirdly, as querists bundled questions together so that it seemed impossible to solve one without addressing the other(s), they often threatened a *universal* war if their questions were not expediently solved. Finally, since bundled questions were presumed to require a *Europe-* or *worldwide* solution, querists frequently proposed federation, or the elimination of borders, as the omnibus solution. Some even viewed the necessity of powers to act together to solve questions as the practical basis for such a federation.

In short, many querists threatened that if there was no omnibus solution, universal war would result. But in order to eliminate existing boundaries and create the conditions for federation, a universal war was required. So querists presented universal war as both a threat and a promise, an outcome to be avoided at all costs and the only means of achieving a desired outcome. The age of questions made the Great War *thinkable*. Querists also increasingly posited a relationship between the geopolitical questions of the East and the social questions of the West, arguing that changing a border in the Balkans to address the Eastern question, for example, could inflame the social question and precipitate a revolution in France.

The Crimean War and later the Great War entranced many querists, who believed that universal war would bring about longed-for solutions. After the postwar peace treaties of 1918–1920, a number of questions were considered "solved," at least in part. But the losers of World War I—dissatisfied with the status quo—became especially active querists during the interwar period. Hitler was one of them. He bundled questions together, insisting they needed to be solved together, and saw universal war and the elimination of boundaries as the path to the great omnibus solution (including but not limited to *the* Final Solution).

The most general characterization of the age, one that encompasses all of the aforementioned features, is that querists used questions to span contradictions. They often argued that a question/problem arose out of a contradiction, or a gap between a universal ideal and a particular reality. Queristic interventions were like large shoes devised to span the gap. They made it possible, in a sense, to be in two places at once. But like large shoes, they left an outsize footprint on the terrain of nineteenth- and twentieth-century history, such that the efforts of querists appear variously as poignant ambition, destructive hubris, and comedic vanity.

Prologue

QUESTIONS AND THEIR PREDECESSORS

All Ages (as if Athens had been the Original) have been Curious in
their Inquiries; ... there is no laying it aside till the whole Frame is
dissolved."[1]

—MEMBER OF THE ATHENIAN SOCIETY (1703)

THE INTERROGATIVE is as old as language. "Questions" are an
essential element of the Socratic method. In the late medieval and
early modern period, scholastics had their "quæstio(nes)," catechisms posed questions to offer scriptural answers, and the national academies that sprang up throughout Europe in the seventeenth and eithteenth centuries organized question competitions.
But in the nineteenth century a new kind of question came into
being, the shorthand for which might be given as "the x question."
Its proliferation was prodigious. Already in 1893 the Russian novelist Leo Tolstoy wrote with undisguised exasperation:

> I constantly receive from all kinds of authors all kinds of pam-
> phlets, and frequently books. [On]e has definitely settled the
> question of Christian gnoseology ... a third has settled the
> social question, a fourth—the political question, a fifth—the
> Eastern question.[2]

8

Beyond the nameless querists who beleaguered Tolstoy, many of the most prominent figures of the time put their pens to questions. Alexis de Tocqueville took on the Eastern, sugar, and fiscal questions; Victor Hugo and George Sand both wrote poems on the social question.[3] Karl Marx and Fyodor Dostoevsky addressed just about every major question; Frederick Douglass spoke passionately about the antislavery question; and the Czech philosopher and politician—and later first president of independent Czechoslovakia—Tomáš Masaryk wrote weighty tomes on the Czech and the social questions.[4] Even Tolstoy himself weighed in on the Eastern question through the character of Levin in the last segment of *Anna Karenina*.[5]

And the trend continued. More-contemporary works range from treatments of "Disraeli and the Eastern Question" to "Freud's Jewish Question" to the relationship between the Jewish and the woman questions.[6] It is difficult to stifle an intellectual yawn upon hearing the phrase "the x question," not because the formulation failed to elicit enthusiastic engagement but because there has been so much of it. Yet somehow we have not wondered: when and why did people start *thinking* in terms of "the x question," and what did it mean?

Definitions

The chapters that follow speak to a particular type of rhetorical formulation that takes the form "the x question" rather than simply any context in which the word "question" appears. Obviously there were "questions" well before the nineteenth century, and there were even a few of the form described above, but the central object of the present analysis is the emergence and spread of "the x question," which began in earnest in the 1830s, continued for more than a century, and has surfaced occasionally in public discussion and quite frequently in scholarship since.

Sharing a habitat in the nineteenth century and inspired by a set of historical catalysts that overlap with those that gave rise to "the x question" were the Russian "accursed questions" (What is to be done? Who is to blame? Whither Russia?[7]). Martin Heidegger's *Fragen* (*The Question Concerning Technology*) after the essence of things or Elias Canetti's "questioning" as "forcible intrusion" offer crooked-mirror reflections of the age, as well.[8] In the chapters that follow, various connections will be explored between some of the above and "the x question." Nonetheless, the reader should guard against conflating every nineteenth- and early twentieth-century appearance of the word "question" with the phenomenon here under scrutiny.[9]

Similarly, although the commodities and material questions, such as the corn, bullion, sugar, and oyster questions, share many common features with the great social and geopolitical questions of the time, the reader should not assume that all querists sought to forge a link between the tuberculosis question, for example, and the longed-for/feared "universal war." The temptation will be to hold every treatment of every question up to the generalizations derived herein, whereas nearly every discrete treatment of every question will fail to live up to generalization in at least one, often in multiple respects. The object here is to glean whether any recurrent patterns can be perceived across the aggregate of "x questions" that appeared in the nineteenth century. It will be for the reader to decide whether it was a worthwhile endeavor to seek such patterns and whether the results of that endeavor warrant further consideration. Far from the definitive work on the subject, the present analysis is but a first foray, which will hopefully produce refinements and corrections as more scholars bring their expertise to bear on the subject.[10]

Finally, on the problem of establishing the origins of particular questions: The astute reader will note that many of the issues discussed under the aegis of a given question—the Jewish question, for example—were discussed well in advance of the actual formulation of the "Jewish question" as such in the 1820s. The matter of Jewish emancipation was raised prior to and during the French Revolution and became an essential feature of many treatments of the Jewish question later on. This is true of many other questions, as well (the Eastern, slavery, woman, Polish, social, etc., questions).

Yet what you have before you is an attempt at a history of the *age of questions*, as opposed to a comparative history of individual questions and their predecessors. The implications of this distinction are as follows: the present work does not trace the content of questions except insofar as their content overlaps significantly with that of other questions of the time. Where the historian of a single question might rightfully consider what issues came to characterize it, and the parameters of the study might therefore justifiably "overflow" its formulation as a question in the temporal sense, this study wonders instead whether there was such a thing as an age of questions; when and why it began; what commonalities can be observed in the way questions were framed and discussed; and to what extent those commonalities hold across all "types" of questions (social, (geo)political, material/economic, scholarly/professional), across national or linguistic contexts, across persons who weighed in on them, across the political spectrum, and over the long century that marked their heyday.

The scope of the project is both very broad—spanning as it does over two centuries and numerous national, imperial, and continental contexts—and also quite narrow. Its narrowness is evident in its methodology; to compensate for the megalomania of the temporal and geographical scope, it chooses to reveal patterns rather than to explain why they emerged in each given context. Party politics and the exigencies of the French Left's, or the Russian Slavophiles', or the German Romantics' engagement with this or that question will be discussed very little or not at all. The reason is simple: because the emphasis is on commonalities across contexts, contextual particularities do not effectively account for why the Spanish and Czech literature should reproduce the same forms and tropes.

Yet context is still important. The chapters offer four loci of contextual particularity: the formal (by analyzing features that emerged within discussions of particular questions, such as the American, social, Jewish, Eastern, Polish, and nationality questions); the personal (with examples from individuals' engagement with multiple questions or with the spirit of the age); the national (with a case study on the "age of questions" in Hungary, as well as some sub-studies on questions' emergence in Britain and the forms they took in places like Russia, France, Germany, Austria, the United States, and Turkey); and the temporal (with a chapter on periodicity and pace in the way questions were discussed). Beyond these particularities, the reader will also find references to publicistic literature representing a variety of languages and contexts (French, Spanish, Russian, Polish, German, Italian, English, Romanian, Hungarian, Bosnian-Croatian-Serbian [BCS], Slovene, Slovak, Czech, Bulgarian, Macedonian, and Turkish), as well as archival sources from Austria, Bulgaria, Britain, Hungary, Germany, Turkey, Serbia, Romania, the United States, Slovakia, and Croatia.

The Reality of Questions

Historians have generally assumed there is a real essence to questions that can be historicized; that the woman question is about the emancipation of women, the social question about gross inequality, the Jewish question about the status of Jews in largely Christian societies and states, and the Eastern question about how to manage the decline of the Ottoman Empire. There is some truth in such general assessments, but it is also true that one essential feature of questions is that they have been chronically, indeed almost reflexively redefined.[11] Since the framing of a question was understood to determine its solution—a phenomenon I will discuss at greater length below—and since offering a definitive and therefore unique solution was the ultimate intervention, reframing or redefining a question was of first-order importance to the serious querist.

Whereas the German theologian Bruno Bauer wrote of the Jewish question that it was "just one part of the great and general question for which our time works on a solution," Karl Marx offered a "critique" of Bauer's Jewish question as a means of solving it; Walter Scott saw it as a component of the Eastern question that would be solved by Christ with the "personal reign of the Messiah," and Theodor Herzl defined it as a "national" question, one essentially about territory.[12] In other words, to borrow a phrase from Fyodor Dostoevsky writing on the Eastern question, "everyone conceives it in his own way, and no one understands the other."[13]

The same has been true of the Polish question, the cause of much reflection and lobbying, and the subject of a massive body of literature that generally assumes everyone knows, or at least should know, what is at issue with the words "the Polish question" (the irony of redefinition was that a new way of seeing a question also had to appear self-evident). Adding to the confusion is the development of a secondary literature about the Polish question, but wherein the author of a monograph or an article, rather than the individuals writing on the Polish question during the period under consideration, determines what is meant by the "Polish question."[14] Hence we find works—such as the 1905 book by a Russian scholar, Mikhail Petrovich Dragomanov, on *Herzen, Bakunin, Chernyshevsky and the Polish Question*— wherein those authors made few if any direct references to the "Polish question."[15]

A historian might wonder who lived in Poland, what those inhabitants' claims to national independence were, what their role in Europe was or should have been, what outsiders projected about Poland's future. But to suggest that the "Polish question" and its "solution" are identical to such considerations is to ignore the very obvious if somehow hitherto obscure fact: the Polish question, like others of the time, was like an arrow-shaped signpost, pointing to a particular querist's preferred "solution." There were certainly commonalities of content across a number of interventions on the Polish question, but if we probe only those commonalities—particular historical interpretations, claims or counterclaims to independence, heroes and villains—we lose sight of what bound the Polish question to other questions of the time and what the ramifications of *thinking in questions* were.

Beyond *Begriff*

The present study shares with conceptual history (*Begriffsgeschichte*) an interest in origins and changes in meaning over time. Furthermore, questions emerged squarely in the period (1750–1850) Reinhart Koselleck designated as a "saddle-period" (*Sattelzeit*), or period of transition wherein concepts emerged that were both abstract as well as future oriented, so studying them may serve to further establish the significance of that time.[16] Nonetheless, this is not a conceptual history, nor does the story follow the plotline laid out by Koselleck.[17]

That Koselleck and his coauthors did not view nineteenth-century questions as "concepts" is evident from their *Basic Concepts in History*, in which certain questions do appear but are taken to describe what the authors considered to be actual historical and political phenomena rather than *concepts*.[18] The present analysis does not place questions below the level of concepts—as Koselleck did—but rather above them, in that it shows how they were both changeable in accordance with historical events and conditions as well as connected to one another through the word *question*, which had its own implied trajectories and constraints. As such, the analysis owes more to Michel Foucault than to Reinhart Koselleck, although admittedly more to an unwitting slip of Foucault than to his ideas about language and structures. In the introduction to his famous essay "What Is Enlightenment?," taking Immanuel Kant's earlier essay by the same title under analysis, Foucault wrote,

> Today when a periodical asks its readers a question, it does so in order to collect opinions on some subject about which everyone has an opinion already; there is not much likelihood of learning anything new. In the eighteenth century, editors pre-

ferred to question the public on problems that did not yet have solutions. I don't know whether or not that practice was more effective; it was unquestionably more entertaining.[19]

He was referring to the eighteenth-century prize competitions run by national academies: academicians would formulate a question and anyone could submit an answer. The best answers were rewarded with publication and distinction (viz. Kant's answer to the question "What is Enlightenment?"). Although Foucault was not alluding to the emergence of nineteenth-century "x questions," the passage demonstrates how thinking in questions is a most peculiar kind of thought that effortlessly spans an abyss between two meanings. In the first part of the passage, Foucault speaks of *questions* requiring *opinions*, whereas in the second, of *problems* to be *solved*. The leap is considerable, and when even someone as sensitive to the subtleties of language makes it without reflection, its naturalness seems doubly affirmed. The history of the "age of questions" begins by wondering: what made this leap feel so natural?

Questions as Problems

The etymology of *question* in several languages reaches back to Latin, and the Latin back to Greek.[20] In those languages, as well as in the word's twelfth-century Middle French and Anglo-Norman incarnations, its meaning encompassed both "query, inquiry" as well as "problem or topic which is under discussion or which must be investigated."[21] These two meanings cohabitate in the words for "question" in French, German, Russian, and most other European languages.[22] There are some telling exceptions, however, which point either to the deep roots of the combined problem/question meanings (Greek) or themselves reveal the imprint left by the age of questions on modern languages (such as Romanian and Polish).

In Greek, the word used for nineteenth-century questions is ζήτημα (issue, matter) rather than ερώτηση (question), but the word ζήτημα also encompasses the meaning of "(object of) inquiry," from ζητέω, meaning "to inquire" or "to investigate."[23] Furthermore, ζήτημα is a synonym of πρόβλημα (problem), ερώτημα (question), and θέμα (subject, issue, matter, topic).[24] In Ancient Greek, the words ζητεύω and ζητίω were the equivalent of the Latin quæro, and ζήτημα was the equivalent of the Latin quæstio.[25]

The Polish word *sprawa*, the most commonly used translation of *question*—in the sense of "x question"—early on, is not identical to the word *question* in English because it means *only* "affair," "problem," or "matter."[26] Yet there is another word that came to be used later in Polish, namely, *kwestia* or *kwestya*, which is related directly to the Latin, French, and English words for "question" and shares their dual meaning insofar as it is a verbatim import from the Latin/French. This fact suggests that the word was endowed with its primary meaning in Polish *during* and *because of* the age of questions, for whereas in most languages the word for "question," with its slippage between "question-to-be-answered" and "problem-to-be-solved," is translatable and translated, this is only partially true in others, such as Polish, Spanish, and Romanian.

In these languages, the most common words for "question-to-be-answered" are *pytanie* in Polish, *pregunta* in Spanish, and *întrebare* in Romanian, whereas the words *kwestia* or *kwestya* (Polish),[27] *cuestión* (Spanish), and *chestiune* or *chestie* (Romanian) have been broadly used to refer to "x questions." In the case of Polish and Romanian, at least, these variants were likely imported from the French with the meaning of "issue," "problem," or "matter" precisely to accommodate the emergence of "x questions" in the nineteenth century. The definition of *chestiune* from a 1939 Romanian etymological dictionary thus included the following elucidation: "A question posed to clarify an issue. A proposal to examine, subject to discuss, matter/affair: *Eastern Question*."[28]

Certainly many before and since Foucault have propagated the conflation of question with problem.[29] Bruno Bauer's 1843 "Die Judenfrage" (The Jewish question) is generally translated as "The Jewish Problem,"[30] and Karl Marx, in his reflections on the Polish question as in the context of the 1848 Frankfurt Assembly, made the same substitution in the course of a single sentence: "As it is closely connected to the Polish question, the Poznan question could only be resolved if merged with the entirety of this problem."[31] An article from 1877 by the American journalist Edwin Godkin calls the Eastern question "the oldest existing problem in European politics"; and shortly after the end of the Great War, John A. Ryan, a priest and professor at Catholic University in Washington, DC, and one of his students, Reverend Raymond McGowan, published *A Catechism of the Social Question*. It begins:

> QUESTION: What do we mean by the social question?
> ANSWER: A *question* denotes a problem or a difficulty which demands solution.[32]

More recently, scholars writing on questions have continued the tradition of conflating "question" and "problem." The English translator of Dostoevsky's *Diary of a Writer* regularly swapped out the Russian writer's вопросы (questions) for the English *problems*.[33] Charles and Barbara Jelavich defined the Eastern question as "[t]he problem of the decline of Turkey and the diplomatic complications which ensued."[34] The late Ottomanist Donald Quataert summarized it as "how to solve the problem posed by the continuing territorial erosion of the Ottoman empire," and the historian L. Carl Brown called it "that very modern problem."[35]

Ennui and Excess

Part of the challenge of undertaking a history of "the age of questions" is that questions appear to exist within an untidy zone between historical phenomenon, period *Begriff*, and historiographical framework. Authors writing about questions in the nineteenth century speak of them as though they are real and clearly defined problems, but in doing so they are also actively seeking to *cast* them as problems to an audience they hope to excite and influence. Then come the historians, who have taken these period authors' books, articles, and pamphlets on a subject such as the Eastern question and made assumptions of their own about what the "real" question is or was, dropped in their own definitions, chronologies, and histories of a question, sometimes at the same time that questions were a regular feature in newspapers, pamphlets, and parliamentary proceedings.

Furthermore, because the Eastern question, the worker question, the Polish question, the Jewish question, et cetera, were the dominant preoccupations of entire fields of scholarship and political activism for decades, if not for over a century, reference to them invariably produces an involuntary historiographical ennui. In his epic history of Poland, *God's Playground: 1795 to the Present*, the historian Norman Davies wrote,

> For 150 years, the Polish Question was a conundrum that could not be solved, a circle that could never be squared. In that time, it generated mountains of archival material and oceans of secondary literature. For the historian of Poland, however, the Polish Question is a singularly barren subject.[36]

Davies' passage reveals how the sense of urgency, indeed *emergency* and feverish agitation that pervades much of the nineteenth-century writing on questions has a peculiar counterpoint: scholarly *ennui*. This work means to leave behind both urgency and ennui, which exude a smug knowing, in favor of simple curiosity, and to ask questions about questions to which we do not already have the answers.

Predecessors and Foils of Questions

Where did the questions of the nineteenth century come from? There are traces of many forms in them, from almanacs to debating societies and legal proceedings. Yet while "the x question" acquired traits from these ancestors, querists also defined their questions *against* the earlier scholastic questions and sought to make way for a new and above all timely form.

Scholastic and Practical Questions

The scholastic question, or *quaestio disputata*, played an outsized if largely invisible role in the age of questions. The *quaestio* was a method of argumentation based on Aristotelian rhetoric commonly used in the medieval universities from the twelfth to the seventeenth centuries. Figures such as Thomas Aquinas and William of Ockham used the method to teach science and medicine.[37] But most of the *quaestiones* were theological and philosophical, possessed of an expansive timelessness that was not easily reconciled with practical, earthly matters. (One other root of the word *question* is the Old English *cwestion*, as in "theological problem."[38]) Aquinas, for example, wondered about the existence of God, the origin of evil, and whether hope is a virtue.[39]

Meanwhile, medieval and early modern mystics wielded questions to suggest a realm beyond human knowledge. In 1620, the German philosopher and theosophist Jakob Böhme wrote his *True Psychology: Explained through Forty Questions*.[40] The questions were put to him by a Doctor Balthasar Walter, and pertained to everything from the essence of the soul to the involvement of the dead in the lives of the living. In the introductory comments preceding his replies, Böhme wrote that "it is not possible for Reason to answer to your Questions: for they are the greatest Mysteries, which are alone known to God ... You shall be answered with a very firm and deep Answer ... not according to outward Reason, but according to the Spirit of Knowledge."[41] The author demurred in the face of divine wisdom: only God knows, but sometimes God reveals his mysteries in unlikely ways, and the question and answer form could be one of them. Revelation—either through reason or through the "Spirit"—were the aim of both the *quaestio disputata* and the mystics' project.

Despite the deep etymological roots of the "question," it was not always or consistently the case that, as problems, they had to be "solved" rather than "answered." The scholastic questions discussed by figures like Aquinas and Ockham, as well as the catechisms that became popular during the Reformation, had questions and answers.[42] Yet with scholasticism in decline in the seventeenth century, questions were becoming more practical and timely than spiritual and timeless: they begged not an answer but a resolution or solution.

The linking of questions to *solutions* is apparent in English in the sixteenth century, and by the seventeenth was being more rigorously applied to "practical" questions.[43] In 1661, the English mathematician Noah Bridges published his *Lux Mercatoria*, offering "a more easie and exact Method for resolving the most Practical and Useful Questions than has been yet published." Bridges's "questions" included "the most Critical Questions of Reduction, Trucks, and Exchanges of Monies, Weights and Measures of Foreign Countries." The semantics of Bridges's work— which was republished in numerous editions over the coming decades—was that of questions to be "resolved" and the method was mathematical.

In effect, the *Lux Mercatoria* was a work of applied mathematics, wherein a number of challenging "questions" were "resolved at one operation."[44] Practice "questions" for the reader were referred to as "useful and pleasant questions to exercise and improve the Learner," with "answers" also given.[45] The exercises appeared after a section on "division," in which Bridges laid out the method of "proof" for a correct operation of division. The "proof" consisted of working backward from the solution. If the solution was correct, it would yield the original terms.[46] (Example: if you divide twelve by three, you can check your answer [4] by multiplying it by three to get twelve). You could derive a solution based on the rules of mathematical manipulation, and you could derive the terms from the solution.

In 1699, Gottfried Wilhelm Leibniz (1646–1716), destined to become the first president of the Prussian academy, wrote a pamphlet arguing for the election of Pfalzgraf Phillipp Wilhelm von Neuburg to the Polish throne. The pamphlet was written at the behest of his patron, the baron Johann Christian von Boineburg, "in the form of a mathematical demonstration which was supposed to convince the electors on the basis of clearly stated, stringent reasons for favouring Boineburg's preferred candidate."[47] In so doing, Leibniz was among those who opened the path to conceptualizing contemporary political and social issues as *problems* requiring mathematical-type *solutions*, and for which only one solution can be correct. The "practical" turn evident in the *Lux Mercatoria* and Leibniz's "proof" foreshadowed a characteristic of nineteenth-century questions that contrasted sharply with the timelessness of scholastic questions.

Nowhere is the contrast more clearly spelled out than in the debates surrounding the bullion question in Britain during the first two decades of the nineteenth century, relating to how Britain should materially back its currency in light of the expenditures of the Napoleonic Wars. By 1816, the regular treatment of the bullion question in the periodical press and pamphlets brought the English poet and historian Robert Southey to disparage the question, as well as the related corn and population questions as "the fleeting fashion of the day." [48]

> The same temper of mind, which in old times spent itself upon scholastic questions, and at a later age in commentaries upon the Scriptures, has in these days taken the direction of metaphysical or statistic philosophy. Bear witness, Bullion and Corn Laws! Bear witness, the New Science of Population! And the whole host of productions to which these happy topics have given birth, from the humble magazine essay, up to the bold octavo, and more ambitious quarto.[49]

Southey feared that the great scholastic questions were being supplanted by practical and timely ones. In the introduction to his *Principles of Political Economy*—written in 1819—the English scholar Thomas Robert Malthus responded to Southey's dismissal of the new questions, mounting a spirited defense of the new

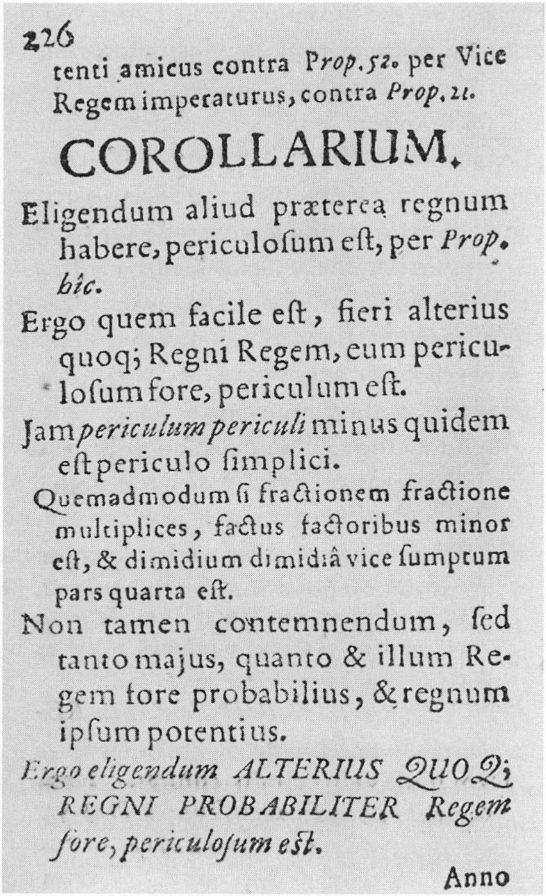

226

tenti amicus contra *Prop. 52.* per Vice
Regem imperaturus, contra *Prop. 21.*

COROLLARIUM.

Eligendum aliud præterea regnum
habere, periculofum eft, per *Prop.*
hic.

Ergo quem facile eft, fieri alterius
quoq; Regni Regem, eum periculofum fore, periculum eft.

Jam *periculum periculi* minus quidem
eft periculo fimplici.

Quemadmodum fi fractionem fractione
multiplices, factus factoribus minor
eft, & dimidium dimidiâ vice fumptum
pars quarta eft.

Non tamen contemnendum, fed
tanto majus, quanto & illum Regem fore probabilius, & regnum
ipfum potentius.

Ergo eligendum ALTERIUS QUOQ;
REGNI PROBABILITER Regem
fore, periculofum eft.

Anno

FIGURE 1. Page from Leibniz's *Specimen Demonstrationum Politicarum*,
which he organized as a series of propositions and corollaries, building
upon one another in the manner of a mathematical proof. Gottfried
Wilhelm Leibniz, *Specimen Demonstrationum Politicarum Pro Eligendo
Rege Polonorum, Novo scribendi genere ad claram certitudinem exactum* [An
essay on political demonstrations for choosing a king of Poland, completed
in a new style of writing for exact certitude] (Vilnius, 1669), p. 226.

political economy as a "practical" science, "applicable to the common business of human life."

> I cannot agree with a writer in one of our most popular critical journals, who considers the subjects of population, bullion, and corn laws in the same light as the scholastic questions of the middle ages, and puts marks of admiration to them expressive of his utter astonishment that such perishable stuff should engage any portion of the public attention . . . The study of the laws of nature is, in all its branches, interesting . . . but the laws which regulate the movements of human society have an infinitely stronger claim to our attention, both because they relate to objects about which we are daily and hourly conversant, and because their effects are continually modified by human interference.[50]

Timeless and universal questions were not to be the stuff of the nineteenth century; "the x question" was self-consciously *of its time*.

Querelle, querist, querulant

The scholastic *quaestio disputata* was—as its name suggests—a form of dispute, a pedagogical conceit of the medieval university crafted to buttress learning through argumentation and repetition. Appropriately then, one of the oldest questions was not a question at all but an argument, the so-called *querelle des femmes* as it was formulated in France in the sixteenth century.[51] The expression would eventually morph into the *question des femmes*, or woman question. It is noteworthy that the term *querelle* (dispute) should give way to *question* if we consider how period authors understood the semantics of questions.

In *querelle*, the largely outdated word *querist* (questioner) overlaps in meaning and application with the "querulant" (malcontent, troublemaker); the word *querist* in historical usage was often

preceded by negative-connotative adjectives such as *impertinent,
insatiable, troublesome.*[52] Over the nineteenth century the "querulant" also became a psychiatric and legal designation for a paranoid
person who obsessively feels wronged or driven to litigate.[53]

During the reign of "the x question," the querulous roots of
questions were well in evidence. In addition to being synonymous
with "problems," questions were also often synonymous with disputes requiring (or resisting) arbitration or mediation.[54] In a
poem from 1831, the Russian poet Alexander Pushkin referred to
the Polish question as "a dispute between the Slavs / A domestic,
age-old argument, too laden with fate / A question that is not for
you [Europeans] to solve."[55] And of the Central American question between Britain and the United States in 1856, the US secretary of state, William L. Marcy, wrote to his British counterpart:

> In a controversy like the present, . . . the matter should be re-
> ferred to some one or more of those eminent men of science
> who do honour to the intellect of Europe and America, and
> who, with previous consent of their respective Governments,
> might well undertake the task of determining such a question,
> to the acceptance as well of Her Majesty's Government as of
> the United States.[56]

Nineteenth-century literary questions—such as the Hamlet,
Shakespeare, Homeric, Madách, Toldi, and Ady questions—were
scholarly disputes; around whether Hamlet's "to be or not to be"
was about suicide or the thought-barrier to meaningful action,
whether Shakespeare/Homer/Madách truly wrote the works at-
tributed to them, whether the character Toldi in the nineteenth-
century poetic trilogy by János Arany was based on a real historical figure, or whether the leftist poet Endre Ady was a saint or a
devil.[57] Such literary disputes carried the mark of the earlier "*Querelle des Anciens et des Modernes*" (quarrel of the ancients and the
moderns) that unfolded in the French Academy in the last decade
of the seventeenth century and spread from there to Britain and

beyond, a quarrel over whether modern knowledge and culture could ever truly outstrip that of the ancients.[58] Some nineteenth-century questions were also designated "querelle," including the German question, occasionally referred to as *la querelle d'allemands*."[59]

Catechism

Beginning in the 1710s, the "querist" appeared as a malcontent in several publications on theological matters in Britain.[60] These interventions speak to another of the likely ancestors of questions, namely, the catechism. As noted above, the Old English *cwestion* meant "theological problem."[61] More pertinent to this analysis is the popular pedagogical role that the catechism played in disseminating religious doctrine, a function outlined by Martin Luther in his "Preface" to the 1529 *Small Catechism*. "Therefore I bid you all for God's sake, my dear lords and brothers, who are pastors or preachers, . . . to help us bring the Catechism unto the people, and especially unto the young."[62]

In 1742, the Unity of the (Moravian) Brethren published a "manual of doctrine" in English that included some telling reflections on the chosen form. Questions were put by the author, Nicolaus Ludwig Graf von Zinzendorf, with "answers" drawn from scripture. Zinzendorf explained the format: "We have reduced them into Questions. For we do not seek for Texts suitable to our Thoughts, but take our Thoughts from the Texts we read . . . This is our Methodus sentiendi. Way of Thinking."[63] The author denied asking questions to prove a point but appealed instead to the authority of scripture. In a subsequent introduction, Zinzendorf observed that some questions "were not always well enough adapted":

> [T]he Reason why they were so as they are, to be the great Attention I had to the Texts of Scripture; for the Questions arose

to me from the Texts of Scripture, and . . . I hastened to make short Questions between them, just to give the whole some Connexion . . . This Reason seemed of Weight; and I feared running into the common Fault, where the Texts are looked out for the Question's Sake; and it made me choose rather to leave my Labour unpolished, that the Holy divine Scripture might retain its native Splendor and Emphasis, and every Reader's Eyes might immediately fall upon the Texts.[64]

Questions, Zinzendorf insisted, came *after* and were *secondary* to the scripture. Yet by flagging the "common Fault," he admitted that it would always be tempting to start with a conclusion and work backward to the question, and ultimately who could tell if the querist was serving God's or his own ends? The quandary is one the age of questions inherited and could never fully resolve.

Furthermore, framing scripture as an "answer," hardly a novelty in the Judeo-Christian theological universe informed by Talmudic contemplation, necessitated the fashioning of a question. The author worked backward from the answer. In this way, the catechistic questions affected the realm of the thinkable by conditioning readers and listeners to expect an authoritative and definitive (which is to say, scriptural) answer. And catechisms were generally published in the vernacular, so laypeople could understand them and, ideally, also study them on their own. The revelatory and popular pedagogical character of many nineteenth-century interventions on questions is therefore at least partially traceable to the catechism.

Finally, it is perhaps also significant that Zinzendorf spared no criticism in passages regarding teachers among the ranks of men: "What do they chiefly amuse themselves with?" The answer from 1 Timothy: "Doting about Questions and Strifes of Words."[65] Here we recognize the malcontent, the *querist* as *querulant*, and a tension between the pedagogical thrust of the catechism (the text) and the manipulative rhetorical skill of the teacher (the person).[66] Later questions would carry unmistakable traces of this tension with authoritative texts (laws, treaties, etc.) as constant referents, often pitted against the skill of pamphleteers, politicians, and orators. Some queristic interventions would even assume the catechistic form explicitly.[67] The revival of *religious* catechistic works in the nineteenth century seems a significant conjuncture, as well, given the sprawl of catechistic thinking.[68]

Pamphlet to Palladium

The catechistic function of establishing what one *ought* or *ought not* do had a corollary in a body of seminal publications framed in a similar vein.[69] In mid-seventeenth-century Britain, publications began to appear on a variety of themes referring to the "grand" or "great" question. In 1643, an anonymous author published a short pamphlet titled *The Grand question concerning taking up armes against the King ansvvered by application of the Holy Scriptures to the conscience of every subject*.[70] Several other "grand" and "great" questions appeared over the coming decades, all of which set out to inform and influence the opinion of readers on a given issue.[71]

Among them were two pamphlets by Daniel Defoe (the author of *Robinson Crusoe*), each addressing "Two Great Questions." The first, from 1700, was on "What the French King will Do, with Respct to the Spanish Monarchy" and "What Measures the English ought to take." The publication elicited two written replies, to which Defoe responded. In 1707, he published a second pamphlet on "What is the obligation of Parliaments to the addresses or petitions of the people" and "Whether the obligation of the Covenant or other national engagements, is concern'd in the Treaty of Union?"[72] In both publications, Defoe laid out the terms of the discussion as questions, which duly implied the necessity of taking a particular action. Similarly, Montesquieu's 1748 *The Spirit of the Laws*, included a chapter on the "applications" of the text's ideas laid out in the form of questions (i.e., "It is a question, whether the laws ought to oblige a subject to accept of a public employment.")

to which the author provided his own proscriptive answer (yes, in a republic, no, in a monarchy) based on the "general principles" outlined in the text.[73]

Another likely forerunner of later questions was the periodical the *Athenian Mercury*—out of which was compiled the *Athenian Oracle*, the *British Apollo,* and later the *Palladium*—featuring a querist as problem- or riddle-maker, or a reader submitting a question to an anonymous "Informer" (who assumed the identity of the god Apollo). In these works, "querist" was a neutral and largely descriptive designation, as in the later Reverend George Berkeley, Lord Bishop of Cloyne's *The Querist: Containing Several Queries, Proposed to the Consideration of the Public,* which first appeared in 1735.[74]

The history of the *Athenian Mercury* dates back to 1691, when a London publicist founded the Athenian Society of scholars, whose members answered questions submitted by readers to a popular periodical by that title.[75] Beginning in 1703, the Athenian Society of London published *The Athenian Oracle Being an Entire Collection of All the Valuable Questions and Answers in the Old Athenian Mercuries.* In its first run, the *Oracle* explained its *raison d'être* as follows:

> The Design is briefly, To satisfy all *ingenious and curious Enquirers* into *Speculations*, Divine, Moral, and Natural, &c. and to remove those Difficulties and Dissatisfactions, that shame, or fear of appearing ridiculous by asking Questions, may cause several Persons to labour under, who now have opportunities of being *resolv'd in any Question*, without knowing their Informer.[76]

Like the catechism, the anonymity of the "Informer"—and the conflation thereof with the god Apollo, just as the query format self-consciously imitated the oracle at Delphi—implied authoritativeness and engaged in a form of popular pedagogy (an advice column *avant la lettre*). The questions in the *Oracle* covered a considerable range: "Whether it was a real Apple our Parents did eat

in Paradice?" (in a manner of speaking, an apple, or perhaps a fig);
"Where and when were Dials, Clocks and Watches first made?"
(ancient Egypt); "Whether it is better to live single, or to marry?"
(probably to marry); "Whether every Angel makes a Species?" (it
depends).[77]

*The British Apollo: Containing Two Thousand Answers to Curious
Questions In Most Arts And Sciences, Serious, Comical, And Humorous, Approved of by Many of the Most Learned And Ingenious of Both
Universities, And of the Royal-Society* first appeared in 1726, and was
based on a similar premise. It included questions submitted by
readers—some mathematical, others inquiring whether to marry
a maid or a chandler's daughter—all answered by "Apollo."[78] The
first *Palladium* appeared in 1752. Collectively, these publications
advanced by degrees the equation of social and other concerns
with mathematical problems or puzzles. Starting with the second
edition, the questions (queries) were submitted by readers, and
the answers/solutions were offered by someone with a pseudonym, implying that there was a different specialist answering
each one.[79]

"That the World is a Riddle has long been agreed, / Who solves
it an Oedipus must be indeed!" Such is the introductory verse to
the *The Gentleman and Lady's Palladium For the Year of our Lord
1753.* The verse opened a volume featuring "new ænigmas, queries
and questions" on a range of topics spanning from the causes of
sodomy to "[w]hether we are influenced to esteem and respect
men for their Riches and Rank they bear in the World, more than
for their innate Worth and Merit." These followed a section of
riddles (or "ænigmas") and were posed to the "Royal Oracle" or
"Querist," along with "questions" that amounted to mathematical
problems (puzzles) submitted by readers. Among the questions
put to the oracle the year prior and answered in the 1753 issue were
how to prevent robberies in London ("by mending the Morals of
the Common People"), whether general naturalization is desirable
(yes and no), and whether women should be allowed to wear
breeches (no).[80]

FIGURE 2. *The British Apollo: Containing Two Thousand Answers to Curious Questions in Most Arts and Sciences, Serious, Comical, and Humorous,*

THE
British Apollo:

Containing Two Thousand

ANSWERS
TO CURIOUS
QUESTIONS
IN MOST
ARTS and SCIENCES,

Serious, Comical, and Humorous,

Approved of

By many of the Moſt Learned and Ingenious of both *Univerſities*, and of the
Royal-Society.

Perform'd by a Society of Gentlemen.

IN THREE VOLUMES.

THE THIRD EDITION.

—————*Per me quod eritque, fuitque,*
Eſque, patet: per me concordant carmina nervis.
Inventum medicina meum eſt ; opiferque per orbem
Dicor ; & herbarum ſubjecta potentia nobis.
Ovid Met. Lib. 1.

LONDON:

Printed for THEODORE SANDERS, at
the *Bell* in *Little Britain*, and Sold by
ARTHUR BETTESWORTH, at the *Red*
Lyon in *Pater-noſter Row.* M,DCC,XXVI.

Approved of by Many of the Most Learned and Ingenious of Both Universities,
and of the Royal-Society, 3rd ed. (London: Printed for T. Sanders, 1726).

Debating Societies and Prize Competitions

The *Palladium* opened a venue in the public sphere similar to the one created by the London debating societies, a forum wherein literate individuals could discuss social, economic, and sometimes even political issues of the day. It was at these societies that the likes of Edmund Burke and William Pitt honed their oratorical skills. Debates were generally advertised as "rational entertainment" in the press, and as many as 650 people of various classes might attend a weekly session. In advance of the session, a question was chosen as the topic of debate, and a debate ended when the audience voted on a winner, sometimes only after several sessions in which any paying member could at least theoretically participate.[81]

In the sources relating to these societies, we find some traits they had in common with the later "x question." A pamphlet dating from 1753, titled *The Other Side of the Question. Being a collection of what hath appeared in Defence of the late Act, in Favour of the Jews,* claimed that

> [a] calm and impartial review of the nature and tendency of the inflammatory libels, which have been of late so industriously circulated through the nation, will enable us to discern, that it is the design of their authors to divert the attention of the public from the true state of the question; and by exciting disturbance in the nation, to accomplish the political schemes of some leading craftsmen in the ensuing elections.[82]

The promise to offer a "calm and impartial" intervention into a heated and overcrowded rhetorical field on a given "question" then before national government was to become a signature feature of the age.[83]

An article in a British daily newspaper from 1788, reporting on the topic of discussion at the Westminster Forum, suggests a link between the activity of the debating societies and the emergence of the later "(anti-)slavery question." "This Evening," we read on the cover of the *Morning Post and Daily Advertiser of London* from March 10, 1788, "the following adjourned Question will be debated: 'Can any political or commercial advantages justify a free people in continuing the Slave Trade?'" The article ended with the notice: "Gentlemen are particularly requested to attend, in order that they may hear the arguments on both sides, and their decision be the result of a fair and free Debate."[84] Though the debating societies were largely unique to Britain, it would not have been uncommon for a gentleman visitor to England from France to attend one or more of these debates—which took place several times a week—as they were a noteworthy spectacle of the time.[85]

A more geographically widespread venue in which questions were raised and discussed and "solutions" proposed during the eighteenth century were the prize competitions of national academies, which Foucault alluded to in his essay "What Is Enlightenment?"[86] These academies were founded mostly in the eighteenth and early nineteenth centuries (in London in 1660, Paris in 1699, Berlin in 1700, Petersburg in 1724, Prague in 1785, Budapest in 1825, Vienna in 1847[87]), and several of them held prize competitions on questions ranging from electricity and winches to using observations to determine the time, "natural inclinations," and "parental authority."[88] These competitions offered a forum for written interventions prompted by a theme or question. Many of the winning entries were published as pamphlets, a common format for the querists of later decades.

Official Venues

Finally, it is essential to note that official settings also lent their forms to the "age of questions." The terms *querelle*, *querist*, and *querulant*, for example, all bear relation to the language of legal procedure, and especially the trial, for much of the argumentation around questions drew on the language of trials and other legal proceedings: proving with evidence (facts and precedents), standing before courts, juries, judges, and the like.

An early pamphlet on the (Roman) Catholic question dating from 1805 speaks of bringing it before "a *Tribunal* and a *Public*" for due consideration.[89] "It will be for the public to judge," the anonymous author of an 1826 pamphlet on the West India question concluded, "whether [the statements and reasonings which appear to belong to a practical consideration of the West India Question] are not sanctioned by common sense and by the experience of history, and above all, whether they are not reconcilable with the true and genuine spirit of the Resolutions of the House of Commons."[90] An early treatment of the Polish question is tellingly titled *The Polish Question before the Court of the Sword and of Politics in the Year 1830*.[91] And in a book from 1863, a Polish nobleman from Russian Poland similarly addressed the "great court known as 'public opinion,'" and noted the status of the "question polonaise" as a "cause célèbre . . . with public opinion as jury and Europe as judge."[92]

But by far the most directly traceable origins of the nineteenth century's "x questions" were the proceedings of representative assemblies (above all, the British Parliament), treaty negotiations, and the official correspondence surrounding them. That story belongs to the age of questions itself, however, and thus to the arguments that follow.

1

The National Argument

THE IMPERIAL TO THE NATIONAL AGE

Denn eben wo Begriffe fehlen, da stellt ein Wort zur rechten Zeit sich ein.
[At the point where conceptions are lacking, a word comes to the rescue.][1]

—THE DEVILISH MEPHISTO TO A STUDENT IN
GOETHE'S *FAUST* (1808) CITED IN SÁNDOR RŐNYI'S
*APPROPRIATE PROGRAM FOR THE LEGAL AND PRACTICAL
SOLUTION OF THE HUNGARIAN QUESTION* (1865)

A Word-Making Age

"At the point where conceptions are lacking, a word comes to the rescue." This is a line from Goethe's *Faust*, which appeared in the first decade of the nineteenth century. The devil Mephisto is explaining to a student—in his devilish way—the opportunities afforded by sophistry and the uses of knowledge for personal gain. Words could possess a magical automatism (*sich einstellen*), the passage implies, offering an escape from failing concepts and perceptions. A word can *substitute* for understanding reality, or, more importantly, it can *create* a new reality ("with words a system can be built," the passage continues). Mephisto possessed the nineteenth century. This argument follows the word-makers.

———

Britain was the birthplace of the age of questions. A prehistory reveals both the centrality of Britain to the emergence and spread of questions, and the particularly British parliamentary stamp they initially bore. Many of the first "x questions"—the American, Catholic (later Irish), Carnatic, Oude, East India, and South American questions—touched upon the form and character of the British Empire and its relationship to the colonies. Later, with the treaty negotiations following the Napoleonic Wars, questions spread far and wide, and found their way into most corners of the globe. They would eventually acquire a different aspect in each language they entered, and each language nurtured its own unique spread of them. Examples from various national-linguistic contexts—German, Russian, Polish, Turkish, and American, to name a few—and a longer case study on the age of questions in Hungary reveal how distinct national contexts gave the same questions a very different character, or the way the same question was defined in comparison with or against the forms it took in other contexts.

An Imperial Prehistory of the Age

"The eighteenth century saw the evolution of the Parliamentary question," wrote the British historian P. D. G. Thomas. These were questions posed by parliamentarians to ministers on matters of policy that came to form the basis of debates around legislative decisions. By the end of the American Revolutionary War, they were an "established custom," Thomas observed. As these questions tended to center on perceived failures, shortcomings, or excess expenditures generated by government policy, it was likely this practice that contributed most directly to the emergence of the shorthand "the x question."[2]

Among the oldest of the "x questions" was the American question. It was a peculiar outlier; in its original form, it had already faded away before the age of questions truly began but later experienced several reincarnations. An early reference to the American question appeared in Thomas Pownall's *The Administration of the Colonies* from 1764.[3] Pownall, a former governer of one of the Thirteen Colonies, argued that "the Colonies, although without the limits of the realm, are yet in fact, *of* the realm . . . and therefore ought . . . to be *united to the realm*, in a full and absolute communication and communion of all rights, franchises and liberties, which any other part of the realm hath, or doth enjoy, or ought to have and to enjoy."[4] "The precise ground on which this dangerous question ought to be settled," wrote Pownall, was:

> how far they are to be governed *by the vigour of external principles*; by the supreme superintending power of the mother country: How far, *by the vigour of the internal principles* of their own peculiar body politic: And what ought to be the mode of administration, by which they are to be governed in their legislative, executive, judicial and commercial departments; in the conduct of their money, and revenues; in their power of making peace or war.[5]

Up until 1793, the American question surfaced mainly in parliamentary debates, albeit with a marked capriciousness of nomenclature, sometimes even within a single source. In 1774, Edmund Burke made mention of "American questions" in a speech before parliament;[6] in reference to a speech before the House of Lords from 1776 by Lord Temple, the editor(s) of a gentleman's magazine recounted Temple's remarks on "the grand American Question," "the question of sovereignty over America," and "debates on American questions."[7]

On the eve of the American Revolution, the American question was most frequently mentioned in parliamentary debates as the issue of how to address the intensifying calls of the Colonies for representation. On February 24, 1775, the British nobleman and military officer John Griffin Griffin charged many of his fellow parliamentarians with having "uniformly shrunk . . . from the great American question; they have wished to defer to the latest hour possible, all discussions of this critical topic," and determined to

offer his own views "[h]owever grating to the ears of some individuals the subject may be."[8] The tone of urgency (that delibera-
tion and action were overdue) and necessary irritation were to
become hallmarks of nineteenth-century questions.

Scientization, or the use of scientific metaphors to render a
question (and its solution) comparable to mathematical problems,
likewise appeared early. In a footnote to one of his sermons from
1769 published in an anthology more than two decades later, Richard Watson, Regius Professor of Divinity at Cambridge, noted,

> A little before the time when this Sermon was preached the
> Colonies had begun to resist the Mother-Country; and I well
> remember, that I, even then, when the American Question was
> scarcely understood by any person, thought the resistance of
> the Colonies so reasonable, that I hesitated in calling them—
> disobedient. I soon after examined the question to the bottom,
> and saw, as clearly as I ever saw a proposition in Euclid,—that
> Taxation without Representation, real or virtual, was robbery
> and oppression.[9]

By the time of Watson's footnote, most who mentioned the American question—including Watson himself—had concluded either
implicitly or explicitly that the American question was "at an end"
or "no more."[10] The Revolutionary War and American independence had "solved" it in the eyes of many earlier querists. Yet with
its origins in Parliament and partial reach in the press, the American question was a true ancestor of the "x question" mania in the
early nineteenth century.

In the last decade of the eighteenth century, the Catholic question made its appearance around the issue of Catholic emancipation then raised in Parliament.[11] In the young United States, a
couple of publications on the Mississippi question appeared in
1803.[12] A later wave of questions discussed in Britain included the
Carnatic, Oude, (East) India, corn, and bullion questions.[13] The
Carnatic and Oude questions emerged in the first decade of the
nineteenth century around the British East India Company's in-

tensifying and controversial involvement in two regions of India (Karnatak and Oudh). Both questions were subjects of intense parliamentary inquiry and discussion, as well as pamphleteering intended to influence public opinion and thereby also the outcome of parliamentary debates.[14]

In 1810, W. Huskisson, who was a member of the Bullion Committee, published a long pamphlet under the title *The Question concerning the Depreciation of our Currency stated and examined.* Although the phrase "bullion question" did not appear in the text, Huskisson did use the "question" formulation, not least of all to justify putting his views into print, "when the many evil consequences of an erroneous, or even an unsettled state of the publick mind upon a question of such vast importance are considered; I trust that I shall be justified in submitting, what was originally prepared for an indulgent and limited circle only, to the examination and judgement of a more extended and impartial tribunal."[15]

Huskisson's reference to a "more extended and impartial tribunal" is symptomatic of how querists would conceive of public opinion as judge or jury in the arbitration of questions.[16] Whereas the preliminary arbiter and forum for discussion of questions had been Parliament, in Britain, at least, the voting public was being called to enter the fray. Pamphlets, newspaper reports on parliamentary proceedings, discussions around expansion of the voting franchise, and the grassroots activities of political parties and debating clubs all contributed to making the fray an expansive one.[17]

In response to Huskisson's pamphlet, the Scottish politician and protostatistician Sir John Sinclair wrote that he had meant to defer propagating his own views on these "important subjects, until the question came to be discussed in Parliament, where the solidity of the arguments to be adduced on either side must ultimately be determined." But he now believed a more timely intervention was warranted:

> It seems to me . . . incumbent upon those, whose attention has been directed to such inquiries, to lay before the public, a clear

and explicit declaration of their sentiments on the subjects of coin and paper currency, and that with as little delay as possible, on two grounds, recognized by Mr. Huskisson; 1. The importance of the question; and, 2. The necessity of having it thoroughly considered, previously to its discussion in Parliament. . . . On the decision of that question depend, not only the interests and the comforts of every class of society, but the very safety and existence of this great Empire.[18]

Sinclair emphasized the magnitude and significance of the question as one demanding serious and urgent public attention; to ignore it would be a catastrophe for society and state alike. It was, he insisted, a matter affecting "every class of society." Adding to the sense of urgency was the rhetoric of ubiquity and threat of harm should no redress be sought and found.

In 1811, the report of the Bullion Committee was discussed in the British House of Commons by Lord Viscount Castlereagh and George Canning, among others, whose speeches were published as pamphlets and later reviewed in the periodical press.[19] While none of the speeches addressed the "bullion question" as such, like Huskisson before them, the "question" formulation, a parliamentary commonplace ("the present question"),[20] was in evidence. "The object of the right honourable gentleman is to settle the publick mind on a question on which there is great division of opinion," declared Canning.[21] "[O]ne cannot well imagine anything more fatally injurious to the prosperity of a state," said Castlereagh, "whose power in war, and whose advancement in peace so intimately rests upon its public credit, than having a question, such as this, hung up in suspense, to be debated from year to year, to the encouragement of the enemy, and to the dismay of our own people, and of those nations in the world who look up to us for protection."[22] The tenor of urgency to solve the question with alacrity *or else* became another common attribute of the way questions were discussed—within a broadly antagonistic genre that used the public sphere to poke and prod legislative bodies.[23]

The earliest explicit mention I have found of the bullion question dates from 1811. Yet although the phrase appears in the title of
Davies Giddy's *A Plain Statement of the Bullion Question in a Letter
to a Friend*, it does not appear in the body of the text.[24] The nearest approximation is on the first page, where Giddy sought to
"induce a wish, and afford a clue, for examining the Question
through all its details of documents, &c."[25] That same year, no less
a figure than the English scholar of political economy and demog-
raphy Thomas Robert Malthus employed the phrase *bullion question* in a review of Giddy's pamphlet and five others.[26] Again,
however, the phrase appeared in the review title, but not in the
body of the text.

Early commentary on the South American question (sometimes called the Spanish-American question[27])—which emerged
in the 1810s around independence movements in South America
during and after the Napoleonic Wars—mirrors the rhetoric put
forward in discussions of the bullion question: namely, that it was
a matter for "everyone." In a parliamentary intervention from 1817,
an MP declared that it "must be considered not as a mere South
American question, but as a European question."[28] Querists' drive
to expand the relevance of their questions did not simply reach
"down" to "every class of society," but also "up" to the level of European affairs and diplomacy.

The Congress of Vienna (1814–1815), meanwhile, brought several questions to prominence simultaneously. There are early references to *la question polonaise*, the maritime question, the Saxon
question, *la question napolitaine, la question jacobine,* and *la question
sicilienne* in correspondence between participants before and during the Congress and in the documents relating to the Congress
itself.[29] The very purpose of the Congress, wrote Russia's chief
negotiator Count Razumovsky to Prince Metternich in December
of 1814, was "that the questions be discussed and decided by mutual agreement."[30]

Outside the chambers of Parliament and European diplomacy,
the real flood of questions into the world of pamphlets, publicists,

and public opinion began in the 1820s. It can hardly be coincidental that it was during this same period, "[b]etween 1815 and the
Reform Act of 1832" in Britain, that "the parliamentary question
gained a new significance as a method by which public opinion,
as formulated over wider and wider areas, could be expressed."[31]
An early example was the West India question, which was mentioned in the London *Times* with considerable frequency starting
in late 1823, and often in connection with the emergent "(anti-)
slave(ry) question."[32] The publication in 1826 of a long pamphlet
on *The West India Question, Practically Considered* was timed to
precede a parliamentary decision on "what may be called the
'West India Question'" by stating that "the actual position of that
Question should be accurately examined and understood in all its
points and bearings" first.[33]

Questions began therefore as items put up for discussion in
representative assemblies or in the course of treaty negotiations
and votes on legislation. Through debates and competitions of
the national academies and debating societies, the periodical
press, and pamphlets, they became items of public debate and concern. A reference from an 1825 pamphlet by T. S. Winn further
clarifies the link between parliamentary debate and the form of
questions. Winn mentioned the British colonial secretary Earl
Bathurst's "speeches in the parliamentary debates on the Slave
question"[34] and offered an early example of question bundling:
"[T]he Parliament of Great Britain took so many years to debate
on the expediency of an Abolition of our Slave Trade with Africa,
the Emancipation of Ireland, the Abolition of Slavery throughout
our dominions, and other equally important questions of such
self-evident solution."[35]

In the discussion of the West India question, its parliamentary
ancestry, the "self-evident" or natural solution, and the bundling
of questions were clearly manifest. All these features would come
to characterize the age of questions. Moreover, Britain's particular
political and diplomatic culture had left an indelible mark on the

age. To the extent we can delineate such an age, it is largely from the attributes it acquired during these moral-political challenges to the expanding hegemony of the British Empire.

International Public Sphere

The eighteenth and nineteenth century saw the emergence of the public sphere, consisting of venues beyond the purview of the state where issues of the time could be discussed and debated.[36] Debating societies, clubs and organizations of various stripes, and the periodical press all contributed to its creation. The emergence of a public sphere was a crucial development in the history of questions, as well, but cannot alone explain their phenomenal reach and peculiar features. Any such explanation must take account not only of the exigencies of political and social interaction but also of international relations and diplomacy.

The early American, Catholic, Carnatic, bullion, and corn questions were domestic matters for Great Britain, at least for as long as the Colonies remained within the British realm. They were largely confined to parliamentary record, treaty negotiations, and pamphlets. The Congress of Vienna and its successor in Verona in 1822 changed all that. By the 1830s, the "(South) American question" (*question americaine*) was appearing regularly in the French Chamber of Deputies debates, in the French and Spanish press, in a history of the Hispano-American revolution, and in the correspondence of the Spanish diplomat and writer Francisco de Paula Martínez de la Rosa Berdejo Gómez y Arroyo.[37]

The internationalization of questions soon became part of their essence, such that by the end of the nineteenth century a typical intervention on the social question first delivered by the Italian patriot and writer Edmondo de Amicis as a speech to university students in 1892 was published the same year in Italian, German, Spanish, Czech, and French. Over the course of the next decade, Bulgarian, Polish, and Russian editions would also appear.[38]

Appropriately, Amicis had opened his speech by talking about what was new about the social question. Though the problems it described might be "as old as the world," he said, one novelty was the proliferation and widespread dissemination of periodicals.[39] The fate of Amicis's lecture came to embody his message. A full two years before his internationally famous novel *Cuore* (*Heart*, 1886) was translated into Czech, the Czech translation of his speech on the social question appeared in Prague in a relatively young periodical called *Athenaeum,* edited by the Czech philosopher and statesman Tomáš Masaryk.[40] Within a few years, Masaryk—who was already writing a book on the Czech question—would write his own work (seven hundred pages!) on the "social question."[41]

The age of questions delineates a period in which the public sphere was *internationalized.*[42] The emergence of questions—indeed, their coincident creation—with the formation of what I would call the *international public sphere* is traceable through querists' relationship to the periodical press and their interest in reaching the literate public, and to that end appealing above all to and through publicistic venues.[43] The translation and reprinting of the debates, proceedings, and speeches of societies, clubs, and representative bodies in the press was a crucial development in this regard. Much of this propagation was self-conscious and tactical.

An early example points to how the public sphere became an international public sphere. The slavery question (as such) likely migrated into French through digests of the British press in French newspapers during the late eighteenth century. An early reference to the "question de l'esclavage" is from February 1788, in a periodical digest of information from the British press. The article offers specific clues as to the method of dissemination, for it appeared in a reprint of a speech delivered on February 19, "[a]t a Society of Friends, assembled in Paris, to pray for the one instituted in London for the abolition of the slave trade."[44]

Writing on the worker question in 1864, the German Catholic theologian Wilhelm Emmanuel von Ketteler was already frustrated with the apparent obliteration of the distinction between party politics and press venues. "Our newspapers are written-down chamber proceedings, and our chamber proceedings are recited newspaper articles," he wrote.[45] The international public sphere also had designs on the distinction between foreign and domestic interests. In 1879, for example, a Romanian politician slipped substantial bribes to French papers to include articles reflecting the Romanian government's official take on the Jewish question.[46]

The National behind the International Public Sphere

But even as the public sphere became internationalized, questions themselves were becoming more national.[47] Three catalysts gave rise to these developments: a sharp uptick in and expansion of the role of diplomacy in policymaking during and after the Napoleonic Wars; the emergence and internationalization of "public opinion" through press venues regularly reprinting articles and the proceedings of representative assemblies from papers abroad, as well as the mobility and activism of those whose plight was wielded to shape "public opinion" during the period under consideration (i.e., Poles, Greeks, Bulgarians, Armenians, Jews, Irish, slaves, etc.); and a sense—also derived from the experience of the Napoleonic Wars—that "public opinion" was a force to be reckoned with and a means to influence policy for those on the "outside." These factors contributed in no small way to the creation of national and territorial states (Greece, Serbia, Bulgaria, Romania, Ireland) as well as intensely politicized territories (Kansas, Macedonia), which then often became national symbols and question farms of their own.

Putting aside for the moment the matter of material and commodities questions, there were two ways of being "outside" in the period leading up to the age of questions: geopolitically and socially. Geopolitically, states that had lost sovereignty or polities that aspired to gain sovereignty were on the outside of the state system. This category included, at various times and in various respects, Poland, the British Thirteen Colonies, the Spanish South American colonies, Greece, Belgium, Serbia, Russia, and the Ottoman Empire, to name a few. Questions formed around these entities in dense clusters, especially where their spheres of sovereign aspiration overlapped. Eastern and especially southeastern Europe acquired layers of questions three or four deep in places.

In the social and domestic political realm, questions adhered to "outsiders" that included Jews, slaves/Negroes, women, workers, peasants, gypsies, and a variety of national-ethnic and religious groups who for various reasons had limited access to influence over state policy. Considered in purely spatial terms, there is a peculiar symmetry in the vectors of social and geopolitical questions; if the matter is framed in terms of emancipation, it appears as though every group and entity to which a question adhered wanted *out*—Poles wanted out of Russia, Prussia, and Austria; Greeks and Serbs wanted out of the Ottoman Empire; peasants wanted out of feudal servitude, Jews wanted out of their ghettos, slaves wanted out of plantations.

But if the matter is framed in terms of *equality*, or the right of *belonging* to and participating in a system, then each of these cases can as readily be seen as aspirations to be allowed *in*—Poles, Greeks, Serbs, Russians, and Ottomans to be allowed into the European state system; Jews, women, slaves, and others to be allowed fuller membership in the state polities to which they were subject. These two ways of viewing the entities and groups that became questions are opposite but equally valid perspectives on the age of questions. One is about exiting a system, the other about entering it, but in both cases, the system itself must change to accommodate the loss and the gain. Insofar as the transformation necessarily affected both the "outsider" and the "system," internationalization was *both the desired result and the tactic deployed to achieve it*. This idea requires some elaboration with examples.

The existence of a public sphere depends on the presumption that "public opinion" exists and is a force of potential influence on the state. Yet either "outsider" positions lacked a native platform or their native platforms could not be wielded to effect changes in policy or sovereignty. Those who weighed in on the Polish question, for example, were generally of the belief that Poland's fate— whether it would reemerge on the map as a fully sovereign entity or be absorbed more perfectly into other states; whether it would become a force for international revolution or conservative reaction—would primarily be decided not in Poland but in Paris, London, Istanbul, St. Petersburg, and later also Vienna and Berlin. Turning public opinion in these places to favor a particular solution to the Polish question was thus comparable to or effectively *a form of* diplomacy.

Even at the Congress of Vienna, before the deluge of pamphlets on the Polish question began, the British foreign secretary Lord Castlereagh told the Russian tsar Alexander I that "the fame of the principal actors" at the Congress would depend on its success, and gently suggested to the tsar that his decisions would fare better "[i]f your Imperial Majesty should have publick opinion behind you."[48] The earliest pamphlets on the Polish question speak of the importance, indeed the overwhelming "force" (*Gewalt*) of public opinion.[49] And in the interest of keeping the question in the public eye in places like France and Britain, among the first undertakings of Polish exiles and would-be statesmen during and after the November Uprising were to send regular dispatches to the *Times*, the *Morning Herald*, and the *Morning Chronicle* in London; to establish (on November 24, 1832) The Literary Association of the Friends of Poland; and to enlist the aid of sympathetic British political writers to found a monthly magazine.[50]

Throughout the life span of the Polish question, but especially in the first decades after its emergence, commentators made repeated reference to the power of the press and Poles' influence on public opinion.[51] In Benjamin Disraeli's 1847 novel *Tancred*, the title character laments that "Parliament was never so great as when they debated with closed doors. The public opinion, of which they never dreamed, has superseded the rhetorical club of our great-grandfathers."[52]

Whether or not it was accurate, the belief was spreading that international public opinion had assumed the role of arbiter in matters of state policy and even diplomacy. "I raise my voice fearlessly before the high tribunal of public opinion,"[53] declared Leopold Leon Sawaskiewicz in a pamphlet from 1840 on the Eastern question as it related to the Polish question. Nor is it a coincidence that the Polish poet Adam Mickiewicz named his weekly magazine, the first issue of which appeared in Paris in 1849, *La tribune des peuples*.[54]

Through these interventions, the international public sphere was cast in the role of stern judge of the action and inaction of governments, a talisman wielded to preempt or shame representative bodies and governments. A French commentator wrote in the mid-1830s that "the Oriental [Eastern] question is one of the most important and urgent that the Press has ever yet been called upon to handle, our Cabinet alone feigns not to comprehend its weight."[55] An early mention of the "Jewish question" in 1830 referred to attempts on the part of letter writers to the London *Times* to influence public opinion in advance of discussion of legislation that would allow Jews to stand for Parliament.[56]

During the Crimean War (1853–1856), the exiled Polish aristocrat Count Walerian Krasiński went so far as to argue that "[a]lthough it may be premature for the cabinets of the allied powers to take up at this moment the cause of our national independence, it is by no means so for the public to discuss this question in all its bearings, because Poland must be reconstructed in the public opinion, before she is restored to the map of Europe."[57] And the British statesman William Gladstone, in his famously inflammatory 1876 pamphlet on *Bulgarian Horrors and the Question of the East* wrote,

> The House of Commons has in the main been ousted from that legitimate share of influence which I may call its jurisdiction in the case . . . [T]he nation will have to speak through its Government: but we now see clearly that it must first teach its Government, almost as it would teach a lisping child, what to say.[58]

Even, and perhaps especially, in autocratic regimes with strict censorship, as in the Russian Empire, public opinion was assumed to possess an almost magical power of which publicists were the primary custodians.[59] And silence was deadly. "All the European press is full of articles on the Polish question," we read in a volume of collected reflections printed in Moscow in 1867. "And are only we, Russians, to be silent when we are better acquainted with it than anyone?"[60] As is evident from the reference to the "European press," as well as from the languages in which appeals to public opinion were made, querists aimed to reach an international audience and questions traveled across national contexts through them.

That states and governments also perceived in the proliferation of pamphlets and newspaper articles around questions at least a periodic threat is evident from their efforts to censor them. Discussion of and debate on the American question effectively ceased in Britain in 1793, at the beginning of the French Revolutionary terror. For the Polish question, suppression was especially harsh in the partitioning states of Russia, Prussia, and Austria.[61] In Hamburg and other parts of Germany in the 1840s, if a work reached a certain length (twenty-one sheets [Bogen]), it was not subject to censorship. The law thus targeted brochures and pamphlets specifically. During times of political upheaval, such as the 1846 uprising in Austrian Poland, the squeeze intensified.[62] For the duration of the January uprising in Russian Poland in 1863–1864, the censorship regime tightened again. In Austria, starting in April 1862, and intensifying throughout the period of the uprising, several titles on the "Polish question" were banned for "high treason" or "disturbing the peace."[63]

States also regularly kept clippings of articles on contested questions published in foreign and rival countries. A folder created by the Ottoman Foreign Ministry in 1867, for example, kept "[p]ress clipping and letter full of ridiculous claims about the Eastern question and the Ottoman state from a French newspaper."[64] During the mid-1890s, a period of especially heated rivalry over the Macedonian question between Serbia and Bulgaria, the Serbian Foreign

Ministry kept press clippings on the question published in Bulgarian newspapers.[65]

Insofar as France, Russia, Germany, Austria, Britain, and the United States did have some power and interest in influencing the course and "solution" of the Polish question, for example, internationalization was a fact built into the question itself. But it was also a tactic; a successful querist had to make the case for the relevance and urgency of a particular question to an international audience. Recall that already in 1817 the South American question was being cast as "a European question."[66] And, in 1829, in the very first pamphlet on the Polish question, we read that "[t]he Polish interest is inseparable from that of Europe."[67]

Rechristening a question as "European" was so common a trope that by the 1830s, the aggregation of questions under the heading of "European questions" was an institutionalized practice. In 1837, the *Augsburger Allgemeine Zeitung* introduced a new regular heading to its readership: "European Questions and Problems." The editors explained the innovation as follows: "Under the heading of questions and problems we mean subjects in which the wellbeing and interests of Europe are heavily implicated, and we will focus on and observe particularly those that are currently on the agenda, or, as they say in parliament, on the table."[68]

Therewith the editors of the *Augsburger Allgemeine* posited a necessary link between European interests and questions, a move that required would-be querists to demonstrate a question's impact on "the wellbeing and interests of Europe." If before it had simply been a strategy of querists to make the case for broader interest in their respective questions, here it became a *necessity*, a prerequisite for entry into the international public sphere.[69]

National Questions

Even as the public sphere was becoming internationalized, it was often on the backs of expressly national questions, such as the Polish and Belgian questions. As the nineteenth century wore on, the continental and overseas empires started shedding subjects; after the Americans in the eighteenth century came the Greeks, Serbs, Bulgarians, and others. The nationalization of questions also meant they became sealed off in political and often linguistic contexts, such that even if they were in conversation with questions by the same name elsewhere (like the social or the Jewish question), they could take on a distinctly national character or simply disappear from, or never penetrate into, particular states and societies.

The exploration of a particular national context will render this phenomenon more visible. Hungary was both a constituent part of the Habsburg Empire as well as a consolidating nation-state, whose statesmen at least periodically sought independence from the empire. Many of them also saw their country as an empire builder itself, an "old" state with established traditions of statecraft, and nonetheless a "new" appearance on the map of Europe after the Great War. As one powerful half of the so-called Dual Monarchy (Austro-Hungarian Monarchy) after 1867, Hungary's political elite participated in some of the most important debates and decisions around the Polish and Eastern questions, in addition to the Balkan, Macedonian, and a number of other "sub"-questions. Furthermore, Hungary shared with Imperial Russia the experience of a battering imperial collapse and a Bolshevik revolution that intensified engagement with the social and nationality questions, as well as a breathtaking array of particular national-territorial questions around its perimeter, ranging from the Ruthenian to the Transylvanian to the Banat questions.

Furthermore, since these questions also engaged Croats, Serbs, Romanians, Slovaks, Ruthenians, and others, a Hungarian case study shows how initially domestic questions were *internationalized* even as they were nationalized by publicistic efforts and the shifting of the boundaries. Finally, the range of sources in which questions surfaced and were discussed is much greater than in many of the aforementioned contexts because Hungary had its own state administration and parliament for at least part of the century and a very active national academy, in addition to a vast array of printing houses and newspapers throughout much of the nineteenth century whose numbers only increased in the twentieth.

Hungary Enters the "Age of Questions"

Predecessors of the "x question" appeared in Hungary in the form of catechisms during the fifteenth and sixteenth centuries, mostly published with the aim of countering rather than propagating Protestantism. One from 1562, translated from the Latin, concluded, "We are not promoting the Evangelium invented yesterday. We are not bringing you knowledge that comes out of Wittenberg, Thuringia, nor Augusta [Augsburg], nor Geneva, but the faith of Saint Peter."[70] In the next century, several more catechisms and Protestant-debunking question books appeared in Hungarian.[71] One of these, a work claiming Catholicism as the true and first religion of the Magyars (Hungarians) and Lutheranism and Calvinism as disastrous for Hungary, even generated a counter-volume, whose author characterized the anti-Protestant querist (*kérdő* or *kérdezkedő*) as a troublemaker.[72]

At the beginning of the nineteenth century, there was a marked shift in the character of question publications. One featured jokes, many of them quite crude. (The most standard format for a joke is, after all, the question: e.g., "Why did the chicken cross the road?" etc.). Like the catechism, jokes and riddles are rhetorical questions: the answer is known in advance and the asking merely provides the occasion for the contest or the comedy, in which invariably a trick, a twist of logic or language, is involved. "What kind of tree is good for the lungs?" the title of the early Hungarian joke book wonders. "The joke" (the word for "joke," *tréfa*, contains the word for "tree," *fa*, in Hungarian, pun intended).[73] Also dating from this period is a question-and-answer book—originally published in French in 1762—on the theme of how to raise healthy, strong children. "It's a good time," the translator wrote, "for this

work, useful to other nations, to be so now to the Hungarian nation in Hungarian translation."[74] The trend toward domestication
(or nationalization) of questions thus arguably predates the age of
questions.

Hungary's entry into the age lagged somewhat behind that of
Britain and France but was very close to that of Germany and Austria. We find some scattered references in publications, letters, diaries, and speeches from before midcentury. As subjects of the
Habsburg Empire, educated and politically involved Hungarian
citizens tracked imperial preoccupations, most prominently the
Eastern question, in which the Habsburg Empire was deeply involved.[75] In a brief, wry diary entry from August 13, 1843, the Hungarian statesman and diplomat István Széchényi reported having
a headache, and then: "Conference sm. Casino. The most important thing in the world. Croatian question.—5–6 arrive very late.
Just about nothing gets done."[76]

The revolutions of 1848–1849, in the course of which Hungary
declared independence from Habsburg rule, brought a burgeoning of the periodical press and publicistic activity in Hungary
as elsewhere, in addition to precipitating friction between the
Magyar (ethnic Hungarian) revolutionaries and some of the leaders of other national movements (Croats, Romanians, Serbs) living in Hungary. The nationality question appeared at this time.[77]
Yet it was not until the second half of the nineteenth century, and
indeed in earnest in the 1850s and 1860s, that the age truly took off
in Hungary.

There are a few reasons why this is the case. Firstly, Hungary, as
part of the Habsburg Empire, did not *qua* Hungary participate in
the diplomatic negotiations around the fallout of the Napoleonic
Wars, wherein several geopolitical questions got their start; nor
was it a pleading plaintiff or emergent independent state at the
time, as was the case with Poland, Greece, and Serbia. That
changed after the 1848 Hungarian Revolution was crushed and its
leaders were executed or sent into exile. The revolutionary leader
Lajos Kossuth fled abroad and began delivering speeches and

appeals to whomever would give him an audience. In one particularly vitriolic speech he delivered in Britain, Kossuth charged Habsburg Austria with being a force that created, or at the very least aggravated, rather than solved questions.

> Let's take a closer look at all the historic great open questions that threaten Europe with unrest [*rázkódtatás*]. There is the Italian question. Who is responsible for its existence? Austria. If the "vampire" were not sucking on the Italian nationality, there would be no Italian question. There is the German question. Who is in the way of its solution? . . . Austria! Always and everywhere Austria. There is the Eastern question . . .[78]

Whereas Austria was the cause, Kossuth argued, an independent Hungary was the solution. Following the failed revolution, it was not until 1861 (briefly) and then again in 1865 that the Hungarian parliament reconvened, and the coincident publicistic deluge around questions confirms the link already discussed between parliamentary issues, public opinion, the rise of an international public sphere, and the emergence and proliferation of questions.

In 1865, Gusztáv Ádolf Ungár referred to the "flood of pamphlets" on the Hungarian question.[79] That same year, an anonymous pamphleteer on the Hungarian question set the goal of clearing up common misunderstandings and prejudices.[80] All kinds of pamphlets had appeared on the question, he wrote, such that a person would think everything had been said already.[81] The 1867 Compromise (*Ausgleich*)—which made Hungary a co-constituent partner in what was now called the Austro-Hungarian or Dual Monarchy, and lent it greater independent state-building capacity—assured the continuation of the publicistic boom.

An 1873 publication on the Muraköz (Međimurje or Medjumurje) question—ecclesiastical jurisdiction in the Međimurje region—highlighted this convergence, offering a compilation of several articles on the question drawn from the periodical press. The introduction noted how absorbed newspapers had been by the question. The editor of the volume then cited Hungary's new governing capacity as the necessary impetus required to solve the question once and for all: "Now that the Hungarian national assembly is settling our nation's affairs, it's high time this question too were definitively solved."[82]

From roughly the 1840s to the 1890s, two questions received outsized attention in Hungary: the aforementioned nationality question and the Hungarian question (the latter relating—at the time—to Hungary's status within the Habsburg Empire). Both were heavily influenced by the fallout of the Hungarian Revolution, in the course of which Hungary was defeated by combined Habsburg and tsarist Russian forces aided by supporters from among the non-Magyar nationalities (above all, Croats, Serbs, and Romanians) of Hungary. Thereafter, Hungary lost its short-lived independence and much of its political representation within the empire for a time. Up until the 1867 Compromise, and even thereafter, the matter of Hungary's status within the empire remained ambiguous, even as the tensions with the various nationalities in Hungary continued. Although the Hungarian and nationality questions bear striking structural similarities to other questions in other national/imperial contexts, they were also marked by the particularities of the Hungarian context.

Nationality Rules

"The most empirical science, history, . . . is the surest witness that ideas [eszmék] have prevailed," wrote the Hungarian politician Ferencz Pulszky in a work from 1840 on the regulation of the Danube and the Eastern question. In a passage that reveals a profound intellectual debt to the German philosopher Hegel, Pulszky wrote: "The existence of great countries and empires is not precipitated so much by large, well-practiced armies, nor by dint of well-organized domestic governance, as by that fatalistic public opinion that inspires and prods [the nation] to its mythical destination."

The words *liberty* and *equality* had broken up Europe's oldest and most venerable dynasties, he continued, and the phrase "unity of all the Slavs"[83] (which could not include Hungarians, who are not Slavs) could do the same now to the Habsburg Empire. "We must derive a different idea to counter this one," Pulszky concluded, but neglected to mention what it should be.[84]

A few years later, Pulszky, who was in Vienna when the Hungarian Revolution began, fled the imperial capital to serve in the revolutionary government and later followed Lajos Kossuth into exile in Britain. Another Hungarian statesman, Count Anton (Antal) Szécsen—a conservative in the Upper House (*felsőtábla*)—stood by Habsburg Austria during the revolution and, after its successful defeat, wrote a book in German titled *Political Questions of Our Time*. The book was an attempt to make sense of the period and "to eliminate the nebulous generalities with which a shallow politics of the everyday [*Alltagspolitik*] thinks it can solve the intricate questions."[85]

It opened with a chapter on "The Ruling Political Ideas and Trends [*Tendenzen*]," those inherited from the upheavals brought on by the Enlightenment and the French Revolution.[86] More recently, those forces had derived a new slogan: "Nationality." Even as Szécsen was writing his *Political Questions of Our Time*, the Hungarian statesman József Eötvös published a two-volume work on *The Ruling Principles of the 19th Century and Their Influence on the State*. Among the "ruling principles" he enumerated were freedom, equality, and nationality, which "stand in contradiction with one another such that their realization must needs result in the undoing of every large state."[87]

In 1865, Eötvös wrote another book on the "nationality question," revisiting the theme of "ruling principles" in the context of a period question of special significance to Hungary.[88] "Such principles," he told his readers, "as have become general principles cannot be repressed, nor can their consequences be averted; and no one people or state, however powerful it may be, can close itself

off from the impact of such principles."[89] For Eötvös as much as
for Szécsen, "nationality" was foremost among those principles.

A few years earlier, a book had appeared (in German in Vienna
and in Hungarian in Pest) on *The Nationality Question in Hungary*.
Its author, who chose the pen name Szombatsági, explained how
"[e]very century has its own dictionary. It creates its own words
just as it creates its own teachings and morals. The words themselves don't change . . . but the meaning is often completely different. One such great word of our time is 'nationality,' which is on
everyone's lips, but which everyone understands differently." And
its meaning had shifted over time, Szombatsági continued, from
referring to the nobility, then to the whole nation, now to a kind
of caste. Like Pulszky, the looming specter for Szombatsági was
pan-Slavism, an ideology hostile to Hungarian aspirations for national and territorial consolidation.[90] The idea of nationality could
be Hungary's undoing.

And yet, "Ideas are the world's sovereigns," he wrote, "and I like
that it is so."[91] Since there was no sense in countering a ruling idea,
Szombatsági proposed clearing up the "confusion of ideas [*eszmezavar*]," a condition he believed was worse than anarchy for a
country. "[W]hat they call freedom renders the kind of order required to sustain society impossible; and what they call order de-
stroys that which I believe is freedom."[92] Freedom in the Hungarian, as opposed to the European sense, meant centralization and
the majority principle.[93] In the place of "nationality," then, which
stood in opposition to the other ideas of liberty, equality, and fraternity, Szombatsági proposed substituting a different ruling idea,
"patriotism."[94]

The "nationality question" received comparable treatment in a
chapter of its own in Szécsen's book, where he set up the problem
posed by the phrase, which concealed within itself two diametrically opposed notions. On the one hand, "*Genuine* and true national feeling is one of the most powerful, indispensable conditions
of the existence and welfare of states." On the other hand, however,

"[T]he pathological nationality-fraud is one of the most ruinous and dangerous errors of the human spirit."[95] The very word *nationality* concealed a potentially disastrous contradiction.

Comparing Questions

Hungarian querists held their nation up to the light of the age of questions, comparing its health and progress, its unexpected jags and comforting rhythms to those of other nations. In so doing, these querists sought reassurance either in company or in condescension: we are not alone; or, we will not make the same mistakes that others have made. "[I]t is not just in our country that there rules an Egyptian darkness and a Babylonian confusion of ideas on this question," wrote Szombatsági in 1861 of the nationality question, "but rather it is mainly other countries that don't get it and conceive of it one-sidedly."[96] Writing in 1896 on the same question, one Hungarian querist reiterated the claim that other countries—Great Britain, Germany, Russia, the Ottoman Empire—had a nationality question but that the Hungarian nationality question was "the oldest, the most shameful, and the most dangerous in perhaps all the world."[97]

Similar comparisons ranged across the Hungarian querists' panoply, from the lighting to the social question.[98] Yet it was the nationality question that evoked by far the most comparison. In 1911, the Hungarian liberal democrat Oszkár Jászi argued that the nationality question in Hungary was not distinct from that in other parts of Europe. "Thus the nationality question is born of itself from the nature of civilization," he concluded, citing the Belgian economist Émile Louis Victor de Laveleye. From the Provence to the Irish to the Polish question in Posen (Poznań), no less than to the Jewish question, he continued, whoever looks to connections rather than "slogans" will conclude that the nationality question had a common basis and a standard, minimal social program required by all nationality questions the world over.[99]

An exchange between two MPs in the Hungarian Parliament revisited these matters in the spring of 1914, just before the outbreak of war. As Ştefan Cicio Pop, an ethnic Romanian deputy, responded to his interlocutor, Albert Berzeviczy, Britain indeed had its Irish question, France its own nationality question, and there was a Ruthenian and a Polish question. "You're right," Pop said of his opponent. "These phenomena really do appear, but no one is pushing them artificially: they have arisen of their own accord." Foreign examples, he continued, showed that force would not solve the nationality question, only constitutional guarantees for the nationalities.[100]

After World War I, the nationality question practically disappeared together with the nationalities themselves when Hungary lost more than two-thirds of its former territory and population with the Treaty of Trianon in 1920.[101] Jászi nonetheless returned to the theme to compare Hungary to the United States and Ireland, where in his view a predominance of national supremacy in the hands of one group (Anglo-Saxons) had solved the nationality question.[102]

During the interwar period, the nationality question morphed into the minority question. Hungary became independent but also shrank considerably as its former territories became part of the new states of Yugoslavia, Czechoslovakia, and Greater Romania. These border changes shifted the preoccupation of querists from non-Hungarians within Hungary to the nearly three million Magyars living *outside* Hungary. In 1937, the Hungarian historian and publicist Miklós Párdányi wrote on the Breton, Basque, and Flemish questions with more than a hint of schadenfreude that France, the leader of the Entente, which had overseen Hungary's truncation with the Treaty of Trianon, was now facing its own nationality question. Párdányi argued that the nationality idea or principle could not be repressed eternally. "Even if it happens with a delay, the modern nationality idea must sooner or later return from its world-conquering journey and realize itself even vis-à-vis its creator: at the turn of the century the spirit of resistance raises its head in one of the peoples comprising the French nation, and the Breton national question comes to life," he wrote.[103]

When the nationality question reemerged during World War II (as Hungary, in alliance with Nazi Germany, regained some of the territories it had lost), comparisons with other countries were also revived. Especially in Hungary, wrote the Hungarian writer and literary scholar László Sziklay in 1941, the words "nationality question," though on everyone's lips, were not well understood. Hungarian public opinion had a long way to go before it grasped, as the consolidating nations—the Germans, English, Italians, and French—had already, what their national idea should be.[104]

Publicistic Diffusion

Such comparisons had a history, in Hungary and elsewhere, and part of that history was one of publicistic diffusion. Translations brought particular perspectives on questions to a Hungarian readership, oftentimes with breathtaking expediency. A book on the worker question by the influential German bishop Wilhelm Emmanuel von Ketteler, first published in 1864, was published in Hungarian translation the same year, before translations in Dutch or French had appeared (and this in spite of the fact that the translator, Gyula Katinszky, prefaced the work by pointing out that there was as yet no worker question in Hungary since there was as yet no working class).[105] There are many similar examples that help explain how the age of questions acquired at least some structural traits that applied across national contexts, while nationally unique forms were defined and developed in reaction to translated texts and assumptions about events unfolding elsewhere.[106]

When the Hungarian journal *Huszadik Század* (Twentieth Century) asked prominent figures to weigh in on the Jewish question in 1916, the editors self-consciously borrowed the conceit from an earlier Austrian publication from 1885, an edited collection of *Letters of Famous Christian Contemporaries on the Jewish Question*. The original volume's editor had solicted responses not just from domestic personalities but from abroad, as well.[107] Implicit and explicit comparisons of the Jewish question between various national contexts were richly represented in the volume, with some claiming there was no Jewish question in Belgium or France, for example, because the Jews had been fully emancipated.[108]

Similar claims surfaced in responses to the Hungarian questionnaire, as in the bank director Sándor Fleissig's assertion that "[i]n Hungary there is no Jewish question nor can there be one. In a country where the laws do not recognize differences between its citizens, it is impossible to speak of a Jewish question."[109] Others, such as the Hungarian-Jewish scholar and publicist Lajos Blau, argued that there was nothing special about the Jewish question in Hungary, that it was the same there as everywhere else, all the more so since the question originated outside the country.[110]

Implicit or explicit comparisons with other countries' questions, or with how one question related to another, were thus the order of the day. It was not only the questionnaires of *Twentieth Century* that highlighted these tendencies, for this was also the era of bibliographies. Compendia of works, oftentimes with a particular informative bent, tracked events of significance to Hungary. The library in the capital, for instance, compiled a bibliography on the Balkan question in 1912, during what would later be called the First Balkan War.[111] Another bibliography on the Hungarian question was published in English in 1938, as the possibility for a revision of Hungary's boundaries was emerging on the horizon with Nazi Germany's dissection of Czechoslovakia.[112] The selection of works itself became an argument for a particular solution insofar as the selected works reveal an unmistakably pro-Hungarian bias.

Storms from Abroad

In 1861, Szombatsági thought that in Europe's recent history, there was nothing but "chaos, disappointment, and planning nipped in the bud." It was therefore unwise to look to the West for a solution to the nationality question.[113] It was much more likely, argued the Hungarian Catholic theologian János Surányi, that Hungary's *problems* would come from the West, and above all from Austria.[114] Another commentator on the Jewish question in Hungary agreed: Austria was the force holding Hungary in a "colonial" status, preventing it from solving its own questions, such as the Jewish question and the nationality question, even following the Compromise of 1867, which had given Hungary nearly full autonomy within the Dual Monarchy.[115]

The emphasis on the need for independence of action in solving questions was echoed in a book on Hungary and the Macedonian Question from 1908, whose author, Felix Gerando, argued that Hungary must become an indispensible member of the "society of cultivated states."[116] This would mean showing "that we are capable of taking a stand on a given question, even if our position directly opposes that in Vienna." Only thus could Hungary win the respect of both East and West, gain full sovereignty, and brace itself for the coming unavoidable storms.[117] But insidious forces were at work inside the country, wrote a pseudonymous pamphleteer (Veridicus) in 1909, forces that were making a business out of keeping the nationality question hot and driving it to a breaking point.[118] The notion that false agitators serving secret interests were behind the persistence of questions was also not uncommon.[119]

The desire to address questions *à la Hongroise* was part and parcel of the frustration with imperfect sovereignty, and left its mark on several patches of the question landscape as Hungarian querists began to see questions primarily in relation to their own identity and interests. In 1900, the *Budapesti Szemle* published a separate volume on the South African question as a matter of increasing interest to Hungary.[120] Meanwhile, even as some querists strained against what they perceived as Austrian imperialism, a parallel Hungarian imperial project was very much on the mind of several querists. In 1916, the globe-trotting writer and theologian Imre Sebők wrote a pamphlet on the "Yellow question" about the future of the Far East, in which he expressed the hope that "our Turanian race's sober and natural expansionism will not seek its path on the part of whites in the destabilized Far East, but in the Balkans and Asia Minor."[121] It was the opinion of the Hungarian nationalist writer and statesman Jenő Rákosi, writing during the Great War, that in order to understand the nationality question, one had to see it for what it was: not a mathematical equation to be solved but a Gordian knot that needed to be cut. Hungary would solve it by successfully establishing Hungarians as the dominant nation of the state, not unlike the English had done in the British Empire.[122]

The Nationalization of Questions

As questions were nationalized, they were also transformed; some nations left a much heftier mark on them than others, a mark that carried over into other national contexts. Much of Hungary's engagement with the age was filtered through translations from the German. This meant that Hungarians' understanding of the nature and stakes of particular questions was often informed by a very Central European sensibility. In fact, some questions came to acquire that sensibility more broadly. Although the Jewish question did not originate in Germany or Austria, by the 1880s, it was discussed in German and Austrian publications far more frequently than in English, French, or other languages.[123]

One means of domesticating a question against any strong pull toward internationalization was to declare it a "social" question. "[T]he Polish question . . . cannot be solved by any (geo)political means," declared Alexander Hilferding, a Slavic linguist and tsarist reformer writing on the Polish question in a Russian military newspaper in 1863. "[T]he Polish question can only be settled . . . by social means," meaning with domestic reform within the Russian Empire.[124] The Irish and Algerian questions, though they came to be as much about moving boundaries as the Eastern or the Polish question—and in fact were sometimes explicitly compared to both by period commentators—were often defined as "social" rather than geopolitical questions.[125] Defining questions as "social" as opposed to national was a means by which imperial apologists sought to keep them domestic, and out of the international public sphere.

If a social question could be more readily domesticated, *the* social question posed more of a challenge. As it migrated into the Hungarian national context, there were numerous attempts to nationalize it, and thus to defang its transformative potential. In December 1842, the publicist and politician Móric Lukács delivered a speech at the Hungarian Academy of Sciences titled "A Few Words About Socialism." He said that the social question was foremost among the questions Hungary would face in the future, for although socialism and communism had little meaning in Hungary now, the ideas of socialists and communists would find their way to Hungary. It was important, therefore, for Hungarian political figures to discuss and debate the social question with the "serious calmness of science" right away.[126]

Hungarian historian István Schlett has noted a series of shifts in the preoccupations of Hungarian politics over the nineteenth century and into the twentieth. Móric Lukács was among those who discussed the social question prior to the revolution of 1848, but the focus soon shifted to other questions, most notably the nationality question, and soon invocations of the worker and social questions were roundly criticized by conservatives.[127] In 1868, Kálmán Törs, who helped found the Budapest Workers Club, noted that the worker question belonged to the realm of "sensitive questions about which it was better not to speak at all."[128] It was not, Schlett argued, until the emergence of a worker's movement in Hungary that the worker question became real.[129] Meanwhile, the literature of the time repeated a refrain of relief that the question had not yet arrived in Hungary.[130] In an 1890 pamphlet, the Hungarian publicist and politician Ágost Pulszky insisted there was still no worker question in Hungary, and what there is of it "is no domestic good, but an imported product."[131]

But even as Pulszky wrote these words, the social question and its frequently cited subquestions, such as the worker and woman questions, were gaining prominence in the Hungarian publicistic realm. In an article that appeared that same year in a major Hungarian daily, the author argued that "no one can say in all honesty that there is no worker question in Hungary."[132] And in 1893, on the occasion of the founding of the Society of National Economy (Nemzetgazdasági Egyesület), industrial expert and politician József Szterényi lamented his own country's penchant for inaction and inertia. If Hungarians continued to ignore economic and social questions, he argued, "A whole deluge of questions is going to rain down on the nation and the country" until a society comes into being that concerns itself with them and takes them up.[133]

A consensus was emerging in Hungary around questions: the only preventative was to be ready, and the only way to be ready was to debate, study, and discuss incoming questions, ideally in advance. This was as true of the less common ones, such as the tuberculosis, sewer (*csatornazási*), or cartel questions, as it was of the political and social ones, where there were lessons to be learned from observing the West, noting its successes, and avoiding its mistakes.[134]

Hungarians also started claiming jurisdiction over particular questions, declaring the sole prerogative to solve them on their own national terms. This impulse had a long history in the region: as far back as the Congress of Vienna, Metternich sought to create "two classes of questions": those that were "Austrian" and those that were "European." Under the category of Austrian questions, he included "those for which the acquiescence of Austria alone could make for a complete solution."[135] Such jurisdictional claims would later surface in many states in interwar Europe, as sovereignty was often declared and tested through states' increasingly competitive assertions of the exclusive right to solve particular questions. The years preceding the outbreak of World War II, in particular, saw a marked proliferation of questions, with

Hungarian statesmen, among others, vigorously proclaiming dominion over several of them.[136]

What's in a Word?

A Hungarian historian reflecting on the history of the worker question in Hungary during the nineteenth century noted that the expression "sober mind" (*józan ész*) was generally used by liberals and conservatives to undercut the socialists and communists.[137] A sober mind—i.e., one not intoxicated by socialist and social democratic ideas—would see that the worker question is really something else, et cetera. Yet the idea that period questions were essentially matters of perception—contradictions that, if looked at differently, would cease to be problems—is present in the leftist literature on questions, as well. The Hungarian philosopher and literary critic György Lukács, writing on the nationality question in 1915, felt that the matter might be approached by the new philosophy, which understood that apparent contradictions and unresolvable problems, when viewed from a different level, actually disappear.[138]

This disappearing act was related to the growing sense that there was a politics behind the names given to questions. Szombatsági, for example, noted a shift that had begun to take place in question designations in his time. Whereas earlier one spoke of the "Hungaria," "tot(h)," "rácz," and "oláh" questions (Latin-based and therefore medieval or early modern designations for some of the different nationalities in Hungary), now these were being modernized: Hungarian (magyar), Slav or Slovak (szláv), Serbian (szerb), and Romanian (román).[139] Szombatsági saw this shift as a turn toward a more exclusivist notion of nationality that, on the one hand, could not encompass (in the case of Hungaria versus Magyar) the entirety of the state's inhabitants and, on the other hand, had designs on Hungarian sovereignty (in the case of "szerb"and "román," both of which pointed to already existing states on Hungary's borders, Serbia and Romania). The shift in terminology was making a reconciliation of the various national aspirations impossible.

The Hungarian writer and publicist Károly Szini made a similar observation five years later by appealing to a different set of "ruling principles"—"Association, alliance, unification!"—in a pamphlet on the Hungarian question.[140] The Habsburg Empire could join in this spirit, but it would have to change its name. [141] A new word should come to take the place of the Habsburg Empire: namely, the *Hungarian* or *Danubian* Empire. "All we want is to swap out one name for the empire for another, a better one. We want to trade a country for just a name."[142] In this way, Szini concluded, together with the Hungarian question, a whole host of questions would be solved.[143]

Hungarian querists often argued that if words and ideas brought about the confusion of ideas (*eszmezavar*) preventing a solution, then new or different words and ideas should be wielded to clear it up. "Thus the mode of thinking must be changed to give healthier principles/ideas a path to influence," the Hungarian bishop Lőrinc Schlauch said of the worker question in an 1891 sermon. [144]

The theme of renaming resurfaced in interwar Hungary with particular intensity. In 1931, the Hungarian Franz Kászonyi wrote a book (published in Vienna) on the "racial" similarities of the Danubian peoples. The nationality question had taken a bitter turn in the East, he wrote, creating divisions where it once forged unity.[145] "Political problems occur when a word is recognized as a collective belief [*Massenglaube*] which divides previously united peoples. A political problem ceases when, instead of the divisive word, the graven image [*Götzenbild*] of a new unifying word comes into play."[146] That word, he concluded, should be *race*, as it would unite the peoples of the Danubian basin in a *"shared 'we'-peoples-consciousness [Volks-Wir-Bewusstsein]."*[147] The longed-for magical automatism was therefore not so automatic—it was willed, very much like Mephisto's rescue word.

A shift in terms, and thus in the spirit of the times, was also on the mind of Ferenc Faluhelyi, a Hungarian professor of international law, when he wrote a pamphlet on the minority question from the Hungarian standpoint in 1937. Faluhelyi was from a part of the Hungarian Kingdom that was lost to Romania in the postwar peace treaties, after which he, like many others of his generation and profile, emigrated to Hungary.[148] In 1936, he established a minority institute with a journal at the University of Pécs in southern Hungary.[149] In his 1937 pamphlet, he quoted Eötvös's claim that the nationality question was the most burning of the nineteenth century, and added that a matter of arguably even greater importance for the twentieth century was the minority question.[150] Then he wondered about the implications of the term *minority*. "There is something in that expression, in that name something new, something of the knowledge that a people that has had the status of a minority thrust upon it can no longer live as it did . . . when it was in the majority, can no longer live life as majority peoples do." With this shift, the Hungarian problem had assumed a new character.[151]

The querists in Hungary were deeply aware that the way a nation framed and understood its questions, the words it used to describe its condition, lent a certain reality to that condition, and it often seemed to them as though words could shift the ground under their feet. As Ármin Beregi, a leading Hungarian Zionist, wrote in 1917 on the Jewish question: "Is there a Jewish question? The answer is in the question. One can only ask if there is one because there is one."[152]

That a question could create a reality by virtue of its mere formulation was a tantalizing and terrifying prospect. "Where conceptions are lacking, at the right moment a word comes to the rescue." Like Mephisto, the querists in Hungary knew they were playing a devilish game. The line from Faust was the epigraph of an 1865 book that offered an *Appropriate Program for the Legal and Practical Solution of the Hungarian Question*.[153]

Epilogue

In May 2014, Vladimir Putin asked, "Can a compromise be found on the Ukrainian question between Russia and America? [T]he question is to ensure the rights and interests of the Russian southeast. It's new Russia." Putin's statement received outsized media attention, with commentators sounding the alarm about his use of the historically charged reference to Ukraine as "new Russia." The phrase suggested Putin was reviving the Russian imperialist project of the nineteenth century.[154] But there was another formulation of a bygone century's vintage in what Putin said that day, one with far more wide-ranging implications: Putin's reference to "the Ukrainian question."

The "Ukrainian question" was not Putin's invention. The phrase had been employed by a variety of figures, from the Ukrainian nationalist Dmytro Dontsov to the Bolshevik revolutionary Leon Trotsky.[155] In broad terms, discussions of the Ukrainain question revolved around whether there was such a thing as Ukraine, or Ukrainians as distinct from other peoples, above all, Russians. The "question" also encompassed discussions of what the geopolitical and social-policy implications of such a distinction could be, both within tsarist Russia and in the neighboring Austro-Hungarian Monarchy, where some of these might-be Ukrainians also lived.

In 1907, a writer on the "Ukrainian question" proposed that it be solved by means of a large-scale "restructuring" (*perestroistva*) of the Russian state, in one fell swoop taking out the broader "national question," as well.[156] The Great War reopened the discussion of the "Ukrainian question" in Russia, Austria-Hungary, and elsewhere, and then it appeared among the first items on the revolutionary agenda of both the February and the October Revolutions of 1917, often discussed under the umbrella of the "national question."[157] Lenin's favored "solution"—granting national autonomy to the various nationalities, including Ukrainians, to win their support for the revolution—was roundly criticized in

1918 by Rosa Luxemburg in her long critique of the Bolshevik Revolution.[158]

This partial sketch of the history of the Ukrainian question reveals the extent to which it became nationalized as a primarily Russian preoccupation. The process began in the nineteenth century, and has now resurfaced from within that Russian context in the twenty-first. It may be that for Austria the phrase is now meaningless, and for Ukrainians it is offensive, but the Russian leadership has self-consciously revived it.

The Eastern question, which has undergone a number of national reincarnations, has followed a comparable trajectory. Although many declared it "solved" with the creation of an independent Turkish republic in 1923, there is little consensus surrounding that conclusion. During the Wars of Yugoslav Succession in the 1990s, some spoke of the return of the Eastern question.[159] German historian Winfried Baumgart later suggested that the Eastern question did not disappear but rather shattered into smaller ones, from the conflict in Israel-Palestine to the wars in the former Yugoslavia.[160] "The Eastern Question still exists," declared Carl Brown in his book on Ottoman diplomacy.[161] As recently as 2015, Tony Barber, an editor of the *Financial Times*, wrote, "Now a second Eastern Question is taking shape. It encompasses issues such as Greece's struggle to reform itself and stay in the eurozone, Kosovo's struggle to survive as a functioning state and Macedonia's struggle to persuade its neighbours, notably Greece and Bulgaria, that its grandiose nation-building effort is no threat to their territorial integrity and cultural identity."[162]

For many Turks, the "Eastern question" came to be synonymous with a threat to their sovereignty.[163] Starting already in the Ottoman period, Ottoman and Turkish commentators denied its existence. What the Great Powers called the "Eastern question" was often understood as a "Western question" by the Ottoman elite and associated with Great Power quarrels rather than anything that was happening within the Ottoman Empire.[164] "If we do not wish for history to repeat itself and for our national territory to once again be shared among the Western Powers as booty," wrote the diplomatic historian and former diplomat Hüner Tuncer, "then I think we must understand very well what the Western states meant by the 'Eastern question' of the past and avoid the misconceptions and mistakes of history."[165]

If the Eastern question was understood as a threat to Ottoman/Turkish sovereignty, then we learn something about its later apparent transmutation in the Turkish Republic from that earlier understanding. For the past several decades, there has been renewed and intense discussion of the "Eastern question" in Turkish media and scholarship, but the phrase is now synonymous with the Kurdish question.[166] That the status of the sizable Kurdish minority inhabiting mainly eastern Anatolia should be given this name is not a coincidence. It is a Turkish nationalist conflation meant to suggest that Kurdish appeals for language rights and autonomy pose a threat to Turkish sovereignty on a par with the threat posed by the Eastern question of the nineteenth century. "THE QUESTION IS NOT A KURDISH QUESTION," declared a Turkish nationalist in an online essay from 2016 on the Turks of Eastern Anatolia, "IT IS AN EASTERN QUESTION! . . . IT IS AN IMPERIALIST WESTERN CHRISTIAN QUESTION!"[167]

The fate of the "Ukrainian question" in Russia and the "Eastern question" in Turkey bear witness to the danger of suggesting that the age of questions was a coherent international phenomenon that has—for better or worse—come to an end. Nor should Russia and Turkey be taken as exceptional cases in this regard. In Hungary, it is still commonplace to hear of the Gypsy question.[168] Elsewhere over the past few years, we have also witnessed the revival of the Catalonian, the English, and the migrant questions.[169] Perhaps the age is alive and well, still moving through time with a markedly national cadence.

2

The Progressive Argument

THE AGE OF EMANCIPATION

[T]he question of emancipation is the question of our time.[1]

—GERMAN THEOLOGIAN BRUNO BAUER IN
AN ESSAY ON THE JEWISH QUESTION (1842)

A Progressive Age

If there was a word that ruled the age of questions, it was *emancipation*. It was the implied solution to most of the great questions: the Jewish, slavery, and woman as much as the Greek, Serbian, Polish, Irish, and Macedonian questions. States, peoples, and individuals all demanded it in equal measure. In his 1842 essay on the Jewish question, Bruno Bauer wrote, "[T]he question of emancipation is the question of our time."[2] Why else would the British statesman and Whig Henry Brougham, advocate and advisor on the Polish question, skip a meeting in 1839 of the London Literary Association of the Friends of Poland to attend to the slavery question?[3] Why else would Adam Mickiewicz, who had himself weighed in numerous times on the Polish question, engage in a deep friendship and prolific correspondence with Margaret Fuller, the American journalist and outspoken advocate for both women's and slaves' emancipation?[4]

The factors that gave rise to the age of questions can be found in the conditions of the late eighteenth century, during which power relations were shifting at both the societal and the international levels. Hitherto marginal classes and nations were gaining a voice and a presence in both domestic and international politics. The growing strength of Russia in the East and of the middle class in Western Europe, especially France, introduced a *moralizing tone* into international and domestic politics that was recognizable already in the 1770s but did not find its expression until half a century later, in the 1810s and 1820s, when the "question" became the byword of moral necessity. These two dimensions of the age of questions—the geopolitical and the social—came into their own roughly simultaneously and asserted themselves in similar terms, in the name of liberty, justice, and equality. The age of questions was thus saturated at its origin with progressive ideals, such that even conflicts among social groups and nations hinged on the opposing sides' relative capacity to represent those ideals.[5]

Rationalization was an additional feature of this fundamentally progressive age. At the commodities level, the sugar, cotton, and oyster questions were about equilibrium: between consumption and production, tariffs and bounties, conservation and exploitation.[6] Many discussions of the cotton question were also about slavery and written by abolitionists.[7] Medical and professional questions relating to diseases such as tuberculosis and cholera, lighting systems, waterways, apartment buildings, and sewage systems posited the necessity of enhancing expertise and precision and producing marked and measurable improvements in people's lives.[8] Meanwhile academic and literary questions served as means of enforcing scholarly rigor and intellectual integrity.[9] A surprising amount of ink was spilled over the so-called dentist question, which one pamphlet defined as the question of the "practice of dentistry itself" and its regulation by law.[10] In sum, questions pointed the way forward to a more just, healthy, discerning, efficient, and knowledgeable society, culture, and international system.

That over the first half of the nineteenth century "the x question" came to be the framing of choice for progressive interventions as much in the geopolitical as in the social realm is evident from Adam Czartoryski's *Essay on Diplomacy* written in 1823 and published in two editions; one in 1830, with the outbreak of the (ultimately unsuccessful) Polish November Uprising against tsarist Russia, and another in 1864, during the (also ultimately unsuccessful) January Uprising against tsarist Russia.[11] Czartoryski was a Polish nobleman and statesman, as well as a close friend and advisor to the Russian tsar Alexander I, who had served as the minister of foreign affairs in the Russian Empire from 1804 to 1806. He would later serve as the president of the Polish National Government during the November Uprising (1830–1831) before it was put down by tsarist forces.[12]

During his tenure as Russia's foreign minister, Czartoryski drafted a ministerial act proposing the total reorganization of the boundaries of Europe, including the creation of an independent Poland under Russian protection. The *Essay* contains many similar ideas for a complete overhaul of the international system, down to the very principles upon which diplomacy is based. It is organized in sections on how diplomacy actually is—namely, chaotic, unjust, and violent—versus how it should be, namely, rational, just, and peaceful.[13] Whereas the diplomatic spirit of the time was characterized by "greed, distrust and envy," Czartoryski argued, it could, if profound reforms were to be initiated by the European cabinets, become "the noblest science and the most useful study."[14] Czartoryski believed that states were effectively "masses of personified individuals" and therefore subject to natural law and entitled to the same forms of liberty and equality as individuals.[15]

The structure of the two editions of the *Essay* is largely identical, but the content of some sections is radically different. Above all, in the earlier edition, "questions" do not appear, whereas in the

1864 version, there are several explicit mentions of the Polish question, including the assertion that there will be no security in Europe until the great iniquity perpetrated against the Poles is re-
paired.[16] The second edition also contains a reference to the Polish
question, retrospectively tying it to the "Negro question" in a segment on the Congress of Vienna.[17] The publication history of
Czartoryski's *Essay* illustrates the extent to which questions became the shorthand of choice for progressive thinkers.

Bundling Questions: For Our Freedom and Yours

Just as Czartoryski linked the Polish to the Negro question, the
emancipatory impulse of the age bundled its causes. "For our freedom and yours" (*Za naszą i waszą wolność*) ran the Polish revolutionary slogan of 1831. Querists cast the Belgian question as related
to the Polish question during the overlapping upheavals in would-
be Poland and Belgium, not least of all because the internationally
agreed-upon solution to the Belgian question had been independence, a solution that many querists favored for Poland, as well.
"[T]he Polish question is identical with that of Belgium," declared
the French royalist newspaper *Le Messager des Chambres*, on December 11, 1830.[18] "Shall we have war or peace?" wrote the Parisian
correspondent of the *London Standard* in late January of 1831.
"People think about nothing else, and talk about nothing else than
this. First of all they are looking to the Belgian question . . . and
next to the Polish question. They do not, however, forget that
there is still outstanding the Greek question."[19] Thus began the
agglomeration of questions into emancipatory bundles.

"'Do you love freedom?' is the question we have startled our
age withal; and we have begun to judge men—of all classes and
conditions,—by the reply their lives make to it," wrote Maria
Weston Chapman in 1839 in *Right and Wrong in Massachusetts*, in
which she commented on the relationship between the slavery
and woman questions:

"May the numerous unpopular questions with which the anti-slavery cause is connected" (thus ran our prayer) "continually come up with it as it is borne onward. So that up to the final triumph, the act of joining an anti-slavery association may be, as it has hitherto proved,—a test act." And so we pray still; for still and forever, TRUTH is one and indivisible. All moral questions are by their nature inseparable, in any other than a mechanical sense, and while we sedulously keep them thus mechanically separate, because to do otherwise would be a sin against the freedom of others, and a betrayal of their confidence, we feel it to be no less a sin against freedom for others to impede any man's course with reproach, on account of this eternal decree of God's providence.[20]

Aggregation also offered the possibility of a universal solution. "Bourgeois society has never been so united as it is united today in the cause of national freedom and independence," wrote the Serbian scholar and statesman Vladimir Jovanović in a pamphlet on the *Serbian Nation and the Eastern Question* in 1863. "It creates bonds not merely between individual people, but between nations, confirmed in that which is called the spirit of the time." He then listed all of the places that had become "questions"—Italy, Greece ("and other Eastern countries"), Poland, Schleswig-Holstein—and that were now locked in a relationship of mutual aspiration that bound their respective questions to a shared solution.[21]

At the same time, during the Polish January Uprising in 1863–1864, other pairings emerged, as querists discussed the Polish question together with the Italian, Mexican, and ever-present Eastern questions, and all the national liberationist undertones the comparison implied. The French historian and publicist Comte de Montalembert wrote in 1863, for example, that "the Eastern question, the Italian question, and the Mexican question cannot permit us to take refuge in indifference and impotence in the face of the Polish question. All of these three issues, despite their extreme gravity, were much less severe and did not take hold of the French heart as much the Polish question."[22]

Just over a decade later, William Gladstone, the British liberal statesman and outspoken advocate of self-government for Slavs in the Ottoman Empire, criticized "one of the latest artifices," which in his view was "to separate the question of Servia from the question of Herzegovina and Bosnia and of Bulgaria . . . they had one root; they must surely have one remedy, I mean morally one; and administered by the same handling; for, if one part of the question be placed in relief, and one in shadow, the light will not fall on the dark places, and guilt will gain impunity."[23]

Critics of the Age

The progressive essence of nineteenth-century question mania is further evident from the commentary of the period's conservative critics. In 1834, in a book by the German Mennonite preacher Leonhard Weydmann on *The Questions of Our Tumultuous Time*, the author noted that querists were intent on destroying the existing hierarchy and setting up in its place "forms whereby the distinction between governing and being governed well-nigh disappears."[24] Conservatives also saw the age of questions as excessively humane. Thomas Carlyle's "Occasional Discourse on the Negro Question" appeared in *Fraser's Magazine* in December 1849. He accused the "Philanthropists" of the age of being "Sunk in deep froth-oceans of 'Benevolence,' 'Fraternity,' 'Emancipation-principle,' 'Christian Philanthropy,' and other most amiable-looking but most baseless, and in the end baleful and all-bewildering jargon,—sad product of a skeptical Eighteenth Century, and of poor human hearts left destitute of any earnest guidance, and disbelieving that there ever was any."[25] The liberal thinker John Stuart Mill responded to Carlyle's charge in a letter to the editor of *Fraser's*. Mill's letter, "The Negro Question," appeared in January 1850 and included his own assessment of the spirit of the age:

Let me say a few words on the general quarrel of your contributor with the present age.... Your contributor thinks that the age has too much humanity, is too anxious to abolish pain. I affirm, on the contrary, that it has too little humanity... It is not by excess of a good quality that the age is in fault, but by deficiency—deficiency even of philanthropy, and still more of other qualities wherewith to balance and direct what philanthropy it has.[26]

This disparity of perception resulted in not a little friction between querists and conservatives, but it bears emphasizing that the language of questions was the terrain of progressives and liberal reformers in that it was they who assumed something was wrong with the status quo that needed fixing. They might have disagreed over the means—as the liberal Italian statesman Camillo Benso, count of Cavour, and the revolutionary Giuseppe Mazzini did over whether liberal reform or national revolution was at the base of the Italian question[27]—but no querist could hold with the status quo.

Most importantly, progressive querists' insistence that period questions were genuine problems demanding expedient solutions started to acquire the authority of consensus, such that in 1941, even Adolf Hitler declared the social question a matter of first-order importance for Nazi Germany, comparing it to the abolition of serfdom: "The decisive matter, I said to myself, is the social question. To evade the question was like in the seventeenth or eighteenth century to believe that it was unnecessary to abolish serfdom," he said.[28]

The Essence of Questions

The Polish, Armenian, woman, Jewish, worker, agrarian, Greek, slavery, and countless other questions were about freedom and independence—for Poles, Armenians, women, Jews, and others. The social, Eastern, nationalities, and European questions were aggregates that encompassed a variety of the aforementioned "smaller" emancipatory questions. The Congress of Vienna placed many of them literally on the table for discussion.[29] Some early references to a "Polish question," for example, appear in correspondence between participants in the 1815 Congress of Vienna and in the documents relating to the proceedings.[30] Their authors were concerned with whether Poland had the right to exist as an independent state following the eighteenth-century partitions that had wiped it off the map of Europe and contributed to the considerable westward expansion of tsarist Russia and the eastward and northward expansion of the Prussian and Habsburg Empires. The South American question (sometimes called the Spanish-American question[31]) that emerged in the 1810s around independence movements in South America during and after the Napoleonic Wars provides another early example.[32]

But the real flood of questions into the world of pamphlets, publicists, and public opinion began in the 1820s. The West India question, which was mentioned in the London *Times* with considerable frequency starting in late 1823 and often discussed in connection with the emergent "(anti-)slave(ry) question," is revealing of the emancipatory momentum behind questioneering.[33] A pamphlet by T. S. Winn from 1825 showcased the progressive character of querists: "[T]he Parliament of Great Britain took so many years to debate on the expediency of an Abolition of our Slave Trade with Africa, the Emancipation of Ireland, the Abolition of Slavery throughout our dominions, and other equally important questions of such self-evident solution."[34] On the West India question, Winn continued, "[H]is Lordship [Earl Bathurst, British colonial secretary] is usually enlightened, liberal, and patriotic enough in his general line of politicks—but possessing West India estate, see his speeches in the parliamentary debates on the Slave question.— Oh what a falling off is there."[35]

In discussions of the West India question of the 1820s, then, social and geopolitical emancipation were offered as "self-evident" or natural solutions. The 1830s mark the full onset of the age, for though the coming of questions was presaged in the decades prior, their explosion around 1829 and 1830 was truly remarkable.[36] Within a few months numerous questions burst onto the scene: the Belgian, Eastern, Polish, Jewish, and Algerian questions all made their broad-circulation debuts in that decade.[37] By the end of the 1830s, the woman and the labor questions were also appearing in pamphlets, parliamentary proceedings, and press venues.

This simultaneity is rooted in the convergence of three factors, all of them related to the emancipationist agenda of querists: the expansion and politicization of press distribution, the expansion of the voting franchise (in Britain), and a tight series of international upheavals around struggles for rights. In the words of British press historian Ivon Asquith, "Perhaps the most important aspect of the history of the press in this period is the decline in the ability of governments to control it."[38] Although up until 1836, the British periodical press was subject to a significant stamp tax, many "unstamped papers" reached readers. The bulk of these were liberal-revolutionary. Compared to the legally stamped press, one historian has observed, unstamped papers were more "consummately impudent" and "self-consciously subversive."[39] These periodicals left their mark on the age of questions from its early years.

Events also played a significant role, including the Greek uprising in the Ottoman Empire (1821–1832), that ultimately resulted in the independence of Greece; the Polish November Uprising in tsarist Russia (1830–1831), crushed by tsarist troops; the Belgian Revolution (1830–1839), resulting in Belgium's independence; the July Revolution (1830) and the June rebellion (1832) which codified popular sovereignty in France; and the debates in the British parliament around the Roman Catholic Relief Act (1829), the Bill for Removal of Jewish Disabilities (1830), and the Reform Act for the expansion of the voting franchise (1832).[40]

Many of these events were causes célèbres of progressives in Britain and France, but it was perhaps the Greek revolt that figured most heavily in cementing the emancipationist character of the age. It inspired liberal romantics across Europe, and the Western Great Powers' ultimate, albeit reluctant, sanctioning of Greek independence gave reformers a foothold back home.[41] The revolt also contributed to the rise of what Alexis de Tocqueville called "la grande affaire du siècle"—the Eastern question, among the most significant and persistent of questions in the nineteenth and early twentieth centuries.[42]

Contradictions and Defects

A question came into being where conditions begged expeditious redress; where something was wrong and badly needed fixing. It is in this aspect that the sensibility of the age was expressed in its purest form: an acute sense of imbalance, disparity, disequilibrium. The history of the social question provides a signature example. A remarkable degree of consensus formed around what had given rise to it: a tension or contradiction between the spirit of the time and the conditions of the time. In the words of the German philosopher Georg Wilhelm Friedrich Hegel from his lectures on the philosophy of history in the 1820s, "nothing is more common today than the complaint that the *ideals* raised by fantasy are not being realized, that these glorious dreams are being destroyed by cold actuality."[43]

In a book on the "social question" published in 1871, the German economist and statistician Hans von Scheel wrote that the "modern culture state" placed "the equality of all before the law and the freedom of the individual ... as fundamental conditions of the spiritual and material development of the people."[44] But because there was a "double organization of the population within the state: a political and an economic," the principle of freedom and equality was unevenly applied across the political and economic realms, producing a contradiction "unique to modern society." "[O]ut of legal freedom and equality there emerged economic un-freedom and inequality." This in turn, von Scheel believed, gave rise to the "social question":

[E]very contradiction, as soon as it becomes conscious, becomes a thought problem: a question. And in this way the formulation of the social question of the present time reveals itself to us very simply and specifically: it is the contradiction between national economic development and the societal development principle—which appears to us as an ideal—of freedom and equality. The study and solution of this contradiction is the study and solution of the contemporary social question.[45]

In 1892, Edmondo de Amicis defined the social question as the tension between the "principle of equality" and the fact of inequality.[46] Two years later, Gustav Müller, a self-declared "common man of the people," wrote that the "social question" was "a consequence of the sharpened capacity to grasp the stark defects [Mißstände] of the present which impose an incontrovertible certainty that conditions as they are today cannot continue to exist for all eternity."[47] Writing in 1895, the German Jesuit canon law scholar and sociologist Joseph Biederlack emphasized that the social question stemmed from "economic and social defects" resulting from the contemporary "one-sided development of money capitalism."[48] And shortly thereafter, Ludwig Stein, a Hungarian-Jewish rabbi, sociologist and philosopher, saw an irreconcilable contradiction between the ideals of freedom and equality at the root of the "social question."[49]

A New Man

The tension between idea and practice—and attempts to reconcile the two—was central to the way the "social question" was discussed in the nineteenth century. To achieve this reconciliation, a number of querists dreamt of common social action that would bring idea and practice into longed-for harmony.[50] As Czartoryski had proposed the remaking of the international system from the ground up, lending it a moral thrust, so too did commentators on the social question posit the necessity of fundamental reform, beginning with the very person, *à la Rousseau*.[51] Only within the person could the contradictions of the time find a common frame and thus a resolution.

In an 1863 essay on William Shakespeare, the French progressive novelist Victor Hugo wrote, "At the point where the social question has arrived, everything should be joint action. Isolated forces cancel, the ideal and the real are integral. Art should help science. Both wheels of progress are turning together."[52] To that end, Hugo intoned the bankruptcy of a strictly economic approach to the "social question," arguing that economics had too long ruled the debate. "The social question was too reduced to the economic point of view, it is time to go back to the moral point of view. . . . Start with: extensive public education [for] if the intellectual condition improves, the material condition will also improve. Rest assured, if your soul grows, your bread also whitens."[53]

In other words, it was not enough to create a new system, one had to create a new kind of person, a *moral person* comparable to the moral geopolitical order conceived by Czartoryski. "The most potent fact of experience now is that the new times require new men, and that the men cannot be furnished fast enough to meet the demand,"[54] wrote the American Unitarian reverend and publicist George Batchelor in a book on *Social Equilibrium* in 1887. Batchelor called for "the training of society to a finer loyalty to the higher interests of humanity."[55]

Nor was it only the social question for which this solution was proposed. In Britain, education itself had long since become a question. In an 1854 pamphlet on the "education question," Reverand George Jamieson of Aberdeen wrote that "*man is according as he has been educated*," and therefore "the best possible education" should be brought "within the reach of the meanest, as well as the greatest."[56] "In our view," wrote the French poet and publicist Léon Deschamps in 1891, "the colonial question has been reduced to an education question."[57]

"In France," wrote Henri de Tourville in 1896 in the preface to a book on *The Labour Question in Britain*, "the education of all the classes is radically and appallingly wrong ... This is essentially the source ... of the whole Social Question. ... A great enterprise has grown up, but there is something wrong with its working. After blaming all the forces of nature, and after appealing to all of them, it has at last been realized that what is wanting is the man." He proposed altering the education of youths to turn out a type of man like the Anglo-Saxon "splendid savage."[58] In 1912, a Hungarian writing on *The Essence of the Social Question* reiterated the argument, citing Tolstoy as saying that in order for society to change, the human heart must change.[59] "Legal and economic remedies would not of themselves solve the social question," wrote Ryan and McGowan in their 1921 *Catechism of the Social Question*. "They are of considerable value, but there must also be a change in the spirit and ideals of men and women."[60]

Popular Pedagogy

Educating the public—*creating* society—was not merely considered to be the form that a solution to the social question should take; it was also the form that discussions of the social question *themselves* took. To that end, a new didactic genre was developed, one that had a precedent in the earliest treatments of the bullion question, wherein commentators stressed the necessity of exposing the matter to public opinion and wondered about the timing and the form of their interventions (parliamentary debate being considered necessary but insufficient).[61] In line with the tendency to at once engage, educate, and convince a reading public on certain questions, a popular pedagogical literature began to emerge, descended from the almanac, the catechism, and the pamphlet, but with shades of the university lecture hall also present.

And yet, initially at least, the university lecture hall was the direct *adversary* of those seeking to raise the profile of the social question. An early reference to the social question appeared in 1831 in the French *Encyclopédie Moderne* under the entry for "Université." The distinction between scholastic versus practical questions discussed by Southey and Malthus can be found here in a critique of the university, where scholastic questions had been born and from whence they were propagated. "Real education, of the sort that created men, that shaped events, no longer has anything in common with this newly restored frame that is still called 'University,'" the authors of the *Encyclopédie* argued. "Intelligence grows through other channels; the developments that moral science has undergone [h]ad the main effect to appreciate the need that mankind has for work. This new knowledge puts the social question where it should be, that is to say, in the position of the highest foresight or the highest theory, the only universal."[62] Here again, the scholastic tradition (of the universities) was supplanted by a new, more *practical* sensibility in the form of the social question.

When the next surge of revolutionary activity began in 1848, its leadership declared that a new kind of universal knowledge was required to solve the social question. In a speech delivered by Adolphe Thiers to the French National Assembly on September 13, 1848, he spoke of it as "a vital question for the future of the republic," one that was not a question of political economy or customs duties or economics but rather "a societal [*gesellschaftliche*], political philosophical, metaphysical question; a question that encompasses all these relationships within itself." As Amicis would later do, Thiers warned his audience that the acuteness of the question was undeniable: "and you know," he continued, "what an enormous significance the social question has attained in the events that have moved France and the world."[63]

In Thiers's speech, as in Hugo's, we find a rejection of political economy in favor of a more all-encompassing mode of understanding and addressing the "social question," one informed by empiricism as much as by idealism. For many who followed the interventions of Thiers and the socialist Louis Blanc in the French National Assembly during the 1848 revolutions, this meant socialism. "Socialism," the German translator of their speeches declared in early 1849, "is a science whose propositions [*Sätze*] were not invented in an academic's study, nor can they be proven by logic quibbles or erudite citations. It is a science that grows directly from the life of the people and can only develop and refine itself in real daily interaction with the world."[64]

But insofar as these thinkers were critical of the out-of-touch nature of university training and demanded a more universal and practical form of education, they also sought to change the university's intended audience, and therewith the language and genres in which it addressed itself to that audience. In a series of lectures, published in Germany in 1856, meant for the general education of women, for example, Karl Biedermann included a lecture on "The Social Question, Its Meaning, and Attempts to Solve It."[65] No one, a range of authors intoned, could afford to ignore the "social question." In the words of von Scheel writing in 1871, "it is the duty of every educated person to inform themselves on the nature of the social question or at least to orient themselves with respect to it."[66] Driven by the same imperative, numerous works on the social question assumed a popular didactic tone, variously seeking to imitate and to transform the university.

The university lecture hall thus became a base of operations for querists. Recall that Amicis delivered his lecture on the social question to students at the university in Turin in 1892. Within months it was translated into Italian, German, Spanish, Czech, and French, and over the course of the next decade, into Bulgarian, Polish, and Russian, as well.[67] In 1895, Joseph Biederlack compiled a series of lectures he had given at the theological seminary in Innsbruck under the title *The Social Question: A Contribution to Orientation Regarding Its Essence and Solution*. Originally, the lectures were intended to prepare future priests for confronting "the great problem of our time," but the book was so popular it went into several editions and was still being published after the Great War.[68] As for McGowan and Ryan's 1921 *Catechism of the Social Question*, the didactic nature is inherent to the form. In the opening remarks on "How Best to Use the Catechism," the authors recommended that "groups of people study it together."[69]

Within the popular pedagogical genre, querists also sought to determine what counted as a venue or means of solving questions and who the primary agents of the solution could and should be. J. A. Hobson wrote *The Social Problem* in 1901, in which he noted that the science of "current political economy" was "defective" for the purpose "of handling the Social Question." The proper method, he determined, "must be that of an organic science, reorganizing organic interaction and qualitative differences, not the purely mathematical or quantitative method which current economic science tends more and more to employ."[70]

Hobson and others worked to shift the scientific metaphor underpinning questions from mathematics/economics to biology. With this shift came a devaluation of day-to-day political "solutions" to the social question. Instead, a longer, broader view was required.

> Turning to concrete politics, [t]he problem drives back into the region of individual character and motive. . . . The ultimate good working of . . . a democracy will depend upon the intelligence and goodwill which the private citizens bring to bear upon public life, and upon the existence of corresponding qualities and sentiments in the public servants . . . The forms and institutions of a State and a society should be so shaped and so sized as to render this free and effective play of moral and intellectual forces possible.

Hobson wrote of the "form" that the solution should take, rather than its particular content, namely, education.

> The Social Question finds, perhaps, its clearest unity in that common education of the intelligence and goodwill of the citizen which, by enlarging the area and extending the time-range of social utility for all citizens alike, tends to assimilate their

private valuations, and so give increased definiteness, coherence and strength to the public standard and the public policy. An organic social policy will be strong precisely in proportion as it expresses the enlightened and enlarged common sense and common feeling of the many . . . Society as an organism must be animated by a common moral and intellectual life, vested in individuals who are working in conscious cooperation for a common end, if any substantial progressive economy of social life is to be attained.[71]

It was everyone's duty to understand and participate in the queristic enterprise, and the progressive spirit saw in each individual a *solution*.

An Answering Being

The German poet and journalist Heinrich Heine was famously excited by questions. Some claim it was he who introduced the "social question" into the German language in his *Paris Correspondence*,[72] and it was undeniably he who scorned the ubiquity of the Eastern question in 1841,[73] and who just over a decade later authored "Zum Lazarus," a poem which coined the phrase "verdammte Fragen" (damned questions).[74]

Laß die heilgen Parabolen,	Leave the holy parabolas,
Laß die frommen Hypothesen—	Leave the pious hypotheses—
Suche die verdammten Fragen	Seek to solve the damned questions,
Ohne Umschweif uns zu lösen.	For us, without wavering.
Warum schleppt sich blutend, elend,	Why does the just man go bleeding, miserable,
Unter Kreuzlast der Gerechte,	Burdened by the heavy cross,

Während glücklich als ein Sieger	While, happy as a conqueror,
Trabt auf hohem Roß der Schlechte?	The unjust man sits on a high horse?
Woran liegt die Schuld? Ist etwa	Wherein lies the blame? Is maybe
Unser Herr nicht ganz allmächtig?	Our Lord not so almighty?
Oder treibt er selbst den Unfug?	Or is He Himself behind this mischief?
Ach, das wäre niederträchtig.	Oh, that would be vile.
Also fragen wir beständig,	So we keep asking
Bis man uns mit einer Handvoll	Until someone finally stuffs our mouths
Erde endlich stopft die Mäuler—	With a handful of dirt—
Aber ist das eine Antwort?[75]	But is that an answer?

"Zum Lazarus" was translated into Russian in 1858, and Russia's own "proklyatye voprosy" (accursed questions) were born, the most prominent of which was the biblical "What shall we do then?" (Luke 3:10); or "What is to be done?" As Isaiah Berlin would later show, the "accursed questions" became the basis for a number of seminal works by the revolutionary and reform movements and a constant preoccupation of Russian literature and politics throughout the second half of the twentieth century, from Nikolai Chernyshevsky to Tolstoy to Lenin, all of whom wrote works with the title *What Is to Be Done?*[76]

The "accursed questions" are a poor fit for the age of questions in one respect: they were actually questions, which is to say interrogatives.[77] They nonetheless deserve a place here because of the relation they bear to the practical and progressive urge behind addressing the "problem complexes" of the time. It is no coincidence, for example, that Chernyshevsky's 1863 novel *What Is to Be Done?* was preoccupied with the idea of the "new man."[78] To further trace this relation we must make a foray into the realm of philosophy, specifically ontology, or the philosophical line of inquiry concerned with the nature of being. This was a field that consumed the Hungarian Marxist philosopher György Lukács toward the end of his life as he wrote the massive, multivolume *Ontology of Social Being*, published in 1972, a year after his death. In it, Lukács wrote that the question forever to be decided was: "What is to be done?"[79]

"We've often said that Man is an answering being [*antwortendes Wesen*]," Lukács wrote, all practical activity has a goal. Furthermore, insofar as humans "give answer" to their condition, they show how the course of history contains within it the potential to *change course* toward a new goal.[80] The individual however faces a "horrible endlessness of isolated individual questions" and tries to bring them together into "a few central" ones, a selection that is at once a "tendency to generalization."[81] This process brings revolutionary transformation, which in turn creates new forms, such that the period *before* the transformation cannot be reconstructed; the words carry a different meaning, the people themselves are transformed. Thus, "[t]he concisely stated central questions lend the 'answering being' a thrust into world-formation and thereby indirectly into self-formation."[82] A "solution" at the level of society does not emerge automatically from conditions but exists solely as a possibility in which practical activity (*praxis*) can play a role.[83]

The footprints of the age of questions are all over Lukács's *Ontology*: in the slippage between "question" and "problem complexes" [*Fragenkomplexe*]; the difficulty of arriving at a workable "solution"; the aggregate or bundling tendency surrounding questions; the emphasis on "practical activity"; the potential for "revolutionary transformation" at the level of the person as much as of the world; and all by means of "concisely stated central questions." The idea that to concisely state a question was transformative in itself is reminiscent of Marx's 1843 response to an article on the Jewish question by the German theologian Bruno Bauer. Marx wrote that "[t]he formulation of a question is its solution."[84] And in Lukács's "answering being," there is another echo of Marx, who wrote in his 1859 *A Contribution to the Critique of Political Economy* that humanity only sets itself tasks that it can solve and that tasks only emerge when the conditions for their solution are already in evidence or at least in a "process of becoming."[85]

Although it was above all ideology Lukács sought to understand, he may have inadvertently written a philosophy for the age of questions. Lukács's *Ontology* is at once a summation of and a retrospective on the age and its visions of a moral transformation of the world, as much as of the person.

The Genre of the Deed

The emergence and proliferation of popular didactic texts—with their emphasis on the whole of society and the practical over the heady and theoretical—hint at the existence of another genre that arose from the age of questions: the genre of the deed. It would be a mistake to neglect nonverbal and nontextual contributions to the age of questions, especially in an era that was keen to emphasize "practical activity." "A satisfactory answer [to the social question]," wrote J. A. Hobson in 1901, "cannot consist in the theoretic solution of a problem; it must lie in the region of social conduct. Not merely the saying what should be done, but the doing, is the solution. The reins of Science and Practice are drawn together; a theory of social conduct which shall take cognizance of all the factors will be likewise the art of social conduct."[86]

Here the response of a Hungarian zoologist, Ferenc Tangl, to a request to weigh in on the Jewish question for a Hungarian cultural journal warrants mention. It was exceptionally brief:

I'm after all just a creature of the laboratory who twenty-five years ago only took a position on the matter in question— which remains unchanged to the present day—insofar as I banished the Jewish question from my institutes! I don't concern myself with the matter of whether the honest person I choose as a colleague is a Christian or a Jew, and I've truly had no cause to complain that the majority of my colleagues were and are Jews.[87]

Tangl's response was categorized by the authors of the questionnaire among those "[w]ho did not give a meaningful answer, but draw attention to one aspect" of the question.[88] Theirs was a disingenuous assessment, coming as it did from a queristic tradition that sought meaning primarily in the practical and the practicable.

Epilogue

The age of questions was status-quo allergic. Querists did not accept that things had to be as they were. They not only posited the necessity of transformation but put their energies into deriving means for *achieving* that transformation.[89] The Great War was the crucible of the age, and querism's emancipationist agenda translated into real revolutionary changes. Some of the most longstanding and seemingly intractable questions of the nineteenth century were considered either solved or at least sincerely addressed during and just after World War I: the Eastern question with the definitive dissolution of the Ottoman Empire and the emergence of the Turkish Republic, the Polish question with the reappearance of Poland on the map of Europe,[90] and the two most significant subquestions under the umbrella known as the social question— the woman and the worker questions—with expanded suffrage for women throughout many Western and European countries and with the creation of a workers' state in the form of the Soviet Union. The Soviet Union was not only the first state to make solving questions part of its *raison d'être* but may also have been the first to formally and officially declare a question *solved*.[91]

A spattering of "smaller" questions that had irritated domestic and international relations for a century had also largely disappeared: the American question with US independence, the slavery question with the abolition of slavery in the British Empire in 1833 and in the US in 1865, the serf question in Russia with the formal abolition of serfdom there in 1861, and the Irish question with Ireland's formal independence in 1922. At both the national and international levels, a remarkable feature of the age was the tenacity and expediency with which veritable armies of politicians, publicists, intellectuals, and even average citizens turned their energies to understanding and deriving solutions to the questions of their time, doggedly debating them in the periodic press, pamphlets, and books, in representative bodies, at treaty negotiations and cabinet sessions, in debating clubs, and atop soapboxes until they were resolved or at least legislatively addressed.

Taking the long view, querists' achievements are undeniable: the proportion of the voting public grew, empires were broken up, and the treaties after the Great War created governing units arguably more in tune with and responsive to their inhabitants' wishes. Furthermore, of the questions that lingered after World War II— among them the black, gay, and environmental questions—many were clearly the progeny of progressive and specifically Marxist political and intellectual traditions.[92]

But the age did not have a categorically triumphant finale. Already in the late nineteenth century some querists used the rhetoric of "progress" to argue *against* emancipation.[93] And few would dare to argue that the Irish question was "solved" with Ireland's independence, that the abolition of slavery effectively eliminated the "Negro question," that Stalinism truly "solved" the woman question, or that the Polish or Jewish questions did not have deeply troubling afterlives following the Great War. Certainly the "*Anschluß* [Austrian annexation] question" of the interwar period, which became the subject of an Austrian question competition in 1927, could not be said to have a progressive underpinning, even if some viewed it as emancipatory at the time.[94]

Furthermore, though it may be that the social question is no longer commonly invoked, the inequality it once sought to address is in the sights of contemporary progressives now as much as it was then. There are periodic mentions of the social question in political rhetoric, but these often coopt the emancipationist and progressive origins and achievements of the queristic endeavor for conservative ends. In 2016, for example, a political slogan of the conservative ÖVP (Austrian People's Party) read: "The social question of our time is the exploitation of the middle class."[95] Are these trajectories at base the fault of the nineteenth century's emancipationist querists or a reaction to their unprecedented success?

In the words of the leftist French philosopher Félix Guattari writing in 1992, "The left and the workers' movement have been built on the social question, on the question of misery." What would bring about a comparable "existential anxiety" today? he wondered. "There has been a social question, which today takes on new forms; an urban question, a non-renewable energy question, a geopolitical question, a demographic question . . . The question of the question is how these questions are articulated." Guattari worried about the "total ambiguity" of the more recent ecological question, which was inherently of neither the Right nor the Left. "If one makes it a natural question, one risks weighting the modes of questioning in the manner of totalitarianism."[96]

The likes of Weydmann and Hitler were conservative critics of the age of questions, who sought first to stand in the way of its goals and later to reverse its principal achievement: emancipation. That the Nazis turned the language of questions to their own purposes is testament mainly to querists' success in setting the terms for transformative action. The Nazis could not defeat the spirit of the age, they could only attempt to roll back its accomplishments by deploying its rhetoric and perverting its emancipatory aims to suit their own agenda. It was in this spirit that the Nazis "solved" the social question; "reopened" the Transylvanian, Macedonian, Polish, Alsace-Lorraine, Croatian, Ukrainian, Slovak, and many other questions; and offered mass death and enslavement as a form of "emancipation," as their Final Solution to the Jewish question. (The slogan wrought in iron over the entrance gates to Auschwitz-Birkenau was, after all, "Work will make you free.")

The end of World War II and the definitive defeat of Nazi Germany restored some of the age's most remarkable achievements, while burying its true essence under the moral taint of the Final Solution. This argument has been an excavation of that essence.

3

The Argument about Force

THE LOADED QUESTIONS
OF A GENOCIDAL AGE

But there is also a third question, and it is also a world one, and is also
rising up and has almost fully arisen already. This question may in part
be called the German one, but in essence, as a whole, it is above all a
pan-European one, and it is completely and organically a part of the
fate of the whole of Europe and of all the other world questions. . . .
[E]veryone in Europe now is busy with his own affairs; everyone has
found his own question of ultimate importance, a question almost as
important as his own existence, a question like "to be or not to be":
and it's that sort of question that has come up in Germany as well, just
at the time the other world questions have arisen.[1]

—FYODOR DOSTOEVSKY WRITING ON THE
SIMULTANEOUS RISE OF THE EASTERN,
CATHOLIC, AND GERMAN QUESTIONS (1877)

In our time, the time of the total collapse of the liberal world of ideas,
the time of democratic institutions' liquidation, when many of the
achievements of the previous century's revolutions are being
abandoned, the time of the ideational reorientation of the European
nations, the reestablishment of internally consolidated communities
and an authoritarian order, the Jewish question cannot be passed over.[2]

—EMMERICH CZERMAK, AUSTRIAN
CHRISTIAN-SOCIAL PARTY (1933)

A Demoralized Age

The arguments put forward in the two previous chapters are half right but nonetheless wholly mistaken. The national and emancipationist motors behind the queristic machine are undeniable, but the *essence* of the age was neither scattered and unique national trajectories nor the progressive triumph of philanthropic good intentions.[3] Nazism was no perversion of the age's lofty ideals but rather the logical culmination of a rampant querism that could neither formulate a clear objective nor admit defeat.

————

In his book *The Main Questions of Modern Culture* from 1914, the German philosopher Emil Hammacher wrote about the questions of his time—among them the social, woman, and worker questions—their causes, and the longstanding desire to solve them and others, tracing their causes and solution-seeking back to Immanuel Kant and other eighteenth-century idealists. "Since people began to be surprised by that which was once considered self-evident, there have been questions and tasks whose solution is felt as a need and a necessity," Hammacher wrote on the eve of the Great War. "[N]ever before have there been so many riddles storming the people as there are today."[4]

Emil Hammacher did not survive the war. He was killed at the front in France, but *The Main Questions of Modern Culture* was celebrated by no less a figure than Thomas Mann, who in 1918 praised Hammacher as "the young philosopher from Bonn ... whom I would very much like to call my posthumous friend" in his conservative defense of Germany's involvement in the war, *Reflections of a Nonpolitical Man*. In spite of Mann's posthumous blessing, Hammacher did not even attain that moderate amount of fame required to be included in the *German Biographical Encyclopedia*. But his thought was as steeped in the problem of action (*What is to be done?*) as the leftist Lukács's, and constitutes a more accurate summation of what the age of questions had wrought: namely, doubt and despair, and a loss of faith in the *Lösung* (solution).

When Hammacher wrote that "never before have there been so many riddles coming at people as there are today," the passage *continues*: "[I]t's not so much that now a question appears with unprecedented intensity, but rather that absolutely all handed-down solutions of world- and life-problems have become doubtful."[5] This loss of faith in solutions did not devolve into pessimism for Hammacher, however. In the place of the *Lösung*, he fantasized about *Auflösung* (dissolution, or giving over). "[T]he self-same conditions that pave the way to the end also lead to the highest maturation of mystical experience; it is in the state of dissolution that individuals can achieve a higher perfection than ever."[6]

When we juxtapose the Polish nobleman and statesman Adam Czartoryski with Hammacher, we see Hammacher engaged in an interrogation rather than a reaffirmation of the Polish statesman's ideals and assumptions. Whereas Czartoryski believed that states were effectively "masses of personified individuals" and therefore subject to natural law and entitled to the same forms of liberty and equality as individuals,[7] Hammacher wondered, "What right does a state have vis-à-vis others and to what extent are its citizens more than a coincidental legal community, a nation? Does the morality of the state operate under fundamentally different norms than those of the individual?" Whereas Czartoryski favored an order that was rational, just, and above all peaceful, Hammacher asked, "Is the war that [a state] fights for its own self-assertion or aggrandizement an amoral or at least fatuous residue of barbarism; is international spiritual culture [*internationale Geisteskultur*] and eternal peace the highest ideal?"[8] His answer to both was no.

It might be argued that Hammacher's perspective was uniquely German, colored by the German idealist and romantic traditions.[9] And indeed Thomas Mann—in his *Reflections of a Nonpolitical Man*, part of a protracted argument with his liberal-progressive and politically engaged brother Heinrich—dubbed Hammacher's book "an astounding synthesis" of "the Germany that had to enter the war."[10] So perhaps in seeking to fathom the age of questions with Hammacher as our starting point, we must conclude either that it came to be dominated by German thought or that we have traced only a specifically *German* trajectory through the age. Is it not possible, as the national argument of the first chapter suggested, that each nation charted its own course through that age, like the Russians with their "accursed questions" and incessant *What is to be done?*

But the ideas in Hammacher's thesis were not uniquely German. The loss of faith in solutions was a more generalized phenomenon. Already in 1853, Marx and Engels wrote of the "eternal 'Eastern question,'" a designation that was repeated by an anonymous pamphleteer in 1860.[11] In 1865, the Hungarian statesman József Eötvös wrote in his book on the nationality question:

> If some question is left open for a longer time, there is no shortage of proposed solutions, and sometimes it is precisely their number that makes for the greatest difficulty of certain questions; partly because—as in other cases, so herein, too—after the barrage of unsuccessful attempts at solution, the question becomes more complicated, and partly because political debates over means [to a solution] push the goal into the background such that those who agree on the goal nonetheless disagree on the means and face each other as enemies.[12]

The possibility that some questions were therefore unsolvable moving targets troubled commentators on questions as much in Hungary as in Germany. "It is said that the question is settled," the English archaeologist and statesman Austen Henry Layard said of the Eastern question in an 1853 speech before the House of Commons. "I contend that it is only a question deferred."[13]

Of the Irish question, the American attorney David Bennett King wrote in 1882: "I have not ventured to suggest a settlement of the Irish Question, nor even to predict very confidently what form it will next assume. One who has read Irish history is not

likely to venture on so rash an undertaking."[14] Later the founder
of modern Zionism, Theodor Herzl, wrote that the solution to
the Jewish question should be sought in constant movement, like
a plane held up by the motion of air around its wings.[15] Richard
Suschka, who worked in the finacial directorship of the Hungarian Agricultural Academy's branch in Magyar-Óvár, noted in
1897 that whenever it seemed as though the tuberculosis question
had been solved, upon closer examination it turned out that it
was not.[16]

In the years to come, similar assertions of insoluability would
be made for the woman, sugar, Jewish, and maid questions, to
name just a few.[17] And though the Great War seemed to promise
a solution to questions, in the eyes of many it merely exacerbated
them.[18] The German philosopher and historian Oswald Spengler,
writing in 1918, lamented that "one was always endeavoring to find
the solution to *the question*, rather than accepting that many questioners will have many answers, that a philosophical question is
merely a thinly veiled desire to receive a particular answer that is
already implied in the question itself, that the ephemerality of the
time's great questions is beyond measure."[19]

Even the featured philosopher from the progressive argument,
György Lukács, was less hopeful of finding solutions by the end
of his life. At war's end, Lukács weighed in when one of the premier Hungarian journals, *Twentieth Century*, ran a discussion
forum on the nationality question. Prominent thinkers from different parts of Hungary were asked to respond to a provocative
essay by the Hungarian political scientist Mihály Réz. The unfolding Bolshevik revolution in Hungary prevented some from submitting their views, but Lukács—though he was a minister in the
revolutionary government—handed in a long essay refuting Réz's
racialized understanding of the nationality question, offering instead a materialist interpretation in line with the views of the
Austro-Marxist Otto Bauer, who felt that national hatred is but
transformed class hatred.[20] The nationality question, Lukács argued, was one that would benefit from the approach of the "new

philosophy," which showed how apparent contradictions and un-resolvable problems, when viewed from a different level, actually disappear.[21]

But decades later, in his *Ontology*, Lukács argued that even a teleological progression could be interrupted by practical action and taken in a new direction. There was no *automatic* disappear-ance of the problem. The shift in Lukács's own thinking is remark-able, and perhaps traceable to the spectacular failure of the Repub-lic of Soviets he served in 1919, after which his position came closer to that of Réz's original essay in the *Twentieth Century*. Réz had characterized the nationality question as an "organic mistake" that could not be solved by "single measures."[22] He noted that the rea-son the question seemed so intractable was that it was forever changing: as one national goal was achieved, a new one emerged on the horizon, and no matter how modest and reasonable their aims appeared initially, those aims would become broader with time until they finally demand to rule.[23] Lukács's ideas about prac-tical action dealt a similar blow—albeit from the left—to the idea that questions could be solved once and for all.

The Hungarian liberal democrat Oszkár Jászi was also dismis-sive of Réz's intervention on the nationality question, viewing it as a theory of imperial competition that sacrificed individual hu-manity.[24] Yet Jászi's own intervention reiterated the idea that the nationality question was in a constant state of developmental flux and therefore required "appropriate flexibility and liberal spirit" on the part of the state.[25] Though otherwise on opposite ends of the political spectrum, Réz and Jászi saw the nationality question as one that could not really be definitively solved, but that had to be repeatedly addressed.[26]

The Dark Side of Emancipation

If *emancipation* was a watchword of the age of questions, it was a mercenary one that anyone could—and did—use. The ideal of emancipation brought with it the longing for an emancipator, an advocate and liberator. The slogan of the 1831 Polish uprising in tsarist Russia—headed by Czartoryski—had been "For our freedom and yours." Its formulation coincided roughly with the emergence of the Polish question and spoke to a desire to cast the Polish cause as a broader one, extending well beyond the boundaries of would-be Poland. In this spirit, Polish exiles joined the forces of Young Poland with those of Young Italy and Young Germany as part of a broader "Young Europe," a community of reform-minded early nationalists who saw a federation of free and consolidated nation-states as an alternative to the existing imperial Concert of Europe. This vision necessitated both a breaking up of empires and a recombination of states into a new international order, something like the one Czartoryski imagined in his *Essay*.[27]

The rhetoric surrounding a "solution" to the Polish question thus assumed a terrific scope. An 1831 essay in the *London Foreign Quarterly Review* expressed sympathy for the cause of Polish independence but anxiety about the language around the "Polish question," which "[i]f acted upon," would "lead to a succession of revolutions, dismemberments of countries, and wars, until all the world, all Europe at least, became constituted under one form of government."[28] The author sought to keep the cause of Polish independence from being confounded with "the monstrous system of political ethics" that had designs on the whole of the European state system.[29]

That the stakes were much higher than one nation's independence is clear from a very different source, an unpublished manuscript on the Polish question written by the Russian philosopher Pyotr Chaadayev. Chaadayev's *Philosophical Letters*, written in 1829, caused a scandal when they were published in Russia in 1836. The stark criticism of Russian backwardness they contained so outraged Tsar Nicholas I (1825–1855) that he had Chaadayev locked up in a mental institution. In Chaadayev's view, missing out on Catholicism had arrested Russia's development, locking it outside of history. Though critical of Russia in the *Letters*, Chaadayev's was a pious (both literally and figuratively) criticism, as he believed in "a chosen people who would lead mankind to its final goal."[30]

Julia Brun-Zejmis has written of Chaadayev's intervention on the Polish question that "Chaadaev saw Russia's historical privileges as enabling her to make truthful judgments and thereby find correct solutions, not only for problems raised in western European history, but for all Mankind."[31] This made Russia's retention of its westernmost (Polish) provinces "a vital question" in the mind of Chaadayev, whose vision of a "Renaissance dream" placed the Polish claim of acting "for our freedom and yours" in direct competition with an emerging Russian-centered pan-Slavic one.[32]

The idea of Russians as liberators would be propagated by many other Russian thinkers, including the Russian philosopher Nikolai Danilevsky, a liberal turned conservative, who wrote on the Eastern question in 1869. Danilevsky believed that a Russian-dominated "[a]ll-Slavic federation" was "the only reasonable, intelligent solution" to the Eastern question.[33] Tsar Alexander II (1855–1881) was heralded as the "tsar liberator," first for his abolition of serfdom in Russia in 1861 but later also following his intervention in southestern Europe resulting in the administrative separation of Bulgaria from the Ottoman Empire. Leading others to freedom was not merely an ideational project but a transformative state-building one, and also a means of preserving and expanding—rather than undermining—Europe's empires.

Even—and perhaps in some cases especially—where emancipationist drives in southeastern Europe were anti-imperial, violence was commonly viewed as a legitimate solution to period questions. The Macedonian question offers a powerful example: whereas Bulgaria, Serbia, and Greece all offered to "solve" the Macedonian question by liberating the people of Macedonia from the Ottoman Empire, starting in the late 1880s and into the 1900s, this "liberation" frequently meant violence on a breathtaking scale, as groups of militants operating on behalf of one or the other neighboring state burned entire villages; pillaged; raped; killed priests, teachers, and civilians; and undertook forced conversions.[34] The vision of emancipation was therefore not uniquely and unambiguously progressive. What can be said of it is that it was visionary, transformative, and zero sum, and quite often resulted in violence and war.

The Dark Side of Bundling

The gathering of questions into bundles meant that proposed solutions were rarely small, localized fixes but rather structural overhauls on a breathtaking territorial and social scale. "Shall we have war or peace?" wrote the Parisian correspondent of the *London Standard* in late January of 1831. "People think about nothing else, and talk about nothing else than this. First of all they are looking to the Belgian question . . . and next to the Polish question. They do not, however, forget that there is still outstanding the Greek question."[35] Questions, in other words, were linked to the possibility of a broader European conflict in the minds of many querists.

Plentiful were the assertions across the lifespan of the Polish question, for example, that it was not merely about Poland but indeed a "European question" with the capacity to make or break the peace of Europe.[36] A pamphlet from 1831, written by a "Polish diplomat," makes the connection between his preferred solution and war explicit in the very title *The Recreation of Poland; or, A General European War.*[37] Nor was it only Polish diplomats and patriots who made such assertions. Also in 1831, a French law student wrote that the cause of Poland was the cause of France because France "must proclaim a war of principles on which her own existence depends" and support those who wished "to follow her example" with "the point of the bayonet."[38] That same year, the Prussian military leader and theorist of war Carl von Clausewitz wrote that "the Polish question, much like the Belgian, touches on our highest and most sacred interests and relates to the matter of our very existence."[39]

Suggesting a necessary link between solution and survival was a means for commentators on questions to cast their preferred solution as a matter of life and death: to be or not to be. In a memorandum from 1815 on the Polish question circulated at the Congress of Vienna, the author(s) argued that the question was not purely a political one but one of "justice and public morality that will doubtlessly influence the future fate of the nations of Europe," whose Great Powers "dream only of the balance of force and the equilibrium of potential violence."[40] And in the closing line of one of the earliest pamphlets on the Polish question, we read: "Poland should be given its due—freedom, [a]nd whosoever is unwilling to sheath their sword should be forced—as the Turks were at Navarino—to do so by violence: Peace! Peace! Peace!"[41] Even if it means war.

It was clear by the uprising of 1830–1831 that many querists viewed conflict and the possibility of its spread as an opportunity for the "solution" of questions, hence the reference to the Battle of Navarino (1827) as decisive in settling Greek independence in the same way the author hoped Polish independence would be secured. Behind every plea for peace lurked a backhanded battle cry.

In a pamphlet from 1840, the French publicist François Dumons wrote of the Eastern question that solving it would require either "a general war and a war of principle, or—what would be better for everyone—a good-natured and rational alliance."[42] That same year, a Polish exile named Sawaszkiewicz wrote of the Polish question: "*[A]ll the leading* political events of Europe, are more or less involved in this question."[43] He averred that the Eastern and Polish questions could only be solved together, and that "[s]ince the fall of Poland . . . it is no wonder that . . . all Eastern commotions have become of *vital* importance to the Western nations, and that the present one should be made a question of a *general war*."[44] In an article from 1849 in his *La tribune des peuples*, the exiled writer and Polish patriot Adam Mickiewicz put forward a similar position: "The Eastern question arises with a somber grandeur, a general war can result from it."[45] We know something about Mickiewicz's views on a "general war" from a poem he composed in the wake of the November Uprising's failure:

"For a universal war for the Freedom of the Peoples, / We beseech thee, O Lord."[46]

In 1851, the conservative Austro-Hungarian politician Anton Szécsen railed against the increasingly "mechanistic"—as opposed to "organic"—approach to solving questions in his book on *Political Questions of the Time*. "Organic politics," he wrote, insists on discussion and reform and achieving practical goals. "Mechanistic politics," by contrast, is machine oriented, idealizing. Discussion works initially, but when rights are denied, discussion ends and a solution is sought through bloody revolution.[47] Several commentators on the Kansas question, noting the escalating violence against residents of the territory along proslavery and antislavery lines in the 1850s, reached a similar conclusion about the relationship between the presumed intractability of rights questions and violence.[48] And a Slovene commentator lamenting the proliferation of "questions upon questions" (social, woman, Eastern) observed that "force" and "the fist" were the language of questions.[49]

Although the violence surrounding the Kansas question was initially localized, it later spun out of control, feeding into the American Civil War. In Europe, bundling often served to internationalize both a question and a preferred solution. So it was that one commentator on the Eastern question linked it to the Alabama question in the United States as a matter of negotiated sovereignty.[50] Furthermore, the belief that individual questions could not be isolated came to be viewed not as a barrier to but as a *catalyst* of their solution. During the First Balkan War in 1912, an article in a German newspaper argued for bundling the Albanian and Adriatic questions "with all the other questions that have been raised by events in the Balkans" to derive a lasting solution.[51] "Were the Balkan problem an isolated one," we read in a 1918 British government history of the Eastern question, "a satisfactory arrangement might well seem impossible; but the introduction of factors outside its strict limits may offer a practicable solution."[52]

Internationalization in turn brought question bundles into rhetorical relation with a generalized conflict: the "universal war" was the nightmarish panacea worship-dreaded by many querists. The Crimean War (1853–1856) appeared to some—including Mickiewicz, who died on his way to taking part in it against Imperial Russia—as the long-awaited universal war. "This is not a little war," Austen Henry Layard told the House of Commons in 1854 in a speech on the Turkish question. "[N]ow you have got into a great war."[53] An 1855 pamphlet by "a German statesman" on *The Polish Question Viewed from the German Perspective* declared that "this colossal struggle cannot be ended other than by a complete change in the alliances of all states, as well as in their boundaries." The war, in other words, had seen to it that "the Polish question is rising imperceptibly to the level of a soluble, indeed, a practical question."[54] Czartoryski, too, weighed in on the possibility that the war would critically raise the Polish question in Russian-controlled Poland.[55]

War and the potential for an even larger, all-embracing conflagration were at the heart of the age of questions. Bundling tendencies were in evidence at three levels: questions were bundled to suggest or combine solutions, wars were magnified or universalized to accommodate the bundles' seething mass, and some questions became mammoth provocations to a "solution-seeking" age, presumed to symbolize the entirety of what was wrong with the time. "Every time the Eastern question arises," wrote Fyodor Dostoevsky in 1876 in his *Diary of a Writer*, "the apparent wholeness of Europe begins, much too obviously, to fall apart into personal, segregatedly national egoisms . . . [s]o that every time this fatal question appears on the scene, all former inveterate political conflicts and ailments of Europe begin to ache and fester."[56]

At the same time, questions could gather all of Europe's troubles under a single rubric to enable a wholesale *solution*, an ultimate, even a definitive peace.[57] In his 1869 *Russia and Europe*, Nikolai Danilevsky believed he had found both a perfectly reduced formula and an omnibus solution to the Eastern question. "The curative events, from which . . . we will learn our saving lessons, have already appeared on the horizon of history, and are called: *The Eastern Question*."[58] The belief that it was possible to reduce questions to a single common denominator and to solve them in one stroke pervaded Dostoevsky's thinking on the Eastern question, as well.[59] An anonymous "Son of the East," writing in 1882, similarly argued that "this Eastern question is not a single question, but a series of many problems and multiform views ... and becomes a political, religious and social question."[60] And a Serbian querist writing in 1915 insisted that "[l]asting peace ... contains within itself also the definitive and just solution of the Balkan question."[61]

In her 1889 book *Lay Down Your Arms!*, for which she later won the Nobel Peace Prize, Bertha von Suttner observed a sinister connection between the very mention of questions and the threat of war. Each question was like a " 'black spot' that arose on the horizon," and "War in sight" was the favored slogan of politicians whenever they did.[62] When "the European situation has no 'pressing question,' " then "peace is secured," was the going assumption, Suttner observed. "What weak logic! Questions can arise at any moment. Only when we keep some other remedy at the ready besides war will we be secured against war."[63]

The Dark Side of Equilibrium

There is a pattern of the age that comes through especially powerfully in the European context, and that is an evolving conception of an intangible and yet almost physical relationship between the geopolitics of the East and the social politics of the West. In 1831, in an early intervention on the Polish question, its author lamented "the confusion between the struggle for ancient privileges in the East and the unfortunately simultaneous revolutionary convulsions in the West."[64] One result: the terms of the Polish question were presented in radically different ways to different audiences, sometimes by the very same people. The domestic politics of the Great Powers—and particularly concerns about revolution—became crucial to the case made for Poland by its advocates during the November Uprising.

The diplomatic campaign initiated by none other than Czartoryski in Austria during the brief existence of a Polish National Government of the November Uprising of 1830–1831, for example, was effectively a legitimist one. It asserted that Tsar Nicholas I of Russia had broken faith with the 1815 Concert of Europe, failing to keep tsarist Russia's promise to maintain the Polish constitution, and that the Poles were not dangerous revolutionaries but interested in preserving their rights in accordance with the terms of the Congress of Vienna. Contained in this appeal was the idea that Russia (not Poland) posed the greater threat to the conservative European order: if the Polish uprising were to be crushed, then the European peoples would be next insofar as Russia was not about to respect the status quo.[65] Meanwhile Czartoryski also courted the liberal press and politicians in Western Europe. At its earliest appearance, the Polish question was crafted to accommodate this dual-track content.

For Czartoryski, the geopolitical questions of the East were intimately related to the social ones of the West. He and others posited not so much an oppositional or mirror model but rather a *relational* model for thinking of Europe's East and West in a common frame. The geopolitical drama unfolding in the East was presumed—even mobilized—to affect the social domain in the West, even as the character of Western Europe's social politics was wielded in the interest of shifting boundaries and state sovereignty in the East. In the words of an anonymous German pamphleteer writing on the Eastern question in 1843, "[I]t is extremely crucial to balance out the Eastern difference before a catastrophe occurs in Western Europe."[66]

In 1847, Benjamin Disraeli, destined to become Britain's first (and still only) Jewish prime minister, was then still climbing through the ranks of the Conservative Party as a member of Parliament. He made speeches by day and wrote fiction by night. That year, a bill was introduced and debated that would have permitted Jews to become MP's without converting to Christianity (as Disraeli himself had done). Disraeli argued in favor of the bill. It failed.

Later that same year he published his novel *Tancred; or, The New Crusade.* The title character travels to the Holy Land and meets a certain Signor Elias de Laurella, the Jewish honorary consul-general of Austria. In chapter seven, the characters engage in a conversation about the Eastern question in which Laurella asks, "But the question is, what is the Eastern question?"[67] The conversation is about the Eastern question, but more importantly (and cryptically) it is about the Jewish Disabilities Bill of 1847, as is shortly revealed when another character answers that "[t]he Eastern question is, who shall govern the Mediterranean." In the ensuing dialogue, it is mentioned that the prime minister of Egypt is Jewish, and later that because Christianity stems from Judaism and it was the Jews who perfected Christianity, they are well suited to govern. In this way, Disraeli used the Eastern question to propose a solution to the Jewish question in Britain, a bundling that linked domestic social policy in Britain to the geopolitics of the Ottoman Empire.

Other nineteenth-century luminaries did the same. Yet although bundling social with geopolitical questions suggested opportunity to some, it spelled calamity to others. On September 20, 1840, the British secretary of state for war and the colonies Lord John Russell wrote a letter to the prime minister Lord Melbourne on the Eastern question, in which he outlined "the great questions relating to the settlement of Europe" and worried that, in the event of a war, conflict "would speedily embrace the other questions" and "leave the East a prey to the ambition of other states, & the freedom & civilization of the west exposed to all the hazards of internal convulsion, and external attack."[68]

A similar argument surfaced more than a decade later, when the threat of war seemed even more acute. On March 23, 1853, with the Crimean War on the near horizon, Britain's newly appointed secretary of state for foreign affairs, George Villiers, fourth Earl of Clarendon, sent a dispatch to Sir G. Hamilton Seymour, then British minister to Russia. The foreign secretary sought to assure the Russian leadership that Britain had no hostile intentions.

The main object of her Majesty's Government, that to which their efforts have been and always will be directed, is the preservation of peace; and they desire to uphold the Turkish empire from their conviction that no great question can be agitated in the East without becoming a source of discord in the West, and that every great question in the West will assume a revolutionary character and embrace a revision of the entire social system for which the Continental Governments are certainly in no state of preparation.[69]

Clarendon's dispatch surfaced a year later and became a matter for public debate when Britain's involvement in the war erupted into a domestic controversy. The debate focused on 1,300 pages of official government documents relating to the period leading up to the war.[70] In April of 1854, Karl Marx, writing on the Eastern question under a pseudonym for the *New York Tribune*, was among those to comment on the British foreign secretary's now-published dispatch. Marx paraphrased Clarendon:

Her Majesty's Government "desires to uphold the Turkish Empire," . . . not from any Eastern consideration at all, but "from their conviction that no great question can be agitated in the East *without becoming a source of discord in the West*." . . . The brave Earl goes further. Why does he fear *a war with France,* which he declares must be the "necessary result" of the dissolution and dismemberment of the Turkish Empire? A war with France, considered in itself, would be a very pleasant thing. But there is this delicate circumstance connected with it. "*Every great question in the West will assume a revolutionary character and embrace a revision of the entire social system.*"[71]

As we know, Marx favored "a revision of the entire social system." Of interest here is that both he and the British foreign secretary—though their politics were diametrically opposed—shared the view that "agitation" of the Eastern question would precipitate a war that would result in such a revision. Tweak a question in the

East, and "[e]very great question in the West" would be affected, as well. "One might formulate the riddle in this way," wrote Dostoevsky in 1877:

> [W]hy does it always happen, and particularly lately—I mean from the middle of the nineteenth century...—that the moment some issue in the world touches on something general and universal, all the other world problems at once rise parallel to it? For instance, in Europe it's now not enough to have just one world problem, the Eastern Question; no—in France, Europe suddenly and unexpectedly raises another question of world importance—the Catholic one. And the Catholic question is there... because it has been accepted here that Catholicism is the common banner under which to unite the whole order of things... against something new and imminent, vital and fateful, against the renewal of the macrocosm by a new order of things, against the social, moral, and radical revolution in all of Western European life.[72]

In their engagement with questions, Czartoryski, Disraeli, Clarendon, Marx, and Dostoevsky all postulated the interconnectedness of domestic social relations in the West with sovereignty issues in the East.

A similar yet even more forceful model of that connection emerged just after the Crimean War and resounded well into the twentieth century. In the 1856 satirical novel *Fritz Beutel* by the German poet and humorist Hermann Marggraff, the title narrator tells two Turkish ministers: "The Eastern question... is about how Eastern barbarism... is holding a fig leaf to conceal its nakedness. It picked this fig leaf from the tree of Western civilization. No true peace can be achieved until the differences have been equalized, i.e., until Western Civilization gives in as much to Eastern barbarism as the latter does to Western Civilization."[73] Marggraff's conception was one of a disequilibrium steadily yielding to homogeneity. Where there had previously been two levels of civilization—the higher West and the lower East—equilibrium was the prerequisite for a solution to the Eastern question.

The German historian Leopold von Ranke, writing around the time of the Berlin Congress of 1878, felt that, with reference to the Eastern question, in particular, "[o]ne saw rightly what was at stake with the question. Eastern and western deviations [*Irrungen*] impact one another in a most dangerous way."[74]

> In our time the inner movements of Turkey directly touch upon the conflicts of European domestic policy. It is clear for all to see that the system that came to dominance after 1815, known as the Holy Alliance, had to be abandoned in the wake of the Greek uprising. [...] Sympathy for the Greeks became a lever for liberal aspirations. The Kingdom of Greece was founded on all the most animated conflicts of domestic and foreign interests of the European powers.[75]

Though securing Greece's independence required shifting boundaries, there was hardly a consensus that "Eastern" questions were to be solved in strictly geopolitical terms. There were repeated attempts over the course of the lifespan of several questions to define them as "social." "The Polish question," Adolf Chaisés wrote in an 1863 pamphlet, "now occupies the first place among all major social problems."[76] And as we learned from the national argument, the Irish question was also periodically labeled a social question.[77]

That querists framed this alignment of the geopolitical and social questions along an East-West axis as a sign that the dividing boundaries between East and West were more generally eroding. One stanza of a satirical poem, first published in the 1883 edition of London's *Mayfair Magazine*, titled "A Lament for Romance" alluded to a dull leveling occasioned by the West's engagement with the Eastern question:

> The East is Occidentalized,
> > By railroads, tramways, and hotels,
> The picturesque is little prized
> > Wherever modern progress dwells;
> The conquering Mussulman of yore
> > Has fallen from his pride of place,

The "Eastern Question" is a bore,
   The record of a waning race—
No more the Crescent blazes red,
  'Tis pale and faint: Romance is dead![78]

A few years later, in an 1887 book on "social equilibrium," the American Unitarian Reverend George Batchelor bound the social to the geopolitical across continents through question-problems. "Once a disturbance of the social equilibrium could be confined to a narrow territory," he wrote. "Now, so rapid and easy is communication, and so great the increase of sympathy, with its mutual attractions and repulsions, that what is felt in one land is quickly felt in another." Social disequilibrium could spread, in other words, resulting in a kind of reverse flow or contamination.[79] In this new interconnected world, he continued, "[t]here is no American problem now. Our problems are also European problems, and the problems of Europe are the problems of Asia."[80]

> The fortunes of the little kingdom of Bulgaria, remote as they are from the thought and interest of the American public, have a most direct and important relation to the welfare of every American laborer . . . because the law of social equilibrium requires that undue pressure in one part of a fluid social system shall be relieved by the distribution of the pressure through all the parts in communication with it.[81]

In 1922, Arnold Toynbee repeated in terms quite similar to Marggraff's and Batchelor's the inevitable "leveling" course he presumed to be underway between the Ottoman Empire and the West around the Eastern (or Western) question. "For good or evil, the barriers between the West and the Near East are down, and the interchange of currents seems certain to go on increasing until the waters find a common level." Nor was this a positive development. "It now looks as if the Near East were infecting conflicts of nationality in Western Europe with the ferocity and fanaticism which it has imported into its own," Toynbee lamented.

Before the War, the ancient conflicts of interest between Ulster-men and Catholics in Ireland or Germans and Poles in Silesia were waged with some restraint, and bloodshed was uncom-mon. In 1921 both these and other zones of national conflict in the West were a prey to revolutionary bands, semi-official bashy-bozuks, regular combatants whose activities were dis-avowed while approved by their governments, and all the other indecencies familiar in the Armenian vilayets or Macedonia. This moral Balkanisation is also unmistakable, and it is more dangerous than the political and economic manifestations of the tendency.[82]

The bundling of questions ceased to be perceived as a means to a solution and instead came to be seen as a source of contamination; the bundles connected West with East, setting both in motion.[83] One Hungarian querist, Miklós Párdányi, writing in 1928, betrayed not a little schadenfreude in a pamphlet on the "Breton, Basque, and Flemish questions." The age of questions would take its re-venge on France in particular, he believed, as punishment for at-tempting to sideline the nationality principle in its own domains (and for the punitive peace it had helped impose on Hungary, in the course of which Hungary lost two-thirds of its territory and 70 percent of its population). Tweak a border in the East and you will have trouble back home in the West, was the subtext of Párdányi's argument. Eventually the Breton, Basque, and Flemish questions would rise again and do to France what France had done to Hungary.[84]

Sanctioned Decontamination: The Jewish Question in the Age of Questions

The questions of the nineteenth century that form the backdrop to Párdányi's Breton, Basque, and Flemish questions are ones like the Macedonian, Ukrainian, and Armenian questions. (Toynbee's reference to "the Armenian vilayets and Macedonia" is also telling in this regard.) These were born in different contexts. The Macedonian question was largely a struggle between Greece, Serbia, and Bulgaria for the souls of the inhabitants of Macedonia; the Ukrainian question was a struggle primarily between Russians, Ukrainians, and Poles for the souls of the inhabitants of Eastern Poland or Western Russia/the Soviet Union; and the Armenian question related to the status of Armenians in the Ottoman Empire, whether they deserved an autonomous existence within or independence from the Empire, and—if so—what shape such autonomy/independence might take. But what is remarkable about all three questions is how violent the attempts to definitively solve them became, especially during the late nineteenth century and above all in the course of that great solution crucible, World War I.

In his memoir, *Hitch-22*, Christopher Hitchens outlined his qualms with the very formulation of the Irish question: "[T]he word 'solution' can be as neutral as the words 'question' or 'problem,' but once one has defined a people or a nation as such, the search for a resolution can become a yearning for the conclusive. *Endlösung*: the final solution."[85] This magical automatism had long been noted by other commentators on questions, among them Karl Marx,[86] as well as Karl May, who wrote in 1882 of the Eastern question: "Whoever can first define it gets to solve it."[87] A few decades later, during the Great War, the German political scientist Adolf Grabowsky wrote that "[o]nce the problems are comprehensively and clearly grasped . . . they will steer themselves toward solution."[88] Of the Yugoslav question, the Croat politician and publicist Franko Potočnjak wrote in 1915 that, once "properly understood," the truth of the question would "categorically lead to its proper solution."[89]

The Hungarian democratic thinker and statesman István Bibó went one step further and assigned a politics to this sort of automatistic thinking. In a long essay on the Jewish question in Hungary from 1944, he argued that it was reactionary forces who had come to see antidemocratic ideas and anti-Semitic nationalism as that which "explains with blinding clarity every problem, interprets every irritating experience as part of a comprehensive system, and naturally finds the solution automatically [*magától*]."[90]

It is especially ironic that the second chapter's argument on progress cited Lukács and his work on ontology to argue that the age of questions was underpinned by a fundamentally emancipatory and progressive impulse. In fact, it was precisely with the *ontological* questions, the ones that spoke to the essence of a people or peoples (Irish, Armenian, Jewish, Macedonian), that the destructive fury of the age was most fully revealed. As Hitchens noted, "once one has defined a people or nation" as a "question" demanding a "solution," that people or nation has been turned into a problem.

This phenomenon has long preoccupied commentators on and historians of the Jewish question in particular. In 1966, the Jewish historian Jacob Toury sought to uncover when the "slogan" of the "Jewish question" first appeared. He noted that although there were tangential semantic near misses during the revolutionary period in France, "a *question juive* did not emerge." He concluded that "neither a tense social situation nor party politics, nor even ideological altercations between conservatism and liberalism were at the root of the later concept of a 'Jewish Question.'"[91]

Ultimately he placed the origins of the slogan in the late 1830s, arguing that "the 'Jewish question' as a slogan did not take root until it had established itself as an anti-Jewish battle-cry," namely, with two long essays published in 1838 in German titled *The Jewish Question*.[92] The anonymous author of the essays argued that, on the basis of their essentially alien characteristics, Jews should not be given political equality in Prussia (as was being debated at the time).[93] A small flurry of publications in 1842 in Germany used the term *Judenfrage* to argue against full and immediate equality. Toury concluded that "the slogan *Judenfrage*, . . . initiated a new phase in the development of anti-Jewish bias. Its ideological connotations foreshadowed the development of those forms of antisemitism that became rampant in Western Europe at the end of the nineteenth century."[94] Therefore, "Jews," he wrote, "could not concede the existence of a 'Jewish question'" which was already loaded with prejudice against them.

Toury's assertion was borne out by the fuller context of Marx's famous 1843 response to Bruno Bauer's essay on the Jewish question, in which he wrote: "How, then, does Bauer solve the Jewish question? What is the result? The formulation of a question is its solution. The critique of the Jewish question is the answer to the Jewish question."[95] It was Bauer's insistence on *formulating the question* that was problematic for Marx. For those who took Jews' right to emancipation as a given—in Marx's case, as part of a more generalized emancipation—there was no "question." "Is there such a question?" wondered the Hungarian-Jewish writer and editor Lajos Szabolcsi in 1917:

> It is only a *question* to those who cannot accept that we, Hungarian Jews, consider this country as much our homeland as do Hungarians of other faiths. It is only a *question* to those who would like to change that. It is only a *question* to those who believe that our being, our existence, our worth, our survival, our development are not facts or plusses, but rather doubtful, wavering uncertainties, in a word: *questions*.[96]

In the words of the Hungarian communist Erik Molnár, writing in 1946 on the history of the "Jewish question," there had long been many voices declaring that "the Jewish question was an artificial creation of politically motivated demagoguery. Without anti-Semitic propaganda, no one would speak of a Jewish question."[97] In this respect, it is telling that the "Judenfrage" appears in Koselleck et al.'s *Basic Concepts in History* only under the entry for "Antisemitismus,"[98] and that the *Encyclopedia Judaica* does not contain an entry for the "Jewish question," while *Antisemitism: A Historical Encyclopedia of Prejudice and Persecution* does.[99]

The *Universal Jewish Encyclopedia*, meanwhile, denies the existence of "a single Jewish question anywhere." Jews "never, at any time or any place considered themselves a problem to themselves or to the people among whom they lived."[100] The writer Jean Améry similarly identified the Jewish question with anti-Semitism, writing after World War II: "Anti-Semitism and the Jewish question as historical, socially determined, and intellectual [*geistige*] phenomena have never had anything to do with me. They are utterly and completely a matter for the anti-Semites, their shame or their sickness. The anti-Semites have to come to grips with it, not I."[101]

At least three other attributes of the age of questions figured into the trajectory from a Jewish question to the Final Solution. One was the early proclivity to think in terms of "final solutions," frustrated by the late nineteenth- and early twentieth-century suspicion that questions might not be solvable. The result was despair, on the one hand, and increasingly radical "solutions" on the other. A second element was the universalization of a question's impact through arguments that a question was not merely a matter of interest or relevance to the group it named (slaves, women, workers, Jews, and others) but to everyone and was therefore in everyone's interest to solve. And finally, the internationalization of questions that accompanied bundling gave rise to megalomaniacal thinking about the necessary scale of a "solution" to the "Jewish question," tying it to universal war. I will briefly treat each of these here in turn.

Final Solutions

Those who spoke in the idiom of questions saw the stakes in finding the best—indeed, the *definitive*—solution as especially high. Even prior to the age, semantically it was quite common for a "question" to be presumed to have a "final solution."[102] Eighteenth-century uses of the phrase "final solution" in English also denoted a cure, as of a disease or fever.[103] The German word *Endlösung* began appearing in the second half of the nineteenth century, generally in reference to mathematical or chemical formulae or equations.[104]

The idea of the single, one-stroke solution enraptured many nineteenth-century thinkers, from the English parson Walter Scott to the Russian general Rostislav Fadeev.[105] In a speech delivered by Napoleon III to the French Chamber of Deputies on the occasion of the opening of the legislative session in November of 1863, for instance, the emperor spoke of the "sugar question" as demanding a "final solution."[106] Not even literary questions relating to characters in fictional texts could escape the rhetoric of the final solution.[107]

The mathematical models for deriving "final solutions" initially implied there could be only *one* possible solution to a given question. This scientized monomania was manifest in the nineteenth-century fascination with "$2 \times 2 = 4$," a common weapon in the rhetorical arsenal of commentators on social and geopolitical issues, especially in the first half of the nineteenth century. In an 1842 piece titled "The Reaction in Germany," the Russian socialist revolutionary (later anarchist) Mikhail Bakunin wrote, "The Left says, two times two are four; the Right, two times two are six; and the middle-of-the-road compromisers say two times two are five."[108] In other words, only the Left had the correct solution.

So prevalent was the use of "$2 \times 2 = 4$" that Fyodor Dostoevsky, in his 1864 novel *Notes from Underground,* gave it a body and an attitude: "Twice two's four watches smugly, stands in the middle of your road with his arms akimbo, and spits."[109] But even Dostoevsky himself would later write ecstatically of formulae and final solutions: "[W]ith the final solution of the Eastern question, all other political strife in Europe will be terminated. [T]he formula—'the Eastern question'—comprises, perhaps unknowingly to itself, all other political questions, perplexities and prejudices of Europe."[110]

As noted earlier, however, toward the end of the nineteenth and into the early twentieth century querists' faith in "final solutions" was slipping. In 1859, the Italian revolutionary Giuseppe Mazzini wrote that the liberals had catastrophically reduced the Italian question to the wrong formula. "Whatever has since impeded the free, logical, and rational development of our movement comes from that malignant formula [*formola malaugurata*]."[111] But what if there was no such thing as the "right" formula, or what if the formula had to change over time? In his 1868 *The Worker Question in Its Present Form and the Attempts to Solve It,* Ernst Becher wrote that "each time has its own tasks to fulfill, its own questions to solve, which sum up the character and meaning of [that time] . . . the struggle and pursuit of what is newer and better, the battle of other ideas and principles against the legacy of vanquished forms of life and axioms, but nowhere yet nearing completion."[112] Becher presented period questions as part of an interminable process, forever incomplete, requiring constant engagement.

With the loss of faith in final solutions, the mathematical fixation behind early questions began yielding to a biological and medical one.[113] "Society is sick," wrote Becher, "because society is the organism that keeps the blood of social life in circulation. Then comes the question regarding the causes, character, and cure of the sickness: *the social question.* The social question is thus now and forever more the question of *establishing harmony in the integral life* [*Gesammtleben*] *of the people*."[114] The biological metaphor could accommodate querists' lust for the legitimacy of science while accounting for previous failures to find definitive solutions. If construed as a sickness or a condition, a question might attenuate or grow acute, but never disappear, or it might show different "symptoms" in different national contexts.

The Austrian theosophist Rudolf Steiner alluded to the limitations of single formulaic "solutions" in his work on the "social question" from 1919, decrying the notion that a scientific messiah would come and offer a grand solution. Even if someone did derive a "perfect theoretical 'solution,'" he wrote, "[w]e are no longer living in a time in which one can believe it possible to operate this way in public life."[115] The social question had to be viewed as periodic rather than fixed, like hunger rather than like a mathematical equation. "Just as an organism becomes hungry some time after being full," he wrote, "so does the social organism proceed from order to disorder. There can no more be a universal medicine for [maintaining] order in social relations than there is a food that will satisfy for all times." The "social question," though hardly a new development in human societies, had to be solved repeatedly and differently each time in accordance with the conditions of that time.[116]

Similarly, the Hungarian-Swiss rabbi and philosopher Ludwig Stein believed that the shift to biology was merely a new approach to an old problem that had preoccupied both Plato and the scholastics. "Every age rather throws up these as yet unsolved questions again in its own fashion," he wrote in 1897. What religious dogma had been in the Middle Ages and mathematics in the seventeenth century, biology was in the nineteenth century, namely, the search for a new path to the universal.[117]

Everyone's Question, an International Question

The search for the universal was not incidental to the age of questions: it was central. When the American political economist and publicist Henry George wrote a book on the "Irish land question" in 1881, he argued that "[I]t is a mistake to consider the Irish Land Question as a mere local question, arising out of conditions peculiar to Ireland, and which can be settled by remedies that can have but local application. On the contrary, . . . it is nothing less than that question of transcendent importance which is everywhere beginning to agitate, and if not settled, must soon convulse, the civilized world." As George's work was translated into several languages, its entry into the international public sphere precipitated a telling transformation of the question itself: the "Irish land question" became simply "the land Question," first in translation, and later even in subsequent editions of George's English-language original.[118]

When speaking to a group of students at the University of Turin in 1892, Edmondo de Amicis warned his audience, on the cusp as they were of entering active economic and political life: "Don't listen to those who claim that the social question is only a question for industrial and agricultural workers ... No, it is a question for everyone." All classes are affected by it, he intoned, including the middle class. Amicis then presaged a constant struggle with a question that transcended events, politics, and even entire movements.[119] That same year the Hungarian Catholic theologian János Surányi made a similar case in a work on the social question, which he dubbed one of the most burning questions of the time, not just for one or the other class, but for everyone. He insisted that the well-being of the whole of society depended on its solution.[120] And in 1915, a Polish querist dubbed the Polish question "Le grand problème international."[121]

Throughout much of their history, querists frequently endowed questions, among them the "Jewish question," with two universalizing features: that every question was at root a *Jewish (Eastern, social, etc.) question*,[122] and that the Jewish (Croatian, woman, or worker) question was not just a problem for Jews (or Croats, or women, or workers) but *everyone's* concern, and insofar as it was everyone's problem, failing to solve it would redound to everyone's harm, and its ultimate solution to everyone's benefit.[123] This strategy prevailed regardless of whether the commentator was for or against emancipation.[124]

"The whole world longs for the solution of the Jewish Problem," wrote the American lawyer and soon-to-be supreme court justice Louis Brandeis in 1915.[125] Similarly, Stephanie Laudyn (Stefanja Laudynowa), in the 1920 book *A World Problem: Jews—Poland—Humanity*, wrote, "In studying the question, I have realized that the relation of the Jews in regard to Poland is exactly the same as their relations to the world at large. For that reason, the problem at issue intimately concerns other nations; in fact, affects their creeds, their ideals and aspirations."[126] And writing in the 1920s, the Hungarian orientalist and philologist Mihály Kmoskó argued that Jewry—as those responsible for Hungary's 1919 Bolshevik revolution—had already achieved the status of an international great power that small nations could not take on alone. Only a great economic and political alliance of anti-Semitic small nations could "solve the Jewish question in accordance with unified principles and on an *international* basis."[127] (A Romanian diplomat told his Bulgarian counterpart something similar during a conversation in March 1939.[128])

By suggesting that the Jewish question could be solved by a reshuffling of alliances, and potentially even the creation of new states and the bending of borders, what had often been construed in the West as a social question increasingly took on the character of a geopolitical one. That it was understood as such is evident from several interventions on the Jewish question in Romania during the Berlin Congress (1878) where Romania's independence was linked to the "solution of the Jewish question" in the form of emancipation of the country's Jews.[129]

Hitler as Question Bundler

Adolf Hitler was very much a creature of the age. The most vehement of his queristic preoccupations was the Jewish question. But what historians of Nazism have hitherto overlooked is how the Jewish question was part of a question bundle, and how its solution was framed in a classic querists' manner, namely, as related to and necessarily contingent on opening or reopening a series of other questions. In a speech he gave in Berlin some months after the Nazis seized power in 1933, Hitler said, "Each of us will pass, but Germany must live, and in order for her to live all questions of the day must be overridden and certain pre-conditions established."[130] His and the Nazis' formulation of the "Endlösung" (Final Solution) unmasked the pathology behind the age's bundling of questions and obsessive desire to see them definitively solved.

Many Germans, and especially the Nazis, did not see the end of the Great War as the end of the age of questions. On the contrary: In a speech he delivered to the Reichstag on May 17, 1933, by which time the Nazis had consolidated their power enough to make the Reichstag a governing body in name only, Hitler asserted that

> all of the problems causing today's unrest lie anchored in the deficiencies of the peace treaty, which was unable to provide a judicious, clear and reasonable solution for the most important and most decisive questions of the time for all ages to come. Neither the national problems nor the economic—not to mention the legal—problems and demands of the peoples were solved by virtue of this treaty in a manner that would allow them to withstand the criticism of reason for all time.[131]

Hitler declared as a Nazi objective to "resolve all suspended questions in such a manner that another conflict cannot emerge, at least for the foreseeable future."[132] This applied not merely to the geopolitical questions but also to the social question. In a late-night conversation with Heinrich Himmler on November 2, 1941, Hitler reminisced to the SS leader about his early dedication to solving the social question. "To have evaded the question would have been like in the seventeenth or eighteenth century to believe that it was unnecessary to abolish serfdom." With the social question solved, he continued, "It was a matter of mathematical certainty that this party would take charge! . . . The same is true now on a larger [international] scale."[133]

Raising the question to a "larger scale" was precisely what Hitler and the Nazis did with other questions, as well, and above all with the Jewish question. "It's entirely natural," Hitler told Himmler on the evening of January 27, 1942, "that we should concern ourselves with the question on the European level. It's clearly not enough to expel them from Germany."[134] In a speech delivered on his behalf on February 24, 1943, Hitler argued that "international Jewry, which instigated this new war, will find out that nation after nation engrosses itself more and more in this question to become finally aware of the great danger presented by this international problem."[135]

The striking pattern that emerges when we view Hitler in the context of the age of questions is how the path to war and mass violence was paved with questions. The Jewish question played a central role but did not of itself constitute a *casus belli* for the Nazis except as part of a question bundle. On January 30, 1939, Hitler gave a speech to the Reichstag in which he said, "During my struggle for power, it was first and foremost the Jewish people who ridiculed my prophesies that I would someday take over the leadership of the German state and the entire German people and that I would push for a solution to the Jewish problem, among many others."[136]

The Nazis opened a chain of questions during the years and months preceding the war. Among the first were the racial and Jewish questions domestically, which by design acquired an international scope (as they became the "emigrant question").[137] Then there was the Saar question regarding the status of the Saarland.[138] In 1935, there was a plebiscite, and the region voted to rejoin Germany. Hitler and Goebbels had placed the matter at the center of the country's domestic and international political agenda of the time, initiating a massive propaganda campaign in favor of reannexation.[139] The thrust of the campaign was that the Saar question was "the last obstacle to amicable relations with France" and that "when the Saar question was settled" in favor of Germany, the result would redound to "the pacification of Europe."[140]

After the Saar question came the Austrian (or Anschluß), Sudeten-German, and Danzig questions (all defined and discussed in the "question" idiom). By 1939, the Nazis had opened or reopened questions all around their periphery, in addition to the social and Jewish questions, both domestically and abroad.[141] More importantly, their reputation as querists *par excellence* caught the attention of those who were dissatisfied with the postwar "solutions," such that even well beyond Germany's borders, querists oriented themselves toward Germany and fascist Italy.[142] The Croatian question, wrote the Croatian fascist Ante Pavelić in a memorandum from October 28, 1936, was not solved in 1918.

It could therefore be useful if the Croatian question were to receive increased attention as a constituent component of the region and Danubian problems in the German Reich, and if it were to be acknowledged: what the essence of the Croatian question is, and what its European significance depends on, [and] how the Croatian people has related and relates to the current political questions affecting Europe and especially Germany.[143]

One need look no further than the pamphlets, diplomatic exchanges, and internal national and parliamentary debates of the period to witness the explosion of questions in the late 1930s and into the 1940s: among others, the colonial, Algerian, Macedonian, Transylvanian, Indochina, Romanian, Czech, Rusyn, Bessarabian, Thracian, Dalmatian, Ukrainian, Somaliland, Albanian, Balkan, Mediterranean, Danube, [Turkish] Straits, Medjumurje (Muraköz/Međimurje), North African, Lithuanian, Banat, Greek, Teschen (Cieszyn/Těšín), and Dobrudja questions saw a spike in discussion.[144] Querists also frequently cast them as "international" or "European" in scope and importance.[145]

Furthermore, in both pamphlets and state correspondence, questions proliferated among Germany's allies and were related to one another in smaller and larger chains.[146] Those who favored the Versailles settlement and its established boundaries, or who feared revisionist neighbors in Hitler's "New European Order," cried foul: "There is no unsolved 'Macedonian' question," declared a Serbian pamphlet in 1940, as Bulgaria intensified its lobbying for recovery of Macedonia. "The Southern Serbia question was solved once and for all in 1913–1918."[147] Similarly, in May 1942, during a documented conversation between the Hungarian ambassador Antal Ullein-Reviczky and the Croatian foreign minister Mladen Lorković in Zagreb, Ullein-Reviczky said that "[t]here is no Medjumurje question as a question, because to us it is not one."[148] Since the territory was under Hungarian state control, its status was—as far as the government was concerned—not in question.

The Germans encouraged the bundling of their own questions with others' in order to gather the greatest possible support behind German claims and grievances. In a conversation over dinner between a secretary in the Hungarian embassy in Berlin and the German ambassadorial advisor Karl Werkmeister, in November 1938, the subject turned to the Ruthenian question. Werkmeister told his Hungarian interlocutor that the final settlement of the Ruthenian question should be tied to that of the Ukrainian question as "a vital question for us Germans," and when that happens "that will be the moment when an opportunity will open up for Hungary to solve the Transylvanian question 'hand in hand' with the German government."[149]

These questions then became matters of Allied interest, as well. In late August of 1938, a Hungarian diplomat reported on the British view of the Czech question. If the British were willing to give Sudetenland to Germany and thereby solve the "German question" there, it would stand to reason, the Hungarian felt, that Britain would also sanction Hungarian territorial aspirations vis-à-vis Czechoslovakia and thereby facilitate the solution of the "Hungarian question."[150] In June 1938, the Polish foreign minister spoke of the importance of showing the Western powers that in Czechoslovakia, "there is not simply a Sudeten-German question but also a Hungarian, Polish, Slovak question, as well."[151] It was in the context of this stiff competition over question jurisdiction that the Slovak nationalist statesman and professor of law Ferdinand Ďurčanský wrote in 1944: "The nature of the order of Central European questions is [c]onditioned by the state of European political relations."[152]

As question followed question, Hitler repeatedly claimed the latest to be the "last," only to raise another. After the Munich Agreement, which gave Germany control of the Sudetenland, thereby "solving" the Sudeten-German question, the German army went on to invade the rest of Czechoslovakia. "The claim that this solution contradicts the Munich Agreement cannot be justi-

fied any more than it can be substantiated," Hitler told the Reichstag on April 28, 1939. "Under no circumstances can the Munich
settlement be regarded as a final one. After all, it makes concessions for the solution of additional questions and the need to resolve them."[153] Later in the same speech, he declared that "one
question remains open": the Danzig question regarding the status
of the Free City of Danzig/Gdańsk, which Hitler claimed should
belong to Germany. "I regard the peaceful resolution of this question as a further contribution to a final relaxation of tensions in
Europe."[154] On September 1, 1939, the German army invaded Poland in an effort to "solve" the Danzig and Polish questions in one
blow: with occupation and annexation. Britain responded with a
declaration of war—and World War II began.

In a conversation with Vyacheslav Molotov, the Soviet minister
of foreign affairs, in November 1940, Molotov noted that Hitler
had "thrown up a series of questions relating not merely to Europe
but also beyond that to other areas [of the world]."[155] Later that
same day, Molotov mentioned the Finnish question to German
foreign minister Joachim von Ribbentrop and asked him for clari-
fication on "all the other questions" that Ribbentrop and the Nazis
had opened or reopened. Ribbentrop began to speak of the Bulgarian question but quickly declared himself "questioned out"
[überfragt].[156] Two years later, in 1942, Hitler himself would reflect
back on that time "when numerous questions stood open."[157]

What had changed by 1942 was that Germany was involved in
a "universal war." As during the period preceding the Crimean
War and the Great War, the conflict itself was viewed as a crucible
of questions and their solutions.[158] In a closed meeting with German generals in November 1937, Hitler said that the "German
question" would have to be resolved "by means of force." It was
only a matter of "when" and "how."[159] When speaking with the
Romanian leader Ion Antonescu in November 1940, the German
leader told him that "historic questions are generally resolved by
violence rather than with phrases."[160] War, in other words, was

part of the plan. Documents produced in the run-up to World War II in Hungary—a soon-to-be ally of Nazi Germany—show not just an intensifying bundling of questions but also repeated consideration of "solving" them by means of military invasion, occupation, expulsion, or forced annexation: opportunities open, weighed, taken, or missed.[161]

The documents also reveal the extent to which the Nazis and others in Europe imagined the various territorial and national questions to be linked and show their efforts to "solve" them together and in their own interest. This inclination drove militarism insofar as the Germans solved or kept questions in suspension in accordance with a friend-enemy formula. In a discussion with the Bulgarian prime minister, Dobri Bozhilov, in November 1943, Hitler told him that the modus operandi of the Third Reich was "to give everything to friends at the expense of foes."[162] Since a "friend" was a state or group that lent Germany military support, competition between states exited the diplomatic and entered the military realm, at least for as long as it looked as though Germany might win the war.[163]

In mid-June 1941, on the eve of the Axis invasion of the Soviet Union, the Hungarian ambassador to Berlin, Döme Sztójay, told the Hungarian regent Miklós Horthy that Romania's involvement in the attack on the USSR counted as a "merit" for the Romanians in German eyes.

> Recently I have heard comments to the effect that in the event of the possible liquidation of the Soviet Union the Reichschancellor wants to give Romania the entire territory of the principality of Moldova. Yet in spite of whether Romania earns "subsequent merits," it is conceivable and does not seem impossible that the Führer will, in turn, want to settle the Transylvanian question in Hungary's favor, either [by giving us] all of Transylvania, or making some more favorable adjustments to the border [settled on in] Vienna. Naturally Antonescu will fight with every means at his disposal against this eventuality. Neverthe-

less, if Hungary also earns subsequent "merits," there is greater hope that the Transylvanian question will be resolved in our favor than without [those merits].[164]

In other words, if Hungarians dedicated themselves to the war against the USSR as the Romanians had done, the Transylvanian question could be settled in their favor. Hungarian prime minister Miklós Kállay was very explicit about the role the Transylvanian question played in the government's decision to join the offensive against the Soviet Union in his a posteriori evaluation of the situation: "If we do not take part in the war against the Soviet Union like Romania, then Hitler will be forced . . . to change his position regarding the Transylvanian question to the Romanians' advantage."[165] There followed another visit to Budapest by German field marshal Wilhelm Keitel on January 20, also to settle the matter of Hungary's military contribution to the summer offensive. Keitel told the Hungarian leadership that the Transylvanian question would be solved in favor of Romania if Hungary did not contribute to the extent expected by Reich officials.[166]

After starting the war, Hitler spoke vaguely of the "New Order," promising the solution of all outstanding questions at the conflict's end.[167] As for the Jewish question, Hitler and other leading Nazis soon began propounding a "radical" and "general" (Europe-wide) "solution": extermination.[168] Nor was it merely its allies' commitment to the war effort that Germans sought in exchange for solving questions in a given nation's favor, but also their commitment to the Final Solution itself. In an all-too-common queristic move, the Nazis tied the solution of the Jewish question to numerous geopolitical questions revived by revision of the post–World War I treaties as well as to the prospect "universal war."

In 1941 and 1942, the Jews of Bulgarian-controlled Macedonia were systematically disenfranchised and stripped of their occupations and property through a series of laws, decrees, and legislative decisions.[169] During discussions of the Bulgarian national assembly around the implementation of anti-Jewish legislation,

assemblyman Petar Shishkov linked the Jewish to the Macedonian, Thrace, and Dobruja questions (territories they had received
or recovered as allies of Nazi Germany): "[J]ust as Bulgaria owes
the liberation of Macedonia, Thrace, and Dobruja to the new
world order, it is also natural that we have an obligation to that
new order to keep up with the pace of the solution of the Jewish
question as is being done everywhere in Europe in one way or
another."[170]

In December of 1942, a Slovak diplomat reported that Reich
officials were pleased that the "solution of the Jewish question"
was proceeding in Slovakia, Croatia, and Romania, but angered by
the fact that Hungary did not seem to recognize the need to act on
it.[171] And in October 1944, the Slovak prime minister, Štefan Tiso,
declared that as part of the Axis alliance, the Slovak nation "will
be able to rid itself of every enemy of the state that has threatened
the state and continues to threaten it politically, biologically, and
morally. Therefore the government will begin to thoroughly solve
the Jewish question, and similarly the Czech question will be
solved in Slovakia."[172]

Just as Tiso had done, several other states discussed connections between the Jewish and other nationality questions.[173] Decades after the war, in 1974, a historian of Romania, Stephen
Fischer-Galaţi, wrote an essay titled "Fascism, Communism, and
the Jewish Question in Romania." He wondered why it was that
the Jewish question rather than the Magyar (Hungarian) or the
Russian questions came to assume such overweening importance
in Romania during the interwar period, when, "[i]n reality, the
Jewish Question was infinitely less significant than the Magyar or
Russian."[174] Fischer-Galaţi was observing one of the peculiar effects of Hitler's and Nazi Germany's question bundling.

In addition to following the Nazis' lead on the Jewish question,
many states also undertook, or at least contemplated, "solutions"
of their other national questions (Ukrainain, Czech, Transylvanian, Macedonian, etc.) in the same vein as the Final Solution,

namely, by deportation and/or extermination of undesirable minorities. In 1942, a Hungarian official wrote that if Hungary were to emerge from the war with sizable military and political capabilities, "the expulsion of the three million Romanians [in Transylvania] can be recommended. Whoever stays in the country in spite of this—and I repeat, if we are strong—we will have a free hand to deal with the masses, deprived of their leaders, or to assimilate them."[175] And in 1941, Henrik Werth, chief of staff of the Hungarian Army, went so far as to propose the expulsion of all non-Magyar and non-German elements from Hungary, a total of about eight million individuals (mostly Slavs and Romanians).[176] Hungarian historian Krisztián Ungváry has noted the links between the Holocaust and plans to expel other minorities from Hungary.[177] Another historian, Andrej Angrick, in a book on the Einsatzgruppe D in the southern USSR, has found that, in 1941, the Romanians considered the "liquidation" of Ukrainians in parallel with the solution to the "Jewish question" in Northern Bucovina.[178] That same year, Mile Budak of the Independent State of Croatia told a closed circle of the necessity to solve the Jewish and Serbian questions together and by the same means.[179]

Epilogue

The Final Solution was no perverse coda to the age of questions but rather its fullest realization. In 1960, the writer Elias Canetti published *Crowds and Power*, in which he sought to fathom how totalitarian systems functioned by appealing to a certain desire within individuals to form a mass. In a section on "Elements of Power," there is a short chapter titled "Question and Answer." Although Canetti was not speaking of Hitler's question bundles, his assessment of questions as "means of power," and particularly as a means to subordinate the answerer (a formulation with a perverse similarity to Lukács's "antwortendes Wesen" [answering being]), resonates with uncanny precision:

All questioning is intrusion. Where it is wielded as a means of power, it cuts into the body of the questioned. . . . For the effect of questions on the querist [*den Fragenden*] is an elevation of his sense of power; they give him the desire to pose still more and more questions. The more he yields to the questions, the more the questioned subordinates himself.[180]

It is appropriate that the Romanian etymological dictionary, published in 1939, noted that the word *chestiune* can mean both matter and affair (as in the "Eastern question") and "[a] torture from the Middle Ages."[181]

4

The Federative Argument

THE AGE OF ERASING BORDERS

Indeed, for any question, there is a solution at the ready. Federalism answers everything because it simplifies everything . . . The federal principle should be the new international law of Europe.[1]

—ELIAS REGNAULT, *THE EUROPEAN QUESTION INACCURATELY CALLED THE POLISH QUESTION* (1863)

An Aggregating Age

The essence of the age of questions was the practical accommodation of physical reality to the attitude of interrelation that the age engendered. "Federation" is one name we can give to that accommodation. The character of the age was not wholly the national one described in the first chapter, nor the emancipationist one of the second, nor the bellicose and destructive one of the third, though it contained elements of all three. Whether we celebrate federation as a triumph of the practical over the passionate and the willed transcendence of seemingly intractable contradictions and tensions, or bemoan its abstracted universality and long for a smaller scale and a greater intimacy, the age of questions has brought us to this: "[F]or any question, there is a solution at the ready. Federalism answers everything because it simplifies everything."[2]

―――――

Both Adam Czartoryski and Emil Hammacher wondered whether states were like individuals and what rights should adhere to them in the community of nations. But whereas Czartoryski argued for states' equality, Hammacher believed the state had the right to assert itself and even expand. And whereas Czartoryski wanted a rational, just, and peaceful international order, Hammacher doubted that "international spiritual culture [*internationale Geisteskultur*] and eternal peace" should be considered "the highest ideal."[3] Note that in either case, existing borders would have to be erased.

Formulating Universalism

In 1923, the Austrian philosopher and geo-politician Richard Coudenhove-Kalergi published a book titled *Pan-Europe*. In it he posed what he called "the European Question," which he formulated as follows: "Can Europe, so long as its political and economic disunion lasts, maintain its peace and independence with respect to the growing World Powers; or is it bound, in order to preserve its existence, to organize itself into a federal union?" Like so many others in the nineteenth century, Coudenhove-Kalergi argued that "[t]o put the question is to answer it," and the answer was that a federal union of European states was an absolute necessity.[4]

When Coudenhove-Kalergi wrote that "[t]o put the question is to answer it," he was echoing—consciously or not—Marx's assertion regarding the Jewish question that "[t]he formulation of a question is its solution. The critique of the Jewish question is the answer to the Jewish question."[5] For those who took Jews' right to

emancipation as a given—in Marx's case, as part of a more generalized emancipation—there was no "Jewish question." The matter
rather became one of figuring out how to achieve the human
emancipation of all people from the structures of capitalism.

Marx had elevated the question to a higher level, as if to say: Of
course the Jews should be emancipated. *Everyone* should be emancipated. The matter of *Jewish* emancipation does not warrant separate consideration, except insofar as—according to Marx—Jewish
proclivities were implicated in the the very structures of capitalism, such that *everyone* had become "Jewish." Human emancipation, Marx believed, could be achieved not by a policy decision in
favor of emancipation but only by the universalization of the very
concept of emancipation. If addressed at this fundamental level,
an apparent opposition gave way to a shared goal.

The move to elevate and universalize a question in order to
make it disappear was one querists regularly employed. "The solution I propose is summarized in these two lines," wrote the French
novelist and publicist Émile de Girardin in 1853: "Elevate the Eastern question to simplify it; simplify it to resolve it."[6] The sweep of
querism was awesome—from global geopolitics, to the national,
the social, the personal—and very often megalomaniacal in its assessment of the scale of transformation required to effect solution.
It was as if the whole trajectory of questions was augmentative:
questions were *everyone's* problem, and it was *everyone's* responsibility to solve them. In *The Jewish State*, published in 1896, Theodor
Herzl wrote:

> I think the Jewish question is no more a social than a religious
> one, notwithstanding that it sometimes takes these and other
> forms. It is a national question, which can only be solved by
> making it a political world-question to be discussed and settled
> by the civilized nations of the world.[7]

Herzl chose the highest, the most overarching of the many manifestations of the Jewish question as the only level at which solution

was possible. Hitler also considered the Jewish question to be an "international problem," and declared that a solution was therefore only possible at the international level.[8] Hitler's, Herzl's, and Marx's treatments of the Jewish question all speak to a feature of the nineteenth-century idiom: the question as *international* problem, as *everyone's* problem, requiring *universal* solution. Every European, Coudenhove-Kalergi argued, would soon "be forced . . . to take a stand in regard to the European Question. Then let it rest with the Europeans whether they want union or disunion, organization or anarchy, resurrection or downfall."[9]

Federated Questions: From Indefinite to Definite

Many querists thought about the world the way they thought about questions, namely, as disparate parts that needed to be bundled into a single whole. In the foreword to *Pan-Europe*, Coudenhove-Kalergi wrote that "[a]lthough in public discussion there is much talk of European questions, there is none of *the* European Question in which all of them are rooted, just as the many social questions are rooted in the Social Question."[10] Therewith Coudenhove-Kalergi made an astute observation regarding the language of questions, correctly observing that umbrella questions—like the European and the social question—had proceeded along a trajectory from indefinite to definite.

The Social Question

The "social question" had two lives: one as a category question ("*a* social question"), the other as a single question or aggregate of many questions ("*the* social question").[11] Just as the nineteenth century gave birth to questions, so did it produce various typologies of them. The most common division was between so-called political and social questions. But some made still finer distinctions, adding a category of national, religious, moral, or economic questions.[12]

One early mention of a social question appeared in French in a review of several books on public education from a royalist periodical, *Friend of Religion and of the King*, published in Paris in 1816.[13] The author noted that M. Dampmartin, who had written a *Letter to the Gentlemen of the Chamber of Deputies concerning Public Education* (1815), "above all wanted to offer some views on education which thoroughly address this major social question."[14] On March 19, 1826, a Parisian newspaper registered the ongoing concern regarding "how to fight a legal question with a social question during revolution."[15] In both instances, the reference is to "*a* social question" in the typological sense rather than to "*the* social question" as a thing unto itself.

The first references I have found to "*the* social question" date to 1831 and are related to the fallout of the July Revolution in France. From French the term likely spread into English through newspaper reports on the events in France, and somewhat later into German.[16] The social question was considered a relative latecomer, both as a problem in itself and as a typology. In a series of lectures meant for the general education of women published in Germany in 1856, Karl Biedermann opened a lecture on "The Social Question, Its Meaning, and Attempts to Solve it" by saying that "Of late the political and national questions have been joined by a third: the social [question]."[17] Biedermann's assertion is at least partly borne out by a comparison of peaks in the prevalence of the social question versus the Eastern and the Polish questions. In French, the peak for the social question is clearly in the 1890s, whereas the peaks for the Eastern and Polish questions come earlier, starting already in the 1840s (Eastern) and 1860s (Polish). The same pattern appears in German and English.[18]

If instead of the peaks, we focus on the raw number of mentions each question received in printed matter across the period, we see that the social-question peak represents a far greater number of total mentions than either of the two others, overshadowing other questions not merely as a typological umbrella but in its overall prevalence.

The European Question

The European question followed a similar trajectory from indefinite to definite. At the Congress of Vienna (1814–1815), the powers enumerated the "questions Européens" they had gathered to settle.[19] Already in the 1830s, when the century's questions were still fresh, the aggregation of questions under the heading of "European questions" was becoming accepted practice. Recall the British MP's intervention on the South American question from 1817, in which he argued that it "must be considered . . . as a European question."[20] In the very first pamphlet on the Polish question, published in 1829, we read that "[t]he Polish interest is inseparable from that of Europe,"[21] and in 1837 a German newspaper introduced the regular heading "European Questions and Problems."[22]

Over the course of the nineteenth century, the ratcheting up of questions to the level of a great "European question" that encompassed all of Europe's unresolved issues grew more pronounced. In 1833, the Polish-Jewish émigré activist Jan Czyński published a pamphlet titled *The Polish-Jewish Question Envisioned as a European Question*, in which he argued that the Polish and Jewish questions could only be solved together and at the European level.[23] "The Polish question," Adolf Chaisés wrote in an 1863 pamphlet, "which now occupies the first place among all major social problems, is naught but an accident of the European question."[24] That same year the French republican political writer Elias Regnault published a pamphlet in Paris whose title ran *The European Question Inappropriately Called the Polish Question*, in which he proposed "a federal Europe—strong, compact, of unified sentiments, morals and intellectual knowledge" as a solution.[25]

Weighing in on the Hungarian question in an 1865 pamphlet, Gusztáv Ádolf Ungár[26] remarked on both the proliferation and the interconnectedness of questions.

[I]n this moment there are about as many "questions" as there are states waiting for the solutions to their questions. However independent these questions may seem to be of one another, their interconnectedness [*egybefüggését*] can nonetheless be readily and consistently shown, and it would not be difficult to offer proof, for example, that the Eastern question stands in a causal relationship with the Greek [question], the Polish question with the Italian, and the Schleswig-Holstein with the Hungarian. We have in fact arrived at the point where there is really only one question, the *great European question* [*az európai összes kérdés*]."[27]

Similarly, in 1882, an anonymous "Son of the East" wrote that "this Eastern question is not a single question, but a series of many problems and multiform views ... and becomes a political, religious and social question."[28] A Russian pamphlet dubbed it an international question in 1878, and a Moscow newspaper related the Eastern question to the European question in 1888.[29] This conflation in turn caught the attention of the Ottoman government, which translated it into Ottoman.[30] The Romanian question was cast as part of the European question in an 1895 pamphlet, and the French historian Albert Sorel, writing in 1898, called the Eastern question in reality a "European question."[31] A year into the Great War, Serbian diplomats submitted to the Entente leadership a memorandum in which they declared that "[t]he Serbo-Croatian question is part of the present European question."[32]

The general procession from indefinite to definite of the social and European questions has an echo in the trajectory of solutions. The pairing of question with solution can be used in the indefinite sense of "a solution," as in one of many possible solutions, or in the mathematical sense, for which only one solution can be correct. The observation of Michel Foucault that eighteenth-century querists "preferred to question the public on problems that did not yet have solutions," while subsequent interventions tended to "collect opinions on some subject about which everyone has an opinion already" suggests that not only questions followed a trajectory from indefinite to definite, so did solutions.[33]

The Question Bundle

The very idea that there was or could be a European question emerged out of discussion and arguments for the various "smaller" questions of the first half of the nineteenth century, and was preceded by a rhetorical bundling of emergent questions. As we have seen, querists identified the Polish with the Belgian question,[34] or with the Italian, Mexican, Schleswig-Holstein, or Eastern questions,[35] as a means of advancing particular solutions and winning the attention of public opinion and the ears of statesmen.

But this kind of lobbying had a peculiar side effect: After defining these early questions as "European" and then suggesting a relationship between them, querists concluded that *solutions* also had to be elevated and expanded to encompass the whole of Europe or beyond. Furthermore, in the process, Europe itself had to make the move from being an adjective (European) to a noun (Europe), from assuming an indefinite to a definite shape. This progression can be traced through two aspects of the age of questions: an increasing anxiety regarding the threat questions posed to "Europe" and the perceived need for coordinated European action to solve period questions.

A Common Irritant, a Common Project

In what the argument of force has called "the dark side of bundling," in the eyes of many nineteenth-century querists, unresolved questions threatened the precarious unity of "Europe" itself. "Every time the Eastern question arises," wrote Fyodor Dostoevsky in 1876 in his *Diary of a Writer*, "the apparent wholeness of Europe begins, much too obviously, to fall apart into personal, segregatedly national egoisms ... [s]o that every time this fatal question appears on the scene, all former inveterate political conflicts and ailments of Europe begin to ache and fester."[36] Yet questions could also gather all of Europe's troubles to enable a wholesale *solution*.[37]

Some querists argued that questions demanded a unified European response, the creation of a true and unified European field of action. At the Congress of Vienna in 1814–1815, Metternich defined a set of "European questions" that had to be solved in agreement with other Great Powers.[38] "The Eastern question will not be settled by one of [the Great Powers]," Alexis de Tocqueville told the French Chamber of Deputies in 1839. "It will be by all of us, or by no one."[39] In a German pamphlet on the Eastern question, published in 1843, the anonymous author argued that "[t]he Eastern question could be thoroughly and permanently solved to the glory and honor of Europe if only the Christian powers united for a truly Christian action."[40] "The refusal of the Porte to accede to the wishes of Europe," wrote the Russian Prince Gorchakov in a dispatch from 1877, "has caused the Eastern crisis to enter upon a new phase. The Imperial Cabinet has regarded it from the outset as an European question, which should and could only be solved by the unanimous accord of the Great Powers."[41] The Scottish liberal George Campbell agreed that a solution could be arrived at "by that concert of the Powers which we now happily have."[42]

Two years later, in 1879, the German ur-historian Leopold von Ranke located such "unanimous accord" in the past actions of Europe's powers around the Eastern question. In his work *Serbia and Turkey in the Nineteenth Century*, he wrote about the near miss of a major European conflagration around the Mehmet Ali crisis in the Ottoman Empire in the 1830s.

A drama without equal—these powers, equipped for war as never before—how they move against one another, engage in disputes, join alliances and counter-alliances, put an end to a distant world's questions at the least irritation [*Berührung*], and thereby avoid entering into open battle with one another! ... And not just one or the other power, but the whole of Europe.[43]

Two years later, in 1881, a pamphlet appeared bearing the title *The Eastern Question Solved: A Vision of the Future* by an author writing under the pseudonym "Budge." The author described the Eastern question as "this European question," sketching an alternative future reality wherein British prime minister William Gladstone's policies around the Eastern Crisis (1876–1878) had been implemented and thereby "the many-sided and knotty Eastern Question" had been solved. The solution was a federated Balkan kingdom and the transformation of Istanbul into a free city, "the International Capital" run by "the hand of united Europe," "the Great Power of the Future, the great majority of Europe." It was "this brotherhood of nationalities, which has so happily solved the great Eastern Question."[44]

A very similar argument had already been put forward by the Irish banker and diplomat J. Lewis Farley in an 1876 pamphlet on *Turks and Christians, a Solution of the Eastern Question*. Farley proposed a federation of Balkan states and shared European sovereignty over Istanbul. "Some such a solution of the Eastern Question is the only one practicable, and, sooner or later, it must be adopted."[45] Europe's unity was thus to be forged together with a Balkan federation as a means of solving the region's questions. Accordingly, in 1907, the British liberal statesman Noel Buxton wrote of the Macedonian question—in a chapter titled "The Real Question"—that

> Macedonia raises thoughts of a nobler cause than the relief of suffering alone, for it recalls no less a matter than that of reviving once more the comity of nations. Cross Europe from end to end, and though you pass through commercial barriers and hostile armies, you see in every land a type of social order which is common to all. It is a type found only in Europe and her daughter States. It is a type which makes Europe, though so small a corner of the world that you can traverse it in three days, foremost of all the continents. The spirit and the source of it are everywhere the same. Who that gives thought to these things can fail to lament the fall that has taken place from the ideal of Charlemagne, from the holy Roman Empire with its theory of

a united Christendom, to the modern make shift of the "balance of power"? We must cherish the germ of unity contained not only in the Hague Conference, but in every common action. In spite of all the rivalries aroused, Macedonia compels the Powers to work together, and to peoples whose officers cooperate in the same police force the thought of war seems increasingly absurd; the very perplexities of the task may be but the birth throes of a new unity.[46]

The message of unity through engagement with the Eastern question, in particular, continued to resonate even after the Great War. In a four-volume work on Greek diplomacy, published in 1925, the French historians Édouard Driault and Michel Lhéritier reflected back on the history of the Eastern question. "Europe has defined itself, as much in 1821 as in 1921, as a federation of Christian states."[47] Federation was thus given as both the *true condition* and *the only solution*; at once already realized in practice and just then coming into being through practice. The troubling questions of the nineteenth century served as both irritants to the status quo and opportunities to forge a greater unity between the European powers.

The Federation Consensus

In the 1830 edition of his *Essay*, Czartoryski argued that small states had a role to play in the international system but were too weak to stand alone, and should therefore unite into federative arrangements.[48] We have already seen that the slogan of the 1830–1831 Polish uprising in tsarist Russia—during which Czartoryski served as the President of the Polish National Government—was "For our freedom and yours," and it was under this banner that Polish exiles propounded a "solution" of terrific scope to the Polish question, necessitating both the breaking up of empires and a recombination of states into a new international order. They united the forces of Young Poland with those of Young Italy and

Young Germany as part of a broader "Young Europe," calling for "the association of free and equal peoples" in place of the existing Concert of Europe.[49]

"Young Europe's" designs on the international system are less significant than the fact that the solution its leaders propounded mirrored the virtues others saw in the Concert itself: both sought to bring European states into partnership and harmony. By the second half of the nineteenth century, federation was very nearly a consensus solution to Europe's questions (or "the European question"). Figures ranging from the Hungarian revolutionary Lajos Kossuth to the Russian Bolshevik Leon Trotsky to the Polish novelist Joseph Conrad all proposed federative solutions to a range of period questions (Hungarian, Balkan, Eastern, Polish).[50] The ideal of federation also found its way into discussions of period social questions, or "*the* Social Question," as Coudenhove-Kalergi noted was the ultimate formulation of "the many social questions" of the time, such as the woman and worker questions.[51] Although these were not first and foremost about geopolitics and the boundaries of states, many had come to see social questions in a geopolitical light. In the words of the Russian anarchist Mikhail Bakunin, "[t]he social question . . . can be resolved only by abolishing State boundaries."[52]

Nor was it only the liberals and the left who thought in these terms. In an 1872 pamphlet, a self-declared "colonist" in Canada argued vehemently that "emancipation" should not be the solution to the colonial question, but rather federation.[53] In 1879, the German philosopher, publicist, and diplomat Constantin Frantz wrote a book titled *Federalism as the Guiding Principle for Social, State, and International Organization*, in which he sought to tap the energy that had built behind the social question to formulate, and similarly solve, what he called the "international question." Only the general "blindness regarding the true meaning of the matter" could be the reason why the international question "was still not in the catalog of the great questions, while . . . nowadays the whole world speaks of the *social* question, and scarcely anyone dares to deny that this question truly *exists*. As if the *international* question *doesn't* exist?"[54] Frantz went on to argue that the solutions to the social and international questions would have to be one in the same. "This is why even [the socialists] have really fixed international organization in their sites."[55]

Frantz proposed a decidedly conservative and anti-Semitic federation of Central European states rooted in religion as an alternative to the socialist and German nationalist federative solutions.[56] Meanwhile, so deep was the federalist consensus that some querists, including the American Unitarian reverend and publicist George Batchelor, even proposed breaking down the barriers between *religions* in the interest of solving period questions.[57]

"Indeed, for any question, there is a solution at the ready," wrote Elias Regnault in his 1863 work on the Polish question. "Federalism answers everything because it simplifies everything . . . The federal principle should be the new international law of Europe."[58] So it was that both the defenders of empires and their most vociferous critics—including left-wing revolutionaries and advocates for new nation-states and their expansionist aspirations—posited competing federalist schemes. In an 1840 pamphlet, the French publicist François Dumons wrote of the Eastern question:

> [T]he present condition of Europe, in a political as well as in the social sense, is rotten at its core and is based on a false premise; it lacks balance and thus can not endure. EUROPE MUST BE RECONSTITUTED, and its future can be conveyed by this formula: EMPIRE OF THE EAST, EMPIRE OF THE WEST . . . Then, and only then, will the peace of Europe and the world be assured.[59]

Dumons imagined a future with two great *empires*. His notion that federation could bring East and West into proper relation—to correct for a lack of "balance"—was a view shared by other querists, as well.

In 1860, an anonymous pamphleteer writing *A Few Words on the Eastern Question* also called for "the creation of a Christian empire in the East" that would unite all the Southeast European successor states of a presumed-to-be-defunct Ottoman Empire. To bring it about, the author posited the "urgent necessity" of calling a "European Congress" with an eye to "terminating this eternal Eastern question." The author acknowledged that such a solution would not be easy, but had Europe's empires not already overcome such difficulties themselves? If all the new states were "united on a footing of perfect equality . . . there would only remain between them the distinction of language, which would not divide them more than the inhabitants of England or of France are divided who speak different dialects."[60] Certainly the difficulty of making a Christian empire out of Ottoman successors would not prove insurmountable for "the creating hand of Europe."

That same year, the Ottoman-Phanariot prince Jakobos Giorgios Pitzipios made an analogous argument in an appeal to Lord Palmerston. The Eastern question could only be solved by a "Byzantine Union" (federation), he wrote.

> Under any other arrangement there can only be on the one hand uneasiness, distrust, disorder, and apprehension, and, on the other hand, revolts, massacres, devastations, and dangerous interventions; and, ultimately, a general war, disastrous in its consequences to all governments.[61]

In 1866, the Hungarian writer and publicist Károly Szini invoked a "European movement, striving for unity" in a pamphlet on the Hungarian question.[62] *"Association, alliance, unification!* This is the slogan of today's better era, the principle, precondition, and catalyst [*rugója*] of all progress and prosperity, for both individuals and peoples," he declared. [63] "Whoever looks to the future and doesn't wish to deceive himself must admit that he sees a great movement there—a movement toward the unity of nations. . . . Let the European movement begin."[64] In this way, Szini concluded, together with the Hungarian question a whole host of others would also be solved.[65] A few years later, during and after the Franco-Prussian War (1870–1871) and at the genesis of the New

Imperialism, a Canadian pamphlet offered "Imperial Federation" as a solution to the colonial question.[66] And the following year a self-declared Canadian "colonist" argued that federation was the one and only "practical solution" to the colonial question, an express *alternative* to emancipation. "It is not Federation in the abstract which we have to consider," he wrote, "but Federation as compared with a disruption of the empire."[67]

The idea of federation also had strong roots in the expressly *anti*-imperial ambitions of states like Serbia, whose two targets for expansion were the Ottoman and the Habsburg empires. In 1867, the German journalist and travel writer Gustav Rasch wrote a book on *The Peoples of the Lower Danube and the Eastern Question* in which he observed that

> "Confederation of the South Slavic Races" is the program of *Vidovdan*, the most widely read newspaper in Serbia—confederation of Serbs, Bosnians, Bulgarians and Croats. Serbia is in a position to realize this program on its own if only the young, blossoming and freedom-loving country is given a hand. In the event of a European conflict in the East, one of its first consequences would be this South Slavic confederation and the liberation of all South Slavic races from under the Turkish yoke.[68]

Two of Serbia's activist statesmen, Ilija Garašanin (1812–1874) and Stojan Novaković (1842–1915), favored a federative or confederative arrangement for the Balkan Peninsula, with Serbia in a leadership role.[69] Meanwhile, Benjamin von Kállay, a rising star among Austro-Hungarian statesmen, hoped for a federation of Balkan states with Hungary playing the leadership role.[70] Opposite national ambitions thus overlapped in their conception of a shared future.

The belief that nation and empire, and even socialist and communist aspirations, could only be fully realized within a federative framework is evident in the perspective of Russian pan-Slavists of the time. The philosopher Nikolai Danilevsky insisted in 1869 that both the Eastern and Polish questions could be solved by an "[a]ll-Slavic federation with Russia at the head."[71] The then-leftist Mikhail Bakunin had a different vision of Slavic unity, which he put forward in his 1848 "Appeal to the Slavs." His plan called for the "dissolution, overturn, and regeneration in the entire North and East of Europe, a free Italy, and as the last result, the Universal Federation of European Republics."[72]

In 1916, the Hungarian statesman and former interior minister of Hungary Gyula Andrássy (the younger) published a volume on *The Problems of the World War* that included chapters on the "The Eastern Question and the World War" and the "Polish question." In it, he proposed the reassembly of the parts of partitioned Poland within a Central European federation (either within Germany or Austria-Hungary, but preferably the latter), adding that if the Polish question were not properly solved in the course of the war and the subsequent peace settlement, the result would be "perpetual conflict."[73]

In a 1918 book on *The Habsburgs and the Serbian Question*, the Austro-German publicist Leopold Mandl argued that only one solution could produce all-around satisfaction: a South Slavic federation within the Habsburg Monarchy.

> Such a magnificent, ethnic process awaits [*harrt*] European statecraft such that she might bring that process to a generally acceptable resolution: the unification of all South Slavs in the interest of general cultural progress under the House of Habsburg as the result of the fateful, troubled, almost four-hundred-year-long period of tutelage [*Sittungsarbeit*].[74]

That same year, Leon Trotsky proposed a federation involving much of the same territory, but in a decidedly *anti*-imperial, and specifically anti-*Austrian* vein. He quoted Marx on the Eastern question: "The governments with their old-fashioned diplomacy," wrote Marx, "will never solve the difficulty. Like the solution of so many other problems, the Turkish problem, too, is reserved for the European Revolution." Furthermore, Trotsky continued, "What is here said of Turkey now applies in a still greater degree to Aus-

THE FEDERATIVE ARGUMENT 151

tria Hungary. The solution of the Balkan question is unthinkable without the solution of the Austro Hungarian question, as they are both comprised in one and the same formula—the Democratic Federation of the Danube and Balkan Nations."[75]

The geopolitics of the East inspired Western imperialists to contemplate federative "pan"-configurations of their own. "I invite all those who are unnerved by their dread of Panslavism or their fears of Tuetonic ascendency on the Continent," wrote the British MP Thomas Brassey in an 1877 pamphlet on *The Eastern Question and the Political Situation at Home,* "to realize the grand but not impracticable vision of the power which might be created by a federation of all the Anglo-Saxon peoples."[76] The congresses at which the Great Powers came together to discuss the solution of geopolitical questions—such as the Eastern question—were viewed by some as institutional vertebra for a new kind of European supranational state. The *Times* called the Berlin Congress "the first example of a de facto parliament of the Great Powers."[77]

Epilogue

Querists drew on scientific insights—specifically in the physical sciences—to describe their perspective on the East-West dynamic.[78] Czartoryski himself had argued that diplomacy could be "the noblest science and the most useful study" and that states were subject to natural law.[79] The protagonists of the age of questions were preoccupied with the notion of an intangible yet somehow *physical* relationship between geopolitical and social questions, and between East and West.[80] For them, the shorthand for equilibrium was federation: a dissolving of boundaries to reach a common level signified the release of longstanding disparities and tensions: a catharsis.

In 1887, when the American Unitarian minister George Batchelor published his *Social Equilibrium and Other Problems Ethical and Religious,* he argued that concerns about "social equilibrium" had become territorialized and that the territory they encompassed had grown larger.[81] He opened his work by suggesting that the "burning questions" of the time were but surface phenomena obscuring "deepest causes."[82] Among the "ills which now affect the body politic," he wrote, was "a disturbance of the social equilibrium."[83] Batchelor concluded that "[b]efore we can reach any solution of the problem which can be accepted as final, some new adjustment of equilibrium must take place among the great nations which hold the control of the world." Such an adjustment should entail the creation of a "peaceful confederation of the nations," the precondition for "any final settlement of the question as to rights of individuals."[84]

Batchelor's solution encompassed both the geopolitical (confederation) and the social (rights of individuals), and he conceived of the two in tight relation to one another. Coudenhove-Kalergi wrote that the "separation between Nation and State" that would accompany the creation of Pan-Europe would "everywhere facilitate economic recovery as well as the solution of the Social Question. It will rid Europe's political atmosphere of its poisonous elements and prepare it for the Pan-European solution."[85]

5

The Argument about Farce

THE FARCICAL AGE

> But now we hear another exclamation: "Oh, if only we were less
> skeptical and could believe that there are world questions and that
> they are not a mirage!"[1]
>
> —FYODOR DOSTOEVSKY (1877)

A Fraudulent Age

What the "crisis" had been to the eighteenth century, the "question" became to the nineteenth: the melodramatic yelp of publicists and politicians in search of an audience.[2] The smartest observers saw that a game was afoot. In 1864, Wilhelm Emmanuel von Ketteler, a German Catholic theologian and Bishop of Mainz, also known as the workers' bishop, wrote a seminal text on the worker question. He declared that the so-called political questions of the day were creations of the "working class of the pen, for that part of it that talks and writes the most and as a result rules both podium and press," in its own interest and for personal gain.[3]

For a long time critics like Ketteler were ignored by the frenzied querists, but eventually even they had to address the charge of insincerity, and then it was only a matter of time before the vacuity of "question"-mania became common knowledge. In the end, the age of questions did not go out with a national flourish, a progressive blast, a federative crescendo, or even a Nazi bang, but with an academic whimper.

The Birth of Questions Revisited

The first matter that should tip off the historian-detective to the possibility that the age of questions was steeped in fraud is the shadowy nature of their origins, and how the expectations of those who have sought their origins affected what they found. Consider Jacob Toury, for example, whose search for the origins of the Jewish question seem to have been undertaken in good faith. In contrast to many earlier commentators on the Jewish question who traced its origins as far back as the very origins of Judaism, Toury's careful research brought him to the (correct) conclusion that the question was very much of nineteenth-century vintage.[4] He also correctly observed that the matter of Jewish emancipation was discussed in several contexts—most notably, the French Revolution—long before a "Jewish question" ever emerged as such.[5] His search was nonetheless colored by the Final Solution as the presumed telos of the Jewish question.

Ultimately he dated the slogan back to 1838, with two long essays published in German titled "The Jewish Question."[6] The anonymous author of the essays had argued that, on the basis of their essentially alien characteristics, Jews should not be given political equality in Prussia (as was being debated at the time).[7] Toury concluded that the question itself was "an anti-Jewish battle-cry." A small flurry of publications in 1842 in Germany used the term *Judenfrage*, all to argue against full and immediate equality, and thus, Toury added, "the slogan *Judenfrage* . . . initiated a new phase in the development of anti-Jewish bias. Its ideological connotations foreshadowed the development of those forms of antisemitism that became rampant in Western Europe at the end of the nineteenth century."[8] "Jews," he declared, "could not concede the existence of a 'Jewish question,'" which was already loaded with prejudice against them.

Toury's work is interesting, but also misguided. Firstly, Germany, and specifically Prussia, was almost certainly *not* the birthplace of the Jewish question. In fact, it was rather a latecomer. A much earlier reference to the Jewish question appeared in 1830 in the London *Times*. It mentions a number of letters addressed to the *Times*, written to influence public opinion in advance of parliamentary debates on legislation calling for the removal of Jewish disabilities. "We must decline the insertion of any of the numerous letters on the Jewish question, about to be decided by Parliament," we read in a brief notice "To Correspondents" from April 23 of that year.[9] We do not know what these letters contained, but we do know that the matter to be decided in Parliament was inspired by the successful "solution" to the Catholic question through the repeal of Catholic disabilities a year earlier.[10] As a successor to the Catholic question, the Jewish question appears in a wholly different light.

Yet because Toury was guided by a search for the origins of the *Endlösung*, he hit upon not only the wrong place (Prussia) but also the wrong time. His mistake was very likely an honest one. But of other querists who misdated the origin of a question, we cannot be so sure. Misdating was not incidental to the age but an essential feature of it from the very beginning. Indeed, the scholar who wishes to approach the age of questions by searching for its origins is immediately struck by a peculiar phenomenon: at the very instant they were born, questions were often endowed with a history that backdated them by decades, sometimes centuries, before their actual emergence.

Whereas querists have often dated the Polish question to the first partition of Poland in 1772,[11] it was only *formulated* as such around the 1810s,[12] in the run-up to the Congress of Vienna, and only commonly *discussed* as such in the early 1830s, during the Polish November Uprising in tsarist Russia.[13] Furthermore, my own attempts to trace the origins of the phrase "Eastern question" and its first usages had to contend with several layers of misleading assumptions and presumptions. The phrase did appear in a 1777 British publication, but the reference is not to the "Eastern question" as it was later known but rather to British India ("So much for the present Eastern question—a question of more importance than is generally imagined and which points at more than meets the vulgar eye.").[14] Although the appearance of the Eastern question in state correspondence and published sources dates back to the 1820s and 1830s,[15] most querists have traced its origins back at least to the emergence of tsarist Russia as a factor in shaping the future of the Ottoman Empire with the Russo-Turkish war of 1768–1774 and the subsequent treaty of Küçük Kaynarca of 1774.[16] A number of querists and historians have gone back farther still, to the seventeenth century, or to the Ottoman expansion into southeastern Europe in the fourteenth and fifteenth centuries, and beyond.[17]

"The 'Eastern question,'" wrote the Croat nationalist politician Eugen Kvaternik in 1868, "[i]s so old that it reaches into the history of Rome."[18] "From time immemorial," wrote the historian J. A. R. Marriott in his 1917 book on the Eastern question, "Europe has been confronted with an 'Eastern Question.'"[19] The *Encyclopedia of the Ottoman Empire* traces the origin of the phrase back to the Congress of Vienna, but the sources cited in the piece do not bear out the assertion.[20] Historian Alexander Bitis wrote that "[n]o one knows for sure when the term 'the Eastern Question' first entered the vocabulary of European diplomacy," yet took issue with *The Encyclopedia Britannica's* dating it to the Congress of Verona (1822), claiming that "the term was commonplace during the Napoleonic Wars," though he cited no source for this assertion.[21]

In fact, I have only encountered one commentator on *any* of the questions I have analyzed who has come close to correctly dating a question's true origin, and that was Otto von Bismarck, who—in a speech to the lower house of the Prussian parliament in 1886— said that "the Warsaw rising of 1830" marked the "emergence of a Polish question, in a European sense, in which other nations were involved and which has never since then wholly disappeared."[22]

Bad Faith

It is clear that establishing a chronology of the Eastern question was bound to the act of defining it: if the "Eastern question" was about Ottoman decline, then the date it emerged was fashioned to correspond to the author's conception of when decline set in.[23] Furthermore, if dating the origins of a question was a way of defining it and—as Marx and others claimed—to formulate a question was to solve it, then questions were often little more than excuses for putting forth particular solutions. In 1863, a pseudonymous Jean Ouvrier declared the "worker question" to be the invention of those who wanted there to be a "worker's movement": "One needed a workers movement, so one created a worker question."[24] Or recall Spengler's observation that a "question is merely a thinly veiled desire to receive a particular answer that is already implied in the question itself."[25]

The fullest manifestation of the bad faith of the age of questions can be found in a nearly imperceptible yet remarkable shift in the way interventions on questions were titled. Whereas early texts (such as William Duane's 1803 writings on the Mississippi question and Davies Giddy's and Thomas Robert Malthus's 1811 writings on the bullion question) had the question in the title and nowhere else in the text, later ones (including Theodor Herzl's 1896 *The Jewish State* and Richard Coudenhove-Kalergi's 1923 *Pan-Europe*) featured the *solution* in the title with the question discussed throughout.[26] The 1921 *Catechism of the Social Question* captured in its very format the reverse engineering that typified the age.[27] Authors merely used questions as rhetorical launchpads for advancing their vision of how things should be.

A few period commentators—among them the Russian novelist Ivan Goncharov in his 1869 novel *The Precipice* (*Обрыв*)—were
conscious of how the word "question" was losing its interrogative
aspect.

> "You mentioned the 'Eastern question,' and in the news-
> papers the Eastern question is also mentioned. What is this
> Eastern question?"
> "[I]n fact . . ." he said thoughtfully, "It's not a question at all!"
> "Now all 'questions' have disappeared!"[28]

And in their place came pompous declarations and shrill manifes-
tos. "Master, what do you make of the Eastern question?" wrote
the popular German author Karl May (a.k.a. Kara ben Nemsi) in
his 1882 travel memoir *From Baghdad to Stambul*. "I think they
should mark it not with a question mark but with an exclamation
point."[29]

Tolstoy, among others, was wise to the age's prolific hubris and
penchant for hyperbole. In 1893, he wrote with undisguised exasperation of all the pamphlets and books he received in which the
authors offered fail-safe solutions to this or that question:

> I think that the time and labour, not only of all these writers,
> but even of many others have not only been wasted, but have
> also been harmful . . . because in the preparation of these writ-
> ings . . . all these authors, instead of feeling their guilt toward
> society, as they would if they played cards or blind man's bluff,
> continue with a calm conscience to do their useless work.[30]

The questions of the nineteenth century resemble large, clown-
like shoes,[31] absurd attempts to span an abyss between what was
and what the querists wished for. With the emergence of questions, it is as if many of the inhabitants of that century donned
such shoes and stumbled ramstam into the twentieth century.
Gaze in wonder at the outlandish tragicomedy that ensued.

Little Beasties

Already at their backdated birth, questions were remarkably exclamatory. A passion mandate seemed to accompany them wherever they appeared, and period observers were quick to note it. In 1805, a pamphlet by the Irish-Catholic writer Theobald MacKenna decried the "clumsy invectives, the hyperbolical conjectures, the fictitious apprehension" that had hitherto attended discussion of the Catholic question.[32] An 1831 pamphlet by "An Englishman," noted the "affectionate anxiety" the Polish question evoked from "all classes" of British society.[33] The apathy of the French and British public "with regard to the Eastern question," wrote a British editor in 1836, "proceeded from an ignorance of facts, in the midst of a confusion of words and phrases."[34]

The fervent appeals and hyperbolic prose that encircled questions were heavily criticized by Friedrich Engels, who in 1848 wrote that "[w]henever the Polish question is debated, almost the entire Left indulges, as usual, in declamation or even in extravagant rhapsody, without discussing the facts and the actual content of the question."[35] And in February of 1854, in a letter to the former French prime minister Léon Faucher, Alexis de Tocqueville compared engagement with the Eastern question to "banging one's head against the wall" (*se faire casser la petite fiole sur la tête*).[36] Meanwhile, the Kansas question was one "under which the country already shakes from side to side," US congressman Charles Sumner told the senate in 1856.[37]

If there was a queristic genre, it was irritative. In a September 1876 entry of his *Diary of a Writer*, Fyodor Dostoevsky called the Eastern question a "piccola bestia" (little beast) that had produced a "condition of general madness."[38] The spider-troublemaker was also the theme of a series of reflections on the Eastern question in a book on *Spiders and Spider Life* from 1919, by the German naturalist Kurt Floericke, who noted that the spider was a holy animal in Islam because one supposedly saved the prophet Mohammed as he was hiding in a cave. "How different the world would look if there had not been a spider on hand back then! There probably would be no Eastern question and the newspapers wouldn't bore one with the Bulgarian conundrum [*Wirren*]."[39]

In addition to *madness*, common words used to describe the effect of questions included *confusion*, *anxiety*, *despair*, and *unease*. "The nationality question," wrote Slovak-Hungarian statesman and publicist Leopold Thull in 1867, "has kept Hungary and indeed the whole of Austria in a state of bated breath for decades."[40] The Czech philosopher and statesman Tomáš Masaryk wrote in 1898 that the "social question" means the "unease (*Unruhe*) and dissatisfaction, yearning and fearing, hoping and despairing, suffering and frustrated fury (*Ingrimm*) of thousands. Millions."[41] And in a 1918 pamphlet on the Ukrainian question, the author dedicated the first section to describing the "lack of clarity" and "chaos" surrounding the question.[42]

Several commentators observed a mood of general agitation bordering on the pathological around questions. An anecdote about Benjamin Disraeli during the period of his premiership related an encounter at a dinner party, when a woman seated next to the statesman pressed him for swift government action on the Eastern question. "I cannot imagine what you are waiting for!" she told him. "At this moment, Madam," came his calm reply, "for the potatoes."[43]

In 1879, the German historian Heinrich von Treitschke wrote of how "Anti-Semitic societies are formed, the 'Jewish question' is discussed in noisy meetings, a flood of anti-Semitic pamphlets appears on the market. There is only too much of dirt and brutality in these doings."[44] Three years later, the Russian-Jewish physician Leon Pinsker wrote, "The age-old problem of the Jewish Question is causing emotions to run high today, as it has over the ages. Like the quadrature of the circle, it is an unsolved problem, but unlike it, it remains the burning question of the day."[45] "When did the 'Jewish question' leap on my back?" wrote the Russian dramatist Leonid Andreyev during the Great War, "I don't know. I was born with it and under it. From the very moment I assumed a conscious attitude towards life until this very day I have lived in its noisome atmosphere, breathed in the poisoned air which surrounds all these 'problems,' all these dark, harrowing alogisms, unbearable to the intellect."[46]

It was not merely that questions were irritating, they were also *ubiquitous*. There is a joke—with many variations—that goes something like this: At an international essay competition where the theme was elephants "the Englishman wrote 'Elephants I Have Shot'; the American wrote 'Bigger and Better Elephants'; the Frenchman wrote 'L'Elephante es Ses Amours'; the Pole wrote 'The Elephant and the Polish Question.' "[47] The phrase "Słoń a sprawa polska" (The elephant and the Polish question) is even an entry in Polish Wikipedia and was the tongue-in-cheek name given to a 2007/2008 Polish-Italian cultural festival in Sicily.[48]

Nor is the aura of obsessive preoccupation unique to the Polish and Eastern questions. As Richard Bernstein wrote of the Jewish question, "I vividly recall that when I was a teenager growing up in Brooklyn (during World War II), there were many local jokes about 'the Jewish question.' 'The Jewish question and—' was a formula where one could simply, imaginatively fill in the blank . . . for example, 'The Jewish question and the Brooklyn Dodgers.' "[49] There are works on "the Jewish question in Poland," on "Freud's Jewish Question," and on the relationship between the "Jewish question" and the "woman question."[50] It seems everyone, from Marx to Freud to Dostoevsky to Goebbels to Sartre, had something to say about it. More recently, the American writer and broadcaster Howard Jacobson wrote a best-selling novel titled *The Finkler Question*, a spoofed slant reference to the Jewish question through a fictional character named Sam Finkler.[51]

The markings and violence done to written sources on the "Polish question" offer proof enough that the phrase touched many a nerve: whole chapters torn with apparent fury out of books, and a goodly supply of shrill marginalia ("Hypocrisy!" "Not for the Poles!").[52] And in a copy of an 1881 Hungarian pamphlet on the

Jewish question, a heated argument rages between two readers in the margins.[53] Similar examples abound.[54] In fact, the very *frenzied and dogged passion* that questions have evoked has contributed to their relegation to the trash bin of history, if not of historical inquiry. Yet even this ennui has a long historical pedigree. One author writing in an evening newspaper in 1881 longed for the "termination" of "this tedious Eastern Question,"[55] and a poem in an 1883 issue of London's *Mayfair Magazine* included a comic-pathetic line declaring that "[t]he 'Eastern Question' is a bore."[56]

The Reality of Questions Revisited

It was not long before questions were overlaid with seemingly intractable negativity, rather like enemies to be defeated. "Ach! How horrid this Eastern question is that sneers at us with every confusion!"[57] wrote the German poet Heinrich Heine in 1841. A commentator in the London *Evening Star* writing in 1881 called it "the hideous nightmare that has been the chief cause of uneasiness amongst the European Powers."[58] To the British publicist and statesman John Morley, the Eastern question was "[t]hat shifting, intractable, and interwoven tangle of conflicting interests, rival peoples, and antagonistic faiths,"[59] while an anonymous author writing in Italian in 1854 described it as a "serious dispute that has shaken Europe for so long."[60]

In an 1877 work on *The Eastern Question, Past, Present and Future*, the English naval officer Captain Bedford Pim wrote what he called "a succinct account of the 'Eastern Question'" for his readers. "Having done this," he concluded, with the swaggering tone of the Arctic explorer he was, "it only remains to look the situation frankly and bravely in the face, and to grapple manfully with the evil."[61] The Turkish writer Namık Kemâl was more despairing when he wrote in 1911/1912: "The Eastern Question is the name of those calamities of politics that have, for two centuries, been feared in the manner of volcanoes that erupt with fire at the least desirable time and change the face of the earth with an earthquake of explosions [or misfortunes]."[62]

In the midst of the general mania around questions, it is little wonder that the more astute observers began to question their legitimacy and even their very existence. During the Crimean War, the Saxon legation to Paris wrote a report claiming that the Eastern question was really just an Anglo-French scheme to prop up Lord Palmerston and Napoleon III against domestic political enemies.[63] In 1858, a character in a German novel phlegmatically declared, "The Polish question still hangs around like a ghost haunting Europe. But it is a silly ghost that no one really believes in any longer."[64] Such ideas were frequently overlaid by not a little satirical commentary on the imaginary character of questions. A German book of anecdotes from 1861 includes the following comic dialogue between two Berliners:

> KRIPPENSTAPEL: We are still far behind the English. . . .
> NANTE: Yes . . . They invent everything a person could want. One invention after the other: steamships, gas lighting, the Eastern question, matches, national debt.[65]

A few years later, in 1863, the Marquess of Salisbury penned his own laconic take on the Polish question. "There are few positions more embarrassing," he wrote, "than that of men who hold moderate opinions in regard to questions upon which excitement is running high."[66] In an 1887 article on "Socialism and Democracy," Woodrow Wilson issued a comparable lament:

> One wearies easily, it must be confessed, of woeful-warnings; one sighs often for a little tonic of actual thinking grounded in sane, clear-sighted perception of what is possible to be done. Sentiment is not despicable—it may be elevating and noble, it may be inspiring, and in some mental fields it is self-sufficing— but when uttered concerning great social and political questions, it needs the addition of practical initiative sense to keep it sweet and to prevent its becoming insipid.[67]

In the second half of the nineteenth century, words such as *moderate*, *sane*, and *sober* became part of the way querists framed their own interventions as a means to set themselves apart from the image of the hysterical, maniacal querist.[68]

The pseudonymous Hungarian Szombatsági opened his work on the nationality question by telling his readers that it had a long history, was hard to solve, but was nonetheless of paramount importance, and that what was needed was a clear understanding and "political sobriety."[69] The theme of sobriety, or the "sober mind," recurs throughout the work.[70] The metaphor of drunkenness and sobriety is revealing, for drunkenness is a temporary condition of impairment. If one is drunk, the problem is not with the world but with one's perception of it; seeing the world clearly—i.e., being sober—makes the question go away. Coming to one's senses is tantamount to solving the problem.

The problem with questions was thus more the frenzy they produced than the reality they portended to describe. In a confidential report on the Eastern question for the British government, the Anglo-Irish major-general G. J. Wolseley wrote in 1876:

> As a man awaking from heavy slumber disturbed by dreams, shakes himself into consciousness of the practical reality around him, so the English people seem now to have cleared away those clouds of sentiment in which the Eastern Question had been enveloped by unpractical enthusiasts actuated by the highest motives, by the designing Russian diplomatists with a view to national aggrandizement, and by the home politicians for party purposes. . . . [O]ur blood has cooled down from the fever heat to which it had been excited, to an ordinary and natural temperature, and we can now hope to reason rationally, and to divest this perplexing question of all false sentimentality.[71]

The passion around questions—the marquess, Wolseley, and others suggested—was part of their fraud. In 1876, Alfred Austin wrote a pamphlet titled *Tory Horrors; or, The Question of the Hour: A Letter to Gladstone*, a scathing critique of William Gladstone's

Bulgarian Horrors and the Question of the East of the same year. Austin lampooned the sensationalism of Gladstone's pamphlet and charged him with cynical political calculation:

> I would invite you, when you have retired from the tumult of public meetings to the recesses of your own conscience, to ask yourself with merciless scrutiny whether, had the name of your pamphlet been regulated either by what it contains or by the emotion which lately invaded your retirement, you would not in candour have been compelled to call it, "Tory Horrors, or the Question between Lord Beaconsfield and myself."[72]

Such skepticism—nay, *cynicism*—cast a lingering shadow over querists' interventions. A year later, a character in an satirical piece by a British journalist declared, "I verily believe that there is no Eastern Question at all, but that the entire thing is an invention got up and maintained by subscription among our newspapers at home, in order to increase their circulation."[73]

Period queristic mania caused more than a few to lose faith in questions' reality. Since questions could be and were defined according the whims and preferences of the querists, a new group of commentators emerged who made it their task to define questions right out of existence. "There is no woman question," Leo Tolstoy wrote in his diary in 1898. "There is a question of the freedom and equality of all human beings. The woman question is just arrogance."[74] For an Austrian author writing during the Great War, the "so-called Ukrainian question" was the malicious construction of an MP who, for "purely personal reasons," invented first a "Ukrainian people" and then a "Ukrainian question," which then grew into a "question of the future of the monarchy" with a "hypnotic effect" on policy makers.[75]

For many Polish Marxists, the Polish question was nonexistent, in much the same way as Marx noted for the Jewish question or Tolstoy for the woman question. "At present there is no 'Polish question,'" wrote Julian Marchlewski in 1923, "there exists instead a question of the emancipation of the Polish proletariat, which should be resolved in a revolutionary manner."[76] And commentators on the social question—including the German revolutionary Karl Heinzen and the Austrian theosophist Rudolf Steiner—kept the phrase at an ironic distance by placing it in quotation marks.[77] Even the so-called "European question" was a diversion. If a question was considered the responsibility of all of Europe, then no individual state could be held to account for failing to address it.[78]

Although in 1875 Lord Stratford de Redcliffe confidently declared in an article in *The Times* that "[t]he Eastern Question is a fact, a reality of indefinite duration," other period commentators were not so sure.[79] In the words of a minor character, an Ottoman statesman, in Benjamin Disraeli's 1847 novel *Tancred*, "For my part, it seems to me that your Eastern question is a great imbroglio that only exists in the cabinets of diplomatists. Why should there be any Eastern question? All is very well as it is." [80] The fictional character's outburst matches another famously uttered by the (real) Austrian diplomat Anton Prokesch: "[I]n Turkey there is no Eastern question!"[81]

The poem that Ambrose Bierce wrote on "The Eastern Question" (perhaps during the crisis in Macedonia in 1903) was appropriately satirical.[82] It suggested that the frothing passions surrounding it were just that: foam with no substance that obscured a deeper, more cynical reality.

> Looking across the line, the Grecian said:
> "This border I will stain a Turkey red."
> The Moslem smiled serenely and replied:
> "No Greek has ever for his country dyed."
> While thus each patriot guarded his frontier
> The Powers stole the country in his rear.

Many were coming to believe that the geopolitical questions of the East, in particular, were but a shadow play of the Great Powers. "The business of diplomacy," wrote Fyodor Dostoevsky in 1877,

> is now to lay hold of the Eastern Question in all repects and to assure everyone . . . that no question whatever has come up,

that these things are nothing more than some litte excursions and maneuvers [and] not only has the Eastern Question not come up but that there never was such a thing at all, that it never existed but is only a fog that was spread a hundred years ago . . . and that this unexplained fog persists to this day.[83]

In 1886, an Ottoman Foreign Ministry official concluded that an "Eastern question" would always emerge out of British-Russian competition.[84] And Arnold Toynbee opened his classic 1922 history *The Western Question in Greece and Turkey: A Study in the Contact of Civilizations* with an evocative image: that the shadow that so frightened Western Europeans in the East was their own, and that the Eastern question would therefore be better understood as a "Western question."[85] An Austrian cartoon from 1872 satirized the Polish question as a crooked mirror into which the Great Powers gazed, thinking they were engaging with a romantic and elusive Poland. A closer look revealed they were gazing at one another.[86]

The seepage of questions into literature and satire (Scherr, Disraeli, Rabener, Bierce) offers a clear indication that period thinkers believed the question genre had an undeniable air of artifice about it that obscured essential truths. They had begun to suspect that the questions of the nineteenth century were naught but elaborate *fictions*.

The Scientization of Questions

Confronted with the possibility that they had gotten all worked up over a mirage, many querists, instead of folding, doubled down and tried to invoke the empirical certainty of science to legitimate their folly. The logic of mathematical questions (what we would now call equations, problems, or formulae) made them operable *in both directions*, a feature with which querists endowed nineteenth-century questions. Insofar as the Eastern, woman, and Jewish questions were construed as problems to be solved, we have seen how period thinkers often reverse engineered an

FIGURE 3. "Wie der Dr. Leopold Herbst ausging, die polnische Frage zu studieren, und wie es ihm hiebei ergangen" [How Dr. Leopold Herbst went out to study the Polish question, and how that went for him], in *Der Floh* (Vienna), February 4, 1872, p. 23.

understanding or definition of questions from their presumed definitive or final solutions.

Although the British mathematician-philosopher George Boole wrote in 1854 that it was "premature" to "speculate . . . upon the question whether the methods of abstract science [specifically algebraic logic] are likely at any future day to render service in the investigation of social problems,"[87] it was also in a very real sense too late. Statisticians and their predecessors had been applying these methods at least since Kant waxed enthusiastic about their potential in his 1784 *Idea for a Universal History with a Cosmopolitan Intent.*[88] In fact, mathematical models for understanding society were already starting to lose their grip, and querists were quick to change tactics.

Over time, and especially toward the end of the nineteenth century, as faith in single, definitive, or "final" solutions waned, querists replaced mathematized equation- or proof-like metaphors with biological and medical ones. Questions were no longer problems that could be definitively and clearly solved so much as ills to be remedied or ameliorated.[89] Querists hypothesized that the disequilibrium or malady that characterized questions could not be "cured"; it would need to be treated over and over again (like hunger), could not be treated at all, or could only be treated with the most extreme and often violent interventions.[90]

The very notion of disequilibrium drew on scientific insights, specifically in the physical sciences. Querists conceived of an intangible and yet somehow *physical* relationship between the geopolitics of the East and the social politics of the West. "[T]he idea of European equilibrium," wrote the German historian Barbara Zielke in her 1931 doctoral dissertation on the *The Eastern Question in the Political Thought of Europe*, was "of decisive significance precisely for the Eastern question."[91] Querists borrowed from theories in fluid dynamics (or hydrodynamics) and especially of equilibrium as expressed in the work of Blaise Pascal and Jean le Rond d'Alembert to advance their claims.[92] They also made frequent references to "dividing barriers," "equilibrium," and "leveling" in interventions on the social, Jewish, and woman questions.[93]

Certain scientized patterns repeat across multiple interventions on nineteenth- and twentieth-century questions: the need to establish first causes or premises, the aggregation of questions into question bundles (combine to solve), and the offering of a "formula" for a great omnibus solution. With these rhetorical nods to the objectivity of science, querists sought to obscure their own agendas by suggesting that the questions themselves provided both the formula and the momentum toward "the only reasonable, intelligent solution."[94] When the precondition for the solution is given as part of the solution itself, *that* is a problem.

The Wages of Passion

As even those who wrote on questions began to lose faith in their reality, the role of the querist began to change: not universally and not overnight, but strikingly and irreversibly. To observe the change, it is important to understand that a nearly ubiquitous formula within the question idiom looked something like this: introductory remarks decrying the confusion of terms and ideas around previous interventions on a given question, followed by a promise to offer a correct, sober, and clear formulation of the question, which should in turn naturally point to the solution.[95]

Writers regularly prefaced their positive, "sober" agenda with a passionate denunciation of the supposed misnomers, misapprehensions, or outright fabrications of preceding querists.[96] And as the argument on force noted, faith in final solutions was slipping. "For as long as I can remember," wrote a Serbian reviewer in a Belgrade-based periodical in 1891, "and God knows I remember as far back as the Crimean War, I've been constantly hearing that the Eastern question will be solved—now, immediately, today, tomorrow, it's here."

But forty years have passed during which people have been solving the Eastern question, and there have been so many wars because of it, so many international conferences and congresses, and it's still not solved. On the contrary. Today four million people are standing in Europe, armed to the teeth, facing each other off, ready to rush to their doom . . . and all this because of the Eastern question and that itty-bitty Alsace-Lorraine.[97]

Questions of the late nineteenth and early twentieth centuries differed from their predecessors in that they appeared more impervious to ready solutions. Even after the Bolsheviks had taken control of a diminished Russian Empire and the Habsburg and Ottoman Empires were definitively dismantled, a Bulgarian legal scholar ended a long history of the Eastern question with the conclusion that "the Eastern question is not solved, because injustice and arbitrariness [произвола] cannot offer a lasting solution to any problem."[98]

Commentators accused the publicistic and political realms of not merely fabricating questions and prematurely declaring them solved but also of offering unrealistic panaceas and "miracle cures." In the 1890s, one Hungarian newspaper, the social democratic daily *People's Word*, noted that everyone weighing in on the worker question offered a "magical potion" [csodaszere] to solve it.[99] Writing on the woman question in 1909, the Catholic theologian Viktorin Strommer complained that feminists were too quick with their "magic potion," such that the problem seemed to essentially solve itself.[100] And the same year, the Hungarian Catholic vicar Béla Mészáros saw a world full of "prophets" claiming to possess the only solution to the social question.[101]

Politics, Mihály Réz stated at the beginning of his famous 1917 essay on the nationality question, are immensely complex, yet in every time, doctrinaires look for a single cause and with it a single, elegant solution.[102] This was a foolhardy mistake. By the outbreak of the Great War, querists from both the Right and Left saw false prophets, quacks, and ideologues lurking behind questions. The more the spirit of the times or the spirit of man sought solutions, the further those solutions seemed to recede, and what had once seemed a straight course now resembled ever more a "vicious circle" or a "Gordian knot," both metaphors which began to appear frequently in the idiom of questions.[103]

An inexorable momentum was building behind this ever-tighter welter and spin. But instead of driving inexorably toward emancipation or war or federation, querists more commonly sought to throw the machine into neutral. Having roundly dele-gitimated final solutions, fewer and fewer querists even offered them, resorting instead to diagnoses of the time. In a 1933 book on *The Spirit of the Time as a Question of the Philosophy of History*, the right-wing Hungarian librarian-historian Tibor Joó wrote that the spirit of the time, much like Lukács's "answering being," was forever trying to solve something, and each era did so over and over again.[104] "[I]t is hopeless to seek a singular 'solution,' a magic potion or an incantation to remedy this situation," wrote the Hungarian democrat István Bibó of the Jewish question in 1944. Instead, he continued, what was required was "a slowing down of the vicious circle."[105]

Querists' Profile in Flux

Given the growing consensus that final solutions were not possi-ble, both the form and the content of interventions on questions began to change. Early interventions tended to be written by mem-bers of parliament, politicians, statesmen, or publicists. During and after the revolutions of 1830–1833, and again in 1848, however, the pamphlet and newspaper venues they employed were opened to a broader range of querists, a trend which continued as press venues proliferated and literacy rates grew in many countries throughout the second half of the nineteenth century.[106] Already in 1840, Lord John Russell wrote to the British prime minister Lord Melbourne on the power of the press in the conduct of di-plomacy around the Eastern question, suggesting that "the articles in the newspapers form part of the conduct of the negociations."[107] And in 1847, in Disraeli's *Tancred*, the title character lamented that "The public opinion . . . has superseded the rhetorical club of our great-grandfathers."[108]

In an 1870 review of a book of *Popular Lectures and Essays on Legal Matters*, the reviewer, Dr. Karl Lemayer, noted that the phrase "popularization of science" is "known to be ... a completely useless catchphrase concealing a shallow nature [*Seichtigkeit*], lack of understanding, or a certain asinine radicalism."[109] He nevertheless defended as "beneficial" the notion that "everyone is offered the gratifying opportunity to light his modest little lamp among the great lights of science." He went on to criticize the book's author for not addressing "questions of the day" (*Tagesfragen*): "[H]e should have addressed the aspects of his themes that most relate to questions of the day and are therefore of interest to the broader public."

Lemayer's critique contained an increasingly common disparagement of the quality of publicistic interventions on questions. The sole original contribution to be made by the popular pedagogical genre was in the realm of a more profound elucidation of "questions of the day"; in other words, snatching them out of the inept clutches of journalistic hacks. "It would make a lot of eyes see more clearly that there are a lot of things between heaven and earth with regard to these questions which the wisdom of our daily press has no clue about and that the decisive points and great difficulties are to be found for the most part in completely different directions than where the leading articles and club speakers seek them."[110]

By the 1870s, questions had indeed started to reach "a lot of eyes." This was the decade of the great attempts to bring the Eastern question, in particular, to bear on domestic political issues: to influence an election in Britain; or to bring the force of public opinion back behind a Russian imperial palace whose strength and popularity seemed to be foundering. A Russian pamphlet from 1878 noted with astonishment how rapidy the Russian public had concerned itself with a question that hitherto had been "no more than a 'subject of information' for the Asiatic Department of the Ministry of Foreign Affairs."[111]

By the 1890s, it was possible for a miller, a timber industrialist, or a self-declared "common man of the people" to enter the querist

fold by means of self-published pamphlets.[112] The Russian writer
Anton Chekhov, in a satirical piece titled "The New Years Drink,"
described the character Semyon Stepanich: "He, like every Russian citizen, has his own views on the Bulgarian question, and if
it were up to him, he would solve it better than anyone else."[113]
In *The Third Staircase*, an 1892 novel by the Baltic German writer
Eduard von Keyserling, there is a scene in which an old shoemaker mounts a podium to give an impassioned speech on the
Eastern question. "He was rather intoxicated and spoke in a confused manner; he wanted to urge the [social democratic] party to
do something to solve the Eastern question; that was a duty."
Even when a fire breaks out and nearby buildings start to burn,
"[a]t the podium the shoemaker was still calling for the solution
to the Eastern question, for the free Balkan states."[114] The absur-
dity of the scene was meant to point to the folly both of question
hysteria and the lower-class elements it had emboldened. "Just
as in politics," wrote the secretary of the Hungarian National
Millers' Association in 1894, "the 'opinion of the street' cannot
offer us guidance."[115]

In 1885, the Austrian-Jewish publicist Isidore Singer edited a
collection of *Letters of Famous Christian Contemporaries on the Jewish Question*. His primary objective—as outlined in the foreword
to the compilation—was to take the discussion out of the hands
of the riffraff of the street (*Strassenpöbel*) and move it from the
"smokey beer halls," and place it instead where it belonged, namely,
in the "consultation chambers of scholars and statesmen."[116] His
compilation was intended to be just such a "consultation chamber" [*Berathungssaal*].

> And in fact it seems high time that the discussion of such seri-
> ous questions be taken out of the hands of half- and uneducated
> people and into those of men whose rich life experience and
> high position in the realm of science and literature entitles them
> to speak the last word on a question that cuts so deeply into the
> entirety of social existence.[117]

Singer solicted responses from domestic (Austrian) elites, as well as from abroad. When the Hungarian journal *Twentieth Century* asked prominent figures to weigh in on the Jewish question in 1916, it self-consciously borrowed the conceit from Singer's *Letters*.[118]

There were thus two forces pulling at opposite ends of the age, one that mourned the passing of elite decision-making and de- cried the "confusion of concepts and tangling of relations" that accompanied the "questions being discussed in our tumultuous time," and the concomitant proliferation of strong opinions as well as the sinking level of public discussion around questions[119]; and another that blamed the self-important megalomania of press and political figures for creating and sustaining question-fictions. Both forces drew attention to an ever more broadly held conception that the age was spinning its wheels and had become all churn and no substance.

The Academic Whimper

The very desire to gather a compendium of differing positions—as Singer and *Twentieth Century* did—points to a mounting unease with the propagandistic isolation of the singular pamphlet coupled with a sense that to understand, which often meant to see from a different perspective or from multiple perspectives, was tanta- mount to solving, and a rhetorical prioritization of "seeking the truth" over "transient tactical opportunism."[120] Some of this is evident from the list of individuals queried for the *Twentieth Cen- tury* questionnaire, which included politicians from various points on the political spectrum (none of whom replied): Zionists, liber- als, populists, and conservatives. The journal, in short, presumed disagreement regarding the existence, nature, and solution to the Jewish question, and sought to offer a representative array of positions. The journal's editors did not offer their own solu- tion. Instead, they immediately initiated another questionnaire in the same vein on the nationality question.[121] A comparable compendium of positions on the colonial question in Germany was compiled by Hans Poeschel of the German Empire's Colonial Office in 1920.[122]

The late nineteenth century also saw the proliferation of subject bibliographies on questions, which reinforced the value of compiling competing perspectives as an aid to "understanding" a given question. In 1885, the Australian folklorist Joseph Jacobs published a bibliography of 1,230 titles in an effort to "collect together all the literary productions emanating from either side of the so-called Jewish question under its protean aspects in Europe and America during the decade 1875–1884." (The titles were in German, English, French, Hebrew, Hungarian, Romanian, Italian, Russian, Dutch, Spanish, Polish, and Danish, which Jacobs then divided them categories including A = Anti-Semitic, P = Pro-Semitic, and C = Conversionist).[123] Several other bibliographies of various questions, ranging from the social to the Balkan questions, also appeared in the last third of the nineteenth century and thereafter.[124]

In their selection, bibliographies provided their own oblique but often quite clear definition of the question. It is worth noting that many works cited in these publications do not explicitly refer to a particular question, and thus we can see the range of issues and concerns that a given editor selectively gathered under a particular question umbrella and how a question was presumed to exist independently of its formulation as such. The implications: that you might well be discussing a question without invoking its name, that you know a question when you see it, and that others will accept a definition you have chosen as self-evident, while often acknowledging in the same form (namely, the variety of the works cited) that there is little agreement on the matter of essence.

Little wonder that with the widespread loss of faith in solutions and the proliferation of compendia highlighting the arbitrariness of definitions came the mounting suspicion that it was not even worth trying to engage with questions. In 1865, Miloš Popović offered a "Serb perspective" on the nationality question in Hungary, in which he also made mention of the Eastern question:

In Europe we've already become so accustomed to the "Eastern question" that it seems as though it will remain forever insoluble, as though it were a thing incapable of further development in accordance with the laws of continuity and progress, and that under its influence we have become as carefree as in some contagious disease after the first flash of fear, and now with shuddering tranquility we look on as it wreaks havoc; with mute desperation we give ourselves over to it.[125]

Robert Musil went one further in an article from 1912. Politics in Austria had been reduced, he wrote, to a one-sided sense of "the difficulty of the nationality question." But it was a difficulty that had "long since become a comfort," and an "unacknowledged evasion and lingering," betraying an "emptiness of the inner life, like the void in an alcoholic's stomach."[126]

In light of the intense rhetoric of conviction surrounding questions, Toynbee's assertion that only the peoples of the East believed that "Western politics turn upon the Eastern Question, and that the Englishman or Frenchman looks abroad on the world with eyes inflamed by a passionate love or hatred, as the case may be, for the Greek or the Turkish nation," seems incongruous.[127] What Toynbee was likely responding to, however, was what he perceived as a real disjuncture between the passion with which questions were discussed in pamphlets and parliamentary speeches, and the indifference with which most people most of the time approached them.

Tolstoy's intervention on the Eastern question through the character of Levin in the last segment of *Anna Karenina* unfolded in a similar key: the Russian people generally did not share the passion of commentators on the Eastern question, and the frenzy surrounding it was mostly the work of a handful of ne'er-do-wells and sensationalist journalists. "Of course the newspapers are unanimous," the old Prince Alexander Shtcherbatsky tells an enthusiastic pontificator on the Eastern question. "That is easily explained. War will double their circulation."[128]

Epilogue

Long after many period commentators of the age of questions stopped believing in the reality of questions and, indeed, questioned the motives of querists, academics in various disciplines continued to treat them as real and assign them histories. It is a querist's intention and folly to insist that questions are real and clearly defined problems. Historians have proven no better in this respect than the querists themselves. They have long read querists' books, articles, and pamphlets on a subject such as the Eastern or the nationality question and proceded to make assumptions of their own about what the "real" question is or was and dropped in their own definitions, chronologies, and histories of the question, sometimes at the same time that questions were a regular feature in newspapers, pamphlets, and parliamentary proceedings. Yet if questions were understood as problems, it was because querists actively sought to *make* them problems for an audience they hoped to excite and influence, oftentimes with very concrete policy agendas in mind.

Perhaps the fraud of the age is beginning to dawn even on historians, however. By now Ottomanists know the Eastern question: they know it well enough to be suspicious of it as a formulation, to enclose it in quotation marks or precede it with a "so-called."[129] They know it well enough to steer clear of it if they hope to say something sensible about Ottoman history; it was for too long the dominant frame for approaches to Ottoman history in the West. Selim Deringil refers to an " 'Eastern Question' paradigm" and "the 'Eastern Question school' " that continues to haunt the historiography of the Ottoman Empire.[130] And even as early as 1922, when Arnold Toynbee published his classic history *The Western Question in Greece and Turkey: A Study in the Contact of Civilizations*, there were clear signs of a weariness with the old "Eastern question" formulation that obscured far more than it revealed.[131]

Ottomanists also know that historians and statesmen have traditionally used the phrase "Eastern question" to talk about many things—the balance of power in Europe, Russian expansion, and Jewish emancipation, for example—*except* the Ottoman Empire.[132] And they have sought to correct for the absence of the Ottoman Empire's policies and protagonists from works on the Eastern question by writing about nineteenth-century European international relations from an Ottoman perspective.[133] "If we do not wish for history to repeat itself and for our national territory to once again be shared among the Western Powers as booty," wrote the diplomatic historian and former diplomat Hüner Tuncer, "then I think we must understand very well what the Western states meant by the 'Eastern question' of the past and avoid the misconceptions and mistakes of history."[134]

Nor has the Eastern question been unique in this respect. In 1946, the Polish writer Edmund Jan Osmańczyk resisted his publisher's suggestion to title his book "New Polish Questions." Osmańczyk considered the title "too emotional" and opted instead for *The Republic of Poles*.[135] More recently, in his history of Poland, *God's Playground: 1795 to the Present*, the historian Norman Davies wrote that "of all the animals to be found in the diplomatic garden of modern Europe The Polish Question is indeed the elephant, if not the dodo." For that reason, historians of Poland must view it as "a singularly barren subject."[136]

In modern Greek, "You've made an Eastern question (out of it)" (Ανατολικό ζήτημα το έκανες) is a common idiom meaning "You've made a mountain out of a molehill." That about says it all.

6

The Temporal Argument

THE AGE OF SPIN

I think there was never a greater need, nor will there be a more
suitable time to realize the idea than the present moment. . . .
The old conditions have been irretrievably lost, and since then
provisional ones have formed: we need a new fundament, a new
organization: A great transformation, a great decision . . . Fortunate
is the age that makes its own man![1]

—HUNGARIAN PUBLICIST AND WRITER KÁROLY SZINI,
WRITING ON THE HUNGARIAN QUESTION (1866)

A Time-Conscious Age

The argument about farce is not unlike Baudelaire's dandy, whose
"aristocratic superiority of mind" obscures what his taste cannot
abide. With laconic wit that betrays "the joy of astonishing others,
and the proud satisfaction of never oneself being astonished" and
"an air of coldness which comes from an unshakeable determination not to be moved," the argument dismisses with a gloved hand
an entire age.[2] Like the dandy himself, we need take that argument
only half-seriously.

The previous chapter was right to chastise the smugness of querism, to call out the querists as spin doctors. The age of questions was indeed an age of spin, but in an entirely different sense of the word. Querists sought control and practiced manipulation, but they also longed to *relinquish* control of the processes their querism had set in motion. Their spin thus became part entropic welter, part death spiral. It was the spin of disengagement.

Timing

The reader of period pamphlets, newspapers, and other interventions on questions may be forgiven for coming away with the impression that it was *very nearly impossible* to get a question right, both in terms of formulation and timing. "The Eastern question," wrote the French novelist and publicist Émile de Girardin in 1853, "remains [as] it was before: a poorly posed question and therefore insoluble."[3] A secret memo from 1870 drafted by the Foreign Ministry in Saxony on the German question argued that it must be solved *before* others could be addressed.[4] In a lecture delivered in 1897 on "Scientific Development in Ancient Greece," Emil Reich, the founder of geopolitics, told his audience at the University of Cincinnati:

> The Grecians were doing in science exactly what we are doing. They raised a question and tried to answer it. Now the trouble is that we frequently ask questions which are either entirely out of place, or immature, or in some other way inappropriate. To ask the right question—why that is the greatest difficulty.... [T]he ancients failed not because of a radical fault in their scientific method, but simply because they wanted to solve problems that were not then or as yet not ripe for solution.[5]

Therewith Reich raised the possibility not only that a question could be wrongly formulated but that a correctly formulated question may come into being *at the wrong time*.[6] We cannot speak of an age of questions without regard for this tyrannical, elusive, and yet ever-ticking metronome that set its meter.

An important effect of backdating questions was to posit an ineluctable momentum toward solution. A tone of urgency overlaid the work of just about every querist, with the implication that it is *high time* to see the question addressed. In a speech on the "anti-slavery question" from 1855, Frederick Douglass argued, "There is no denying it, for it is everywhere admitted, that the anti-slavery question is the great, moral and social question now before the American people. A state of things has gradually been developed by which that question has become the first thing in order. It has got to be met."[7] An anonymous pamphleteer writing *A Few Words on the Eastern Question* in 1860 similarly spoke of the "urgent necessity" of "terminating this eternal Eastern question."[8] "There seems to be a rare opportunity for a settlement of the Eastern question, such as may not occur again for many a long day if we allow events to march," wrote the Scottish liberal politician George Campbell in 1877.[9] "The misery of the Jews is an anachronism," wrote Theodor Herzl in his famous 1896 pamphlet *The Jewish State*: a solution to the Jewish question was already long overdue.[10]

That this sense of urgency became, paradoxically, timeless is evident from a brief excursus into the history of the Macedonian question. In 1895, the cover of a Bulgarian newspaper, *The Macedonian Voice*, featured an article on "Macedonia and Europe," in which the author declared that the Macedonian question "day by day takes on ever greater and ever more serious proportions." In the near future, the article continued, "it will be solved."[11] Nearly half a century later, in 1941, a Bulgarian propaganda pamphlet declared in German that "[a] definitive and just solution of the Macedonian question is urgently necessary under the present circumstances."[12]

The metronome of the age did not mark out an acceleration across the nineteenth century and into the twentieth but rather set a frantic pace at the start that could not but remain so, driven by an anxiousness that the time had come or, worse, that it had already passed—a sensibility that spun into a rhythmic, increasingly detached automatism.

The American Question Revisited

I ask the reader to indulge in the reprisal of one of the earliest questions—from the national argument—from which we might perceive the pace and rhythm of the age: the American question. An early reference to it appears in Thomas Pownall's *The Administration of the Colonies* (1764).[13] Pownall argued that "the Colonies, although without the limits of the realm, are yet in fact, *of* the realm . . . and therefore ought . . . to be *united to the realm*, in a full and absolute communication and communion of all rights, franchises and liberties, which any other part of the realm hath, or doth enjoy, or ought to have and to enjoy."[14] Here the question was about the status of the Colonies within the British Empire. On February 24, 1775, on the eve of the American Revolution, John Griffin Griffin charged many of his fellow British parliamentarians with having "uniformly shrunk . . . from the great American question" and having deferred "to the latest hour possible, all discussions of this critical topic."[15]

After the American Revolution, when the Colonies had become the United States of America, most publicists who mentioned the American question concluded either implicitly or explicitly that it was "at an end" or "no more."[16] Yet it resurfaced soon thereafter, this time relating to the merchant interests of Britain, the United States, and France after the French sought to blockade Britain and the British to prevent the United States from trading with France (1806–1807).[17] During the War of 1812, and up until the peace signed at Ghent in late 1814, the question was *again* transformed—as the United States declared war on Great Britain after thousands of US subjects had been impressed into the British navy by force—and *again* hotly debated.[18] The American question was reincarnated once more in the 1850s and 1860s, but this time in relation to the "question of slavery" during the Civil War.[19]

By now another pattern should be evident, namely, that of chronic redefinition. Questions morphed, appeared under various names, or took divergent forms under the same name. A very different context—the Hungarian—reveals the extent to which this is true. The Hungarian question referred initially to Hungary's status within the Habsburg Empire, later to Hungary's territorial losses during the Great War, and during the Cold War to the possibility of "rolling back" the Soviet occupation of Hungary, or was conflated with the minority question.[20]

Another question with many iterations was the Transylvanian question, which was initially about the status of the principality of Transylvania vis-à-vis the Hungarian Kingdom (specifically, the possibility of full unification with the Kingdom). After Hungary lost the territory to Romania with the postwar Treaty of Trianon in 1920, the question became a matter of the region's future (specifically, the possibility of it being reannexed to Hungary).[21] When part of Transylvania *was* reannexed to Hungary with the territorial changes mediated by Nazi Germany and fascist Italy during World War II, it was related again to the region's future, either as part of Romania or Hungary or both, and was as regularly discussed in Romanian national circles as in Hungarian ones.[22]

The rhetorical thrust behind redefinition came partly from events but partly also from a common three-part formula within the querist genre: (1) firm condemnation of the general attitude of frenzy that had hitherto surrounded the question; followed by (2) comprehensive dismissal of all previous interventions on the question as either wrong-headed, compromised by bias, or both; and finally (3) the offer of a calm, sober, and objective redefinition of the question that naturally points to the means of effecting its solution.[23] From an 1805 pamphlet on the Catholic question:

1. "The press of this metropolis presents, indeed, instructors and guides; but they are of that description, who have long

misled the Empire . . . All the clumsy invectives, the hyperbolical conjectures, the fictitious apprehension . . . all the
legends with which a prejudice, insatiably vindictive, had
glutted itself . . ."[24]

2. "There certainly exist upon this subject honest and candid
prepossessions . . . I conceive these conclusions to be
founded in misapprehension, and erroneous . . ."[25]

3. "I shall, therefore, with every possible deference, lay down
in the plainest and most simple form, and in the narrowest
compass, the scale of argument which produced my own
conviction."[26]

This rhetorical strategy, although not present in all queristic interventions, was nonetheless elemental to the genre.

Periodicity

The quest for international visibility left its mark on the way questions emerged and evolved over time, and indeed explains three
aspects of that emergence: the backdating of questions already
mentioned, the near simultaneity of their birth, and the anxious
rhetoric that swaddled them. The Polish question, for example,
emerged more or less simultaneously and was often discussed
together with at least two others: the Eastern question and the
Belgian question.[27] This simultaneity is rooted in the cluster of
events around 1830 mentioned earlier.[28] Around these events there
emerged an international public sphere conceived as a factor in
domestic political and diplomatic decision-making, a sphere in
which the skilled querist reigned supreme.

Yet none of the century's questions occupied the publicistic or
political realm with consistent frequency or intensity, nor were
they always as important in one country or context as they were
in others. As measured by the sheer magnitude of attention and
mania lavished upon it—in the press, pamphlets, discussion
groups, and representative assemblies; among diplomats and royal

courts; in fiction; and occasionally even on handkerchiefs—the Eastern question was arguably the grandest of all nineteenth-century questions.[29] "All eyes and thoughts are fixed on the Eastern Question," wrote Lord William Russell to his brother Lord John Russell, who had recently become Britain's secretary of state for war and the colonies, in September 1839.[30] Writing in the London *Times* in 1876, Lord Stratford de Redcliffe declared that "[t]he Eastern Question has by degrees assumed such large proportions that no one can be surprised at the space it occupies in all public discussions whether of the tongue or of the pen."[31] A Russian pamphleteer made a similar assertion two years later: "The Eastern question is, without exaggeration, in our historical moment the soul and essence of the international life of the countries of Europe."[32] It was especially so for Russia, the author continued.

The question was repeatedly cast as a *vital* one for various other European states, as well as social and ethnic groups.[33] In 1839, the Austrian writer Franz Grillparzer called it a "vital question for Austria," and a decade and a half later, William Henry Trescot pressed the importance of the Eastern question on the American public.[34] Manjiro Inagaki, writing in 1890, made a similar argument for Japan.[35] Yet there were stretches of years when the Eastern question practically disappeared from the press of some countries and slackened across all of them, when commentators could merely hope it would be "reopened."[36]

These examples highlight another feature of the age: the irregularity with which questions commanded the international spotlight, not surprisingly around wars and uprisings. If we examine the appearance of the phrase "Polish question" in publications spanning the nineteenth and twentieth centuries using the Google Books and the HathiTrust Research Center databases, a few patterns appear: first, that the question emerged in different languages at roughly the same time, so it was international from the beginning. Nonetheless, some languages—though we should be careful not to confuse languages with state interests alone—were more "interested" in certain questions at certain times than others

(German-language commentary on the Polish question largely began in earnest in the years preceding the 1860s uprising, for example).[37]

In general, the concentration of interest in the Polish question shot up during periods of conflict: 1830–1831 (November Uprising—Russia), 1846 (Greater Poland Uprising—Austria), 1848–1849 (1848 revolutions and war), 1854–1855 (Crimean War), 1863–1864 (January Uprising—Russia), and 1914–1918 (World War I). We also see that the question was revived with the rise of Nazism and the disappearance of Poland (again) from the map in 1939 and indeed throughout World War II.[38]

It is therefore not a coincidence that as wars threatened or broke out, questions seemed to surge with renewed strength. "The Russo-Turkish War of 1877–1878," wrote a Turkish historian, "marks the commencement of the 'Armenian question' in Turkey."[39] Many observers of the Balkan Wars of 1912–1913 believed they marked the emergence or at least intensification of several questions.[40]

But it was with the outbreak of the Great War that a true deluge of questions flooded the publicistic realm and saturated political rhetoric. "There is such an opportunity for getting a settlement of the Irish question in present circumstances," wrote the Scottish political commentator in early August of 1914.[41] "The world war broke out and with it the 'Ukrainian question' came out of its ideational into its real stage," we read in an anonymous Austro-Hungarian manuscript.[42] It is remarkable to note how many questions seemed to surface or resurface simultaneously in both government correspondence and the publicistic realm during the war.[43] In Serbia, the state-run press published a number of pamphlets as part of a series titled "Contemporary Questions." In the words of the series editor, "[e]ven as the European war rages . . . still in every European nation many books and pamphlets are being written . . . about the different questions that are the order of the day, or that could be of interest to public opinion in the near future."[44]

As we learned from the argument on force, World War II saw a similarly sharp uptick in questioneering.[45] Numerous queristic interventions propagated a tone of eager anticipation of a great international coming-to-a-head and, furthermore, played no small part in bringing it about.[46] In November of 1941, addressing the Bulgarian National Assembly on the Macedonian question, Dimitar Peshev told his fellow assembly members that "certainly there will come an auspicious moment when the international conditions will allow for this question to be addressed."[47] A pamphlet from earlier the same year on the Macedonian question was timed to be published in German just after the Germans invaded Yugoslavia, and to help create an opening for Bulgaria's occupation of Macedonia. Its author declared emphatically that "[t]his Macedonian question has played the most important role in each and every military conflict on the Balkan Peninsula, and will certainly play a similar role in the present circumstances."[48]

After the war, a series of questions relating to decolonization appeared, or reappeared, on the queristic landscape, among them the Indochina (Vietnam), Algerian, and India-Pakistan and/or Kashmir questions.[49] And the "question algérienne" experienced a surge in discussion during the Algerian war (1954–1962), peaking in 1958, around the May coup and the fall of the Fourth French Republic.[50] Soviet Premier Nikita Khrushchev even invoked the "combine-to-solve" dynamic of questions in a speech to the fifteenth session of the United Nations General Assembly on September 23, 1960, where he said of the colonial, Korean, and disarmament questions, "One might say these are complex questions, that they cannot be solved in one stroke. But . . . they must be solved before it's too late. To avoid solving them is impossible."[51]

In between conflicts and congresses, however, there were long stretches of indifference and even silence. Giuseppe Mazzini, writing on the Polish question in 1836, noted, "For some time in Europe hearts have stirred for Poland. At least so they would have us believe. The sympathies that once seemed to have been extinguished were suddenly revived."[52] Yet during the January Uprising in 1863–1864, attention to the Polish question was so intense that it eclipsed other events, not least of all the US Civil War.[53] In a book on *Germans, Russia, and the Polish Question* (*Niemcy, Rosja i kwestia polska*) from 1908, the Polish politician Roman Dmowski—then a member of the tsarist Russian duma—made note of the fickleness with which the attention of both the international community and Poles themselves turned to the Polish question, such that it periodically disappeared from the international and indeed national public eye.[54] Other questions fared similarly. An 1839 pamphlet on the Belgian question, for example, opened with the observation that it had seemed to "go to sleep" for five years before being reawakened.[55]

So tenuous did questions' claim to international and domestic attention seem that sometimes their very existence was called into question. In 1856, just as the Crimean War had ended, a piece in an Austrian satirical magazine asserted that "the Polish question" no longer existed because "there are no more Poles," meaning that the Poles who lived in the territory of the former Polish-Lithuanian Commonwealth were no longer allowed to be Poles but rather had to identify as Slavs or Germans as the partitioning powers demanded.[56] "When the French speak of the Polish question," an anonymous author in a British weekly wrote in 1861, "they can only mean that in Western Europe a very warm sympathy is felt for the Poles. There is no Polish question in the sense in which there is a Hungarian question or a Turkish question."[57]

The implication in these passages is that in order for there to be a "question," there had to be some likelihood of a change in policy, action, or intervention that would alter the status quo. Questions were inherently status-quo allergic; they implied both the possibility and the necessity of moving beyond the present state.[58] If a matter did not possess this peculiar allergy, it was not a question. Querists had a disparaging expression for people who favored maintaining the status quo: "ostrich policy," or burying one's head in the sand rather than facing the imperative of transformation.[59] An 1886 draft speech by the Viennese populist and anti-Semitic politician Karl Lueger went one further, declaring that the liberals who prevented a solution to the national question were hell-bent on "destruction." "Any attempt to solve the national question is cunningly defeated," he wrote. "[A]ll that just so the sharks among the people can complete their destruction undisturbed."[60]

Cathartic Futures

Querists arrived at the conclusion that to (correctly) formulate a question was to solve it, on the one hand, because they were aware of bias in previous formulations and that formulations came pre-loaded with particular solutions but, on the other, because they sensed there was a real structure to be apprehended beneath the frenzy, the contradictions, and the anxious meditations and that, when properly apprehended, the tension and contradictions of the time would simply disappear.

In short, querists dreamt of catharsis. Even when they gave up on final solutions, the dream of catharsis was the dream of either achieving calm in spite of failing to find a solution (calm *as* a solution) or achieving calm through indifference or denial of questions' reality. Catharsis was only meaningful as a final phase of previous developments. This explains why historical overviews of particular questions often accompanied querists' interventions and even became a genre in themselves.[61] It also explains why some queristic interventions went one step further, imagining the shape of brighter futures on the *other side* of their preferred solutions.

In 1881, a pamphlet appeared bearing the title *The Eastern Questions Solved: A Vision of the Future* by an author using the pseudonym "Budge." The author sketched an alternative future wherein British prime minister William Gladstone's policies around the Eastern Crisis (1876–1878) had been implemented and the "the many-sided and knotty Eastern Question" had been solved.[62] The solution was a great Balkan kingdom and the transformation of Istanbul into a free city. Even the problem of dirty streets, stray

FIGURE 4. Budge, *The Eastern Question Solved: A Vision of the Future* (London: W. H. Allen, 1881).

dogs, and beggars had disappeared, thanks to the fact that the Great Powers had "so happily solved the great Eastern Question."[63] Another utopian projection by a Jewish satirist in Hungary, Adolf Ágai, delighted in the solution of the Jewish question in the Budapest of the future, where out of five million inhabitants, twenty million are Jews. But since both Christians and Jews are converting en masse to Buddhism, the question is considered solved.[64]

More often than promising utopian futures, however, querists imagined profoundly dystopian ones. Though the ostensible goal of "solving" questions—in a manner desirable to the author—was peace and catharsis, the threat of war was the necessary precondition for the "solution" of peace. This was evident already in 1829 with the first pamphlet on the Polish question, which drew attention to "the dangers that threaten the political balance of Europe, the independence and nationality of peoples."[65] Another querist writing in 1897 on the social question in Hungary argued that if legal and social reform were not undertaken, the changes required would take place one way or another through violent revolution.[66] The promise of utopia with the proper solution of the social question was frequently accompanied by a threat of disaster on a vast international scale should the solution not be found.[67] Even in the conclusion to his fantastical description of postsolution Istanbul, "Budge" warned that "[i]f this work be not done by peaceful means, it will be accomplished in a deluge of blood."[68]

A Question of Genre: The Constraints Imposed by Timeliness

A character in Tolstoy's *Anna Karenina* tells an enthusiastic pontificator on the Eastern question that the reason the newspapers were unanimous on the Eastern question was that "[w]ar will double their circulation."[69] Similarly, a character in a British satirical piece cries out: "I verily believe that there is no Eastern Question at all, but that the entire thing is an invention got up and maintained by subscription among our newspapers at home, in order to increase their circulation."[70] Both were pointing to the age's meter of urgency and timeliness, but also to questions' potentially *fictional* nature.

In spite of their apparent ubiquity in the nineteenth century, questions were largely restricted to a small range of venues and genres that did *not* often include fiction. Questions were the stuff of publicists and politicians. The pamphlet and newspaper article were their natural and original habitat, as these were the venues of timeliness and periodicity. Fiction's presumed timelessness rendered it ill-suited to querism, just as the scholastic questions' timelessness was the foil for the timeliness that characterized the age of questions.[71] The bulk of the interventions on the bullion question were in pamphlet form, and although writings on questions became lengthier with time—some in the form of books running into several hundred pages—even these later interventions retained some of the stylistic tics, function, and structure of pamphlets.[72] But if the pamphlet was the primary vehicle of the age of questions, it soon faced competition from the burgeoning of genres competing for new audiences.

Literary texts provide an especially piquant example of both the expansiveness and hard boundaries of the age. The nineteenth century was after all the century of the great novel and Romantic poetry. Yet although there are countless poems and reams of passionate prose on the cause of martyred Poland in the nineteenth and twentieth centuries, for example, I have only found one poem with any mention of the Polish question, and even that makes only an oblique and incomplete reference to it.[73] This is not to say that literary and cultural figures kept their distance from questions—far from it. The age was densely populated by diplomats and statesmen who wrote poetry and novels, poets and novelists who addressed diplomats and statesmen, and publicists who were also poets.[74]

But when cultural figures spoke in questions, they were generally speaking or writing in a *publicistic* rather than in an artistic vein. The earliest mentions of the social question in the French periodical literature show the extent to which the literary genre was initially *not* considered suitable for engagement with questions. In 1832, M. Nault, writing on James Fenimore Cooper, opined, "In the great social question that today stirs the people and separates them into two opposing camps of the intellect and the will, it seems that the field of letters is as sacred territory reserved in the time of the ancients for kindness and harmony."[75] Literature, in other words, was insufficiently pugnacious and, indeed, too necessarily beautiful to be a field of engagement with irritating questions. But Cooper was an exception, Nault believed, and more were to come.

With the flourishing of the free press during the 1848 revolutions, in addition to pamphlets and newspaper articles, a passionate surge of revolutionary poetry engulfed the social question, as well.[76] The French poet George Sand's "La question sociale" from May 4, 1848, opened with a warning: "Flee, flee, citizen, the house is burning!" The warning goes unheeded until the "citizen" is forced to jump to his death to escape the flames and collapsing building.[77] Sand's poem relayed the spirit of urgency and call to action common to engagement with questions in the publicistic vein. The fact that these injunctions were cloaked in metaphor hardly separates them from pamphlets, which were also rich in metaphors (of drunkenness, Gordian knots, viscious circles, ostriches, little beasties, spiders, flaming volcanoes, magical potions, prophets, and miracle cures).[78] But the poetic genre remained a rare vessel for questions.

Less than a decade after the revolutions, Karl Biedermann would write of the social question that "[n]ot only science, but also literature has frequently taken possession of this question."[79] The examples he offered included works of literature, drama, and art. Nonetheless, many of the works do not contain explicit mention of the social question. The same was true of the mid-nineteenth-century American poet and journalist William Cullen Bryant. An article in the Richmond *Enquirer* from 1860 spoke of him as an individual "whose vocation it is to write poetry without the inspiration; as a poor indicter of mean doggerel." To this a writer for the Charleston *Mercury* stepped in to defend Bryant: "Bryant is an Abolitionist, and his journal, the *Evening Post*, an unscrupulous organ of his abominable creed; but it is simple justice to say that, unlike Longfellow, Whittier, Lowell, and a host of less distinguished bards, he has never polluted the works of his imagination by the introduction of the slavery question in any form."[80] It is worth noting that the "slavery question" as such was also not addressed in the literary works of the aforementioned Longfellow, Whittier, and Lowell, although their abolitionist proclivities are in clear evidence, and the question is mentioned in some of Lowell's publicistic works.[81]

In 1863, the German novelist and poet Theodor Fontane and his friend Friedrich Eggers, an art historian, traded off writing stanzas of satirical verse that spoofed the burning "oyster question" of the time, though only in a subsequent scholarly footnote was the phrase actually deployed to describe their exchange.[82] And when the novelist Joseph Conrad, who prior to 1914 "had never even voiced his personal ideas on any aspect of the Polish question," did finally decide to write a political memorandum, in 1916, he more than likely based it heavily on a text prepared by his friend Józef Retinger, a prominent political advisor and advocate for European unity.[83]

So although the wall partitioning the literary from the queristic realm at times appeared porous, it was still a wall. The individual who introduced the social question into the German language may have been the poet Heinrich Heine, but it was in his nonfictional *Paris Correspondence* rather than in his poetry.[84] As for the French writer Victor Hugo, though he would eventually write a poem with the title "La question sociale,"[85] his interventions on the social question were delivered largely in the revolutionary

French National Assembly of 1848–1849.[86] The Polish poet in exile Adam Mickiewicz, though he dedicated much of his life to the cause of Polish independence and even died trying to fight for it, wrote very little about the "Polish question" as such, and when he did, it was in his own weekly political magazine.[87] It was far more common for literary figures—Hugo, Dostoevsky, Joseph Conrad, and others—to offer their views on period questions through non-literary venues.[88]

One notable exception was Tolstoy, who channeled his own views on the Eastern question through the character of Levin in the last installment of *Anna Karenina*.[89] For this, he was roundly criticized by Fyodor Dostoevsky, not least of all for breach of genre: "[T]he author uses Levin to express many of his own views and convictions, putting them into Levin's mouth . . . I still refuse to confuse the author himself with the figure of Levin as his creator depicted him. As I say this, I find myself in a painful quandary, because even though very much of what the author expresses through Levin evidently concerns only Levin himself as an artistically depicted character, I still did not expect this from such an author!"[90] In Dostoevsky's earlier novel *Crime and Punishment*, "social questions" are discussed at two different points in the story (in addition to sporadic mentions of the "woman question" and the "cesspool question"), though in neither case obviously channeling the views of the writer himself.[91] At the time of his attack on Tolstoy, Dostoevsky was writing reams on the Eastern question, albeit in the more accepted publicistic vein.[92] (An irony: although he was careful to preserve the purity of genres with regard to questions, in his publicistic endeavors, Dostoevsky ascribed novelistic attributes to the development of the Eastern question, implying that a novelist could comprehend the question's true significance far better than a diplomat.[93])

Nonetheless, in terms of genre, it seems only satire could comfortably bring literature and querism into a common frame. Although the "Eastern question" would be the subject of poems by

Ambrose Bierce and Algernon Charles Swinburne, Bierce's was markedly satirical.[94]

Zeitfragen

Literature and philosophy were supposed to be timeless. What business did they have mucking about in the field of questions, which was inherently and at its origin about relevance, utility, and urgency (if we consider its roots in parliamentary deliberations and treaty negotiations)? When the political economist Thomas Malthus and the poet Robert Southey argued over the significance of the bullion question in second half of the 1810s, theirs was essentially an argument about the relative value of timeliness and timelessness.[95] As Malthus's own trajectory shows, whole new disciplines (political economy and later sociology) formed—at least in part—around engagement with questions so that philosophy and literature could retain their timelessness. Timeless questions were not the stuff of the nineteenth century, whose questions were self-consciously *of their time*.

The Social Question: A Case Study

"They say the social question is as old as the world," Edmondo de Amicis told students at the University of Turin in 1892. "It may well be," but "what is not as old as the world," he continued, "is the stature obtained by the principle of equality," or the gross *inequality* of power that gold had given to those who possess it in great quantities, power even over the state. Nor was the organization of workers as old as the world, or the proliferation and widespread dissemination of periodicals. "The social question may well be as old as the world," Amicis concluded,

> [h]owever, what in my opinion is really just of our age . . . is
> the dissatisfaction of mind and heart, that dark and constant

struggle between consciousness of civic duty and the benefit of the individual, the confused feelings of guilt, the uncertain notion of something great and fateful.[96]

Two patterns emerged within the discussion of questions, both of which are present in Amicis's lecture, that produced an emphasis on the uniqueness of "now." The first relates to the way questions were historicized (and backdated) even as they were invented, but missinterpreted. The second is in the way period commentators used questions to define what made their own time distinct from earlier ones. Amicis's elaboration of what was new about the "social question" makes more sense if considered in light of the earlier self-conscious divergence of querists like Malthus from their scholastic predecessors.

Close study of the trajectory of the social question draws out the cadence of the age especially elegantly. It was an umbrella question under which several smaller subquestions were ranged.[97] Amicis himself understood it as being comprised of an assortment of others, such as the worker or labor, woman, and agrarian questions.[98] In 1871, the German economist and statistician Hans von Scheel observed the variety of subquestions that were variously ranged under the category of the social question: "the worker question, the woman question, the apartment question," even the "oyster question," et cetera.[99]

The omnibus character of the social question was also stressed by the German Jesuit canon law scholar and sociologist Joseph Biederlack in an address to future Catholic priests in 1895. "The worker question is just a part, and the workers' pay question is even just a small part of the social question," wrote Biederlack.[100] He went on to define different parts of the "social question."[101] The "social question," he argued, takes on a tremendous scope once one grasps the roots of today's social and economic defects; it extends even into the realm of morals and ethics, law, science, and the state.[102] It is therefore also a "religious question," "because it encompasses within itself the most important questions of ethics, philosophy of law, and political science [*Staatslehre*]."[103] In the preface to a Spanish translation of a French textbook on social economy written in 1896, we read that "the principal questions arising in our time all fall under the generic name of the social question."[104] And in 1901, the French scholar-priest Louis Garriguet called it "the great question of the present hour, which preoccupies all the world."[105] As if to demonstrate his point, within months Garriguet's book was being copied by hand by an Ottoman bureaucrat in Istanbul.[106]

The trajectory of the social question was therefore not unique to that question but encompassed an array of others. Analyzing that trajectory can bring us to a more general understanding of the age.

First Causes

In addition to tracing origins and offering definitions, querists were similarly preoccupied with causes. What gave rise to the social question? As Amicis understood it, the "principle of equality" and the fact of inequality rendered a paradox that was the "social question" of the time. Contradictions, paradoxes, and defects were the essence of the age.[107] It is worth pausing here to consider a couple of features of the way "now" was defined against previous times in discussions of the causes of the social question. One is the repeated reference to contradictions and defects, and the other related phenomenon is how these contradictions and defects were viewed as stemming from a disjuncture between ideas or principles, namely, the principle of equality (and freedom) and economic reality.

The first—which amounted to a pathologization of the present—was regularly manifest in agitation, confusion, despair, and disorientation of the sort described by Amicis, Masaryk, and other querists, and one did not have to be on the left to feel it.[108] As for the perceived disjuncture between ideas (or ideals) and reality, it is worth noting how forceful was the concomitant sense that principles or ideas had themselves become agents in human history. It was a belief that pervaded many of the late nineteenth-century discussions of the social question in particular. A passage from the preface to an 1896 book on *The Labour Question in Britain* by the French sociologist Henri de Tourville, disciple of the French Catholic sociologist and economist Pierre Guillaume Frédéric le Play, is especially revealing of this tendency.

> A great event occurs which gradually reconciles the most opposed sentiments. Who did it? No one and yet every one, not through any conscious desire preceding and preparing the issue, but through some need which demanded a solution and through the satisfaction of which greeted it when found. Powerful forces are at work, overruling the will of the masses as well as of the classes, and pointing to the influence of the laws which shape the conditions of human life.

De Tourville concluded that "[n]o one now leads the world, either from above or from below."[109] Instead, it was ideas that ruled the day.

The notion of a "ruling idea" is likely descended from an array of sources: the "genuis saeculi" (spirit of the century) that became the "Zeitgeist" (spirit of the times) with Herder in the 1760s, which Goethe then satirized in his *Faust* (1808) as none other than the "rulers' own spirit."[110] This notion of the rulers' spirit was reversed in Hegel's *Elements of the Philosophy of Right* (1821), when he wrote of the "Weltgeist" (world spirit): "states, nations, and individuals . . . are forever the unconscious tools and organs of the world spirit at work within them."[111] One was either being ruled *by* or being ruled *through* the spirit of the time, according to several discussions of the "social question."

"Ruling ideas" also lie at the very heart of socialist thought. In 1845 and 1846, Karl Marx and Friedrich Engels wrote *The German Ideology*, in which they put forward the notion that every age had its own "ruling ideas" (*herrschende Gedanken*), which were the ideas of the ruling classes. These could then be separated ("abstracted") from the ruling individuals and relations of the time such that "one could, for example, say, that during the time of aristocratic rule, the notions of honor, loyalty, et cetera, reign, while under bourgeois rule the notions of freedom, equality, et cetera, reign."[112] But there was a problem, Marx and Engels noted: that "although every shopkeeper can tell the difference between what someone says they are and what they really are, our historiography has not yet come to this trivial realization. It takes every epoch for its word, what it says about itself and imagines of itself."[113]

With Marx and Engels, the inherent disjuncture between the explicit and implicit nature of "ruling ideas" resembled what von Scheel would later call "a thought problem": the seed of a question. *The German Ideology* was never published during the lifetime of its coauthors, or rather only in part. But, as we have seen, the explication it contained of the contradiction between the "ruling ideas" of the time and reality was at the core of discussions of the social question.

And there were others around mid-century who spoke of "ruling ideas" in connection with other questions. In the early 1850s, the Hungarian statesman József Eötvös published his two-volume work on *The Ruling Principles of the Nineteenth Century and Their Influence on the State*. Among the "ruling principles" he enumerated were freedom, equality, and nationality, which "stand in contradiction with one another such that their realization must needs result in the undoing of every large state."[114] It was nevertheless the contradiction *between* ruling ideas, rather than between the ideas and the reality, that constituted the problem of the time, according to Eötvös.

About a decade later, in 1865, Eötvös wrote another book on the nationality question, revisiting the theme of "ruling principles" in the context of a period question of special significance to Hungary.[115] "Such principles," he told his readers, "as have become general principles cannot be repressed, nor can their consequences be averted; and no one people or state, however powerful it may be, can close itself off from the impact of such principles."[116] Resistance was futile; the principles of the time would have their way with the states, societies, and individuals of the time.

Although Eötvös was especially concerned with the nationality question, his belief that the "ruling principles" of the time had an inexorability all their own appeared in subsequent treatments of the social question, such as de Tourville's, and elsewhere. In 1894, a member of the Hungarian National Assembly called the social question "the ruling idea of the future society."[117] "The planet that reigns over the principles of our time is the social problem,"[118] wrote the Hungarian priest and politician Sándor Giesswein in 1907. He, like others of his time and before, believed that the "solution" to the "social question" must be rooted in the *present conditions*: the "ruling ideas" demanded it. And should the tensions and contradictions between "ruling ideas" be successfully managed, a great benefit would redound to all. If not, the result would be catastrophic for all.[119]

Querists were giving themselves over to automatism, an idea that both comforted and horrified them. The very people who insisted most vehemently on the necessity of action to move away from the present state of affairs were simultaneously developing a view of the world wherein they were helpless to act, and could only seek to comprehend the direction the world was taking. In reflections from 1877 on what he called the mysterious "simultaneity" of questions, Dostoevsky wondered,

Is there not [s]uch a phase, such a point in every question when it can no longer be resolved ... by applying little patches to it ... ? [I]sn't there at a given moment such a point in the course of events, such a phase when there suddenly appear some strange new forces—incomprehensible and mysterious ones, let's assume—that suddenly take hold of everything, that at once seize everything as a whole and draw it away irresistibly, blindly, as if down a slope, or, perhaps, into an abyss?[120]

Mutatis Mutandis

In seeking to explain why action was necessary *now* and what was *different* about *now* as compared to earlier times, a number of querists offered a variation on the Hegelian historical dialectic. An early reference to the social question appeared in an article by the Romantic writer Charles Nodier in the Paris *Revue Politique* from 1831. Nodier wrote, "I believe in Saint-Simon, the god of the nineteenth century, and I firmly believe that no other god of the same kind is going to come and simplify the social question and reduce it to its most basic terms."[121] The idea that the "social question" did not lend itself to reduction and simplification not only is comparable to the way Malthus spoke of the bullion question but also foreshadowed some of the later thinking—inspired by Hegel—that the "question" had changed over time and that it must be rethought again. It was in this climate that commentators on the social question arrived at biological metaphors, such as illness or hunger, as opposed to mathematical formulae, to explain the recurrence of questions.[122] In this way the question acquired a timelessness to which querists had otherwise long been averse.

Three great ironies emerge from this analysis. First, what gives coherence to the age of questions is its *incoherence* across time (namely, the chronic redefinition of questions). Second, the urgency and momentum toward definitive solution ultimately produced a sense that such a solution was impossible, without losing a whit of urgency. And, third, the firm belief that there was something special about "now" that made questions "of their time" coexisted with an emergent belief that they were also interminable (timeless). All of these speak to a single conclusion: that time was of the essence. Querists wanted to take what was unique about questions—namely, their practical, timely nature—and reconcile it with or read from it general, universal patterns. In other words, although the age came about *in conscious opposition* to scholasticism, its *real object* was to win a stake in the universal. One further forray into the relationship between the age and the development of scholarly disciplines will serve to clarify this aim.

A Question for Philosophy?

Just as literature defined the outer limits of what questions could be made to do, in the realm of other disciplines, a flirtation with philosophy as an analytical frame for the social question also played such a role. The debate that ensued around one such attempt to think philosophically about questions offers a vantage onto how sociology came to be legitimized as a field unto itself.

In 1897, Ludwig Stein—a rabbi of Hungarian-Swiss origin who worked as a journalist and publicist in addition to writing works in philosophy and sociology—published a series of lectures he had given over the course of the 1890s, the overarching title of which was *The Social Question in the Light of Philosophy: Lectures on Social Philosophy and Its History*. In it, he sought to offer a philosophical treatment of the social question in the popular pedagogical genre.[123] Stein opposed what he saw as the "Prostitution of the intellect [*Prostituirung des Geistes*] that puts on the make-up of science and wants to show off with sociological phraseology." In line with the critique of day-to-day politics offered by many other commentators on questions, Stein felt that philosophy lengthened and expanded the perspective on the "questions of the day" (*Tagesfragen*).[124] The "partisan thinker" (*Parteimann*), he wrote, "gets drunk on the political orgies of his time and lurches blindly on to the nearest goal. Meanwhile, the philosopher in the midst of the political bacchanalia surrounding him, calls for foresight and sobriety."[125] In other words, extracting oneself from the moment offered the longed-for calm; sobriety as solution.

A reviewer of Stein's book, Erich Adickes—himself a German Kantian philosopher—was not impressed. He criticized Stein's approach much as Dostoevsky had criticized Tolstoy's, for breach of genre and discipline. He noted Stein's "Ostentation of words or tintinnabulation of Phrases" (*Wortgepraenge oder Phrasengeklingel*).[126] Stein himself had written half-apologetically of his "lectures" that they "not only display a somewhat unphilosophical vivacity of expression, but also rhetorical expressions erupt forth."[127] In his review, Adickes retorted that "It sounds as though a serious philosopher . . . is duty-bound to write in a dry, ponderous and boring fashion, and as if rhetorical verbiage were allowed at the lectern that would not look well in print."[128] But if Stein's book had failed to be a true work of philosophy—which Adickes believed it had[129]—it was not because he had used colorful language but rather *"because of its sociological content it should not be considered philosophy insofar as sociology should be considered an autonomous science."*[130]

Adickes claimed that the legitimacy of philosophy as a discipline was threatened by works such as Stein's. The philosopher's "universalist tendency" must be preserved, but not by having philosophers "play the master" and "interject" in every area of scientific inquiry, seeking to "reach the top" of an area of knowledge without making the difficult ascent via "experience." Instead, there must be a kind of division of labor between disciplines, one in which their areas of competence do not significantly overlap, for the position of the philosopher could only be secure "if it is apportioned a particular jurisdiction [*Arbeitsgebiet*]," Adickes concluded.[131] In this way, every discipline could have its own particular stake in the universal. "Every discipline must study its object, pose its questions, exploit its discoveries and solutions in light of the ideal of a scientific *generalized view* [*Gesammtansicht*] of the world of experience," he wrote.[132] In other words, if Stein wished to reach this ideal in the idiom of questions, he could do so only as a sociologist, not as a philosopher.

The Czech statesman and philosopher Tomáš Masaryk also read Stein's book and in his own work on the social question included a footnote on the relationship of sociology to philosophy, especially philosophy of history (*Geschichtsphilosophie*). "Nowadays in Germany," he wrote in 1899, "sociology is penetrating more decisively into the older history of philosophy [*Geschichtsphilo-sophie*] and the juridically treated political science [*Staatswissen-schaft*]." He noted the "confusing terminology"—*Socialphiloso-phie, Gesellschaftswissenschaft*—that surrounded the formation of the sociological discipline. "[I]ndeed," he wrote, "it is a matter of the constitution of sociology vis-à-vis the older philosophy of history and the German-developed fields of political and social sciences."[133] And so questioneering contributed in no small way to cleaving sociology from philosophy—none of the universalizing, cathartic outlets of old (religion through scholasticism, literature, philosophy) would allow it in. In 1901, the French scholar-priest Louis Garriguet published an *Introduction to the Study of Sociology* in Paris. Its opening chapter is titled "La question sociale."[134]

Epilogue

In *The Questions of Our Tumultuous Time* from 1834, the German Mennonite preacher Leonhard Weydmann noted the "zeal" and "impatience" and the "confusion of concepts and tangling of relations" that accompanied the "questions being discussed in our tumultuous time."[135] Weydmann offered a return to tradition and authority, and above all to God, as the solution. Although their proposed "solutions" were different, in engaging with the querists, detractors such as Weydmann were drawn into the pathologization of the present. For them, the irritation and anxiety caused by questions were the problem with "now."

This negative consensus on the status quo became more general and pervasive with time. When J. A. Hobson wrote *The Social Problem* in 1901, he noted in the introductory pages how "[t]he early political economists and social reformers assumed the positive attitude concerning themselves primarily with wealth in a narrower or wider sense; but it is significant of our more critical age that a Social Question has become almost synonymous with the treatment of want, the cure of disease rather than the enlargement of health."[136] A "more critical age" was the age of questions, in the course of which the opportunity and aspiration of some revolutionary-era thinking had yielded to a form of thought-protestantism; a constant correction with a parallel striving for fundamental renewal. As the very title of Hobson's book reveals, there were no more genuine questions, only problems. Whereas the work set out to address the "Social Question," the title announces a treatment of *The Social Problem*.

Hannah Arendt noted "the tremendous intellectual change which took place in the middle of the [nineteenth] century," namely, "the refusal to view or accept anything 'as it is' and . . . the consistent interpretation of everything as being only a stage of some further development."[137] The irritation with the status quo became, through the formulation and discussion of questions, a *general* one. The pseudonymous Hungarian Szombatsági wrote in his book on the nationality question in 1861 that the time was a transitional one. "Everything is in a state of boiling, moving, developing. Everything that exists is under attack, and that which is coming into being, because it is unknown, is precarious. I could say we have words without meaning, or that we at least do not understand, and we have feelings that we don't know how to put in words."[138]

In the words of Ernst Becher writing on the "worker question" in 1868, "[i]t is a time . . . [w]hich . . . [m]ust bring the renewal process that has long been in the making to completion. . . . [W]e therefore cannot view anything that the present confronts us with as a complete structure [*Gebilde*], but rather we must see in everything only the formations of transition."[139] "This is a period of Drift," wrote the Canadian Edward Jenkins in a compilation of pamphlets on the colonial question. "Swept along by wind and current, our political and social tendencies appear to be escaping from our governance and to be manoeuvred by fate. [T]he idea of Drifting is clearly recognized as a thing of the age."[140]

The attraction of "Drift," or to automatism and catharsis; the diffusion of queristic tensions into juxtapositions and compilations—with questionnaires and bibliographies; sobriety and clarity serving not merely as a state of mind required to address questions, but solutions themselves: all of these had become features of an age that could not fathom how to accomplish the mission it had set for itself. Or perhaps there were fewer true believers in that mission, and more who clung to the status quo even as they wielded the question idiom. In 1874, the German diplomat and writer Oskar Meding wrote a novel titled *European Mines and Counter-mines*, set a few years earlier in 1867. In one scene, the Emperor Napoleon III, while curling his goatee around his fingers, tells the French minister of foreign affairs, Marquis de Moustier, "we must not tolerate that the Eastern question should be somehow brought to a definitive solution, or even to a temporary accord." Instead, he continued, we must act "so that everything remains as it is."[141]

In Robert Musil's novel *Man without Qualities*, written during the 1930s and early 1940s, the narrator writes of the character Ulrich that he had been "accustomed his whole life long to expect politics to bring about not what needed to happen, but rather at best only what should have happened long ago."

> Even the social question . . . appeared to him not as a question, but rather as an omitted answer. But he could name a hundred other such "questions" on which the mental files had long since been closed, and yet . . . awaited manipulative processing in the Office of Dispatch in vain.[142]

This passage comes from a chapter sketch that is not included in published versions of Musil's novel. The novel itself remained unfinished.

7

The Suspension-Bridge Argument

THE AGE OF SPANNING CONTRADICTIONS

To understand a certain obtuseness is required. One must be obtuse to understand. He likened it to needing big shoes to cross a bridge with cracks in it. One mustn't ask questions.[1]

—THE PHILOSOPHER OETS KOLK BOUWSMA
RECALLING A CONVERSATION WITH LUDWIG
WITTGENSTEIN (ITHACA, NY, 1949)

Contradictions between theories show that these theories have reached their natural limits; they must therefore be transformed and subsumed under even wider theories in which the contradictions finally disappear.[2]

—GYÖRGY LUKÁCS, "WHAT IS ORTHODOX MARXISM?" (1919)

A Paradoxical Age

Adam Czartoryski's *Essay on Diplomacy* was published in two editions: one in 1830 and another in 1864 (three years after his death). Both dates were significant: the first corresponded to the November Uprising against tsarist Russia, which Czartoryski headed for a short time before tsarist troops definitively crushed it. The second was the January Uprising of 1863–1864, also against tsarist Russia, which also ended in the decisive defeat of the insurgents. The previous arguments have noted a number of differences in the two editions of the *Essay*, but there is one difference they have overlooked. Although Czartoryski did not live to see the failure of the second uprising, there were some lessons he had drawn from the fallout of the first edition that found their way into the second. As we learned from the progressive argument, the question idiom was absent from the first edition—he had written it in 1823, before the age had begun in earnest—but was very present in the second, where many of the hitherto discussed features of the age (bundling, urgency, questions as a threat to European security, etc.) also figured prominently.[3]

With the new idiom, however, something was also lost. By the 1850s, the fickleness of public attention to the Polish question was already apparent, as was the decline in support—especially among liberal Germans—for Polish aspirations. The 1864 edition conceded that public opinion in Britain had little effect on policymaking, a pessimism that is not present in the 1830 edition.[4] The near unanimous support of European public opinion for the 1830 uprising had not, after all, resulted in Great Power intervention on behalf of Poland. In fact, the *Essay* closed on a melancholy note: "Notre voix est trop faible, trop isolée pour en eveiller même l'espérance" (Our voice is too weak, too isolated to even awaken hope).[5]

The *Essay* was written in French, partly as it was meant to appeal to statesmen and astute readers across the continent. Even after the January Uprising was put down, there were those who still believed in the transformative capacity of public opinion, but they were more likely to be French than Polish. Around the same time the second edition of the *Essay* appeared, the Frenchman Alfred Briosne wrote on the Polish question, highlighting the "impotence of diplomacy" to prevent war and that public opinion of "civilized Europe" should be able to participate in international debates "irrespective of their nationality" in the interest of peace.[6] The popular pedagogy of the querists had kept such a hope alive, but for the likes of Czartoryski, an essential promise held out by the question idiom and querists' creation of the international public sphere—that international public opinion mattered in the resolution of questions—had proven illusory. It is telling that just as the idiom appeared in Czartoryski's *Essai*, its very progeny, namely, his faith in the power of public opinion, disappeared. Thus we are confronted with yet another paradox of the age.

In addition to the paradox of the international public sphere, four other great paradoxes have emerged from the foregoing analyis. First, what gives coherence to the age of questions is its incoherence (namely, the age is defined by the chronic redefinition of questions). Second, the urgency and momentum toward a definitive solution that querists propounded was fully compatible with their belief that a solution was elusive or simply impossible. Third, the belief that there was something special about "now," which made questions timely, came to coexist with the belief that they were also timeless. And fourth, the age of questions gave rise simultaneously to both the belief that a universal war would be the result of a failure to solve them and the belief that only a universal war could solve them.

Is there a system of rules that could be said to govern the age of questions in all its particular aspects, a pattern that integrates all disparate patterns, a chorus to unite the disparate voices heard thus far?

Automatism

In 1887, the American Unitarian reverend George Batchelor published his work on social equilibrium. He observed that "by the tremendous leap made by modern knowledge, a great chasm has suddenly been opened between our actual and our possibile condition,—a chasm which can be crossed only slowly, if we would go safely."[7] To that end, questions were like large shoes spanning the chasm: anyone who wore them had a heel on the real and a toe on the possible, existing in two places at once. Querists were prophets with one foot in the present and another in some imagined future. Technically speaking it is impossible to proceed quickly in large shoes, but since one is in a sense already with a toe in the possible, there is an illusion of speed and of momentum that underpins the urgent tone of the age, for as one advances, so does the possible.

In the negotiations of the Concert of Europe following the Congress of Vienna, and specifically at the secret meeting of the four Great Powers (Russia, Prussia, Austria, and Britain) at Aix-la-Chapelle on November 20, 1818, the signatories agreed to cooperate militarily in the event of further revolutionary convulsion in France. This nebulous conditional future event was refered to in the protocols as "the Question." ("That resolutions derived from this overview of the Question will be recorded to this Protocol, provided that they relate to the *casus belli et foederis*, established by the Treaty of Nov. 20, 1815.")[8] The agreement literally underscored "casus foederis et belli," where the "foederis" mandated concertedness in negotiation and action, and the "belli" the eventuality that such concerted action should entail making war. The "concert" was thereby bound to the "war" from the start.[9]

A solution to the Eastern question could easily be implemented, wrote an anonymous German pamphleteer in 1843, if the Great Powers were to unify to undertake it. But, "it could come quickly and automatically [*freithätig*] to the world conflagration [*Weltkampfe*] that certainly awaits us if we allow matters to continue in accordance with their own will." This "world conflagration," the author concluded, "will be all the more terrible the longer it is put off."[10] What is remarkable about this text is that the querist wrote of the threat of war in the simple future—this *will* happen—and the peaceful solution in the conditional: this *could* happen.

In November 1849, François Dumons, a French publicist who had in 1840 posited the necessity of solving the Eastern question by means of a complete transformation of the international system, pressed the case in even more general queristic terms. "The

situation of Europe and France has perhaps never been more serious," he wrote in an open letter to the French president. "[T]he
most difficult and delicate social and economic questions impe-
riously demand prompt satisfaction."[11] The scope of his vision for
their solution is evident from the title of the pamphlet itself:
*Situation: The Reconstitution of Europe and Social and Political Re-
organization, or a New Governmental, Financial, Administrative, and
Judicial System Submitted to the French People.*

Dostoevsky, writing in 1877 on the uncanny "simultaneity" of
questions, predicted that "something colossal . . . elemental and
dreadful, and also changing the face of this world" would end "the
present age." The days when questions could be solved by "patches,
little patches, and more little patches!" were nearing an end.[12] The
Eastern and Catholic questions, he continued, had already arisen
"and are now being moved not by human wisdom but by their own
elemental force, by their own fundamental, organic need; and they
can no longer remain unsolved."[13] Theodor Herzl, in his 1896 *The
Jewish State*, declared: "If . . . this attempt to solve the Jewish Question is to be designated by a single word, let it be said to be the
result of an inescapable conclusion rather than that of a flighty
imagination."[14]

"Time presses," wrote Coudenhove-Kalergi in *Pan-Europe*:

> Tomorrow perhaps it may be too late for the settlement of the
> European Question; and it is better, therefore, to begin today.
> The rapidity of the movement toward the unification of Europe
> is quite as important as its existence: for it depends upon the
> rapidity of this movement whether Europe will be a union of
> states or a collection of ruins.[15]

The injunction of the age was to think backward from a future
heap of ruins, quickly; to possess retrospective foresight.

And furthermore, the imagined "collection of ruins" appeared
as both a threat and a promise, both the reason why question
bundles needed to be resolved and the means by which they could
be resolved:

For a universal war for the Freedom of the Peoples,
We beseech thee, O Lord.[16]

Though the ostensible goal of "solving" questions—in a manner desirable to the querist—was peace, the threat of war was the necessary precondition for the "solution" of peace.[17] Question bundling produced not one but *two* parallel and perfectly commensurable imperatives: federation and war. Neither the one nor the other is the "truest" manifestation of the age, for both exemplify the effect of bundling, which mandated a great omnibus solution, one that could only be achieved by a social and geopolitical reset on a massive social and geopolitical scale.

The federal "solution" to nineteenth-century questions neither precluded violence nor adhered exclusively to a leftist or even liberal ideological agenda.[18] Joseph Conrad's proposed solution to the Polish question, laid out in his 1916 *Note on the Polish Problem*, was a plea not for Poland's independence but rather for the Polish territories of the three partitioning powers to be united under the Habsburg crown as part of a broader vision of a united Europe.[19] And his appeal for European peace sounds a good deal more like a threat of violence.[20] The Poles' persistent "power of resistance" created a "moral obligation" to aid them, he wrote, as "[t]here is always risk in throwing away a tool of proved temper."[21] The Polish question, therefore, was a problem "justifying the employment of exceptional means for its solution ... [T]here are psychological moments when any measure tending towards the ends of concord and justice may be brought into being."[22]

Hitler also described a way to bring the states and peoples of Europe together. "To this end all the contradictions [*Gegensätze*] between the members of this community of interest [*Interessengemeinschaft*] must be eliminated, or at the very least neutralized. For that, it's necessary to clarify a whole series of questions." No stranger to "exceptional means" himself, Hitler then told the Soviet foreign minister Vyacheslav Molotov that he had found the "formula" to do just that.[23]

Even as that formula mandated universal war, advocates of Hitler's "New European Order" rhetorically set peace and reconciliation between nations as the ultimate goal. In Article 1 of his proposal for the "Creation of the 'European Union of States,'" formulated in March 1943, German foreign minister Joachim von Ribbentrop asserted that the primary objective of the union was "that wars should no more take place between European peoples."[24] All of these common and oft-repeated goals of federative scheming made for conflations of "liberal" interwar federative fantasies—such as Coudenhove-Kalergi's "Pan-Europe"—with the Nazi plan.[25] A Bulgarian specialist on international law, Georgi Genov, thus wrote in 1941 that "the idea ... of a so called Pan-Europe, that [Europe] should turn into a single federation, stressing the solidarity of European nations [is] precisely what Germany is calling for today."[26] In his plan to create a "United Lands of Hungaria" the Hungarian Nazi Arrow Cross leader Ferenc Szálasi argued that confederation was necessary to preserve peace in the region.[27]

A Shift in Register

But once unity is achieved, a greater unity becomes thinkable, even necessary. Part of the story of the age is thus about how an idea of deliverance—for Slavs, Catholics, Poles, Jews, Serbs, Bulgarians, and/or Greeks—was transformed into an idea of Europe's or the world's deliverance. It began from the premise that the status of these peoples was everyone's concern and was bound up with European or international peace by the transformation of the Eastern question into what Dostoevsky, writing in 1877, called a "world" question, "one of the principal divisions of the worldwide and imminent resolution of the fates of humanity, their new and approaching phase."

We know that this matter concerns not only the East of Europe, not only the Slavs, the Russians, and the Turks, or, specifically, the Bulgarians over there, but that it concerns also the whole of the West of Europe, and not only in relation to the seas and the straits, access and egress, by any means; it is much deeper, more fundamental, more elemental, more necessary, more essential, more primary.[28]

As we learned from the federative argument, other questions soon followed a similar pattern. When Theodor Herzl, the father of modern Zionism, wrote *The Jewish State* in 1896, he described the "Jewish question" as a "political world-question to be discussed and settled by the civilized nations of the world."[29] Leon Trotsky wrote in 1914 that, unless promptly addressed, "the chaos at present prevailing in Southeastern Europe" around the Balkan question could spread "in fact through the whole of Europe."[30] "Europe cannot find peace before it has dealt properly with the Jewish question," said Hitler.[31]

These assertions amount to a queristic fantasy turned grotesque mandate ("A great event occurs which gradually reconciles the most opposed sentiments. Who did it? No one and yet every one, not through any conscious desire preceding and preparing the issue, but through some need which demanded a solution and through the satisfaction of which greeted it when found. Powerful forces are at work, overruling the will of the masses as well as of the classes, and pointing to the influence of the laws which shape the conditions of human life . . . No one now leads the world, either from above or from below."[32]), but also a shift in register. There is no more agonizing indicator of this shift than Coudenhove-Kalergi's assertion in *Pan-Europe* that "[t]oday the European Question signifies to the world what for more than a century the Balkan Question signified to Europe: a source of endless insecurity and unrest." With that claim, Coudenhove-Kalergi sought to transform Europe into a world problem, "not merely of local but of international import; until it is solved there can be no possibility of a peaceful development of the world."[33]

In 1946, the Belgian Trotskyist Ernest Mandel (a.k.a. Germain), writing on the Jewish question in the immediate aftermath of the Holocaust declared that "what Auschwitz and Maidanek mean for the Jews, the atomic bomb signifies for all humanity. The perspective of the disappearance of the Jews from the earth is part of the perspective of the destruction of the human species." Thus, "if the Jewish tragedy is only the symbol and to a certain measure the 'mirror of the future' for humanity, the only way out which still remains open to humanity is at the same time the solution of the Jewish question."[34] This appeared in a subsection with the heading, "The Jewish Question Can Be Resolved Only as Part of the Solution of the World Crisis."

Querists tended to seek a higher vantage: a grander question affecting *everyone* and a grander solution involving *everyone*. Insofar as many querists saw universal war as an alkahest to solve all questions, and the solution of all questions as a precondition of preventing universal war, they contributed in no small way both to federalist thinking and to what Carl Schmitt called the "manifest fraud" of a war to end all wars.[35] Close study of the age confronts the historian with the history-moving power of large shoes spanning opposites, traversing a rickety suspension bridge of contradictions. Slowly, of necessity, and very fast, also of necessity and because the toe has already arrived where the heel has not yet been. By the age's apex, the gait acquired a pointed silliness, a toe-heel: place the toe where you wish to be and the heel will follow.

There are many manifestations of this reversal. In Coudenhove-Kalergi's *Pan-Europe* and Herzl's *Der Judenstaat*, the solution trades places with the question. Driven by his fascination with what he saw as the self-correcting essence of nature and biology, the Russian naturalist and philosopher claimed to have found both a perfectly reduced formula and an omnibus solution to the Eastern question. "If we look at Russian life," he wrote, "we quickly see that it is not in complete health. . . . [The] curative events, from which . . . we will learn our saving lessons, have already appeared on the horizon of history, and are called: *The Eastern Question*."[36] The question *itself* provided the momentum toward solution, which for Danilevsky meant the creation of a Russian-dominated "[a]ll-Slavic federation" as "the only reasonable, intelligent solution" to the Eastern question.[37]

The reversal was also manifest in querists' romantic fascination with the inexorable solution-seeking capacity of language itself, as in the Viennese satirist Karl Kraus's intervention on the woman question from 1909: "Language decides everything, including the woman question"[38]; or Adolf Grabowsky's insistence that "[o]nce the problems are comprehensively and clearly grasped . . . they will steer themselves toward solution"[39] since "[l]anguage thinks in a very subtle manner here: it calls the correct answer to a question a 'solution'; the unraveling is thus at once the achievement, and hence language views the amalgamation of successful unraveling toward a beneficial result as a completely natural achievement."[40]

Finally, the reversal could also take the especially cynical form of placing the solution cart before the question horse, like Adolf Hitler's admonition that "[i]n the handling of the Danubian problems, our generation must remember that not all the questions of rights which arise were successfully answered by the peace treaties. Any responsible statesman should, indeed must, leave his successor a whole drawer full of somewhat nebulous claims, so that the latter can be in a position, should the need arise, to conjure up these 'sacred' rights as the pretext for any conflict which may seem necessary."[41]

In Two Places at Once

To observe a contradiction was to suggest the existence of a structure, as well as a way of spanning the components of the structure so as to *overstep* the contradiction. In the wake of the failed 1848 Revolution, the Hungarian statesman, József Eötvös, set out to write a history of the causes of the French Revolution. It became instead a two-volume work—published in Hungarian and German—on *The Ruling Principles of the Nineteenth Century and Their Influence on the State*.[42] Among the "ruling principles" he enumerated were liberty, equality, and nationality, which "stand in contradiction with one another such that their realization must needs result in the undoing of every large state."[43]

In 1865, Eötvös wrote his book on the nationality question, revisiting the theme of "ruling principles."[44] "Such principles," he told his readers, "as have become general principles cannot be repressed, nor can their consequences be averted; and no one people or state, however powerful it may be, can close itself off from the impact of such principles."[45] The national idea, in his view, was naught but the result of frustrated attempts to achieve individual liberty and equality, so the subject nationalities should be granted these and the nationality question would disappear.[46]

Eötvös contemplated the future of Hungary, Austria, and Europe in a polemical field that seemed to him wholly hostile to Hungarian interests. Two other Hungarian politicians shared this view, Ferencz Pulszky and Anton Szécsen. Yet while their proposed solutions were very different, the structure of their proposals was remarkably similar. Pulszky, raising the specter of pan-Slavism, wanted Hungary to assume her place as "the heart of Europe, that never ceases beating for all that is great and good."[47] Szécsen, while making a distinction between organic reform and machinistic (revolutionary) overhaul, and as a conservative favoring the former, nonetheless argued for a great inner transformation, "a newly strengthened public spirit, a newly awakened sense for justice and truth."[48] Eötvös, while arguing that the threat posed by the national idea should not be ignored nor the debate around it silenced,[49] and that the force of general principles—foremost among them nationality—could not be repressed, nonetheless believed that "in the great movement that is flowing around Europe's holiest interests, we should stand our ground."[50]

In each case, there is a desire to simultaneously go with the times and restrain them, to rush forward and hang back, to magnanimously give and selfishly hoard, in short, to take two directions at once. How else can we explain the fact that a critic of the French and Hungarian Revolution (Szécsen) and a champion of the same (Eötvös) were able to maintain a fundamental political opposition to one another while understanding not only events in the same terms (as ruling ideas born out of the French Revolution, and framed in the question idiom) but also solutions (favoring the "practical")?[51] The historian must pause in wonder at a time wherein such consensus on words, ideas, and their overweaning significance prevailed, yet wherein such intense and ever-fracturing differentiation filled a rhetorical field to overbrimming with contradictions and paradoxes, without threatening the coherence of the structures they had conjured to hold them in place. Small wonder it seemed possible to occupy two opposite positions at once.

The Function and Fiction of the Age

At roughly the same time that Hitler concluded that solving the social question was an imperative not unlike the abolition of serfdom in the eighteenth century, a character in Robert Musil's *Man without Qualities* told an interlocutor who was going on about the social question to pipe down: "If that's what we're going to talk about, I'm out of here and going home; it bores me to death."[52] A question reached the status of ultimate legitimacy and well-acknowledged tedium simultaneously: an incontrovertible truth and a plaything of fiction. The assumption of the previous arguments has been that the age of questions was either in deadly earnest or a grand joke, either over or ongoing, either progressive or reactionary, either national or international, either timely or timeless. These are false dichotomies, but the age was also not simply "all of the above." Its objective was to overcome contradictions, such that all of the aforementioned opposites found a common frame in the question idiom, a place where their opposition became part of the structure itself, what held it together. Virginia Woolf knew that to exist is to hold together contradictions. There is an essential historical reality to this feat. Insofar as there was an "age of questions," perhaps this was its function.

It was a poignant wish. But there was also a physical world, real people, and events; and there was that *word*, that shoe that could extend so far and already be where one wanted to go. Those very large shoes that seemed to overstep distressing contradictions right and left often came down all the more squarely—and sometimes with deadly force—on the greatest of all question bundles and problem complexes: human beings.

NOTES

Preface

1. Henry George Liddell, Robert Scott, Henry Stuart Jones, and Roderick McKenzie, *A Greek-English Lexicon* (Oxford: Clarendon Press, 1996), p. 756.

2. From the first chapter of *Between States*: "Far from being a modern manifestation of long-standing antagonisms between Hungarians and Romanians, the Transylvanian Question is thus a product of changes in the European geopolitical landscape that began in the mid to late nineteenth century with the decline of the Ottoman Empire. These changes raised questions about the rights of the nation and the individual within it; about the terms of citizenship and national belonging; about the nation's role in 'Europe' and the international order; about the structure of society; about overlaps and fractures between class, religious, race, linguistic, and gender categories; about challenges to state sovereignty over territories and populations; and about relations with neighboring states and Great Powers. These dilemmas often clustered around particular people and places, taking on lives of their own. Hence the proliferation of 'questions' in the nineteenth century: the Polish Question, the Eastern Question, the Jewish Question, the Macedonian Question, and the Transylvanian Question. And as these questions moved into the twentieth century, it became apparent that resolving them would require reconciling boundaries with ideas—ideas not only about nations, but about Europe." Holly Case, *Between States: The Transylvanian Question and the European Idea during World War II* (Stanford, CA: Stanford University Press, 2009), p. 11.

3. See ibid., "The 'Jewish Question' Meets the Transylvanian Question," pp. 175-198; Wendy Brown, "Tolerance and/or Equality? The 'Jewish Question' and the 'Woman Question,'" in *differences* 15, no. 2 (2004): 1–31.

4. See, for example, Jacob Toury, "'The Jewish Question': A Semantic Approach," in *Leo Baeck Institute Yearbook*, no. 11 (1966): 85–106.

5. See the National Archives of the UK, Kew (hereafter cited as TNA), FO 417/1, Negotiations respecting Poland Correspondence, pp. 14, 48–49 (the Saxon question is also mentioned on p. 49); Österreichisches Staatsarchiv, Wien (Austrian State Archive, Vienna, hereafter cited as AT-OeStA), HHStA StK Kongressakten 2,

Protocoles des Conférences séparées, appelées des quatre, Vienna, December 29, 1814, p. 69; ibid., Conférences des Quatre, Séance, October 30, 1814, p. 4; "Fair Draft Memorandum—Instructions for the Duke of Wellington, September 14, 1822," in *Despatches, Correspondence, and Memoranda of Field Marshal Arthur Duke of Wellington*, vol. 1 (London: John Murray, Albemarle Street, 1867), p. 285.

6. *London Medical and Surgical Journal* 8–9 (1836): 11.

7. Walter Russel Mead and staff, "Russia Signs Agreement while Putin Talks Empire to Russian Audience," *The American Interest*, April 17, 2014, http://www.the-american-interest.com/blog/2014/04/17/russia-signs-agreement-while-putin-talks-empire-to-russian-audience/; Pamela Engel and Gus Lubin, "Putin Makes Worrying Comments about Novarossiya," *Business Insider Australia*, April 17, 2014, www.businessinsider.com/maps-of-novorussia-and-old-russian-empire-2014-4.

8. Steven Erlanger, "A Proud Nation Ponders How to Halt Its Slow Decline," *The New York Times*, August 24, 2013, http://www.nytimes.com/2013/08/25/world/europe/a-proud-nation-ponders-how-to-halt-its-slow-decline.html?pagewanted=all; Brian Standberg, "The French Question," *Historical Perspectives* (blog), August 25, 2013, http://briansandberg.wordpress.com/2013/08/25/the-french-question/.

9. Mead and staff, "Russia Signs Agreement"; Engel and Lubin, "Putin Makes Worrying Comments"; Sean Curran, "Scottish Referendum: What Is the 'English Question'?" *BBC News*, September 19, 2014, http://www.bbc.com/news/uk-politics-29281818; James Landale, "The Politics of the English Question," *BBC News*, September 19, 2014, http://www.bbc.com/news/uk-politics-29274379; Bettina Schulz, "Die Irlandfrage" [The Irish Question], *Zeit Online*, November 29, 2017, http://www.zeit.de/wirtschaft/2017-11/brexit-grossbritannien-irland-eu-aussengrenze-baileys; Simon Wilson, "The Catalonian Question," *Money Week*, September 19, 2014, http://moneyweek.com/the-catalonian-question/.

10. See, for example, "Staatsbesuch des portugiesischen Premiers: Meinungsunterschiede über Migrantenfrage" [State visit of the Portuguese premier: Differences of opinion on the migration question], *Luxemburger Wort*, October 22, 2014, http://www.wort.lu/de/photos/staatsbesuch-des-portugiesischen-premiers-meinungsunterschiede-ueber-migrantenfrage-54477f25b9b398870807d7cf; Moritz Böse, "Der DFB und die Migrantenfrage: Kurswechsel aus Überzeugung oder durch (Erwartungs-)Druck?" [The German Soccer League and the migrant question: Change of course out of conviction or from (peer) pressure?], *Unsere Zeit, sozialistische Wochenzeitung*, July 10, 2015, http://www.unsere-zeit.de/de/4728/vermischtes/368/Der-DFB-und-die-Migrantenfrage.htm; and "EU nimmt am UN-Gipfel zur Flüchtlings- und Migrantenfrage sowie an 71. Vollversammlung der Vereinten Nationen teil" [The EU to take part in the UN summit on the refugee and migrant question as well as in the 71st general assembly of the United Nations], *Eu-*

ropäische Union Nachrichten, September 2016, https://europa.eu/newsroom/events /eu-attends-un-summit-refugees-and-migrants-and-71st-united-nations-general -assembly_de.

11. Liddell, Scott, Jones, and McKenzie, *A Greek-English Lexicon*, p. 756; John Oswald, Joseph Thomas, James Lynd, and John M. Keagy, *An Etymological Dictionary of the English Language* (Philadelphia: E. C. & J. Biddle; Claxton, Ramsen & Haffelfinger, 1868), pp. 357–358, 360.

12. See Thomas Mann, *Betrachtungen eines Unpolitischen* [Reflections of a nonpolitical man] (Berlin: S. Fischer Verlag, 1920), pp. 203–205; Christa Wolf, *Nachdenken über Christa T.* [The quest for Christa T.] (Frankfurt am Main: Suhrkamp, 2007), p. 21.

Introduction

1. *Deutsches Wörterbuch von Jacob und Wilhelm Grimm* [German dictionary of Jacob and Wilhelm Grimm], "Frage," accessed October 3, 2016, http://woerterbuch netz.de/DWB/?sigle=DWB&mode=Vernetzung&lemid=GF07898#XGF07898.

2. To call them "querists" is misleading in some respects. It was not a term they self-applied, and furthermore, as their questions were not real interrogatives, using a word that means "questioner" is imprecise. Yet I use the term for two reasons: to avoid the over-repetition of awkward constructions, such as "those who weighed in on questions," and because the word *querist* implies an insatiability that permeated the tone of many discussions around questions. *Oxford English Dictionary*, s.v. "querist, n."

3. Fyodor Dostoyevsky, "Never Has Russia Been as Powerful as Now—A Nondiplomatic Judgment," trans. K. A. Lantz, in *A Writer's Diary*, vol. 2 (Evanston, IL: Northwestern University Press, 2000), p. 1002.

Prologue: Questions and Their Predecessors

1. Member of the Athenian Society, *The Athenian Oracle Being an Entire Collection of All the Valuable Questions and Answers in the Old Athenian Mercuries . . . By a Member of the Athenian Society* (London: Printed for Andrew Bell, 1703), p. 1. (The whole of the text cited is italicized with the exception of the above-italicized text.)

2. Leo Tolstoy, "The Non-acting," in *The Complete Works of Count Tolstoy*, vol. 23 (Boston: Dana Estes, 1905), p. 50.

3. See Alexis de Tocqueville, *Oeuvres complètes* [Complete works], vol. 3, pt. 2, *Écrits et discours politiques* [Political writings and speeches] (Paris: Gallimard, 1985), pp. 255–265, 288–301, 708–709, 734–737; Victor Hugo, "XIV: La question sociale," in *Toute la lyre* [The whole lyre], T. 2 (Paris: Hetzel [u.a.], 1888), pp. 321–323; and

George Sand, "La question sociale," in *Souvenirs de 1848* [Memories of 1848] (Paris: C. Lévy, 1880), pp. 75–78.

4. The references for Marx and Dostoevsky are too numerous to list exhaustively here, but see, for example, Karl Marx, *La question polonaise devant l'Assemblée de Francfort* [The Polish question before the Frankfurt Parliament] (Paris: F. Alcan, 1929); Marx, "On the Jewish Question," accessed September 23, 2016, http://www .marxists.org/archive/marx/works/1844/jewish-question/; Marx and Frederick Engels, *The Russian Menace to Europe: A Collecton of Articles, Speeches, Letters, and News Despatches*, ed. Paul Blackstock and Bert Hoselitz (London: George Allen and Unwin, 1953), p. 122; F. M. Dostoievsky, *The Diary of a Writer* (New York: George Braziller, 1954), pp. 428–430, 434–435; Dostoyevsky, "Never Has Russia Been as Powerful as Now," p. 1002; Frederick Douglass, *The Anti-slavery Movement: A Lecture by Frederick Douglass before the Rochester Ladies' Anti-slavery Society* (Rochester: Lee, Mann, 1855); Tomáš Garrigue Masaryk, *Otázka sociální: základy Marxismu sociologické a filosofické* [The social question: Foundations of sociological and philosophical Marxism] (Prague: Nákl. Jana Laichtera, 1898); and T. G. Masaryk, *Česká otázka: snahy a tužby národního obrození* [The Czech question: Efforts and aspirations of the national revival] (Prague: Nákl. Času, 1895).

5. Lyof N. Tolstoï, *Anna Karenina* (New York: Thomas Y. Crowell, 1899), p. 386; see also pp. 340–341, 344–347, 384–388. See Jelena Milojković-Djurić, *The Eastern Question and the Voices of Reason: Austria-Hungary, Russia, and the Balkan States, 1875–1908* (Boulder, CO: East European Monographs, 2002), pp. 32–47, 36–37.

6. Jay Geller, "*Atheist* Jew or Atheist *Jew*: Freud's Jewish Question and Ours," in *Modern Judaism* 26, no. 1 (February 2006): 1–14; Miloš Ković, *Disraeli and the Eastern Question* (Oxford: Oxford University Press, 2010); Brown, "Tolerance and/or Equality?," pp. 1–31. For a treatment of the relationship between the Jewish and Transylvanian questions, see Case, *Between States*, pp. 175–198.

7. It should be noted that there is no agreement among scholars as to what the "accursed questions" actually were. While some insist they were the "eternal questions" on the existence of God, the immortality of the soul, and meaning (viz. Victoria Frede, *Doubt, Atheism, and the Nineteenth-Century Russian Intelligentsia* (Madison: University of Wisconsin Press, 2011), p. 209), others assert they were of a more practical and timely bent, like the ones listed above, which inspired individuals such as Nikolai Chernyshevsky, Leo Tolstoy, and Vladimir Ilyich Lenin (viz. Robert Daniels, "The End of the Soviet Union," in *A Companion to Russian History*, ed. Abbott Gleason [Chichester, UK: Wiley-Blackwell, 2009]: pp. 451–468, p. 458).

8. Elias Canetti, *Masse und Macht* [*Crowds and Power*] (Hamburg: Claassen Verlag, 1960), pp. 327–333; Martin Heidegger, "Die Frage nach der Technik," [The question concerning technology] in *Die Technik und die Kehre* [Technology and the turn] ([Pfullingen]: Neske, 1963), pp. 5–36.

9. In particular, except as a matter of translation, the phrase "the question of x" is not consistently identical with "the x question." In French, for example, "question d'Orient" and "querelle des femmes" are the most common renderings of "the Eastern question" and "the woman question," respectively, whereas the "Polish question" appears as the "question polonaise." My reason for emphasizing "the x question" over "the question of x" is that the former is much more common, is uniquely typical of the nineteenth century, and constitutes a traceable phenomenon, whereas the latter does not. There are some notable and sticky exceptions, such as when a question that generally takes the form "the x question" slips into "the question of x," I feel I must take it to be as much of the former as of the latter character. For example, when a Missouri congressman delivered a speech in 1858 in the House of Representatives on "the Kansas question," he began: "The attitude of the present Administration on this Kansas question, and upon the question of slavery generally, has been discussed in almost every conceivable aspect." Francis Blair, *Speech of Hon. Francis P. Blair, Jr., of Missouri, On the Kansas Question* (Washington: Printed at the Congressional Globe Office, 1858), p. 3. When Stefan Collini writes of "the question of intellectuals," comparing it to the Eastern and the Irish questions, however, the comparison strikes me as off the mark. The "Eastern question" and "Irish question" were heavily used expressions in the nineteenth and twentieth centuries, whereas "the question of intellectuals" in Britain was not really, except as a modifying phrase ("the question of intellectuals' role in . . ." etc.). There was a "question of intellectuals" in Mao's China after World War II, however, for which the comparison is more apt, in my view, and would warrant further exploration. Stefan Collini, *Absent Minds: Intellectuals in Britain* (Oxford: Oxford University Press, 2006), p. 51. Special thanks to Miloš Vojinović for drawing Collini's book to my attention.

10. Especially in those areas wherein the present author is at best an amateur enthusiast and at worst a shameful interloper (i.e., historical etymology, history of philosophy, history of science, and an array of "national" and "imperial" histories beyond my areas of strength).

11. My first book supposes that the essence of the Transylvanian question was who should have control of Transylvania: Hungary or Romania? Case, *Between States*, p. 1. It turns out that the question had earlier been very differently defined— namely, as a question of whether Hungary should formally integrate Transylvania into the Hungarian Kingdom as opposed to keeping it as a separately administered province. See Lajos Hajnald, *Felsőházi beszéde az erdélyi unió tárgyában: (junius 17- kén). . . .* [Speech to the upper house on the subject of union with Transylvania (June 17th)] (Pest: Lampel R., 1861), p. 4; and Gyula Szekfű, *A magyar állam életrajza: történelmi tanulmány* [Biography of the Hungarian state: A historical study] (Budapest: Dick Manó, 1917), p. 154.

12. Bruno Bauer, *Die Judenfrage* [The Jewish question] (Braunschweig: Friedrich

Otto, 1843), p. 3; Marx, "On the Jewish Question"; Walter Scott, *The Eastern or Jewish Question Considered: And, What the Bible Says About Coming Events* (London: Alfred Holness, 1882), p. 3; Theodor Herzl, *The Jewish State* (Rockville, MD: Wildside Press, 2007), p. 56.

13. Dostoievsky, *The Diary of a Writer*, p. 429.

14. On historiography relating to the Polish question, see, for example, Louise Schorn-Schütte, "Polnische Frage und deutsche Geschichtsschreibung," [The Polish question and German historiography] in *Zum Verständnis der polnischen Frage in Preussen und Deutschland 1772–1871* [Towards an understanding of the Polish question in Prussia and Germany, 1772-1871], ed. Klaus Zernack (Berlin: Colloquium Verlag, 1987): 72–107. Schorn-Schütte tellingly cites a work by Jerzy Topolski on "The Partitions of Poland in German and Polish Historiography" as an earlier intervention on the same subject, thereby confounding the partititons with the "the Polish question" (p. 73).

15. The work is essentially these writers' views on Poles or, rather, on the "Western provinces" of Russia. М. П. Драгоманов, *Герцен, Бакунин, Черныышевский и Полский Вопрос* [Herzen, Bakunin, Chernyshevsky and the Polish question] (Kazan: Д. М. Гранъ, 1906); see esp. p. 3.

16. See, for example, Reinhart Koselleck, "Einleitung" [Introduction], in Otto Brunner, Werner Conze, and Reinhart Koselleck, *Geschichtliche Grundbegriffe* [Basic concepts in history], vol. 1 (Stuttgart: Klett-Cotta, 1992), pp. xiii–xxviii.

17. In general, I read Koselleck as looking at much of the same period, but primarily from the standpoint of the second ("An Answering Being") and the fifth ("Zeitfragen") chapters of the present analysis, insofar as he pointed out the perceived widening disjuncture between experience (*Erfahrung*) and expectation (*Erwartung*) attributable to the emergence of "progress" (*Fortschritt*), perceived a future orientation in the shift in concepts, and discussed federation schemes in terms of concept-driven expectations. The word "perceived" is significant, as Koselleck himself noted in connection with the conclusion "that modernity can first be grasped as a new time once expectations have distanced themselves ever more from all previous experience," and that "the question of whether it's a matter of objective history or only of its subjective reflexion is still not thereby settled." See, for example, Reinhart Koselleck, " 'Erfahrungraum' und 'Erwartungshorizont'—zwei historische Kategorien" [The 'space of experience' and 'horizon of expectation'—two historical categories], in *Vergangene Zukunft: zur Semantik geschichtlicher Zeiten* [Futures past: On the semantics of historical time] (Frankfurt am Main: Suhrkamp, 2000), pp. 349–375, esp. pp. 359–360, 362, 370–372. This was not a blindness on his part but rather a perspectival difference partly dictated by the chosen category of analysis (namely, the *Begriff*), which further reaffirms my conviction that a history of the age

of questions cannot be undertaken solely by means of employing the methodology of *Begriffsgeschichte*.

18. Most prominent are the social question (*soziale Frage*) and the German question (*deutsche Frage*). See, for example, Brunner, Conze, and Koselleck, *Geschichtliche Grundbegriffe*, vol. 1, p. 151 (Judenfrage), 227, 506, 820 (soziale Frage); ibid., vol. 2, pp. 148 (deutsche Frage), 790 (soziale Frage); ibid., vol. 3, pp. 193, 360, 559, 563, 943, 1011 (soziale Frage), 300 (nationale Frage); ibid., vol. 4, pp. 85 (Arbeiterfrage, Handwerkerfrage), 758 (deutsche Frage); ibid., vol. 5, pp. 65 (Arbeiterfrage), 768, 977, 979, 1011 (soziale Frage), 1024 (Arbeiterfrage); ibid., vol. 6, pp. 826 (soziale Frage); and ibid., vol. 7, p. 353 (deutsche Frage), 371n, 427 (nationale Frage). The list is not exhaustive.

19. Michel Foucault, "What Is Enlightenment?," in *The Foucault Reader*, ed. Paul Rabinow (New York: Pantheon, 1984), pp. 32–50.

20. On the Greek origins of the Latin *quæro*, see F. E. J. Valpy, *An Etymological Dictionary of the Latin Language* (London: Printed by A. J. Valpy, sold by Baldwin, 1828), p. 385. The definition of the Latin *quæstio* offered by Gesner's 1749 Latin thesaurus is given as "ζήτημα," which is the Greek word used in speaking of the "Eastern question" in the nineteenth century ("ανατολικό ζήτημα"). See Johann Matthias Gesner, *Novus linguae et eruditionis Romanae thesaurus* [New treasure of the Roman language], vol. 2, within which vol. 4, Q–Z (Naples: La scuola di Pitagora), p. 11.

21. *Oxford English Dictionary*, 2nd ed., vol. 13 (Oxford: Clarendon Press, 1989), pp. 7-8, s.v. "question, n." See also Pierre Larousse, *Grand Dictionnaire Universel du XIX. Siecle, Francais, Historique, Geographique, Mythologique, Bibliographique, Litteraire, Artistique, Scientifique, etc., par Pierre Larousse* [The great universal dictionary of the nineteenth century, French, historical, geographical, mythological, bibliographical, literary, artistic, scientific, et cetera, of Pierre Larousse], vol. 13 (Geneva: Slatkine, 1982), p. 526.

22. The relevant term in various languages is *question* (French), *Frage* (German), *вопрос* or *вопросъ* (Russian), *questione* (Italian), *kérdés* (Hungarian), *otázka* (Czech), *pitanje* (Bosnian-Serbian-Croatian), and *въпрос* (Bulgarian). Several languages adopted a variation on the French in connection with the nineteenth-century questions (a word distinct from the word for "question" in those languages), for example: *chestiune* (Romanian, instead of *întrebare*), *kwestia* or *kwestija* (Polish, instead of *pytanie*), *cuestión* (Spanish, instead of *pregunta*). Several languages also occasionally use the word for "issue," in addition to a variant on "question," in reference to nineteenth-century questions. For example: *soru* (question) or *mesele* (issue) (Turkish), *kwestia* or *sprawa* (Polish). Finally, in Greek there is just one word used as a rule, and that is *ζήτημα* (issue, matter) rather than *ερώτηση* (question). The case of Greek, Romanian, and Polish will be discussed in more detail below.

23. See R. S. P. Beekes and Lucien van Beek, *Etymological Dictionary of Greek* (Leiden: Brill, 2010), pp. 500–501; Liddell, Scott, Jones, and McKenzie, *A Greek-English Lexicon*, p. 756.

24. Αριστοτέλειο Πανεπιστημίο Θεσσαλονίκης, *Λεξικό της κοινής νεοελληνικής* (Lexiko tēs koinēs Neoellēnikēs) [Dictionary of standard Modern Greek] (Thessaloniki: Αριστοτέλειο Πανεπιστημίο Θεσσαλονίκης, Ινστιτούτο Νεοελληνικών Σπουδών, 1998), p. 561.

25. Henri Estienne, Charles Benoît Hase, G. R. Ludwig von Sinner, Theobald Fix, and Michelangelo Costagliola, *Θησαυρός τής Ελληνικής γλώσσης* (Thēsauros tēs hellēnikēs glōssēs) = *Thesaurus graecæ linguæ* [Thesaurus of the Greek language], vol. 5 (Naples: La scuola di Pitagora editrice, 2008), pp. 33–34. (This work was initially published in the 1830s–1860s).

26. See, for example, Antoni Bukaty, *Sprawa Polski wywołana przed sądem miecza i polityki w roku 1830*, cz. 1 [The question of Poland brought before the court of the sword and of politics in 1830, pt. 1] (Paris: w druk. P. Baudouin, 1833); and R. Cutlar Fergusson, *Sprawa Polski ujarzmionéj na Parlament W. Brytanji, przez R. C. Fergusson* [The question of subjugated Poland in the British parliament] (Paris: nakladem associacji liter. Londynskiéj przyjaciół polski, 1834), the Polish translation of speeches delivered by Robert C. Fergusson before British Parliament in 1832 and 1833. In addition to Polish, some other languages also occasionally use the word for "issue," in addition to a variant on "question," in reference to nineteenth-century questions. In Turkish, for example: *soru* (question) or *mesele* (issue); and in Greek, there is just one word used as a rule, *ζήτημα* (question, issue, matter) rather than *ερώτηση* (question).

27. Sometimes also *kwestija*.

28. "A question posed to clarify a matter. A proposal to examine, topic to discuss, an item of business: Eastern question. A medieval torture." August Scriban, *Dicționaru limbii românești: Etimologii, înțelesuri, exemple, citațiuni, arhaizme, neologizme, provincializme* [Dictionary of the Romanian language: Etymologies, definitions, examples, citations, archaisms, neologisms, colloquialisms] (Jassy: Inst. de arte grafice "Presa Bună," 1939), p. 266.

29. A notable meta-analysis of this phenomenon is Jean-Claude Milner's *Les penchants criminels de l'Europe démocratique* [The criminal inclinations of democratic Europe] (Paris: Editions Verdier, 2003). Milner sees modern history since the eighteenth century as defined by the "problem/solution" as opposed to the "question/answer" pairing. Milner's particular interest is in tracing the modern European historical trajectory toward the "final solution." The present analysis, by contrast, views this teleology of the "final solution" as a partial and ultimately insufficient exploration of the "problem/solution" pairing's implications. European unification, which Milner views as the by-product of the Holocaust's expurgation of the Jews, has different

origins in the present analysis, bound up with the agglomerative zeal of the age of questions rather than as a chronic problematization of the "name of the Jew."

30. See Bruno Bauer, *The Jewish Problem* (Cincinnati: Hebrew Union College-Jewish Institute of Religion, 1958).

31. From an article published in the *Neue Rheinische Zeitung*, August 19, 1848, cited in Marx, *La question polonaise devant l'Assemblée de Francfort*, p. 26. See also the 1920 book *A World Problem: Jews—Poland—Humanity*, wherein the author writes, "In studying the question, I have realized that the relation of the Jews in regard to Poland is exactly the same as their relations to the world at large. For that reason, the problem at issue intimately concerns other nations; in fact, affects their creeds, their ideals and aspirations." Underlining is my own. Stephanie Laudyn, *A World Problem: Jews—Poland—Humanity* (Chicago: American Catalogue Printing, 1920), pp. 5–6.

32. Edwin L. Godkin, "The Eastern Question," in *The North American Review* 124, no. 254 (January 1877): 106–126; John A. Ryan and R. A. McGowan, *A Catechism of the Social Question* (New York: Paulist Press, 1921), p. 5.

33. See, for example, Dostoyevsky, "Never Has Russia Been as Powerful as Now," pp. 1001–1002. The phrase "мировые вопросы" is translated here as "problems of world importance," whereas the more literal translation is "world questions." See Фёдор Михайлович Достоевский, *Дневник писателя, 1877 год, Май-июнь* [Diary of a writer, May–June 1877], https://ru.wikisource.org/wiki/Дневник_писателя ._1877_год_(Достоевский)/Май-июнь/ГЛАВА_ВТОРАЯ_III.

34. Charles Jelavich and Barbara Jelavich, *The Balkans* (Englewood Cliffs, NJ: Prentice-Hall, 1965), p. 34.

35. Donald Quataert, *The Ottoman Empire, 1700–1922* (Cambridge: Cambridge University Press, 2005), p. 56; L. Carl Brown, *International Politics and the Middle East: Old Rules, Dangerous Game* (Princeton, NJ: Princeton University Press, 1984), pp. 25.

36. Norman Davies, *God's Playground: 1795 to the Present* (New York: Columbia University Press, 2005), p. 11.

37. See Brian Lawn, *The Rise and Decline of the Scholastic* Quaestio Disputata*: With Special Emphasis on Its Use in the Teaching of Medicine and Science* (Leiden: Brill, 1993), esp. pp. 70, 74, 86. It is worth noting that the scholastic method of disputation has even deeper roots, in Aristotle's *Metaphysics*, for example.

38. See *Oxford English Dictionary*, s.v. "question, n."

39. From his *Summa Theologiæ*, completed in 1273.

40. It would later appear in Latin in 1632, in German in 1648, and in English in 1665. Johann Angelius von Werdenhagen and Jakob Böhme, *Psychologia vera I.B.T. XL quaestionibus explicata et rerum publicarum vero regimini ac earum maiestatico iuri applicata a Iohanne Angelio Werdenhagen, I.C.C.* (Amsterdam: Apud Iohann. Ianssonium, 1632); Jacob Böhm and Balthasar Walther, *Viertzig Fragen von der Seelen*

Urstand, Essentz, Wesen, Natur und Eigenschafft, was sie von Ewigkeit in Ewigkeit sey?
(Amsterdam: Fabel, 1648); Jakob Böhme, *Forty Questions of the Soul Concerning Its
Original, Essence, Substance, Nature or Quality and Property, What It Is from Eternity
to Eternity: Framed by a Lover of the Great Mysteries, Doctor Balthasar Walter, and
Answered in the Year 1620* (London: L. Lloyd, 1665).

41. Jakob Böhme, *Forty Questions of the Soul*, pp. 5, 7.

42. Most famously, Martin Luther's *Enchiridion, Der kleine Katechismus* [*The
Small Catechism*] from 1529. It's also worth noting that there was something like a
revival of catechistic works in the nineteenth century. See, for example, the introduction to an 1853 edition of Luther's small catechism. Martin Luther, *D. Martin Luthers
kleiner Katechismus, Nach den Originalausgaben kritisch bearbeitet. Ein Beitrag zur
Geschichte der Katechetik von Lic. K. F. Th. Schneider* [Dr. Martin Luther's small catechism, critically annotated in accordance with the original edition, with a contribution to the history of the catechetic by Licentiate K. F. Th. Schneider] (Berlin: Verlag
von Wiegandt und Grieben, 1853), p. vii.

43. From 1526: "The solution of a questyon moued of his sayd blessed deth"; and
from 1509: "Now have I answered you your question, and I pray you of a lyke solu-
cion." See *Oxford English Dictionary*, s.v. "question, n."

44. Noah Bridges, *Lux Mercatoria: Arithmetick Natural and Decimal* (London:
R. I. for Thomas Johnson, 1661), pp. 220, 272, 274.

45. Ibid., pp. 77–86.

46. Ibid., p. 70.

47. Maria Rosa Antognazza, *Leibniz: An Intellectual Biography* (Cambridge: Cambridge University Press, 2009), pp. 115.

48. The corn question was raised and discussed in broad relation to the so-called
Corn Laws put in place in 1815 as a protectionist measure that severely restricted grain
imports. The population question was also discussed in connection with the corn
and bullion questions and related to the country's capacity—or lack thereof—to
provide a material existential basis for its population based on population figures in
relation to agricultural production.

49. Robert Southey, "The Poor," in *Quarterly Review*, no. 29, article 8 (1816):
187–235, 235.

50. Thomas Robert Malthus, *Principles of Political Economy considered with a View
to Their Practical Application* (London: W. Pickering, 1836), pp. 9–10.

51. Maria Magro writes of the "querelle" that it had its origins around 1540. See
Maria Magro, *Robert Herrick's "Hesperides" and the Renaissance "querelle des femmes"*
(Windsor, Canada: University of Windsor, ProQuest Dissertations and Theses, 1995),
p. iii. Koselleck et al. also cite a document from 1426 wherein the German "Frage"
appears to suggest dispute or cause of war. See Brunner, Conze, and Koselleck,
Geschichtliche Grundbegriffe, vol. 5, p. 684n.

52. *Oxford English Dictionary*, s.v. "querist, n." The Latin *querela* or *questus* both

mean "complaint." See Valpy, *Etymological Dictionary of the Latin Language*, pp. 388–389.

53. The term in French is *quérulent* and in German *Querulant*. See Gerhard Köbler, *Deutsches etymologisches Wörterbuch* [German etymological dictionary] (1995), p. 322, http://www.koeblergerhard.de/der/DERQ.pdf. On the "Querulant" in psychiatric thought, see Theodor Tiling, *Individuelle Geistesartung und Geistesstörung* [Individual mentality and mental disorder] (Wiesbaden: Verlag Von J. F. Bergmann, 1904), pp. 27–28, 35; August Finger, A. Hoche, and Joh Bresler, *Juristisch-psychiatrische Grenzfragen: zwanglose Abhandlungen* [Juridical-psychiatric boundary questions: Informal essays], vol. 6 (Halle a.S.: C. Marhold, 1908), p. 40.

54. This also explains why commentators often spoke of "settling" a question. See, for examle, Henry George, *The Irish Land Question, What It Involves, and How Alone It Can Be Settled: An Appeal to the Land Leagues* (New York: D. Appleton, 1881).

55. Александр Сергеевич Пушкин, "Клеветникам России," [To Russia's detractors] in Александр Васильев, *Интертекстуальность. Прецедетные феномены: учебное пособие* [Intertextuality. Precedent-setting phenomena: a textbook] (Moscow: Издательство «Флинта», 2013), pp. 200–202.

56. TNA, FO 881/557, United States: Desp. Central American Question (Mr. Marcy), May 24, 1856, pp. 2, 6–7: "[Lord Clarendon] had offered to refer the whole question to the arbitration of any third Power" (p. 2); "[The president of the United States] would greatly prefer that, in a controversy like the present, turning on points of political geography, the matter should be referred to some one or more of those eminent men of science who do honour to the intellect of Europe and America, and who, with previous consent of their respective Governments, might well undertake the task of determining such a question, to the acceptance as well of Her Majesty's Government as of the United States" (p. 7).

57. See, for example, on the "Hamlet question" (Гамлетовский вопрос), James H. Billington, *The Icon and the Axe: An Interpretive History of Russian Culture* (New York: Knopf, 1966), p. 354; Bernhard ten Brink, *Five Lectures on Shakespeare* (New York: H. Holt, 1895), p. 9; Gerhard Joseph, *John Barth* (Minneapolis: University of Minnesota Press, [c. 1970]), p. 15; Ottó Hóman, *A homéri kérdés jelenlegi állása* [The present status of the Homer question] ([Budapest]: [Franklin Ny.], [1872]); Vilmos Tolnai, *A Madách-"kérdés" körül* [Regarding the Madách question] (Budapest: Franklin Ny., 1934); Gyula Győri, *A Toldi-kérdés* [The Toldi question] (Pápa: Ev. Ref. Ny., 1896), p. 3; and Ferenc Zsigmond, *Az Ady-kérdés története idézetekben* [The history of the Ady question in quotes] (Mezőtúr: Török, 1928).

58. Francis Bacon played a central role in the quarrel in its British incarnation. See, for example, Richard Foster Jones, *Ancients and Moderns: A Study of the Rise of the Scientific Movement in Seventeenth-Century England* (Berkeley: University of California Press, 1965), pp. 41–61.

59. See, for example, Stanisław Tarnowski in Julian Klaczko, *Studya dyplo-*

matyczne: Sprawa polska—sprawa duńska (1863–1865), część pierwsza [Diplomatic studies: The Polish question—the Danish question, 1863-1865, part one] (Kraków: Spółka Wydawnicza Polska, 1903), p. xv; Adolphe Pieyre, *L'Épreuve* [The test] (Paris: Librairie Molière, 1905), p. 133.

60. See, for example, John Jackson, *A Collection of Queries: Wherein the Most Material Objections From Scripture, Reason, And Antiquity, Which Have As Yet Been Alleged Against Dr. Clarke's Scripture-doctrine of the Trinity, And the Defenses of It, Are Proposed And Answered. With an Appendix: In Which Are Offered to the Consideration of the Learned, Some Queries . . . Concerning the Vulgar Scholastick Explication of the Doctrine of the Trinity And Incarnation* (London: Printed for James Knapton, 1716), pp. 78, 86, 105, 120–125; and Samuel Fuller, *A serious reply to twelve sections of abusive queries, proposed to the consideration of the people called Quakers; concluding the works of Joseph Boyse* (Dublin: Printed and sold by S. Fuller, 1728), p. vi (and throughout).

61. See *Oxford English Dictionary*, s.v. "question, n."

62. Luther, *D. Martin Luthers kleiner Katechismus*, p. 4.

63. Nicolaus Ludwig Graf von Zinzendorf, *A Manual of Doctrine; or, A second essay to bring into the form of question and answer as well the fundamental doctrines, as the other scripture-knowledge, of the Protestant congregations who for 300 years past have been call'd the Brethren (reserving a Liberty to alter and amend again, what at any Time shall be found needful.) Written in High-Dutch, by the author of the first essay; and now translated into English. With an introduction* (London: for James Hutton, at the Bible and Sun, in Little-Wild-Street, near Lincoln's-Inn-Fields, 1742), p. 8.

64. Ibid., p. 18.

65. Ibid., p. 83.

66. A further instance of this can be found in Jackson, *A Collection of Queries*, p. vi.

67. See, for example, *The Oude Catechism; or, Answers to Questions Concerning Oude, Its History and Its Wrongs* (London: J. Davy & Sons, 1857); *The Carnatic Catechism, with Letter Addressed to Their Graces the Archbishops, &C. &C. on the Carnatic Question. (Resumé and Sequel No. 1[-3].) [On the Claims of 'Azīm Jāh Bahādur to the Throne of the Carnatic. By C. Purushottama, Mudaliyār.].* ([London]: J. Davy & Sons, 1862); *Catechism of the Eastern Question. Reprinted from the 'Pall Mall Gazette' (1877)*; Maltman Barry, *The Catechism of The Eastern Question: Being an Historical Retrospect, from 1710 to 1878* (London: Effingham Wilson, 1880); J. H. Stevenson, *The Money Question: A Catechism* (Pittsburgh, PA: Gleaner, 1893); *A Short Catechism on the Ulster Question* (Westminster, 1893); John D. Spence, *A Shorter Catechism of the Land Question* (London: Liberty and Property Defence League, 1894); *Die Tiroler Frage: ein Katechismus* [The Tirol question: A catechism] (Innsbruck: Der Bundesvorstand des Andreas Hofer-Bundes für Tirol, 1919); John A. Ryan and R. A. McGowan, *A Catechism of the Social Question* (New York: Paulist Press, 1921); Joseph Tarcisius Och, *Social Politics and the Social Question: A Catechism* (Columbus, OH: Pontifical

College Josephinum, 1923); G. E. Bunning, *The Cattle Tick Question: A Catechism on Tick Control and Eradication* ([Sydney]: Dept. of Agriculture, 1932); Jean-Marie Laureys, *Catéchisme des questions sociales actuelles* [A catechism of contemporary social questions] (Brussels: Secrétariat Général, 1937); Antal Mihalovics, *Mindenki könyve: a szociális kérdés lényeges részeinek népies kátéja* [Everyman's book: A popular catechism of the essential aspects of the social question] (Rožňava-Rozsnyó: Sajó-Vidék, [1937]), p. 7.

68. See, for example, the introduction to an 1853 edition of Luther's *Small Catechism*. Luther, *D. Martin Luthers kleiner Katechismus*, p. vii.

69. In addition to republication of Luther's catechism and the texts mentioned below, there was also Richard Challoner, *The Catholick Christian Instructed, in the Sacraments Sacrifice, Ceremonies, and Observances of the Church: By Way of Question and Answer* (London, 1747). See also, for example, John Goodwin, *Impvtatio fidei; or, A treatise of justification wherein ey imputation of faith for righteousness mentsioned Rom. 43.5. is explained & also ey great question largly handled whether, ey active obedience of Christ performed to ey morall law be imputed in justification or not : or how it is imputed : therein likewise many other difficulties and questions touching ty great business of justification : viz, ty matter & forme thereof etc are opened & cloared* [sic] *: together with ey explication of diverse scriptures with partly speake partly seeme to speake to the matter herein dicussed* (London: Printed by R. O. and G. D. and are to be sold by Andrew Crooke, 1642).

70. *The Grand question concerning taking up armes against the King ansvvered by application of the Holy Scriptures to the conscience of every subject* ([Oxford], 1643).

71. See, for example, John Marsh, *An argument or debate in lavv of the great qvestion concerning the militia as it is novv settled by ordinance of both the Houses of Parliament by which it is endeavoured to prove the legalitie of it and to make it warrantable by the fundamentall laws of the land: in which answer is also given to all objections that do arise either directly or collaterally concerning the same* (London: Printed by Tho. Paine and M. Simmons for Tho. Underhill, 1642); William Sclater, *An exposition vvith notes on the whole fourth chapter to the the Romanes wherein the grand question of justification by faith alone, without works, is controverted, stated, cleared, and fully resolved . . . by William Sclater, Doctor in Divinity, sometimes minister of Gods word at Pitminster, in Summerset; now published by his son, William Sclater, Batchelar in Divinity, minister at Collompton in Devon* (London: Printed by J. L. for Christopher Meredith, 1650); Denzil Holles, *The grand question concerning the judicature of the House of Peers, stated and argued And the case of Thomas Skinner merchant, complaining of the East India Company, with the proceedings thereupon, which gave occasion to that question, faithfully related. By a true well-wisher to the peace and good government of the kingdom, and to the dignity and authority of parliaments* (London: Printed for Richard Chiswel, at the two Angels and Crown in LittleBrittain, 1669); and *The grand question resolved viz. a*

king having protested to defend to the uttermost of his power, the true Protestant religion, with the rights and liberties of all his subjects: but if they, fearing that he will violate this his protestation, take up arms to prevent it, what may be judged hereof? (London: Printed for B. Pratt, 1681).

72. Daniel Defoe, *The Two Great Questions Considered* (London: Baldwin, 1700); Defoe, *Remarks Upon a Late Pamphlet Intitul'd, the Two Great Questions Consider'd: I. What the French King Will Do with Respect to the Spanish Monarchy. II. What Measures the English Ought to Take* (London, 1700); Defoe, *The Two Great Questions Further Considered: With Some Reply to the Remarks* (London, 1700); Defoe, *Remarks Upon the Two Great Questions. Part II. Wherein the Grand Question of All Is Considered, Viz. What the Dutch Ought to Do at This Juncture? [a Reply to "the Two Great Questions Further Considered, Etc." by Daniel Defoe.]* (London, 1701); Defoe, *Two Great Questions Considered, I. What Is the Obligation of Parliaments to the Addresses or Petitions of the People, and What the Duty of the Addressers? II. Whether the Obligation of the Covenant or Other National Engagements Is Concern'd in the Treaty of the Union?: Being a Sixth Essay at Removing National Prejudices against the Nation* ([London], 1707).

73. See book 3, chapter 19, "New Consequences of the Principles of the Three Governments," in Charles de Secondat Montesquieu and Thomas Nugent, *The Spirit of Laws* (Dublin: Printed for G. and A. Ewing, and G. Faulkner, 1751), pp. 97–102.

74. E.g. "The Querist dreamt he saw a Comet . . ." etc.; Member of the Athenian Society, *Athenian Oracle*, p. 27. Reverend George Berkeley, Lord Bishop of Cloyne, began publishing *The Querist* in 1735. George Berkeley, *The Querist: Containing Several Queries, Proposed to the Consideration of the Public* (Dublin: R. Urie, 1760), p. iii.

75. John Dunton, *The Athenian Mercury* (London: Printed for P. Smart, 1691).

76. Member of the Athenian Society, *Athenian Oracle*, p. 1. (The whole of the text cited is italicized with the exception of the above-italicized text.)

77. Ibid., pp. 36–37, 190, 231–232.

78. *The British Apollo: Containing Two Thousand Answers to Curious Questions In Most Arts And Sciences, Serious, Comical, And Humorous, Approved of by Many of the Most Learned And Ingenious of Both Universities, And of the Royal-Society,* 3d ed. (London: Printed for T. Sanders, 1726). It should be noted that *The British Apollo* began publication already in 1708 as a calendar or almanac of sorts. Richard Saunders, *Apollo Anglicanus: The English Apollo* (London: Printed by J. Wilde for the Company of Stationers, 1708). Several of the questions were apparently written by women.

79. See Robert Heath, *The Gentleman and Lady's Palladium For the Year of our Lord 1753* (London: for J. Fuller, at the Bible and Dove in Ave-Mary-Lane, 1753).

80. Ibid., pp. 2, 10–11, 18–19.

81. Mary Thale, "London Debating Societies in the 1790s," in *The Historical Journal* 32, no. 1 (March 1989): 57–86, pp. 57–8, 60.

82. *The Other Side of the Question. Being a collection of what hath appeared in De-*

fence of the late Act, in Favour of the Jews. To which is prefixed, a Word or Two by the Editor (London: R. Griffiths, 1753), p. iv.

83. There are countless examples of this, but here are just a few: Theobald MacKenna, *An Abstract of the Arguments on the Catholic Question* (London: Printed by Cox, Son, and Baylis, 1805), p. 3; "Die Arbeiterfrage" [The worker question], *Politisches Blatt, als Extra-Beilage zur Laibacher Zeitung* [Political journal, as an extra supplement to the Ljubljana Newspaper], no. 21 (December 14, 1848): 42; and Szombatsági, *A nemzetiségi kérdés Magyarországban* [The nationality question in Hungary] (Pest: Pfeifer Emich Ny., 1861), pp. 3, 65–66.

84. *Morning Post and Daily Advertiser* (London), March 10, 1788, p. 1.

85. Thale, "London Debating Societies in the 1790s," pp. 57–86, 58, 61.

86. See Toury, " 'The Jewish Question,'" pp. 85–106, 87.

87. Hans-Heinrich Müller, *Akademie und Wirtschaft im 18. Jahrhundert: Agrarökonomische Preisaufgaben und Preisschriften der Preußischen Akademie der Wissenschaften (Versuch, Tendenzen, und Überblick)* [Academy and economy in the eighteenth century: agrarian-economic prize competitions and prize essays of the Prussian Academy of Sciences (experiment, trends, and overview)] (Berlin: Akademie-Verlag, 1975), p. 41.

88. See, for example, Adolf von Harnack, *Geschichte der königlich preussischen Akademie der Wissenschaften zu Berlin: Im Auftrage der Akademie bearb.* [History of the Royal Prussian Academy of Sciences in Berlin: Compiled at the behest of the Academy], vol. 2 (Berlin: Reichsdruckerei, 1900), pp. 305–309.

89. MacKenna, *Catholic Question*, p. 2. This passage from MacKenna was later cited in [Alexander Dolrymple], *On the Catholic Question, properly Roman-Catholic Question* (London: William Ballintine, 1807), pp. 9–10. Dolrymple wrote that MacKenna's pamphlet "cannot be admitted as an impartial *Statement* of the *Arguments* on the question; but The Author is rather to be considered as The *Champion* of The *Roman-Catholic Claims.*"

90. *The West India Question, Practically Considered* (London: John Murray, 1826), p. 110.

91. Bukaty, *Sprawa Polski wywołana przed sądem miecza i polityki w roku 1830*, cz. 1.

92. Fedor Ivanovich Fircks, *La question polonaise au point de vue de la Pologne de la Russie et de l'Europe* [The Polish question from the point of view of Poland, of Russia, and of Europe] (Paris: E. Dentu, 1863), pp. 85, 5–6.

1. The National Argument: The Imperial to the National Age

1. The words of Mephisto, devilishly instructing a student in the arts of manipulation of knowledge, in Goethe's *Faust*. Cited in Sándor Rónyi, *Indokolt programm a magyar kérdés törvényes és praktikus megoldását illetőleg* [Appropriate program for the

legal and practical solution of the Hungarian question] (Pest: Hartleben, Emich Ny., 1865), p. 5.

2. See P. D. G. Thomas, *The House of Commons in the Eighteenth Century* (Oxford: Clarendon Press, 1971), pp. 30, 36. Regarding the focus on shortcomings/failures of government policy, see ibid., p. 31.

3. Thomas Pownall, *The administration of the Colonies*, vol. 1 (London: J. Walter, 1764), p. vii.

4. Ibid., p. x (italics in the original).

5. Ibid., p. ix.

6. Edmund Burke, *Speech of Edmund Burke, Esq., On American Taxation, April 19, 1774* (London: J. Dodsley, 1775), p. 7.

7. *The Gentleman's Magazine, and Historical Chronicle*, vol. 46 (London, 1776), p. 585.

8. Reprinted in *Debates of the House of Commons Containing an Account of the Most Interesting Speeches and Motions, Accurate Copies of the Most Remarkable Letters and Papers, of the Most Material Evidence, Petitions, &C. Laid Before and Offered to the House*, vol. 1 (London: Reprinted for John Stockdale, Piccadilly, 1802), p. 245.

9. Richard Watson, *Sermons on Public Occasions, and Tracts on Religious Subjects* (Cambridge: Printed by J. Archdeacon, 1788), p. 25.

10. Watson's own reference to it was in the past tense. See also *The Gentleman's Magazine*, May 1783, p. 383; *The Parliamentary Register; or, History of the Proceedings and Debates of the House of Commons . . . during the Third Session of the Fifteenth Parliament of Great Britain*, vol. 26 (vol. IX) (London: J. Debrett, 1883), pp. 39, 283; John Jebb and John Disney, *The Works Theological, Medical, Political, and Miscellaneous of John Jebb* (London: Sold by T. Cadell, 1787), p. 552; and John Wilde, *An Address to the Lately Formed Society of the Friends of the People* (Edinburgh: Printed for P. Hill, 1793), p. 512.

11. Great Britain, Parliament, *The Parliamentary register: or, History of the proceedings and debates of the House of Commons [and of the House of Lords] containing an account of the interesting speeches and motions . . . during the 1st session of the 14th [-18th] Parliament of Great Britain*, ser. 2, vol. 42, 1794–1795 (London: Printed for J. Almon, 1795), p. 437; [Dolrymple], *On the Catholic Question*; and TNA, PRO 30/9/3/8, Charles Abbot, 1st Baron Colchester: Papers. Political papers of the 1st Lord Colchester, dealing with Catholic Emancipation; the Public Records; and the Irish question; see letters dated January 1, 1801, and March 9, 1813.

12. William Duane, *The Mississippi Question Fairly Stated And the Views and Arguments of Those Who Clamor for War, Examined in Seven Letters; Originally Written for Publication in the Aurora, at Philadelphia* (Philadelphia: Printed by William Duane, 1803); and William Duane, *Mississippi Question: Report of a Debate in the Senate of the United States on the 23d, 24th, & 25th February, 1803, on Certain Resolutions concerning*

the Violation of the Right of Deposit in the Island of New Orleans (Philadelphia: Printed by W. Duane, 1803).

13. On the "corn question," see, for example, Henry Parnell, *The Substance of the Speeches of Sir H. Parnell, Bart., in the House of Commons, with Additional Observations, on the Corn Laws* (London: Printed for J. Ridgway, 1814), p. 3.

14. See, for example, *The Carnatic Question Considered: In a Letter to a Member of Parliament* (London: R.H. Evans, 1806), p. 2: "If, by any fortunate turn of circumstances, a portion of the substance of these voluminous documents could be impressed on the public mind, or the understanding of the House, the result would be obvious. Show but the *merits* of the *cause*, and *advocates* must necessarily *abound!*"; *Remarks on the Oude Question* (London: Printed for W. I. & I. Richardson, Royal Exchange, 1806), p. v: "A public discussion of such questions, even while they are under the investigation of Parliament, is always thought allowable . . ."; and "Commons Sitting of Monday, January 26, 1807," *Hansard Parliamentary Debates*, 1st series (1803–1820), pp. 552–557, accessed September 22, 2016, http://hansard.millbank systems.com/commons/1807/jan/26/conduct-of-lord-wellesley. Discussion of the East India question (also sometimes simply called the India question) was especially pronounced in 1813, around discussion of the renewal of the East India Company's charter. See, for example, *East India Question: A Short Abstract of the Argument in Support of the East India Company's Petition to Parliament for a Renewal of Their Charter* (London: Printed for Black, Perry, 1813); Charles Maclean, *Abstract of the East India Question: Illustrating in a Concise Manner the Controversy between the East India Company and His Majesty's Ministers* (London: Printed for J. Mawman, 1813); and Civis, *Letters of Civis Upon the India Question* (London: Printed for C. Chapple, 1813).

15. W. Huskisson, *The Question concerning the Depreciation of our Currency stated and examined* (London: Printed for John Murray, 1810), p. ii. It is also worth noting that a year earlier, on May 1, 1809, Huskisson engaged in an exchange on the "Spanish question" in the House of Commons. See *Hansard Parliamentary Debates*, 1st series (1803–1820), p. 290.

16. There are many examples of this, of which I will offer here two. "I raise my voice fearlessly before the high tribunal of public opinion," declared Leopold Leon Sawaskiewicz in a pamphlet from 1840 on the "Eastern question" as it related to the "Polish question." Leopold Leon Sawaskiewicz, *Why the eastern question cannot be satisfactorily settled: or, reflexions on Poland and France* (London: J. Ridgway, 1840), p. iv. A book from 1863 by a Polish nobleman from Russian Poland similarly addresses itself to the "great court known as 'public opinion'" and notes the status of the "question Polonaise" as a "cause célèbre . . . with public opinion as jury and Europe as judge." Fircks, *La question polonaise*, pp. 85, 5–6.

17. Already in the 1740s, for example, the *Gentleman's Magazine* published reports

on the matters discussed in Parliament. See Stephen Koss, *The Rise and Fall of the Political Press in Britain*. Vol. 1, *The Nineteenth Century* (London: Hamish Hamilton, 1981), p. 30. It is worth noting that many political parties eventually had their own associations that weighed in on period questions. See TNA, ZLIB 15/16, "Presentation of Addresses from the conservative Associations to the Earl of Beaconsfield, K.G. and the Marquess of Salisbury, K.G. at the Foreign Office, August 6th, 1878—Report of Proceedings 1878," in "The Policy of the Government on the Eastern Question, by a Member of the Council of the National Union of Conservative and Constitutional Associations."

18. John Sinclair, *Remarks on a Pamphlet Intitled, "The Question Concerning the Depreciation of the Currency Stated and Examined" by William Huskisson, Esq., M.P. Together with Several Political Maxims Regarding Coin and Paper Currency, Intended to Explain the Real Nature, and Advantages, of the Present System* (London: Printed by W. Bulmer and co., sold by T. Cadell and W. Davies [etc.], 1810), pp. 24–25.

19. See Robert Stewart Castlereagh, *The Substance of a Speech Delivered by Lord Viscount Castlereagh In a Committee of the House of Commons, May 8, 1811; on the Report of the Bullion Committee* (London: Printed for J.J. Stockdale, 1811); and George Canning, *Substance of two speeches, delivered in the House of Commons, by the Right Honourable George Canning, on Wednesday the 8th, and Monday the 13th of May, 1811, in the committee of the whole house; to which was referred, the report of the committee, appointed in the last session of Parliament "To inquire into the cause of the high price of bullion, and to take into consideration the state of the circulating medium, and of the exchanges between Great-Britain and foreign parts"* (London: Printed for J. Hatchard, 1811); for reviews of the above, see *The Monthly Review or Literary Journal*, vol. LXVI (1811), pp. 326–328.

20. See, for example, Canning, *Substance of two speeches*, pp. 36, 46

21. Ibid., p. 126.

22. Castlereagh, *Substance of a Speech Delivered*, p. 4.

23. A French commentator wrote in the mid-1830s, for example, that the "[Eastern] question is one of the most important and urgent that the Press has ever yet been called upon to handle, our Cabinet alone feigns not to comprehend its weight." From the *Courier Français*, cited in David Ross of Bladensburg, ed., *Opinions of the European Press on the Eastern Question* (London, 1836), p. xxviii. See also George Campbell, *The Blue Books, and What Is to Come Next* (London: Cassell, Petter, and Galpin [Published for the Eastern Question Association], 1877), pp. 49–50.

24. This was also true of two pamphlets on the Mississippi question from 1803. See Duane, *The Mississippi Question Fairly Stated*; and Duane, *Mississippi Question*.

25. Davies Giddy, *A Plain Statement of the Bullion Question in a Letter to a Friend* (London: John Stockdale, 1811), p. 1.

26. See Thomas Robert Malthus, "Pamphlets on the Bullion Question," in *Edinburgh Review or Critical Journal*, vol. 18 (May–August 1811): 448–470.

27. See, for example, the letter from Stratford Canning to the British minister at Madrid from December 31, 1823, cited in Henry Mann, *The Land We Live in, or, The Story of Our Country* (New York: The Christian Herald, 1896), p. 243n.

28. *Hansard Parliamentary Debates*, 1st series (1803–1820), p. 1197.

29. For example, in a confidential letter from Prince Metternich to Prince Hardenberg on October 22, 1814, Metternich mentions "la question polonaise." TNA, FO 139/13, Prince Metternich, Baron Wessenberg, Austria. Vienna, October 22, 1814, p. 13 (on "la question napolitaine," "la question jacobine," and "la question sicilienne," see ibid., Metternich to Baron Vincent, Vienna, February 18, 1815, pp. 80, 83v; "Remarques sur les Articles du Memorandum Confidentiel" [Remarks on the articles of the confidential memorandum], p. 87). See also on "la question polonaise," TNA, FO 139/27, Protocols, 1 to 7. Vienna, Hardenberg's note, December 29, 1814, pp. 22v, 24. On the Maritime question, see TNA, FO 139/1, Viscount Castlereagh, Paris, "Memorandum of Cabinet," December 20, 1813, p. 1. On the Saxon question, see, for example, TNA, FO 417/1, Negotiations respecting Poland Correspondence, 1814–1815, p. 49. In a letter from the German statesman Ernst Friedrich Herbert von Münster addressed to Hans Christoph Ernst von Gagern: "The Polish question is very important for Germany." In Baron Hans Christoph Ernst von Gagern, *Mein Antheil an der Politik, II. Nach Napeons Fall, Der Congreß zu Wien* [My involvement in politics, part II, after the fall of Napoleon, the congress at Vienna] (Stuttgart: J. G. Cotta'schen Buchhandlung, 1826), p. 46; Report on a conversation with an unnamed "Russian gentleman": "Yet from then on, switching to the politics of the moment, he wanted me to understand how it was necessary to explain the Polish question in terms of the character, education, and manner of Emperor Alexander." In ibid., p. 75.

30. TNA, FO 139/13, Count Rasoumoffsky to Prince Metternich, December 27, 1814, p. 59v. See also ibid., p. 87v. See also TNA, FO 139/22, Count Nesselrode, Count Stackelberg, etc., Russia. Vienna, Capodistrias—Vienna, August 4, 1814, p. 17.

31. Patrick Howarth, *Questions in the House: The History of a Unique British Institution* (London: Bodley Head, 1956), p. 72. Howarth notes that, during this period, the earlier mainstays of parliamentary questions, "war and foreign affairs," were soon joined by others like the corn and cotton questions. Ibid.

32. See, for example, *The Times* (London), November 21, 1823, p. 2; March 18, 1824, p. 2; May 14, 1824, p. 2, among others. On its relation to the slavery question, see T. S. Winn, *A Speedy End to Slavery in Our West India Colonies: By Safe, Effectual, and Equitable Means for the Benefit of All Parties Concerned* (London: Sold by W. Phillips, 1825), p. 99. See also *The West India Question, Practically Considered* (London: John Murray, 1826). The pamphlet comes close to mentioning the slavery question ("the

question of slavery," see p. 45), but stops just short. The pamphlet is a criticism of Britain's involvement in maintaining slavery there by its policies.

33. *West India Question*, p. 1.

34. Winn, *A Speedy End to Slavery*, p. 99.

35. Ibid., p. 98.

36. Jürgen Habermas, for example, defines a *bourgeois public sphere* as "the sphere of private persons assembled to form a public," developed mostly through print media. Jürgen Habermas and Steven Seidman, eds., *Jürgen Habermas on Society and Politics: A Reader* (Boston: Beacon Press, 1989), p. 233.

37. *Journal des débats politiques et littéraires* [Journal of political and literary debates] (Paris), March 29, 1834, p. [3]; *Diario de Avisos de Madrid* [Madrid daily advisor] (Madrid), April 5, 1833, p. 397; Mariano Torrente, *Historia de la Revolución Hispano-americana* [History of the Spanish-American Revolution] (Madrid: Impr. De L. Amarita, 1830), p. 408; letter of Martínez de la Rosa reprinted in *Journal des débats politiques et littéraires* (Paris), July 5, 1834, p. [1].

38. See Edmondo de Amicis, *Osservazioni sulla questione sociale: Conferenza di Edmondo de Amicis detta la sera di giovedì, 11 febbraio 1892 all'Associazione universitaria torinese* [Observations on the social question: Lecture of Edmondo de Amicis delivered on the evening of Thursday, February 11, 1892 at the Turin University Association] (Turin: Roux, 1892); Amicis, *Über die soziale frage* (Vienna: E. Pernerstorfer, 1892); Amicis, *De la question sociale* (Lausanne: Benda, 1892); and Amicis, *Amor y gimnástica; La cuestión social; Garibaldi y otros trabajos* (Madrid: Sáenz de Jubera, 1892). For the Bulgarian translation, which itself was translated from the German edition; see Едмондо де Амичис, *По социалния въпрос* ([s.l.]: Мутафов, 1894). Another German translation appeared in Leipzig in 1896; see Amicis, *Der Student und die soziale Frage* (Leipzig: Rassherg, 1896). A second Czech edition was published in Jičina in 1897; see Amicis, *Student a otázka socialni: Řeč Edmonda de Amicis, kterou měl ve spolku italských studentů v Turině* (Jičina: L. Sehnal, 1897). A Polish translation appeared in 1900; see Amicis, *O kwestyi społecznej: Mowa wygłoszona na zebraniu słuchaczów Uniwersytetu w Turynie w roku 1892* (Lviv: "Promienia," 1900). Russian editions appeared in 1902 (in Geneva) and 1905 (in Russia); see де Амичис, *Студенты и социальный вопрос* (Geneva: Изд. Союза Р.С.-Д., 1902); де Амичис, *Студенты и социальный вопрос: Речь к туринским студентам* (St. Petersburg: Книгоиздательство "Молот," 1905); де Амичис, *Студенты и социальный вопрос* (Rostov-on-Don: Издание "Донская Речь," 1905). See Masaryk, *Otázka sociální.* The book was first published in Czech in 1898, then in German a year later. T. G. Masaryk, *Die philosophischen und soziologischen Grundlagen des Marxismus: Studien zur socialen Frage* [The philosophical and sociological foundations of Marxism: Studies on the social question] (Vienna: C. Konegen, 1899).

39. Edmond de Amicis, "Úvahy o socialné otázce" [Reflections on the social

question], in *Athenaeum, Listy pro literaturu a kritiku vědeckou* (October 15, 1892): pp. 8–13, 10–12.

40. This is all the more peculiar as the novel—originally published in Italian in 1886—was really de Amicis's international claim to fame. For the first Czech edition, see Edmondo de Amicis and Václav Marek, *Srdce* [Heart] (Prague: V. Neubert, 1894).

41. Masaryk, *Otázka sociální*. The book was first published in Czech in 1898.

42. Interestingly, the bulk of the discussion of the transnational public sphere in media studies seems to be on a much more recent phenomena, specifically, the creation and expansion of the European Union after World War II. See Michael Brüggemann, Andreas Hepp, Katharina Kleinen-von Königslöw, and Hartmut Wessler, "Transnationale Öffentlichkeit in Europa: Forschungsstand und Perspektive" [Transnational public sphere in Europe: State of the field and perspectives], in *Publizistik* 54 (2009): pp. 391–414, esp. p. 394. Certainly, international exchanges of ideas were common among theologians and academics of the medieval and early modern periods, but during the age of questions publicistic endeavors sought to reach foreign publics to influence foreign public opinion and thereby policymaking (through the newly expanded voter franchises, particularly in Western Europe).

43. See, for example, [Aleksander Ignacy Jan Piotr], *Briefe eines polnischen Edelmannes an einen deutschen Publicisten über die jüngsten Ereignisse in Polen und die hauptsächlich bisher nur vom deutschen Standpunkte betrachtete polnische Frage* [Letters of a Polish nobleman to a German publicist on recent events in Poland and on the Polish question, which has thus far mainly been considered from the German perspective] (Hamburg: Hoffman und Campe, 1846), which speaks of the "pending Polish questions" being discussed, in English and French cabinets, and hopes that the "more educated" Germans will support Polish aspirations (p. 103). See also Tomasz Wentworth Łubieński, *Kwestya Polska w Rosyi: list otwarty do rosyjskich publicystów* [The Polish question in Russia: Open letter to Russian publicists] (Kraków: Spółka Wydawnicza Polska, 1898), first published in Russian in Leipzig as it was not allowed to be published in Russia under its censorship regime (see p. 5). Also, in Austrian official correspondence relating to the "Jewish question and the recognition of Romanian independence" from 1878–1879, it is noteworthy that the "Jewish question" as such initially appears primarily in translations of Romanian newspaper articles from whence it moves into the correspondence itself. See, for example, AT-OeStA/HHStA PA XVIII 49, "Judenfrage und Anerkennung Rumäniens," 1879, p. 4. See also pp. 33v, 68. Incidentally, there are many other examples of document collections being labeled with the name of a particular question where the question as such does not appear. See, for example, ibid., p. 20; MOL, K64a., 67/a. tétel Muraközi kérdés, 1941, 510/Res. Pol./1941; TNA, FO 881/5658X, Minutes, &c. International Conference on the Sugar Question, 1888; Sächsisches Staatsarchiv,

Hauptarchiv Dresden (Hereafter HStA Dresden), Bestand 10730, Sächsische Gesandtschaft für Österreich, Vienna, Signatur 428, Türkei, Orient-Frage, Kreta-Frage, Bosnische Frage, Tripolis-Frage, Bl. 1–7; and ibid., Bestand 10707, Sächsisches Hauptstaatsarchiv, Signatur 1365, Geheimakte Verschlusssachenanweisung, "Geheimbefehl (Abschrift) Görings zur 'Judenfrage' vom 28.12.1938."

44. "Dans une Société de quelques Amis, rassemblés à Paris, à la prière de celle instituée à Londres pour l'abolition de la traite des Nègres" [At a society of some friends, gathered in Paris, at the request of the one established in London for the abolition of the Negro slave trade], *Analyse de papiers Anglois, depuis le 19 jusqu'au 22 Fevriér 1788*, no. 25, p. 24. A British periodical from the same year also includes mention of the "slave question" in a book review. See *The Gentleman's Magazine and Historical Chronicle for the Year 1788, Part the Second*, vol. 43 [alternatively 64] (London: John Nichols, 1788), p. 629.

45. Wilhelm Emmanuel von Ketteler, *Die Arbeiterfrage und das Christentum* [The worker question and Christianity] (Mainz: F. Kirchheim, 1864), p. 8.

46. AT-OeStA/HHStA PA XVIII 49, "Judenfrage und Anerkennung Rumäniens," 1879, p. 20.

47. Two early treatments of the nationality and worker questions in the Ljubljana press from 1848 and 1849 provide an illustration of this phenomenon. The German-language daily *Laibacher Zeitung* [Ljubljana newspaper] in 1848 published part of a new translation of a book on the worker question by the French economist Michel Chevalier, even as the translator had commented in a foreword on the generally stark differences of approach between French and German authors on the subject of the social question. See "Die Arbeiterfrage" [The worker question], *Politisches Blatt, als Extra-Beilage zur Laibacher Zeitung*, no. 21, December, 14, 1848, p. 42; and Franz Hauser, "Vorbemerkung" [Prolegomena], in *Michel Chevalier über die Arbeiterfrage* [Michel Chevalier on the worker question] (Aachen: Joh. Heinr. Schulz, 1848), front matter, unnumbered. The following year, an article in the local, and increasingly national-oriented, Slovene daily *Novice* included a review of a German-language treatment of the nationality question that the reviewer criticized for favoring German domination. "Dr. Wildnerjeve bukve," [Dr. Wildner's beeches] *Kmetijske in rokodelske Novice*, February 21, 1849, list 8, p. 34.

48. TNA, FO 139/22, Count Nesselrode, Count Stackelberg, etc., Russia. Vienna, Castlereagh to the Russian Tsar, October 12, 1814, pp. 26–26v.

49. *Un mot sur la question polonaise en 1829* [A word on the Polish question in 1829] (Paris: Alexandre Mesnier, 1829), p. 8; the reference to the "force of public opinion" is from *Ueber die polnische Frage* [On the Polish question] (Paris: Carl Heideloff, 1831), p. 3. Attempts to sway public opinion in favor of Poland go back farther than the origin of the Polish question as a matter of public discussion and

debate, and indeed began in earnest during the negotiations of the Congress of Vienna. One result was a pamphlet by Henry Brougham, *An appeal to the allies, and the English nation, in behalf of Poland* (London: J. Harding). Brougham had advised a Polish envoy of sorts (Biernacki, sent to London by Czartoryski in 1814) to "enlist the interest and sympathy of prominent journalists, poets, and other writers on behalf of Poland, so as to induce them to write in her favour." See Adam Jerzy Czartoryski, *Memoirs of Prince Adam Czartoryski and his correspondence with Alexander I: with documents relative to the prince's negotiations with Pitt, Fox, and Brougham, and an account of his conversations with Lord Palmerston and other English statesmen in London in 1832*, edited by Adam Gielgud (London: Remington, 1888), pp. 257–258.

50. Czartoryski, *Memoirs*, pp. 247, 332–4. The monthly magazine was originally called *Polonia*, but later became the *British and Foreign Review*.

51. In 1915, a German pamphlet shrilly denounced the "[i]ntrigues and tricks of Polish journalists in the service of the anti-German news factory, on all five continents against the empire of the European center." M. Kranz, *Neu-Polen* [New Poland] (Munich: J. F. Lehmanns Verlag, [1915]), p. 54.

52. Benjamin Disraeli, *Tancred; or, The New Crusade*, vol. 1 (New York: M. Walter Dunne, 1904), pp. 175–176.

53. Leopold Leon Sawaskiewicz, *Why the Eastern Question Cannot Be Satisfactorily Settled; or, Reflexions on Poland and France* (London: J. Ridgway, 1840), p. iv.

54. See esp. "Notre Programme" [Our program], *La tribune des peuples*, March 15, 1849, p. 1.

55. From the *Courier Français*, cited in David Ross of Bladensburg, ed., *Opinions of the European Press on the Eastern Question* (London, 1836), p. xxviii.

56. "We must decline the insertion of any of the numerous letters on the Jewish question, about to be decided by Parliament," we read in a brief notice "To Correspondents" from April 23 of that year. *Times* [London], April 23, 1830, p. 4.

57. Valerian Krasinski, *Is the Power of Russia to Be Reduced or Increased by the Present War?: The Polish Question and Panslavism* (London: Chapman and Hall, 1855), p. 129.

58. W. E. Gladstone, *Bulgarian Horrors and the Question of the East* (London: John Murray, 1876), pp. 10–11.

59. Łubieński, *Kwestya Polska w Rosyi*, pp. 10–11, 19. A particularly piquant example of this is the incredible trial of Vera Zasulich for shooting a government minister. She was ultimately acquitted by a sympathetic court and jury, in the presence of an enthusiastic public. See Richard Pipes, "The Trial of Vera Z." in *Russian History* 37, no. 1 (2010): v–82.

60. М. П. Погодин, *Полской вопрос, собрание разсуждений, записок и замѣчаний* [The Polish question: A collection of arguments, notes, and remarks] (Moscow:

Типографиа газета "Русский," 1867), p. iii. Similarly, Łubieński writes "silence strikes me as damaging, for *qui tacet consentire videtur* [he who remains silent is assumed to give his consent]." Łubieński, *Kwestya Polska w Rosyi*, p. 17.

61. One 1833 pamphlet by a Pole praised the "courageous voices" favoring Poland, such that not even "the censorship in Vienna and Frankfurt could stifle the general advocacy" for the Polish cause. See Karol Boromeusz Hoffmann, *Lettre d'un Polonais à MM. les pairs et les députés de la France, suivie de deux écrits, savoir: 1. de l'état actuel de la Pologne, 2. Débats de la chambre des communes* [Letter from a Pole to the peers and deputies of France, followed by two writings, namely: 1. The present state of Poland, 2. Debates in the House of Commons] (Paris: H. Fournier, 1833), p. 5.

62. "It's high time that the German press rise above incendiary newspaper articles and brochures to a thorough illumination of the Polish malady in this matter of such fateful significance for Germany. But for that we need freedom from censorship." *Deutsche Allgemeine Zeitung* (April 5, 1846) no. 95, Leipzig, p. 3.

63. *Oesterreichische Buchhändler-Correspondenz*, April 20, 1862, no. 12, p. 101; ibid., May 20, 1863, no. 15, pp. 142–143. Among the banned titles were *Sprawa polska w roku 1861; list z kraju* [The Polish question in the year 1861; letter from the country] (November 1861) (Paris: Martinet, 1861); Litwin, *Kilka słów z powodu listu z kraju pod tytułem: Sprawa polska w 1861 r.* [A few words on the letter from the country under the title: The Polish question in the year 1861] (Paris: Martinet, 1862); *Sprawa Polska w roku 1862* [The Polish question in the year 1862] (Leipzig: Wolfgang Gerhard, Centralna Księgarnia Krajów słowiańskich, 1862).

64. Başbakanlık Osmanlı Arşivi, Istanbul (hereafter cited as BOA), HR.SFR.3 (Hariciye Nezâreti Londra Sefareti Belgeleri), Dos. 121, Göm. 1, (1867).

65. Arhiv Srbije, Belgrade (hereafter cited as AS), Ministarstvo Inostranih Dela, Političko Prosvetno Odelenje (hereafter cited as MID-PP), 50B, red. 35, 1895, Bulgarska štampa o makedonskom pitanju.

66. *Hansard Parliamentary Debates*, 1st series (1803–1820), p. 1197.

67. *Un mot sur la question polonaise en 1829*, p. 13.

68. "Europäische Fragen und Probleme" [European questions and problems], *Augsburger Allgemeine Zeitung, Außerordentliche Beilage*, nos. 91 and 92, February 27, 1837, pp. 362–363. From a special Beilage to the February 27 edition.

69. Robert Cecil, marquess of Salisbury, satirized the pervasiveness of this tactic in an essay on the Polish question from 1863: "[T]o all these claims upon our close and anxious interest the contest adds yet this other—that upon it the destinies of Eastern Europe hang." Robert Cecil marquess of Salisbury, *Essays by the late Marquess of Salisbury* (London: J. Murray, 1905), p. 5.

70. Miklós Telegdi, *Az kereszteynsegnec fondamentomirol valo röuid keonywechke, ki az szent irasnac külömb külömb heleiből kerdes es feleles keppen irattatot, es Telegdi Miklos mester altal deac nyelwből magyar nyelwre forditatot* [A short booklet on the

foundations of Christianity, which was written in the form of question and answer drawing on different places in the scripture, and translated from the Latin to the Hungarian by Master Miklos Tegledi] (Vienna: Raphael Hofhalter, 1562), unnumbered.

71. György Zvonarics, *Rövid felelet, mellyben Pecseli Imrenec, ersec ujvari calvinista praedicatornac tanacsa meghamisséttatic, és az több doctoroc irásira-is válasz adatic im ez kérdés felöl: az keresztyén embernec kellesséke lutheranusnac avagy calvinistánac neveztetni ez végre, hogy az igaz tudomány avagy hitnec vallása azhamistul meg külömböztessék. Mellzet Isten igéjéből, és az szent irás magyarázo kefesztyén Doctoroknak irésokbul szedegetet és az egyigyű hiveknek eppülettyekre közönségesse tött* [A short answer in which the counsel of Imre Pecseli, the pastor of Érsekújvár/Nové Zámky, is falsified, and in which several scholars also give answer to the following question: Should the Christian person be called Lutheran or Calvinist in order that the true knowledge and faith can be distinguished from the false one? With an appendix drawing from the word of God and the exegetical writings of Christian scholars offered for the edification of the simple man] (Csepregben: Farkas Imre nyomtatta, 1626); Mátyás Sámbár, *Három jdvösséges kérdés. Elsö: A lutteránosok és cálvinisták igaz hitben vadnake? Masodik: Csak az egy pápista hité igaz? Harmadik: A' pápisták ellenkézneké a' Sz. Irással, avagy inkáb a' lutterek és cálvinisták?* [Three edifying questions. First: Are Lutherans and Calvinists of the true faith? Second: Is only the one papal faith the true one? Third: Are the papists against the scripture, or rather against the Lutherans and the Calvinists?] (Nagyszombat: az academiai bötükkel Schneckenhaus Menyhárt Venceszló által, 1661).

72. Original: Sámbár, *Három jdvösséges kérdés*, pages unnumbered. Countervolume: János Pósaházi, *Svmmas valasz-tetel. Amaz tsalóka könyvecskére: Kinek tzégére hogy már. Harom idvesseges kerdes. Irattatott egy Xeno-cosmus szerzetén levö Fráter által* [Answer to the treatise.That misleading booklet whose title is: Three edifying questions. Written by a monk of the xenocosmic order] ([Kassa]: [Johann David Türsch], [1666]), pages unnumbered.

73. *Kérdés: Mitsoda fa terem legjobb gyümöltsöt a tüdőknek?: Felelet: a tré-fa: ebéd után poszpász helyett* [Question: What sort of tree (*fa*) produces the best fruit for the lungs?: Answer: The *tré-fa* (joke): for after lunch in lieu of sweets] ([s.i.]: [s.n.], [180?]).

74. Jaques Ballexserd, *Fontos kérdés, miképpen kelljen a gyermekeket úgy nevelni, hogy . . . hosszú életűek lehessenek?* [Important question: How to raise children in such a way that they might have a long life?] (Poson; Pest: Landerer Ny., 1807), p. 5.

75. Hungarian involvement in the issue was through the matter of regulating the Danube (a question in itself in the 1830s). See István Széchenyi and Antal Zichy, *Gróf Széchenyi István beszédei* [The speeches of Count István Széchenyi] (Budapest: Athenaeum Irodalmi s nyomdai R. Társulat, 1887), p. 164 (speech from 1840);

Ferencz Pulszky, *Töredékes észrevételek a Dunaszbályozás s keleti kérdés iránt* [Fragmentary observations on the regulation of the Danube and the Eastern question] (Pozsony: Schid Ny., 1840); and István Széchenyi, *A' kelet népe* [The people of the East] (Pozsony: K. Friderik, 1841), pp. 66–67. The Fiume question was another from this time; see István Széchenyi, *A Jelenkorban Megjelent: Adó és Két Garas* [Newly published: "Taxes" and "Two Groschen"] (Buda, 1844), pp. 260, 265, 270–271.

76. István Széchenyi and Gyula Viszota, eds., *Gróf Széchenyi István naplói (1836–1843)* [The diaries of Count István Széchenyi, 1836–1843], vol. 5 (Budapest: Magyar Történelmi Társulat, 1937), entry for August 13, 1843. From *Gróf Széchenyi István minden írása*, Arcanum CD.

77. Lajos Steier, *A tót nemzetiségi kérdés 1848–49-ben, II. okmánytár* [The Slovak nationality question in 1848-1849, second document collection] (Budapest: Magyar történelmi társulat, 1937), p. 618. This source is a letter in German from a Hungarian Habsburg loyalist officer relating to a memorandum of grievances submitted by a group of Slovaks. It is dated October 21, 1849. There are likely earlier such references, but this is the earliest I have found.

78. Lajos Kossuth, *Irataim az emigráczióból* [My writings from emigration], vol. 2 (Budapest: Az Athenaeum R. Társulat Kiadása, 1881), pp. 230–232.

79. Gusztáv Ádolf Ungár, *Egy szó a maga idejében: adalék a magyar kérdés megoldásához* [A timely word: addendum on the solution of the Hungarian question] (Lipcse: Wigand, 1865), p. 1.

80. *Szózat a magyar kérdés érdemében* [Speech on the subject of the Hungarian question] (Budapest: Hartleben, Kertész ny., 1865), p. 18.

81. Ibid., p. 21.

82. Lajos Bátorfi, *A Muraközi kérdés, külön lenyomat a "Zala-Somogy Közlöny"-ből* [The Muraköz question, special imprint from the "Zala-Somogy Gazette"] (Nagy-Kanizsa: Wajdits József Ny., 1873), pp. 7, 11.

83. Hungarians are not Slavs, so the reference to pan-Slavism here is meant to allude to a serious threat to Hungary's status and position in the region.

84. Pulszky, *Töredékes észrevételek a Dunaszbályozás s keleti kérdés iránt*, pp. 64–65.

85. Anton Szécsen, *Politische Fragen der Gegenwart* [Political questions of today] (Vienna: Jasper, Hügel & Manz, 1851), p. 1.

86. Ibid., p. 3.

87. József Eötvös, *A XIX. század uralkodó eszméinek befolyása az álladalomra* [The ruling principles of the 19th century and their influence on the state], vol. 1 (Pest: Emrich Gusztáv Könyvnyomdája, 1854), pp. 574–574.

88. József Eötvös, *A nemzetiségi kérdés* [The nationalities question] (Pest: Ráth Mór, 1865), p. 9.

89. Ibid., pp. 7, 158.

90. Szombatsági, *A nemzetiségi kérdés Magyarországban*, p. 5.

91. Ibid., p. 15.

92. Ibid., p. 12.

93. Ibid., p. 55.

94. Ibid., p. 65.

95. Szécsen, *Politische Fragen der Gegenwart*, p. 67.

96. Szombatsági, *A nemzetiségi kérdés Magyarországban*, p. 54.

97. [M. Sándor], *A nemzetiségi kérdés és chouvein-érzelem Magyarországon* [The nationalities question and chauvinist sentiment in Hungary] (Komárom: Rónai Ny., 1896), p. 3.

98. J. K. Kraus, *A világítási kérdés megítélésére szolgáló új adalékok: Kőszén-gáz-vízgáz-acetylén-villanyosság* [New contributions to the evaluation of the lighting question: Coal—gas—water-vapor gas—acetylene—electricity (Bécs: [Szerző], 1899), p. 17. In a pamphlet on the lighting question from 1899, Kraus compared Hungary's approach to that of Germany, Great Britain, the United States, and other parts of the Dual Monarchy. On the social question, see Károly Tamás, *A polgári iskola és a társadalmi kérdés* [The secondary school and the social question] (Beszterce: Botschar Ny., 1908), p. 14.

99. Oszkár Jászi, *A nemzetiségi kérdés és Magyarország jövője* [The nationalities question and Hungary's future] (Budapest: Galilei Kör, 1911), pp. 11–12, 16–17. Sándor Giesswein is cited as having concurred with the view that every nation had its own nationality question (p. 51).

100. *Az 1910. évi június hó 21-ére hirdetett országgyülés képviselőházának naplója* [Proceedings of the Chamber of Deputies as constituted on June 21, 1910], vol. 23, session 521 on March 13, 1914 (Budapest Athenaeum, 1914), p. 37.

101. In their stead, the new minority question arose, which will be discussed later.

102. Oszkár Jászi, Péter Ágoston, et al., *A nemzetiségi kérdés a társadalmi és az egyéni fejlődés szempontjából; a Huszadik század körkérdése* [The nationality question from the standpoint of societal and individual development: Survey conducted by the journal *Twentieth Century*] (Budapest: Kiadja az Új Magyarország R.t., 1919), p. 93.

103. [Miklós Párdányi], *A breton-, baszk-, flamand-kérdés* [The Breton/Basque/Flemish question] ([Budapest]: Pesti Könyvny., [1928]), p. 1.

104. László Sziklay, *Közvéleményünk és a nemzetiségi kérdés* [(Hungarian) Public opinion and the nationalities question] (Kecskemét: Szerző, Első Kecskeméti Hírlapkiadó és Ny., [1941]), p. 3.

105. von Ketteler, *Die Arbeiterfrage und das Christentum*; Manó Vilmos Ketteler, *A munkások kérdése és a kereszténység* [The worker question and Christianity] (Eger: Lyc. Ny., 1864). On the timing of the translations, see István Schlett, *A "munkás-kérdés" és a szocializmus a magyar politikai gondolkodásban, 1848–1906: adalékok a politikai ideológiák jelentésváltozásához* [The "worker question" and socialism in

Hungarian political thought, 1848-1906: Contributions to changes in the meaning of political ideologies] ([Budapest]: Kossuth, 1987), pp. 85–86.

106. See, for example, Viktorin Strommer, *A női kérdés és korunk* [The woman question and our time] (Győr: Összetartás, Győregyházmegye Ny., 1909), pp. 38–39; Paolo D'Agostino Orsini, *A gyarmati kérdés az új rendben: a holnap Afrikája* [The colonial question and the new order: The Africa of tomorrow] (Budapest: [Stádium Ny.], 1941), from the Italian Paolo D'Agostino Orsini di Camerota, *La colonizzazione africana nel sistema fascista: i problemi della colonizzazione nell'Africa italiana* [African colonization in the fascist system: Problems of colonization in Italian Africa] (Milan: Bocca, 1941); and József Szabó, *A fogtechnikus kérdés, különös tekintettel Ausztria és Magyarország viszonyaira* [The dentist/dental technician question: With special attention to conditions in Austria and Hungary] (Budapest: Stephaneum Ny., 1907), who offers a comparison between Austria and Hungary, with some text in German and translated in parallel format.

107. Huszadik Század, *A zsidókérdés Magyarországon* [The Jewish question in Hungary] ([Budapest]: [Huszadik század], 1917), p. 77. Mentioned by the respondent Győző Concha.

108. Isidore Singer, ed., *Briefe berühmter christlicher Zeitgenossen über die Judenfrage* [Letters of famous Christian contemporaries on the Jewish question] (Vienna: O. Frank, 1885), pp. 13, 118.

109. Huszadik Század, *A zsidókérdés Magyarországon*, p. 10; see also p. 28.

110. Ibid., pp. 5–6.

111. Fővárosi Könyvtár, *Balkán kérdés* [Balkan question] ([Budapest]: Székesfőv. Ny., [1912]).

112. Jenő Horváth, *The Hungarian Question: A Bibliography on Hungary and Central Europe* (Budapest: Sárkány, 1938).

113. Szombatsági, *A nemzetiségi kérdés Magyarországban*, p. 14. The original reads: "zavart, csalódást, és dugába dőlt tervezést."

114. See János Surányi, *A socialis kérdés s néhány javaslat annak megoldásához* [The social question and a few recommendations for its solution] (Győr: Czéh S. Ny., 1882), pp. 18–19.

115. Ödön Farkas, *A zsidó kérdés Magyarországon* [The Jewish question in Hungary] (Budapest: L. Aigner, [1881]), pp. 11–12.

116. Felix Gerando, *Magyarország és a szandzsákvasút: Magyarország külpolitikája és a macedoniai kérdés* [Hungary and the Sandjak railway: Hungary's foreign policy and the Macedonian question] (Kolozsvár: Ellenzék-Könyvnyomda, 1908), p. 28.

117. Ibid., p. 29.

118. Veridicus, *A magyarországi nemzetiségi kérdés mint—üzlet: egy angol röpirat* [The Hungarian question as—business: An English pamphlet] (Budapest: Légrády Ny., 1909), p. 4. There was no reason for the nationalities to be unsatisfied, as the

Hungarian state had proven itself more than generous in its distribution of rights to them, so the only explanation was that bankers among the nationalities were agitating around the nationality question for financial gain.

119. Another pamphlet author, the Slovak teacher and publicist Adolf Pechány, writing a postmortem/revival of the Tót (Slovak) question in 1933, argued that it was Czech propagandists who had actively blocked the implementation of a workable solution in the past when the Slovaks were part of the Kingdom of Hungary. Adolf Pechány, *A tót-kérdés alakulása 1918-ig* [The development of the Slovak question up to 1918] (Budapest: M. Nemzeti Szövetség, 1933), p. 11.

120. Pál Hegedűs, *A dél-afrikai kérdés, különlenyomat a "Budapesti Szemle" 1900. évi számaiból* [The South African question, special offprint of the *Budapest Review* from the year 1900] (Budapest, 1900), p. 4.

121. Imre Sebők, *A sárga kérdés: emberföldrajzi és politikai tanulmány* [The yellow question: A study in human geography and politics] (Budapest: Lampel, Korvin Ny. 1916), p. 61.

122. In Jászi et al., *A nemzetiségi kérdés a társadalmi és az egyéni fejlődés szempontjából*, pp. 86, 94–95.

123. Joseph Jacobs, *The Jewish Question, 1875–1884: Bibliographical Hand-List* (London: Trübner, 1885), pp. v, x–xi, 1.

124. А. Ф. Гильфердинг, *Собраніе сочиненій А. Гильфердинга*, т. II, *Статьи по современнымъ вопросамъ* [Collection of works by Alexander Hilferding, vol. 2, Articles on contemporary questions] (St. Petersburg: Печатня В. Головина, 1868), p. 360. Originally from *Russkii Invalid*, the official publication of the tsarist ministry of war, on December 4, 1863. Ibid., p. 291.

125. For comparisons with other questions, see, for example, Viscount Wellesley, *The Irish Question Considered in Its Integrity* (Brussels: Meline, Cans, 1844), p. 259. See also ibid., pp. 267, 288–289. On the Irish question as a social question, see, for example, the Irish nationalist Charles Stewart Parnell's 1881 letter to Victor Hugo in Charles Higgins, *The Irish Land Question: Facts and Arguments* (Manchester: J. Heywood, 1881), p. 171. The Irish socialist James Connolly wrote in 1910 that "the Irish question is a social question." James Connolly, *Labour in Irish History* (Dublin: Maunsel, 1910), p. 214. The French socialist deputy Jean Capdeville said in 1954 that "the Algerian problem is, above all, a social problem." Cited in Todd Shepherd "Algeria, France, Mexico, UNESCO: a Transnational History of Antiracism and Decolonization, 1932–1962," in *Journal of Global History* 6 (2011): 273–297, 290.

126. Cited in Schlett, *A "munkáskérdés" és a szocializmus a magyar politikai gondolkodásban*, p. 19.

127. Ibid., pp. 73, 85.

128. Ibid., p. 81.

129. Ibid., p. 78.

130. Manó Vilmos Ketteler, *A munkások kérdése és a kereszténység* [The workers' question and Christianity] (Eger: Lyc. Ny., 1864), p. 7. See Schlett, *A "munkáskérdés" és a szocializmus a magyar politikai gondolkodásban,* p. 85.

131. Cited in Schlett, *A "munkáskérdés" és a szocializmus a magyar politikai gondolkodásban,* p. 137.

132. Cited in ibid., p. 153.

133. Cited in ibid., p. 196.

134. Richard Suschka, *Tuberkulin-kérdés mai állásáról* [The current state of the tuberculosis question] (Magyar-Óvár: Czéh Ny., 1897), p. 2; [László Zelovich], *A kartel-kérdés* [The cartel question] ([Budapest]: [Franklin Ny.], 1928), p. 3; Károly Beivinkler, *A budapesti csatornázási kérdés* [The Budapest sewer question] (Budapest: Rudnyánszky Ny., 1874), p. 16.

135. AT-OeStA/HHStA StK Kongressakten 2, Conférences des Quatre, Séance, December 29, 1814, discussion verbale, p. 1–1v.

136. See, for example, MOL, K64a., 7/a. tétel Cseh kérdés, 448/Res. Pol./1938, p. 97; ibid., 277/Res. Pol./1938, p. 127; ibid. 33/a. tétel Ruszinszkói kérdés, 1938–1939, 1413/Res. Pol./1938, p. 70; ibid., 1352/Res. Pol./1938, p. 19; ibid., 1467/Res. Pol./1938, pp. 141–142 (on working in alliance with Poland); ibid., 236/Res. Pol./1939, p. 250–251; and ibid., K64a., 67/a. tétel Muraközi kérdés, 1942, Muraköz vonatkozó nem Res. Pol. Feljegyzések s másolatok, p. 562.

137. Schlett, *A "munkáskérdés" és a szocializmus a magyar politikai gondolkodásban,* pp. 31–33.

138. Jászi et al., *A nemzetiségi kérdés a társadalmi és az egyéni fejlődés szempontjából,* p. 61.

139. Szombatsági, *A nemzetiségi kérdés Magyarországban,* p. 27.

140. Károly Szini, *Magyar irodalom: Javaslat a magyar kérdés megoldására* [Hungarian literature: Recommendation for solving the Hungarian question] (Pest: Szerző, Trattner-Károlyi Ny., 1866), p. 36.

141. Ibid., pp. 39–40, 43–44.

142. Ibid., p. 40.

143. Ibid., pp. 14–15, 58.

144. Cited in Schlett, *A "munkáskérdés" és a szocializmus a magyar politikai gondolkodásban,* p. 166.

145. Franz Kászonyi, *Rassenverwandtschaft der Donauvölker* [The racial relationship of the Danubian peoples] (Zurich: Amalthea Verlag, 1931), pp. 23–47.

146. Ibid., p. 11.

147. Ibid., p. 270.

148. See Ottó Szabolcs, *Munka nélküli diplomások a Horthy-rendszerben, 1919–1944* [Unemployed college graduates in the Horthy regime, 1919–1944] ([Budapest]: Kossuth Könyvkiadó, 1964).

149. Ágnes Kenyeres and Sándor Bortnyik, *Magyar életrajzi lexikon* [Hungarian biographical dictionary] (Budapest: Akadémiai Kiadó, 1967), http://mek.oszk .hu/00300/00355/html/ABC03975/04062.htm.

150. Ferenc Faluhelyi, *A kisebbségi kérdés eredete és jelentősége általános és magyar szempontból* [The origins and significance of the minority question from the general Hungarian perspective] (Pécs: Taizs József könyvnyomda, 1937), p. 3.

151. Ibid., p. 6. See also István Fenczik, *A kárpátaljai autonomia és a kissebségi kérdés* [The autonomy of the Carpathian Basin and the minority question] (Pécs: Elsö Kecskeméti Hirlapkiadó és Ny. Rt., 1941), p. 3.

152. Huszadik Század, *A zsidókérdés Magyarországon*, p. 48.

153. Rőnyi, *Indokolt programm a magyar kérdés törvényes és praktikus megoldását illetőleg*, p. 5. The text was cited from Goethe's *Faust*, when the character of Mephisto says: "At the point where conceptions are lacking, a word comes to the rescue." *Faust: Eine Tragödie*, p. 19.

154. See Mead and staff, "Russia Signs Agreement"; Engel and Lubin, "Putin Makes Worrying Comments."

155. See Dmytro Dontsov, *Die ukrainische Staatsidee und der Krieg gegen Russland* [The Ukrainian state idea and the war against Russia] (Berlin: C. Kroll, 1915), p. 67; Leon Trotsky, "Problem of the Ukraine," April 22, 1939, https://www.marxists.org /archive/trotsky/1939/04/ukraine.html.

156. Мыхайло Грушевськый, *Освобождение России и украинский вопрос: статьи и заметки* [The liberation of Russia and the Ukrainian question: Articles and notes] (St. Petersburg: Тип.т-ва "Общественная Польза," 1907), p. vi.

157. On the Great War and the Ukrainian question, see AT-OeStA/HHStA SB Nl Flotow 3–7/I, "Die 'ukrainische Frage' in ihrer wahren Gestalt," p. 143; and К. Вышевичъ, *Украинскій вопросъ, Россія и Антанта* [The Ukrainian question, Russia and the Entente] (Helsinki: Гельсингфорская Центральная типографія, 1918).

158. Rosa Luxemburg, "The Nationalities Question," in *The Russian Revolution* (1918), accessed September 27, 2016, https://www.marxists.org/archive/luxem burg/1918/russian-revolution/ch03.htm.

159. Stefan Troebst, "Die 'Wiederkehr der Orientalischen Frage'? Krieg auf dem Balkan" [The return of the Eastern question? War in the Balkans], accessed October 20, 2012, http://www.oeko-net.de/kommune/kommune8-99/TTROEBST.HTM.

160. Winfried Baumgart, "Die 'Orientalische Frage'—redivivus? Große Mächte und kleine Nationalitäten, 1820–1923" [The 'Eastern question' revisited? Great powers and small nationalities, 1820-1923], in *Neue politische Geschichte*, Universität Tel Aviv, Fakultät für Geisteswissenschaften, Forschungszentrum für Geschichte. Hrsg. im Auftr. des Instituts für Deutsche Geschichte von Dan Diner, *Tel Aviver Jahrbuch für deutsche Geschichte*, vol. 28 (1999): 33–55, p. 55.

161. Brown, *International Politics*, p. 7.

162. Tony Barber, "Balkan Turmoil Raises Europe's Second Eastern Question," *Financial Times*, May 13, 2015, http://www.ft.com/intl/cms/s/0/26f1dc1e-f962-11e4 -ae65-00144feab7de.html#axzz3ZqEgMKXP.

163. Rendered in Ottoman as "şark meselesi" or in modern Turkish as "doğu sorunu."

164. See, for example, Haşim Nahid, *Üç muamma: Garp meselesi, Şark Meselesi, Türk meselesi* [Three riddles: The Western question, Eastern question, Turkish question] (Istanbul: Kader Matbaası, 1921); Kahraman Şakul, "Eastern Question," in *Encyclopedia of the Ottoman Empire*, ed. Gábor Ágoston and Bruce Masters (New York: Facts on File, 2009), p. 191; and Selim Deringil, *The Well-protected Domains: Ideology and the Legitimation of Power in the Ottoman Empire, 1876–1909* (London: I. B. Tauris, 2011), p. 6.

165. Hüner Tuncer, *Osmanlı Devleti ve Büyük Güçler, 1815–1878* [The Ottoman state and the Great Powers, 1815-1878] (Istanbul: Kaynak Yayınları, 2009), p. 12.

166. See, for example, Selami Saygın, *Yeni şark meselesi* [The new Eastern question] (Istanbul: Ülke Kitapları, 2003), p. 6; Doğu Ergil, *Doğu sorunu* [The Eastern question] (Istanbul: Akademi Kültür Sanat Yayıncılık, 2008); Kemal Melek, *Doğu Sorunu ve Millî Mücadele'nin Dış Politikası* [The Eastern question and the foreign policy of the national liberation struggle] (Istanbul: Boğaziçi Üniversitesi Yayınları, 1978); and Mehmet Turgut, *"Doğu Sorunu" Raporu Üzerine* [On the 'Eastern question' report] (Istanbul: Boğaziçi Yayınları, 1996).

167. See, for example, "Doğu Anadolu'nun Türklüğü: Kürt meselesi mi şark meselesi mi? . . ." [The Turks of Eastern Anatolia: Kurdish question or Eastern question? . . .], accessed July 23, 2016, http://www.angelfire.com/tn3/tahir/trk26a.html.

168. The Gypsy question has a long history in Hungary. See Albert Fáy, *A vándor- vagy oláh-czigány kérdés* [The nomadic- or Vlach-Gypsy question] ([s.l.]: , [1904]); Móricz Zsigmond, "A mai cigánykérdés," in *Nyugat* [West], no. 7 (1932), accessed July 23, 2016, http://epa.oszk.hu/00000/00022/00534/16638.htm. As with the Eastern question in Turkey, it appears that now—as indeed earlier—it is largely the purview of the Right to speak of a "Gypsy question" in Hungary. Krisztina Morvai, A prominent figure in Hungarian politics and a favorite of the far-right Jobbik party, uses the term. See Krisztina Morvai, "Cigánykérdés" [The Gypsy question], November 3, 2014, http://www.morvaikrisztina.hu/index.php?option=com_content&view =category&layout=blog&id=144&Itemid=334.

169. Sean Curran, "Scottish Referendum: What Is the 'English Question'?" *BBC News*, September 19, 2014, http://www.bbc.com/news/uk-politics-29281818; James Landale, "The Politics of the English Question," *BBC News*, September 19, 2014, http://www.bbc.com/news/uk-politics-29274379; Simon Wilson, "The Catalonian Question," *Money Week*, September 19, 2014, http://moneyweek.com/the -catalonian-question/; "Staatsbesuch des portugiesischen Premiers: Meinungsun-

terschiede über Migrantenfrage" [State visit of the Portuguese premier: Differences of opinion on the migration question], *Luxemburger Wort*, October 22, 2014, http://www.wort.lu/de/photos/staatsbesuch-des-portugiesischen-premiers-meinungs unterschiede-ueber-migrantenfrage-54477f25b9b398870807d7cf; Moritz Böse, "Der DFB und die Migrantenfrage: Kurswechsel aus Überzeugung oder durch (Erwartungs-)Druck?" [The German Soccer League and the migrant question: Change of course out of conviction or under peer pressure?], *Unsere Zeit, sozialistiche Wochenzeitung*, July 10, 2015, http://www.Unsere-Zeit.de/de/4728/vermischtes/368/Der-DFB-und-die-Migrantenfrage.htm; "EU nimmt am UN-Gipfel zur Flüchtlings- und Migrantenfrage sowie an 71. Vollversammlung der Vereinten Nationen teil" [The EU takes part in the UN summit on the refugee and migrant question and in the 71st United Nations plenary session], *Europäische Union Nachrichten*, September 2016, https://europa.eu/newsroom/events/eu-attends-un-summit-refugees-and-migrants-and-71st-united-nations-general-assembly_de.

2. The Progressive Argument: The Age of Emancipation

1. Bruno Bauer, "Die Judenfrage" [The Jewish question], in *Deutsche Jahrbücher für Wissenschaft und Kunst*, no. 274–282 (1842):1119f.

2. Ibid.

3. One member, Edmond Bales, decried Brougham's absence, saying that Poland "is an object deserving of as much sympathy and consideration as the enslaved son of Africa." *Report on the Proceedings of the Seventh Annual General Meeting of the London Literary Association of the Friends of Poland* (London: M. Wilczewski, 1839), pp. 36–7.

4. See Roman Robert Koropeckyj, *Adam Mickiewicz: The Life of a Romantic* (Ithaca, NY: Cornell University Press, 2008), pp. 363–369. Fuller was a journalist who wrote extensively on the women's rights and abolition.

5. In their respective arguments around the Polish question, for example, both the Poles desirous of recovering their state and the partitioning Russians claimed an emancipationist agenda. See the section on the Polish slogan "Za naszą i waszą wolność" (For our freedom and yours), from 1831. For a Russian example, see И. С. Аксаков, *Польский вопрос и западно-Русское дело; Еврейский вопрос, 1860–1886*, Томъ третий [The Polish question and the cause of western Russia; Jewish question, 1860–1886, vol. 3] (St. Petersburg: Издание императорской пыбличной библотеки, 1900) pp. 262–263.

6. See, for example, Yves Guyot, "The Sugar Question in Europe," in *North American Review* 174, no. 542 (January 1902): 85–94, 85; and Albert J. Allom, "The Oyster Question," in *New Zealand Herald* 44, no. 13499 (May 28, 1907): 3.

7. Lambda, *The Great Cotton Question: Where Are the Spoils of the Slave?: Addressed to the Upper and Middle Classes of Great Britain* (Cambridge: Macmillan, 1861), pp. 4–5.

8. See, for example, Suschka, *Tuberkulin-kérdés mai állásáról*; A. Lydtin, *Die Wandlungen in der Tuberkulose-Frage* [Transformations in the tuberculosis question], Deutsche Landwirtschaftliche Tierzucht, no. 3/4 (Leipzig: Schmidt, 1902); Hendrik Willem Middendorp, *La question de la tuberculose devant la Société médicale des Praticiens de Paris, oct. 1902—déc. 1904* [The tuberculosis question before the Medical Society of Practitioners in Paris, Oct. 1902–Dec. 1904] (Paris: A. Maloine, 1905); András Gaál, *Néhány fontosabb tuberculosis-kérdés az újabb kutatások megvilágításában* [Some more important tuberculosis questions in light of the latest research] (Budapest: Egyet Ny., 1933); John Pierrepont Codrington Foster, *The Relationship of the State to the Tuberculosis Question* (Baltimore, MD: Johns Hopkins Hospital, 1906); Philipp Biedert, *Der neueste Stand der Cholera-Frage* [The latest status of the cholera question] (Berlin: Dtsch. Medizinal-Zeitung, 1885); Max von Pettenkofer, *Über den gegenwärtigen Stand der Cholera-Frage und über die nächsten Aufgaben zur weiteren Ergründung ihrer Ursachen* [On the current status of the cholera question and on the upcoming tasks for further establishing its causes] (Munich: Oldenbourg, 1873); Gyula Sgalitzer, *Egy égető kérdés* [A burning question] (Budapest: Singer és Wolfner, 1887) (on cholera); S. H. Scheiber, *A tabes-syphilis kérdés és Virchow állásfoglalása* [The syphilis question and Virchow's position on it] ([s.l.], [1898]); Dr. Viquerat, "Beitrag zur Tuberkulinfrage" [Contribution to the tuberculosis question], in *Centralblatt für Bakteriologie, Parasitenkunde und Infektionskrankheiten* 26, no. 10 (Jena, September 29, 1899): 293–294; Beivinkler, *A budapesti csatornázási kérdés*; Klaudyusz Angerman, *Sprawa kanałowa* [The sewer question] (Rzeszów: Drukarna J. A. Pelara, 1911); Kraus, *A világítási kérdés megítélésére szolgáló új adalékok*; Carl Schwalbe, *Beiträge zur Malaria-Frage* [Contributions to the malaria question] (Berlin: Salle, 1900); Hugo Hollaender, *A malaria-kérdés jelen állása* [The current status of the malaria question] (Budapest: Dobrowsky és Franke, 1902); Gyula Benczúr, *A "rheuma"-kérdés kutatásának perspectivái* [Research perspectives of the rheumatism question] (Budapest: Egyet. Ny., 1928); László Székely, *Az appendicitis-kérdés mai állása* [The current status of the appendicitis question] (Sárospatak: Fischer, [1931]); László Miltényi, *A mutáció-kérdés jelenlegi állása: összefoglaló ismertetés* [The current status of the mutation question: Summary description] (Debrecen: Debreceni Szemle, 1933); [Imre Zárday], *A vérnyomás-kérdés mai állása* [The current state of the blood pressure question] ([Budapest]: Athenaeum Ny., 1935); Béla Katona, *Javaslatok a rokkant-kérdés megoldására* [Recommendations for solving the cripple question] (Budapest: Benkő Gyula, 1915); László Fényes, *A társadalom és a nemi kérdés* [Society and the sex question] (Budapest: Molnárok Lapja Ny., 1907); Ágoston Forel, *A nemi kérdés: Természettudományi, lélektani és egészségtani tanulmány a jövendő fontos*

szociális feladatainak megoldási kísérleteivel [The sex question: A scientific, psychological, and health study on trying to solve the important social tasks of the future] (Budapest: Vass, Markovits—Garai Ny., 1907); Tibor Verebély, *A nemiség mint sebészi kérdés* [Sexuality as a surgical question] (Budapest: Stephaneum Ny., 1933).

9. See Gerhard Joseph, *John Barth* (Minneapolis: University of Minnesota Press, 1970), p. 15; Bernhard ten Brink, *Five Lectures on Shakespeare* (New York: H. Holt, 1895), p. 9; Karl Bleibtreu, *Die Lösung der Shakespeare-Frage: eine neue Theorie* [The solution to the Shakespeare question: A new theory] (Leipzig: Theod. Thomas, 1909); Bruno Eelbo, *Bacons entdeckte Urkunden: Die Lösung der Bacon-Shakespeare-Frage in der Shakespeare-Folio-Ausgabe vom Jahre 1623* [The discovered documents of Bacon: Solution to the Bacon-Shakespeare question in the Shakespeare folio edition from the year 1623] (Leipzig, 1914); Ottó Hóman, *A homéri kérdés jelenlegi állása* [The current status of the Homer question] ([Budapest]: [Franklin Ny.], [1872]); Ferenc Zsigmond, *Az Ady-kérdés története idézetekben* [The history of the Ady question in quotes] (Mezőtúr: Török, 1928); Vilmos Tolnai, *A Madách-"kérdés" körül* [Around the Madách question] (Budapest: Franklin Ny., 1934); Győri, *A Toldi-kérdés*, p. 3.

10. Szabó, *A fogtechnikus kérdés*, p. 1; Murray Raybin, "Morris High School and the Dental Question," in *Journal of the American Dental Association* 22, no. 3 (1922): 504–509, 504.

11. Adam Czartoryski, *Essai sur la diplomatie, manuscrit d'un philhellène: publié par M. Toulouzan* [Essay on diplomacy, manuscript of a philohellenist, published by M. Toulouzan] (Paris: F. Didot, 1830); Czartoryski, *Essai sur la diplomatie, par le prince Adam Czartoryski* [Essay on diplomacy, by Prince Adam Czartoryski] (Paris: Amyot, 1864). On when it was written (1823), see ibid., p. ii.

12. After the failure of the uprising, he was forced into exile. In Britain he was responsible for the creation of the Literary Association of the Friends of Poland. He spent most of the rest of his life in France, where he died in 1861.

13. The form of Czartoryski's argument is likely as significant as its context, for this strategy of juxtaposition was common among religious reformers of the Central European pre-Reformation, who juxtaposed images and descriptions of the Roman Church next to those of the primitive church in order to demonstrate the former's deviation from the latter's teachings. See Howard Kaminsky, Dean Loy Bilderback, Imre Boba, Patricia N. Rosenberg, and Nicholas of Dresden, "Master Nicholas of Dresden: The Old Color and the New: Selected Works Contrasting the Primitive Church and the Roman Church," in *Transactions of the American Philosophical Society*, n.s., 55, no. 1 (1965), pp. 1–93.

14. Czartoryski, *Essai sur la diplomatie, manuscrit d'un philhellène*, pp. 23, 418–419.

15. Ibid., p. 157.

16. Ibid., pp. iv, 83, 86, 87, 89, 94.

17. Ibid., p. 94.

18. Translation in *Courier* (London), December 13, 1830, p. 2. (Also in *Morning Chronicle* [London], December 14, 1830, p. 1, and *London Morning Post*, December 14, 1830, p. 4.)

19. *London Standard*, January 24, 1831, p. 3.

20. Maria Weston Chapman, *Right and Wrong in Massachusetts* (Boston: Dow & Jackson's Anti-Slavery Press, 1839), pp. 153–154.

21. Vladimir Jovanović, *Srbski narod i istočno pitanje* [The Serbian nation and the Eastern question] (Belgrade: Državna štamparija, 1863), p. 1.

22. Comte de Montalembert, *L'Insurrection Polonaise* [The Polish insurrection] (Paris: E. Dentu, Libraire-Éditeur Palais-Royal, 1863), p. 19. See also C. Damotte, *Solution mexicaine: question polonaise, union européenne* [The Mexican solution: The Polish question and the union of Europe] (Tonnerre: impr. de Hérisé, 1863), pages unnumbered.

23. W. E. Gladstone, *Bulgarian Horrors and the Question of the East* (London: John Murray, 1876), p. 46.

24. Leonhard Weydmann, *Die Fragen unserer bewegten Zeit im Lichte des Evangeliums und mit beständiger Rücksicht auf die Urtheile der Reformatoren betrachtet* [The questions of our tumultuous time in light of the Gospel and with constant consideration for the judgments of the Reformers] (Frankfurt am Main: Heinr. Ludw. Brönner Verlag, 1834), pp. 1–2.

25. Thomas Carlyle, "Occasional Discourse on the Negro Question," in *Fraser's Magazine for Town and Country* 40 (1849), p. 671.

26. John Stuart Mill, "The Negro Question," in *Essays on Equality, Law, and Education* (Toronto: University of Toronto Press, 1984), http://oll.libertyfund.org/titles /mill-the-collected-works-of-john-stuart-mill-volume-xxi-essays-on-equality-law -and-education/simple.

27. Giuseppe Mazzini, *La questione italiana e i repubblicani* [The Italian question and the republicans] (Milan: Tipografia di Angelo Ciminago, 1861), pp. 5–7.

28. Adolf Hitler, Heinrich Heim, and Werner Jochmann, *Adolf Hitler: Monologe im Führerhauptquartier, 1941–1944: Die Aufzeichnungen Heinrich Heims* [Adolf Hitler: Monologues in the main residence of the Führer, 1941–1944: The notes of Heinrich Heim] (Hamburg: A. Knaus, 1980), p. 122.

29. See, for example, AT-OeStA/HHStA StK Kongressakten 2, Protocoles des Conféerences séparées, appelées des quatre, Séance du December 29, 1814, p. 2v.

30. For example, in a letter from the German statesman Ernst Friedrich Herbert von Münster addressed to Hans Christoph Ernst von Gagern: "The Polish question is very important for Germany," in von Gagern, *Mein Antheil und der Politik*, p. 46; and in a report on a conversation with an unnamed "Russian gentleman": "Yet from then on, switching to the politics of the moment, he gave me to understand that it

was necessary to explain the Polish question in terms of the character, education, and manner of the Emperor Alexander," in ibid., p. 75.

31. See, for example, the letter from December 31, 1823 from Stratford Canning to the British minister at Madrid, cited in Henry Mann, *The Land We Live In; or, The Story of Our Country* (New York: The Christian Herald, 1896), p. 243n.

32. *Hansard Parliamentary Debates*, 1st series (1803–1820), p. 1197.

33. See, for example, *The Times* (London), Nov 21, 1823, p. 2; Mar 18, 1824, p. 2; May 14, 1824, p. 2; and others. See also *The West India Question, Practically Considered* (London: John Murray, 1826). The pamphlet comes close to mentioning the slavery question ("the question of slavery," see p. 45), but stops just short. See also chapter 1, pp. 241–242, note 32.

34. T. S. Winn, *A Speedy End to Slavery in Our West India Colonies: By Safe, Effectual, and Equitable Means for the Benefit of All Parties Concerned* (London: Sold by W. Phillips, 1825), p. 98.

35. Ibid., p. 99.

36. A prime example is the Polish question, which truly took off in the 1830s, though there were a handful of sporadic mentions of it prior to that. The oldest I have found are from the run-up to the Congress of Vienna. See, for example, TNA, FO 417/1, Negotiations respecting Poland Correspondence, pp. 14, 48–49 (the Saxon question is also mentioned on p. 49); "Fair Draft Memorandum—Instructions for the Duke of Wellington, September 14, 1822," in *Despatches, Correspondence, and Memoranda of Field Marshal Arthur Duke of Wellington*, vol. 1 (London: John Murray, Albemarle Street, 1867), p. 285; TNA, FO 139/22, Count Nesselrode, Count Stackelberg, etc., Russia. Vienna, "Memorial" on the proposed annexation of the Dutchy of Warsaw to Russia, September 1814–September 1815, p. 125v; Gagern, *Mein Antheil and der Politik*, p. 46; ibid., p. 75; Poland, *Constitutional Charter of the Kingdom of Poland, in the Year 1815 with Some Remarks on the Manner in Which the Charter, and the Stipulations in the Treaties Relating to Poland, Have Been Observed* (London: J. Ridgway, 1831), p. 49; *Allemannia: für Recht u. Wahrheit [Allemannia: For law and truth]*, vol. 5 (1816), p. 146; and Christophe-Guillaume Koch and Frédéric Schoell, eds., *Histoire abrégée des traités de paix, entre les puissances de l'Europe depuis la paix de Westphalie* [Abridged history of the peace treaties between the powers of Europe since the peace of Westphalia], vol. 11 (Paris: Gide Fils, 1818), p. 621. The publicistic deluge around the question did not begin until 1829–1831. See, for example, *Un mot sur la question polonaise en 1829*; and *Ueber die polnische Frage*.

37. The first reference I have found to the "question algérienne" is from 1832, in L.-P. Brun d' Aubignosc, *La Haute Police, ou Police d'État sous le régime constitutionnel: Son application spéciale aux départemens de l'ouest et du midi de la France, et à la nouvelle possession d'Alger* [The high police, or state police under the constitutional regime:

It's particular deployment in the departments in the west and south of France, and in the new possession in Algeria] (Paris: Ferra, 1832), pp. 133, 139.

38. Ivon Asquith, "The Structure, Ownership and Control of the press, 1780–1855," in *Newspaper History from the Seventeenth Century to the Present Day*, ed. George Boyce, James Curran, and Pauline Wingate (London: Constable, 1978), p. 111.

39. Stephen Koss, *The Rise and Fall of the Political Press in Britain*, vol. 1, *The Nineteenth Century* (London: Hamish Hamilton, 1981), pp. 51–52. The stamp tax was significantly reduced from four pence to a penny in 1836 but not entirely repealed until 1855.

40. The claim of hypocrisy in international intervention played a role in how discussion of the Polish question relates to the events in France, for it was the Bonapartist general Lamarque's funeral that was the occasion for the outbreak of the June rebellion in Paris, not least of all because the general had been a vocal critic of the French state's failure to mobilize in support of the Polish November Uprising.

41. On the Greek revolt and international public opinion, see Oliver Schulz, *Ein Sieg der zivilisierten Welt?: Die Intervention der europäischen Großmächte im griechischen Unabhängigkeitskrieg, 1826–1832* [A victory for the civilized world? The intervention of the European Great Powers in the Greek War of Independence, 1826–1832] (Munster: LIT, 2011), pp. 235–252.

42. de Tocqueville, *Oeuvres complètes*, vol. 3, pt. 2, p. 282. For more on the significance of the Eastern question in the nineteenth century, see Baumgart, "Die 'Orientalische Frage'—redivivus?," pp. 33–55, 35; Dostoyevsky, "Diplomacy Facing World Problems," in *A Writer's Diary*, vol. 2, p. 995. It should be noted that the Greek revolt, though it inspired public opinion and ultimately won the favor and support of the Great Powers, was only part of the reason why the Eastern question became so important and so hotly discussed in the 1830s. Likely the more significant events of the time for turning the attention of statesmen to think in terms of the Eastern question was the near collapse of the Ottoman Empire resulting from the Mehmet Ali crisis, which led to Great Power intervention to prevent the Ottoman Empire's demise.

43. G. W. F. Hegel and Leo Rauch, *Introduction to The Philosophy of History* (Indianapolis: Hackett, 1988), p. 38. In a much later attempt to identify the forces moving history, Reinhart Koselleck argued that "[i]t is the tension between experience and expectation that provokes new solutions in different ways and thus drives historical time forward." Koselleck, " 'Erfahrungsraum' und 'Erwartungshorizont' " ['Space of experience' and 'horizon of expectation'], in *Vergangene Zukunft: zur Semantik geschichtlicher Zeiten* (Frankfurt am Main: Suhrkamp, 2000), p. 358.

44. Hans von Scheel, *Die Theorie der sozialen Frage* [The theory of the social question] (Jena: F. Mauke, 1871), p. 8.

45. Ibid., pp. 15–16.

46. Amicis, "Úvahy o socialné otázce," pp. 8–13, 10–12.

47. Gustav Müller, *Die einzig mögliche und wahre Lösung der sozialen Frage: Ein Lichtblick in dem wirren Getümmel der Welt in der Gegenwart* [The only possible and true solution of the social question: A ray of hope in the confused tumult of today's world] (Leipzig: Verlag von Max Spohr, 1894), p. 7.

48. Joseph Biederlack, *Die sociale Frage: Ein Beitrag zur Orientierung über ihr Wesen und ihre Lösung* [The social question: A contribution toward orientation regarding its essence and solution] (Innsbruck: F. Rauch, 1921), pp. iii, 1.

49. Ludwig Stein, *Die soziale Frage im Lichte der Philosophie, Vorlesungen über Sozialphilosophie und ihre Geschichte* [The social question in the light of philosophy, lectures on social philosophy and its history] (Stuttgart: Ferd. Enke, 1897), p. 466.

50. "The social question is thus now and forever more the question of *establishing harmony in the integral life* [*Gesammmtleben*] *of the people.*" (Italics in the original.) Ernst Becher, *Die Arbeiterfrage in ihrer gegenwärtigen Gestaltung und die Versuche zu ihrer Lösung* [The worker question in its present form and attempts to solve it] (Pest: A. Hartleben's Verlag, 1868), pp. 2–3.

51. On the Enlightenment origins of the idea of the "new man," see Yinghong Cheng, *Creating the "New Man": From Enlightenment Ideals to Socialist Realities* (Honolulu: University of Hawai'i Press, 2009), pp. 8–11.

52. Victor Hugo, "William Shakespeare," in *Oeuvres complètes de Victor Hugo, philosophie* [*Complete works of Victor Hugo, philosophy*], vol. 2 (Paris: Albin Michel, 1937), p. 173.

53. Victor Hugo, "Post-scriptum de ma vie," in *Oeuvres complètes*, vol. 2, p. 534.

54. George Batchelor, *Social Equilibrium and Other Problems Ethical and Religious* (Boston: G. H. Ellis, 1887), p. 17. On Batchelor, see "Rev. George Batchelor," in *Cambridge Tribune* 46, no. 17 (June 23, 1923), p. 5.

55. Batchelor, *Social Equilibrium*, p. 6.

56. Rev. George Jamieson, *The Education-Question, Philosophically and Practically Considered, in its bearing upon Individual Development and Social Improvement; in a Letter to His Grace the Duke of Argyll, &c. &c.* (Aberdeen: John Smith, 1854), pp. 10, 42 (italics in the original).

57. Léon Deschamps, *Histoire de la question coloniale en France* [History of the colonial question in France] (Paris: E. Plon, Nouritt, 1891), p. 388.

58. Henri de Tourville, "Preface to the French Edition," in Paul de Rousiers, *The Labour Question in Britain* (London: Macmillan, 1896), pp. xi, xiii.

59. Lajos Fodor and Oszkár Jászi, *A társadalmi kérdés lényege* (Budapest: Benkő, 1912), p. 13.

60. John A. Ryan and R. A. McGowan, *A Catechism of the Social Question* (New York: Paulist Press, 1921), p. 46.

61. See, for example, W. Huskisson, *The Question concerning the Depreciation of our*

Currency stated and examined (London, 1810), ii; John Sinclair, *Remarks on a Pamphlet Intitled, "The Question Concerning the Depreciation of the Currency Stated and Examined" by William Huskisson, Esq., M.P. Together with Several Political Maxims Regarding Coin and Paper Currency, Intended to Explain the Real Nature, and Advantages, of the Present System* (London, 1810), pp. 24–25.

62. M. Courtin, ed., *Encyclopédie Moderne ou Dictionnaire Abrégé des Sciences, des Lettres et des Arts* [Modern encyclopedia, or abridged dictionary of the sciences, letters, and arts], vol. 23 (Paris, 1831), 275.

63. Adolphe Thiers, "Rede in der National-Versammlung, am 13. September 1848," [Speech in the National Assembly on September 13, 1848] in Adolphe Thiers and Louis Blanc, *Louis Blanc und Thiers über die sociale frage . . . Aus dem französischen* [Louis Blanc and Thiers on the social question . . . from the French] (Breslau, 1849), pp. 7–8.

64. In Thiers and Blanc, *Louis Blanc und Thiers über die sociale frage*, iii.

65. Karl Biedermann, *Frauen-Brevier: kulturgeschichtliche Vorlesungen* [Women's breviary: Lectures in cultural history] (Leipzig, 1856), 334.

66. von Scheel, *Die Theorie der sozialen Frage*, 1.

67. See chapter 1, note 36.

68. Biederlack, *Die sociale Frage*, p. iii.

69. Ryan and McGowan, *A Catechism*, 4.

70. J. A. Hobson, *The Social Problem: Life and Work* (London: J. Nisbet, 1901), p. 91.

71. Ibid., pp. 298–299.

72. Eckart Pankoke, *Sociale Bewegung, sociale Frage, sociale Politik; Grundfragen der deutschen Socialwissenschaft im 19. Jahrhundert* [Social movement, social question, social policy: Fundamental questions of German social science in the nineteenth century] (Stuttgart: E. Klett, 1970), p. 49f.

73. Heinrich Heine, *Lutetia*, I. Teil [Lutetia, part one], article 30, Paris, January 31, 1841, http://www.heinrich-heine-denkmal.de/heine-texte/lutetia30.shtml.

74. See Heinrich Heine, "Zum Lazarus," in *Heinrich Heines Sämtliche Werke*, vol. 4 (Philadelphia: Verlag von John Weik, 1856), p. 321.

75. Ibid.

76. See Isaiah Berlin, *The Hedgehog and the Fox: An Essay on Tolstoy's View of History* (Princeton, NJ: Princeton University Press, 2013), p. 13f; Николай Гаврилович Чернышевский, *Что дѣлать?* [What is to be done?] (Vevey: B. Benda, libraire-éditeur, 1867), written in 1863; Лев Толстой, *Так что же нам делат?; Исповедь* [What then shall we do? A confession] (Moscow: Либроком, 2009), written in 1886; and Владимир Ильич Ленин, *Что дѣлать? наболевшіе вопросы нашего движенія* [What is to be done? Burning questions of our movement] (Stuttgart: Verlag von J.H.W. Dietz, 1902), written in 1901.

77. A pamphlet from 1895 published in London in Russian and titled *The Vital Question* actually posed a series of real questions about bringing the ideals of social-

ism into the real world. See А. И. Богданович, *Насущный вопросъ* [The vital question] (London: Russian Free Press Fund, 1895), pp. 6–7.

78. The subtitle of the novel, in fact, was *"Из рассказов о новых людях"* (From stories about the new people). Николай Гаврилович Чернышевский, *Что делать? Из рассказов о новых людях* [What is to be done? From stories about the new people] (Leipzig: Новое Изд., 1863).

79. György Lukács, *Zur Ontologie des gesellschaftlichen Seins; Hegels falsche und echte Ontologie*, 2. Halbband [Ontology of social being: Hegel's false and his genuine ontology, second half-volume] (Darmstadt u. Neuwied: Luchterhand, 1986), pp. 398–399.

80. Ibid., p. 415.

81. In the original, these are rendered as: "schlechte Unendlichkeit von isolierten Einzelfragen" and "Tendenz zur Verallgemeinerung."

82. Lukács, *Zur Ontologie des gesellschaftlichen Seins*, p. 455.

83. Ibid., p. 453.

84. Marx, "On The Jewish Question." The idea is present in a more general form already in Hegel in his lectures on the philosophy of history from the 1820s. "If we think of Reason in its relation to the world, then the question of the *definition* of Reason in itself coincides with the question about the *final goal* of the world." (Emphasis in the original.) Hegel and Rauch, *Introduction to The Philosophy of History*, p. 19.

85. Karl Marx, "Vorwort," *Zur Kritik der Politischen Ökonomie* [Preface, Critique of political economy], accessed August 16, 2017, http://www.mlwerke.de/me/me13/me13_007.htm.

86. Hobson, *The Social Problem*, pp. 3–5.

87. Század, *A zsidókérdés Magyarországon*, p. 154.

88. Ibid., p. 152.

89. Querists were also eager to see questions settled and to declare victory. Already in 1840, for example, the liberal French historian and statesman François Guizot told the Chamber of Deputies that he considered the Belgian and Italian questions solved. "Deputiertenkammersitzung, November 25, 1840" [Session of the chamber of deputies, November 25, 1840], from *Der Adler*, December 5, 1840, p. 2315–6.

90. "The Polish question has been solved," declared an internal US report from June 4, 1918, on conditions in Austria and Germany. National Archives and Records Administration, Washington, DC [NARA], Record Group 59, General Records of the Department of State, 1763–2002, Central Decimal Files, 1910–1963, File Unit 763.72/9001: April 30–June 11, 1918, June 4, 1918, p. 15.

91. In 1930, Stalin declared the "woman question" solved. Philip Ross Bullock, *The Feminine in the Prose of Andrey Platonov* (London: Legenda, 2005), p. 101.

92. See, for example, R. F. Ivanov, *American History and the Black Question*

(Moscow: Novosti Press Agency, 1976); Bob McCubbin, *The Gay Question: A Marxist Appraisal* (New York: World View, 1976); Bay Area Communist Union, *The Gay Question* ([San Francisco?]: [Bay Area Communist Union], 1973); and Adela Barungi, *The Environmental Question in Global Economics: The African Story* (Kampala, Uganda: African Research and Documentation Centre, Uganda Martyrs University, 1999).

93. See, for example, AT-OeStA/HHStA PA XVIII 49, "Judenfrage und Anerkennung Rumäniens" [The Jewish question and the recognition of Romania] 1879, Graf Hoyos an Graf Andrassy, July 9, 1879, p. 366v.

94. See Dr. Edmund Wengraf, "Zur Anschlussfrage. Die Preisausschreibung der 'Concordia'" [On the annexation question: Prize competition of the 'Concordia'], *Neues Wiener Journal*, no. 12/191 (November 1, 1927), in AT-OeStA/HHStA SB, Nachlass Rudolf Wolkan, Mappe I, p. 98.

95. See APA Nachrichtenagentur, "ÖVP Wien-Parteitag 11: Blümel: Die soziale Frage unserer Zeit ist die Ausbeutung des Mittelstandes," accessed September 28, 2016, http://www.ots.at/presseaussendung/OTS_20160402_OTS0038/oevp-wien-parteitag-11-bluemel-die-soziale-frage-unserer-zeit-ist-die-ausbeutung-des-mittelstandes. Even on the left, there is controversy over what the social question should mean now. See Walter Ötsch, "Die soziale Frage: Individuell, völkisch, kollektiv?" [The social question: Individual, folkish, collective?] in *Der Standard*, accessed August 14, 2017, http://derstandard.at/2000062318319/Die-soziale-Frage-individuell-voelkisch-kollektiv.

96. Félix Guattari, "La question des questions" [The question of questions] in *Terminal*, no. 56 (February–March 1992): 8–9. Special thanks to Danilo Scholz for drawing my attention to this text.

3. The Argument about Force: The Loaded Questions of a Genocidal Age

1. Dostoyevsky, "Never Has Russia Been as Powerful as Now," p. 1002.

2. Emmerich Czermak and Oskar Karbach, *Ordnung in der Judenfrage* [Order in the Jewish question] (Vienna: Reinhold Verlag, 1934), p. 5 (italics in original).

3. The word "progressive" is hardly the most apt to describe many queristic interventions. See, for example, Weydmann, *Die Fragen*; Dr. Antonio Górski, *Sprawa mieszkań oraz uwagi towarzystwa właścicieli realności z powodu reformy podatku od domów* [The housing question and the concern of the Property Owners' Association about the tax reform on houses] (Kraków: Czcionkami Drukarni "Czasu," 1903), incidentally published by the Conservative Club; Sándor Csia, *A nemi kérdés orvosi s bibliai szempontból* [The sex question from the medical and biblical standpoint] (Budapest: Bethánia, [1912]); L. von der Decken, *Die Geschlechtsfrage und die neue*

Zeit [The sex question and the new era] (Nowawes: Buchhandlung des Weissen Kreuzes, 1921); Ferencz Kiss, *A szekszuális kérdés* [The sex question] (Budapest: Magyar Evang. Ker. Diákszövetség, Ábrahám és Sugár Ny., 1935).

4. Emil Hammacher, *Hauptfragen der Modernen Kultur* [The main questions of modern culture] (Leipzig: B. E. Teubner Verlag, 1914), p. 3.

5. Ibid.

6. Ibid., p. iv.

7. Czartoryski, *Essai sur la diplomatie, manuscrit d'un philhellène*, p. 157.

8. Hammacher, *Hauptfragen der Modernen Kultur*, p. 6.

9. And indeed he himself saw the "task of modern culture" to be to recognize "the most effective result of all previous attempts at solution" yielding "a new idealism." Ibid., pp. 37–38.

10. Thomas Mann, *Betrachtungen eines Unpolitischen* [*Reflections of a Nonpolitical Man*] (Berlin: S. Fischer Verlag, 1920), p. 223.

11. Karl Marx and Frederick Engels, *The Russian Menace to Europe: A Collection of Articles, Speeches, Letters, and News Despatches [by] Karl Marx and Friedrich Engels*, ed. Paul Blackstock and Bert Hoselitz (London: George Allen and Unwin, 1953), p. 122; Marx and Engels, *A Few Words on the Eastern Question* (London: James Ridgway, 1860), pp. 39, 55–56.

12. Eötvös, *A nemzetiségi kérdés*, p. 59.

13. Austen Henry Layard, *The Turkish Question. Speeches Delivered in the House of Commons on Aug. 16, 1853, Feb. 17, and March 31, 1854* (London: John Murray, 1854), p. 13.

14. David Bennett King, *The Irish Question* (London: W. H. Allen, 1882), p. vii.

15. Cited in Carl E. Schorske, *Fin-de-siècle Vienna: Politics and Culture* (New York: Vintage, 1981), p. 164.

16. Suschka, *Tuberkulin-kérdés mai állásáról*, p. 2. On Suschka, see *Hof- und Staats-Handbuch der Österreichisch-Ungarischen Monarchie für das Jahr 1906* [Court- and State Handbook of the Austro-Hungarian Monarchy for the year 1906], vol. 32 (Vienna: Druck und Verlag der k.k. Hof- und Staatsdruckerei, 1906), p. 1007.

17. Writing on the woman question in 1902, the Hungarian pedagogue Imre Neményi noted that it was "constantly debated, already addressed with every imaginable solution, and yet still awaiting its final solution." Neményi, *A nő-kérdés a múltban és a jelenben* [The woman question in the past and present] (Budapest: Hornyánszky Ny., 1902), p. 8. A British government overview of the sugar question from 1903 referred to it as "this hitherto insoluble problem." TNA, CUST 155/19, Sugar duty: "The Sugar Question," p. 5. In 1910, Mrs. Henrik Wüsztner sought to address the maid question in a work appropriately titled *The Eternal Question* (*Az örök kérdés*). The more we concern ourselves with it, she lamented, the more difficulties appeared in the way of its solution. Wüsztner, *Az örök kérdés* [The etermal question] (Budapest:

Stephaneum Ny., [1910]), p. 3; "What if," wrote the writer Lajos Bíró in 1916, "the Jewish question is among those for which there is no solution?" Bíró was quick to add that he thought there was one, even if it were two hundred years off in the future. Huszadik Század, *A zsidókérdés Magyarországon*, p. 55.

18. Just after the war, for example, Bulgarian diplomats wondered how Woodrow Wilson was going to address the unresolved Turkish, Thracian, and Fiume questions. Tsentralen Dŭrzhaven Arkhiv, Sofia (hereafter cited as TsDA), Ministerstvo na Vŭnshnite Raboti i Izpovedaniiata (hereafter cited as MVRI), f. 176K, op. 6, a.e. 63, March 1920, s. 56v.

19. Oswald Spengler, *Der Untergang des Abendlandes: Umrisse einer Morphologie* [The decline of the West: Form and actuality], vol. 1 (Vienna: Wilhelm Braumüller, 1918), p. 34; emphasis in the original.

20. Jászi et al., *A nemzetiségi kérdés a társadalmi és az egyéni fejlődés szempontjából*, p. 70.

21. Ibid., p. 61.

22. Mihály Réz and Oszkár Jászi, *A nemzetiségi kérdés a politikai tudomány szempontjából* [The nationality question from the standpoint of political science] ([Budapest]: [Új Magyarország, Világosság Ny.], [1918]), p. 14.

23. Ibid., pp. 16–17.

24. Ibid., p. 21.

25. Ibid., p. 29.

26. Ibid., pp. 14, 29.

27. Czartoryski, *Essai sur la diplomatie, manuscrit d'un philhellène*, pp. 412–414n. See also Marian Kukiel, *Czartoryski and European Unity, 1770–1861* (Princeton, NJ: Princeton University Press, 1955), p. 156.

28. From *Foreign Quarterly Review* 7 (January and April 1831), p. 527.

29. Here he referred explicitly to a faction of Polish patriots, whom he called the "Arimanes of modern liberty," and French "ultra-liberals." The Napoleonic Wars weighed heavily on such discussions.

30. The text of Chaadayev's manuscript was published (in the original French) with an introduction in English in Julia Brun-Zejmis, " 'A Word on the Polish Question' by P. Ya. Chaadaev," in *California Slavic Studies* 9, ed. Nicholas Valentine Riasanovsky, Gleb Struve, Thomas Eekman (Berkeley: University of California Press, 1980): 25–32, 27.

31. Ibid., p. 29.

32. Pyotr Chaadayev, "Un mot sur la question polonaise" [A word on the Polish question], in Ibid., p. 31. This competition is evident from the overlapping visions of Adam Czartoryski (in his 1830 *Essai sur la diplomatie*) and the Decembrist Pavel Pestel (in his1824 *Русская Правда* [Russkaia Pravda]). See M. K. Dziewanowski, "Czartoryski and his *Essai sur la diplomatie*," in *Slavic Review* 30, no. 3 (September 1971): 589–605, 595.

33. Nikolai Iakovlevich Danilevskii and Stephen M. Woodburn, *Russia and Europe: The Slavic World's Political and Cultural Relations with the Germanic-Roman West* (Bloomington, IN: Slavica, 2013), p. 332.

34. See, for example, İpek Yosmaoğlu, *Blood Ties: Religion, Violence, and the Politics of Nationhood in Ottoman Macedonia, 1878–1908* (Ithaca, NY: Cornell University Press, 2014), pp. 209–288. One might also argue that the Kansas question took on similar dimensions, as pro-slavery activists cast their violent raids as part of an effort to "liberate" the territory from abolitionist ambitions, even as abolitionist groups used the language of emancipation to justify violence against proslavery settlers. In the words of the US senator Charles Sumner to the US Senate from March 13, 1856, the Kansas question was one "under which the country already shakes from side to side, and which threatens to scatter from its folds civil war." See, for example, James Ford Rhodes, *History of the United States from the Compromise of 1850*, vol. 2, *1854-1860* (New York: Macmillan, 1902), p. 126.

35. *The London Standard*, January 24, 1831, p. 3.

36. See, for example, "Arnold Ruge gegen den Anschluß Posens 1848" [Arnold Ruge against the annexation of Posen/Poznań] in *Politische Reden I: 1792–1867*, ed. Peter Wende and Inge Schlotzhauer (Frankfurt am Main: Deutscher Klassiker Verlag, 1990), p. 361; André Chéradame, "La question polonaise et l'equilibre européen, lettre ouverte à Henryk Sienkiewicz" [The Polish question and European equilibrium, open letter of Henryk Sienkiewicz], in *Le Petit Journal* (February 2, 1910), p. 1; M. Kranz, *Neu-Polen* [New-Poland] (Munich: J. F. Lehmanns Verlag, [1915]), p. 53; and Elias Regnault, *La question européenne improprement appelée polonaise: réponse aux objections présentées par MM. Pogodine, Schédo-Ferroti, Porochine, Schnitzler, Solowiew, etc., contre le polonisme des provinces lithuano-ruthènes et contre le non-slavisme des Moscovites* [The European question inappropriately called the Polish question: Response to the objections presented by Pogodine, Schédo-Ferroti, Prochine, Schnitzler, Solowiew, etc., against the Polishness of the Lithuanian-Ruthenian provinces and against the non-Slavic character of the Muscovites] (Paris: E. Dentu, 1863). Nor was this true of the Polish question alone. Many other questions were discussed in this manner. See, for example, Александар Белић, *Србија и jужнословенско питање* [Serbia and the south Slavic question] (Niš: Државна штампарија Краљевине Србије, 1915), pp. 7, 99.

37. "The Polish question keeps coming back, presenting the same difficulties for as long as it is not solved with the independence of the nation." *Die Wiederherstellung Polens oder ein allgemeiner europäischer Krieg, von einem polnischen Diplomaten* [The resurrection of Poland or a general European war, from a Polish diplomat] (Nuremberg: Joh. Leonh. Schrag, 1831), p. 17.

38. Lucien de Saint-Firmin, *La question polonaise, par Lucien de St. Firmin, étudiant en Droit* [The Polish question, by Lucien de St. Firmin, student of law] (Paris: H. Fourniér, 1831), p. 9. It may be worth noting that Saint-Firmin also wrote an earlier

pamphlet on "serious questions" of the day the year before (1830), which may offer some clues as to how questions emerged, especially as the ones discussed in the pamphlet are unlike those that came to define the nineteenth century and of a markedly noninternational and ephemeral nature: "Should the Chamber be immediately dissolved? Or should it, by passing a provisional electoral law, fill the voids that exist within it?" See Lucien de Saint-Firmin, *Un mot sur de graves questions, par L. St.-Firmin* [A word on serious questions, by L. St. Firmin] (Paris: Impr. de David, 1830), p. 2.

39. Carl von Clausewitz, "Die Verhältnisse Europas seit der Teilung Polens (1831)" [European relations since the partition of Poland (1831)," in *Carl von Clausewitz: Geist und Tat; das Vermächtnis des Soldaten und Denkers. In Auswahl aus Seinen Werken, Briefen und unveröffentlichten Schriften* [Carl von Clausewitz: Spirit and action, the legacy of the soldier and thinker, in a selection of his works, letters, and unpublished writings] (Stuttgart: A. Kröner, 1941), p. 218. Ironically, given the content of the above passage, von Clausewitz died in 1831 while trying to contain a cholera epidemic at the Polish frontier, the result of the conditions created by the November Uprising. It is worth noting that this piece was not published until later. He submitted another piece he wrote at around the same time, *Reduction of the Many Political Questions Occupying Germany to the Basic Question of Our Existence*, to the *Ausburger Allgemeine Zeitung*, but it was rejected. The rejection, suggests Peter Paret in an article published in 1970, was likely the result of the fact that this perspective (that intervention could be done for one's own sake rather than others) was foreign to the liberal press of the time. Certainly it became a central feature of publicistic intervention on questions very quickly. See Peter Paret, "An Anonymous Letter by Clausewitz on the Polish Insurrection of 1830–1831," in *Journal of Modern History* 42, no. 2 (June 1970): 184–190, 185.

40. TNA, FO 139/22, Count Nesselrode, Count Stackelberg, etc., Russia. Vienna, "Memorial" on the proposed annexation of the Dutchy of Warsaw to Russia, September 1814–September 1815, p. 125v.

41. *Ueber die polnische Frage*, p. 32. Many were the claims across the lifespan of the Polish question, for example, that it was not merely about Poland but indeed a "European question" with the capacity to make or break the peace of Europe. See, for example, "Arnold Ruge gegen den Anschluß Posens 1848," in *Politische Reden I: 1792–1867*, ed. Peter Wende and Inge Schlotzhauer (Frankfurt am Main: Deutscher Klassiker Verlag, 1990), p. 361; Chéradame, "La question polonaise," p. 1; Kranz, *Neu-Polen*, p. 53; and Regnault, *La question européenne*. A pamphlet from 1831, written by a "Polish diplomat," makes the connection between his preferred solution and war explicit in the very title, *The Recreation of Poland or a General European War*. "The Polish question keeps coming back, presenting the same difficulties for as long as it

is not solved with the independence of the nation." *Die Wiederherstellung Polens oder ein allgemeiner europäischer Krieg,* p. 17.

42. F. Dumons, *Un mot a propos de la question d'Orient sur le devoir de la France et l'Avenir de l'Europe* [A word about the Eastern question on the duty of France and the future of Europe] (Bordeaux: Imprimerie de A. Pechade, 1840), p. 10. Total reorganization was high on Dumons's agenda. See also François-Marie-Ernest Dumons, *Situation: Reconstitution de l'Europe et nouvelle organisation sociale et politique, ou nouveau système gouvernemental, financier, administratif et judiciaire, adressé à M. le président de la république [14 novembre]; Exposé des motifs du projet de nouvelle organisation sociale et politique, ou nouveau système gouvernemental, financier, administratif et judiciaire, soumis au peuple français (29 décembre); par Dumont de La Fontaine* [Situation: The reconstitution of Europe and social and political reorganization, or a new governmental, financial, administrative and judicial system, addressed to the president of the republic, November 14; Explanatory memorandum of the project for a new social and political organization, or a new governmental, financial, administrative and judicial system, submitted to the French people, December 29, by Dumont de la Fontaine] (Paris: au Bureau spécial de publication des brochures, livraisons et journaux, 1849).

43. Leopold Leon Sawaszkiewicz, *Why the Eastern Question Cannot Be Satisfactorily Settled; or, Reflexions on the Respective Genius and Missions of Poland and France* (London: J. Ridgway, 1840), p. 84.

44. Ibid., p. 1.

45. "Politique Général," October 11, 1849, Adam Mickiewicz, *La tribune des peuples* [The people's tribune] (Paris: Ernst Flammarion and G. Gebethner et Compagnie, 1907), p. 323.

46. From one of a series of messianic poems—published in the form of a prayer book—in 1832, part of his response to the failure of the November Uprising. In one poem, "Litania pielgrzymska" (The pilgrim's litany), The original reads: "O wojnę powszechną za Wolność Ludów! / Prosimy cię Panie." Adam Mickiewicz, *Księgi narodu polskiego, I. Pielgrzymstwa polskiego* [Books of the Polish nation, the first Polish pilgrimage] (Paris: A. Pinard, 1832), p. 93.

47. Szécsen, *Politische Fragen der Gegenwart,* pp. 12–13.

48. Both sides in the conflict used rights-based arguments: the abolitionists for the rights of the human being/individual and the proslavery figures for "constitutional" rights. See, for example, Charles Sumner, *The Kansas Question: Senator Sumner's Speech, Reviewing the Action of the Federal Administration Upon the Subject of Slavery In Kansas; Delivered In the Senate of the United States, May 19th And 20th, 1856. Including the Debate Which Followed; Remarks of Senators Douglas, Cass, And Mason; And Mr. Sumner's Reply* (Cincinnati: Published by Geo. S. Blanchard, 1856), pp. 5, 29. On the violence in "Bleeding Kansas" that began in 1854 over whether the new state

should be a slave state or free, see United States, William Alanson Howard, and Mordecai Oliver, *Report of the Special Committee Appointed to Investigate the Troubles in Kansas: With the Views of the Minority of Said Committee* (Washington, DC: C. Wendell, 1856).

49. Dr. Frančišek Lampe, "Vprašanje nad vprašanje!" [Question upon question], in *Dom in Svet* 8, no. 1 (1895), pp. [33–34].

50. See Türr Tábornok, *A keleti kérdés* [The Eastern question] (Budapest: Fanda József Könyvnyomdájában, 1878), p. 30.

51. Reprinted in *Neue Freie Presse Morgenblatt* (Vienna), November 26, 1912, "Die 'Norddeutsche Allgemeine Zeitung' über die Möglichkeiten einer friedlichen Lösung" [The "Northern German General Newspaper" on the possibilities of a peaceful solution], p. 2. It should be noted that the government in Vienna was reportedly disinclined to bundle the questions in this way and rather hoped to solve them in isolation, such that the publicistic pressure behind bundling was perceived as unwelcome. See HStA Dresden, Bestand 10730, Sächsische Gesandtschaft für Österreich, Vienna, Signatur 428, Türkei, Orient-Frage, Kreta-Frage, Bosnische Frage, Tripolis-Frage, Bl. 91–92; Report of the Sächsische Königliche Gesandtschaft on November 27, 1912. See also ibid., Bl. 113, from December 8, 1912.

52. TNA, FO 373/1/17, "History of the Eastern Question," handbook prepared under the direction of the historical section of the foreign office, no. 15 (1918), p. 56. The author(s) then mentioned the "racial question" in Macedonia and the Bulgarian question. Ibid., pp. 57, 60.

53. Austen Henry Layard, *The Turkish Question. Speeches Delivered in the House of Commons on Aug. 16, 1853, Feb. 17, and March 31, 1854* (London: John Murray, 1854), p. 62.

54. *Die polnische Frage vom deutschen Standpunkt betrachtet, von eineim deutschen Staatsmann* [The Polish question viewed from the German standpoint, by a German statesman] (Leipzig: Verlag von Otto Wigand, 1855), p. 3.

55. "If the Polish question should be raised by the war," Adam Czartoryski wrote to London on December 18, 1854, he would vouch for limiting its spread from Russian Poland into Austrian and Prussian Poland. Czartoryski, *Memoirs*, p. 357.

56. Dostoievsky, *Diary of a Writer*, p. 430.

57. For example, in a Memorandum to Viscount Palmerston from François Guizot (then France's ambassador to London) from July of 1840, Guizot linked the solution of questions to "equilibrium between the states of Europe." TNA, PRO 30/22/3D/68, July 24, 1840, p. 364v.

58. Danilevskii and Woodburn, *Russia and Europe*, pp. 225, 256.

59. At around the same time Dostoevsky wrote that "in the solution of the Eastern question all sorts of combinations are being admitted with the exception of the clearest, sanest, simplest, the most natural one." Dostoievsky, *Diary of a Writer*, p. 435.

Furthermore, at one point earlier in the diary entry, he wrote of the need for "a direct and clear solution—the only one which is possible." Ibid., p. 434.

60. A Son of the East, *The Eastern Question; or, An Outline of Mohammedanism, Its Rise, Progress, and Decay* (Boston: A. Williams, 1882), p. 8; see also p. 58: "The Eastern question is of such a complicated nature that it cannot be touched in one of its branches without affecting the entire series of problems which compose its entirety."

61. The author, Aleksandar Belić, also called the Yugoslav question a part of the great "European question." Белић, *Србија и јужнословенско питање*, pp. 7, 99.

62. Bertha von Suttner, *Die Waffen nieder! Eine Lebensgeschichte* [Lay down your arms! A life history] (Dresden: E. Pierson, 1892), p. 209. Special thanks to Tamara Scheer for drawing my attention to this text.

63. Ibid., pp. 240–241.

64. *Ueber die polnische Frage*, p. 31.

65. See Endre Kovács, *A lengyel kérdés a reformkori Magyarországon* [The Polish question in Reform-era Hungary] (Budapest: Akadémiai Kiadó, 1959), pp. 114–115.

66. *Die Orientalische das ist Russische Frage* [The Eastern, which is to say, the Russian question] (Hamburg: Hoffmann und Campe, 1843), p. 73.

67. Disraeli, *Tancred*, pp. 107, 111.

68. TNA, PRO 30/22/3E/100, Lord John Russell: Papers; Correspondence and Papers, vol. 3E, September 20, 1840, p. 46.

69. James MacQueen, *The War, Who's to Blame?; Or, the Eastern Question Investigated from the Official Documents* (London: James Madden, 1854), p. 199.

70. See ibid., p. 5.

71. Karl Marx, *The Eastern Question*: A Reprint of Letters Written 1853–1856 Dealing with the Events of the Crimean War (London: S. Sonnenschein, 1897), pp. 310–311; emphasis in the original.

72. Dostoyevsky, "Diplomacy Facing World Problems," p. 996.

73. Hermann Marggraff, *Fritz Beutel* (Paderborn: Antigonos Verlag, 2012), p. 329.

74. Leopold von Ranke, *Serbien und die Türkei im neunzehnten Jahrhundert* [Serbia and Turkey in the nineteenth century] (Leipzig: Duncker & Humblot, 1879), p. 332. In addition to the Eastern question, von Ranke also made frequent mention of other questions: the Western question, the Serbian question, and the Syrian question. See ibid., pp. vii, 150, 166, 345, 348, 375, 381–382, 428, 488, 517.

75. Ibid., p. 332.

76. Adolf Chaisés, *La question polonaise et européenne; le congrès et Napoléon III* [The Polish and European question: The congress and Napoleon III] (Paris: Dentu, 1863), p. 5.

77. Recall that the Irish question, though it was as much about moving boundaries as the Eastern or the Polish question—and in fact was explicitly compared to both

by period commentators—was regularly defined as a "social" rather than a geopolitical question. For comparisons with other questions, see, for example, Viscount Wellesley, *The Irish Question Considered in Its Integrity* (Brussels: Meline, Cans, 1844), p. 259; see also ibid., pp. 267, 288–289. On the Irish question as a social question, see, for example, the Irish nationalist Charles Stewart Parnell's 1881 letter to Victor Hugo in Higgins, *Irish Land Question*, p. 171.

78. W. P., "A Lament for Romance," in *Mayfair Magazine* (London), December 1883, p. 29.

79. "Napoleon saw the danger of this rapid opening of the vast unknown continents of Asia and Africa. He saw that England, in her haste to open India and China to civilization, was also opening civilization to the uncivilized and preparing future troubles in abundance." Batchelor, *Social Equilibrium*, p. 13.

80. Ibid., p. 14.

81. Ibid., pp. 21–22.

82. Arnold J. Toynbee, *The Western Question in Greece and Turkey: A Study in the Contact of Civilizations* (London: Constable, 1922), pp. 26–27.

83. Toynbee on the "Western question": "both societies [West and East] are moving along the same road in the same direction" but "it is easier to regard objects of thought as constants than as variables. One slips into thinking of Western, Near Eastern, and Middle Eastern civilization as each something with an unchanging identity . . . Yet relativity is as fundamental a law in human life as it now appears to be in the physical universe, and when it is ignored, a true understanding of past history or contemporary politics ceases to be possible." Ibid., p. 14.

84. [Párdányi], *A breton-, baszk-, flamand-kérdés*, p. 1.

85. Christopher Hitchens, *Hitch-22: A Memoir* (New York: Twelve, 2010), p. 372.

86. Who argued in 1843 that "[t]he formulation of a question is its solution." Marx, "On The Jewish Question."

87. Karl May, *Von Bagdad nach Stambul: Reiseerzählungen* [From Baghdad to Istanbul: Travel stories] (Vienna: Karl-May-Bücherei, 1882), p. 408.

88. Adolf Grabowsky, *Die polnische Frage* [The Polish question] (Berlin: C. Heymann, 1916), p. 3.

89. Франко Поточњак, *Југословенско питање*, Савремена питања 9 [The Yugoslav question, vol. 9 of Contemporary questions] (Niš: Државна штампарија Краљевине Србије, 1915), p. 3

90. István Bibó, *Válogatott tanulmányok, 1945–1949, II. Kötet* [Selected studies, 1945-1949, vol. 2] (Budapest: Magvető Könyvk, 1986), p. 714.

91. Toury, "'The Jewish Question,'" pp. 85–106, 89–90.

92. Ibid., pp. 85–106, 92.

93. G. Phillips and G. Görres, eds., "Die Jüdische Frage" [The Jewish question],

in *Historisch-politische Blätter für das katholische Deutschland* [Historical-political papers for Catholic Germany], vol. 2 (Munich, 1838) pp. 377–397.

94. Toury, " 'The Jewish Question," pp. 85–106, 100.

95. Marx, "On The Jewish Question."

96. Század, *A zsidókérdés Magyarországon*, p. 30.

97. Erik Molnár, "Zsidókérdés Magyarországon" [The Jewish question in Hungary], *Zsidókérdés, Asszimiláció, Antiszemitizmus: Tanulmányok a Zsidókérdésről a Huszadik Századi Magyarországon* [Jewish question, assimilation, anti-Semitism: Studies on the Jewish question in twentieth-century Hungary], ed. Péter Hanák (Budapest: Gondolat, 1984), pp. 121–134, 121.

98. Brunner, Conze, and Koselleck, *Geschichtliche Grundbegriffe*, vol. 1, pp. 150–151.

99. Richard S. Levy, *Antisemitism: A Historical Encyclopedia of Prejudice and Persecution* (Santa Barbara, CA: ABC-CLIO, 2005), p. 377.

100. Cited in Alex Bein, *Die Judenfrage: Biographie eines Weltproblems* [The Jewish question: Biography of a world problem], vol. 2 (Stuttgart: Deutsche Verlags-Anstalt, 1980), p. 6.

101. Jean Améry, "Über Zwang und Unmöglichkeit, Jude zu sein" [On the necessity and impossibility of being a Jew], in *Werke* [Works] (Stuttgart: Klett-Cotta, 2002), p. 164. Similarly, and more recently, Mary Gluck has argued that "[i]n 1900 the problem of anti-Semitism . . . was then called the 'Jewish question.' "; see Gluck, *Georg Lukács and His Generation, 1900–1918* (Cambridge, MA: Harvard University Press, 1985), p. 59.

102. See, for example, W. Hawkins, *Tracts in Divinity*, vol. 1 (Oxford: W. Jackson, 1758), p. 288. "He has borrowed that the Distinction of that great and illustrious Writer from whom only we are to expect a full and final Solution of the several Difficulties relating to this Question."

103. John Coakley Lettsom, "Reflections on the General Treatment and Cure of Fevers," in *Monthly Review* 48 (1773), p. 304. Relevant passage: "a speedy and final solution of the disease may be effected." See also *Encyclopædia britannica; or, A dictionary of arts, sciences, and miscellaneous literature* (Edinburgh: A. Bell and C. Macfarquhar, 1797), pp. 105, 130. Relevant passages: "to obtain a final solution of the disease"; "it is seldom, however, that vomiting is found to produce a final solution of fevers."

104. See, for example, in Hugo Schiff, "Berechnung des specifischen Gewichts starrer und gasförmiger Substanzen für den flüssigen Zustand" [Calculating the specific gravity of solid and gaseous substances for the liquid state], in *Annalen der Chemie und Pharmacie*, Bd.113–14, n. Reihe Bd. 37–38 (1860), pp. 187, 191; Domenico Chelini, "Determinazione analitica della Totasione de' Corpi liberi secondo

i concetti del S. Poinsot" [Analytical determination of the totality of free bodies in accordance with the concepts of S. Poinsot] in *Heidelberger Jahrbücher der Literatur* 58 (1865), p. 95.

105. For example, Walter Scott wrote that "to hope for a final solution of the Eastern Question from the Berlin or any other Conference is a sad delusion"; see Scott, *The Eastern or Jewish Question Considered: And, What the Bible Says About Coming Events* (London: Alfred Holness, 1882), p. 3. And the Russian general Rostislav Fadeev, wrote in 1869: "What, then, would be the consequences, if the Eastern Question should now come to a *final solution?*" (italics in the original); see Fadeeff, *Opinion on the Eastern Question* (London: Edward Stanford, 1871), p. 16. See also Г. Е., *Восточный вопросъ и условия мира съ Турціей* [The Eastern question and conditions of the peace with Turkey] (Odessa: Тип. П. Францова, 1878), p. 57.

106. A translation of Napoleon III's speech is in FRUS, United States Department of State, Message of the president of the United States, and accompanying documents, to the two houses of Congress, at the commencement of the first session of the thirty-eighth congress(1863), Supplement: France, pp. [1321]–1329, p. 1323.

107. Győri, *A Toldi-kérdés*, p. 26.

108. Mikhail Bakunin, *Bakunin on Anarchism* (Montreal: Black Rose Books, 1980), p. 56.

109. Fyodor Dostoevsky, *Notes from the Underground, and The Gambler*, trans. Jane Kentish (Oxford: Oxford University Press, 1991), p. 34.

110. Dostoievsky, *The Diary of a Writer*, p. 428. See also Dmitry Merezhovsky's contribution on the Jewish question, "in spite of the pain and the shame we cry out and reiterate and declare to the people around us, who are ignorant of the table of multiplication, that two and two make four, that the Jews are human beings like us; that they are neither enemies nor traitors to their country." Merezhkovsky, "The Jewish Question as a Russian Question," in *The Shield*, ed. Maxim Gorky and Leonid Andreyev. (New York: Knopf, 1917), pp. 116–117. See also Leonid Andreyev, "The First Step," in ibid. p. 21.

111. Mazzini, *La questione italiana*, pp. 3, 5.

112. Becher, *Die Arbeiterfrage*, pp. 1–2.

113. In his *The Decline of the West*, first published in 1918, Oswald Spengler was, in his own way, cued to this shift. "For Kant knowledge is mathematical knowledge. . . . That there is, beyond the necessity of cause and effect—which I might call the *logic of space*—in life also the organic necessity of destiny—the *logic of time*—is a fact of the deepest inner certainty . . . that has not yet penetrated into the domain of theoretical formulation." Spengler, *Der Untergang des Abendlandes*, p. 9.

114. Ibid., p. 3 (italics in the original).

115. Rudolf Steiner, *Die Kernpunkte der sozialen Frage in den Lebensnotwendigkeiten*

der Gegenwart und Zukunft [The crux of the social question in the vital necessities of the present and future] (Stuttgart: Der kommende Tag, 1920), p. 5.

116. Ibid., p. 10.

117. Stein, *Die soziale Frage*, pp. 515–517.

118. See George, *The Irish Land Question*, pp. 12-13. "In order to better indicate the general character of this subject, and to conform to the title under which it had been republished in other countries, the title was subsequently changed to 'The Land Question,'" we read in the preface to the 1912 edition of the book. George, *The Land Question, What It Involves, and How Alone It Can be Settled* (New York: Doubleday, Page, 1912), p. 3. Among the aforementioned translations, see George, *La cuestión agraria* [The land question] (Buenos Aires, 1884); and Джорджъ, *Земелниятъ въпросъ, неговата сжщность и единствено разрешение* [The land question, its essence and only solution] (Sofia: Книгоиздателство 'Възраждане', [n.d.]), although it seems the Bulgarian translation appeared only after the title had already been changed in English. See ibid., p. 9.

119. Amicis, "Úvahy o socialné otázce," pp. 8–13, 10–12.

120. Surányi, *A socialis kérdés*, p. 3.

121. Michel Lempicki, *Grand problème international* [The great international problem] (Lausanne: Agence polonaise de presse à Rapperswil, 1915), p. 8. He also cited Napoleon I as having said, "Poland is the key to the European vault" (La Pologne, c'est la clef de la voûte européene). Ibid., p. 9.

122. See, for example, Otto Glagau (1878) cited in Brunner, Conze, and Koselleck, *Geschichtliche Grundbegriffe*, vol. 1, p. 136. Lajos Bíró's intervention in Huszadik Század, *A zsidókérdés Magyarországon*, p. 53. See also Alexis Nour, "Rusia în 1915, Chestiunile poloneză, evreiască și ucraineană. Existența Ucrainei contestată de d-nii Take Ionescu și Nic. Iorga" [Russia in 1915, the Polish, Jewish and Ukrainian questions. The existence of Ukraine contested by Take Ionescu and Nicolae Iorga], in *Viața Romînească, Revistă literară și științifică* 39, no. 10 (1915): 230–241, 237. And Alexander Mach, former head of the Hlinka Guard and Interior Minister of Slovakia (1939–1945), said that "[i]n the Jewish Question, we had already for a long time seen (in our country) a Hungarian Question." Cited in MUDr. Gabriel Hoffmann et al., *Zamlčaná Pravda o Slovensku: Prvá Slovenská republika, Prvý slovenský president Dr. Jozef Tiso, Tragédia slovenských židov podľa nových dokumentov* [The supressed truth about Slovakia: The first Slovak Republic, the first Slovak president Dr. Josef Tiso, the tragedy of Slovak Jews according to new documents] (Radošina: Garmond, 1996), p. 548.

123. In his memorandum on the Croatian question from October 28, 1936, the Croation fascist Ante Pavelić argued that no other political or social question could be solved until the Croatian question was solved, "because the entire life of the state

is suffocating under the burden of the Croatian question." Nor was it just a domestic problem in his view: "Time and again it has proven to be a serious international problem, a source of conflict that can give rise to unforeseeable tremors." Ante Pavelić, *Die kroatische Frage* [The Croatian question] (Berlin: Inst. f. Grenz- u. Auslandstudien, 1941), pp. 10–11.

124. In offering the "Jewish state" as "an inescapable conclusion," the necessary solution to the Jewish question in 1896, the founder of modern Zionism Theodor Herzl declared, "The world will be freed by our liberty, enriched by our wealth, magnified by our greatness. And whatever we attempt there to accomplish for our own welfare, will react powerfully and beneficially for the good of humanity." Herzl, *Jewish State*, p. 55.

125. Louis Brandeis and Felix Frankfurter, *Brandeis on Zionism: A Collection of Addresses and Statements* (Union, NJ: Law Book Exchange, 1999), p. 34.

126. Laudyn, *World Problem*, pp. 5–6. First published as Laudynowa, *Sprawa światowa; Żydzi-Polska-ludzkość* (Chicago: [The Two Little Printers], 1917). Note that she also wrote on the "Polish question" in a piece that was first published in 1904, later as a stand-alone publication. Laudynowa, *Kwestja polska i inne: listy polityczne "Polki"* [The Polish question and others] (Warsaw: Druk L. Bilińskiego i W. Maślankiewicza, 1908)

127. Mihály Kmoskó, *Zsidó-keresztény kérdés* [Jewish-Christian question] (Budapest: Stephaneum Ny., [192?]), p. 16.

128. TsDA, MVRI, f. 176K, op. 7, a.e. 753, March 1939, p. 17.

129. See Paul Dehn, *Diplomatie und Hochfinanz in der rumänischen Judenfrage* [Diplomacy and high finance in the Romanian Jewish question] (Berlin: W. Giese, 1901), p. 23.

130. Adolf Hitler, *My New Order* (New York: Reynal & Hitchcock, 1941), p. 229. Speech of December 11, 1933, in Berlin. It is interesting to note that, on the eve of the Nazi seizure of power, officials in the German Foreign Office were discussing what they called a "Fragenkomplex" of interrelated questions. In TNA, GFM 33/3347/9214, pp. E647985, E647986, E647990, E647992, E647993, E647990-E647993. (The questions discussed included the Disarmament, corridor, debt, and Eastern boundaries questions [Abrüstungsfrage, Korridor-Frage, Schuldenfrage, Ostgrenzen-Frage], among others.)

131. Max Domarus, *The Essential Hitler: Speeches and Commentary*, ed. Patrick Romane (Wauconda, IL: Bolchazy-Carducci, 2007), p. 586.

132. From a conversation between Hitler and Molotov, November 12, 1940. Andreas Hillgruber, *Staatsmänner und Diplomaten bei Hitler* [Statesmen and Diplomats with Hitler], vol. 1 (Frankfurt am Main: Bernard u. Graefe, 1967), p. 299.

133. Hitler, *Monologe im Führerhauptquartier*, p. 122.

134. Ibid., p. 260.

135. Domarus, *Essential Hitler*, p. 410.

136. "Das Jahr 1939," in *Hitler. Quellen 1924—1945* [Hitler, sources, 1924-1945] (Berlin: De Gruyter, n.d.), p. 1058, accessed August 12, 2016, http://www.degruyter .com/view/HITQ/MXD-0021.

137. See, for example, TNA, GFM 35/149, Code 13 Jewish question 1933–1936, August 29, 1935, Doc. 13093/1, pp. 8–10; ibid., November 23, 1933, Doc. 13056, pp. 1, 4; February 1934, Doc. 13070, pp. 1–13 (captured/confiscated German documents in the British Archives).

138. The Saarland had come under British and French occupation after World War I and was set up as a mandate under League of Nations auspices (known as the Territory of the Saar Basin) as part of German war reparations and in an effort to prevent Germany from using its outsized industrial capacity and natural resources— specifically coal—to rearm.

139. See especially H. Diehl, Kurt Vowinckel, and Adolf Hitler, *An die Saarländer* [To the inhabitants of the Saarland], 1934); Fritz Hellwig, *The Saar Basin and the Saar Question* [*Einführung in die Saarfrage*] (Berlin: Anglo-American, 1934); Paul Ostwald, *Die Saarfrage* [The Saar question] (Frankfurt am Main: Diesterweg, 1934); Werner Frauendienst, *Die Saarfrage im Lichte der Geschichte* [The Saar question in the light of history] (n.p., 1935); Viktor Bruns, *Die Volksabstimmung im Saargebiet* [The referendum in the Saarland] (Berlin: C. Heymann, 1934); Fritz Karl Roegels, *Deutsches Schicksal an der Saar* [German destiny on the Saar] (Breslau: Korn, 1934).

140. From an interview Hitler gave to the American journalist Pierre Huss, correspondent for the Hearst Press, on January 16, 1935. Domarus, *Essential Hitler*, p. 547.

141. See, for example, ibid., pp. 625, 643, 741. See also TNA, GFM 35/149, Code 13 Jewish question 1933–1936, August 29, 1935, Doc. 13093/1, pp. 8–10; ibid., November 23, 1933, Doc. 13056, pp. 1, 4; February 1934, Doc. 13070, pp. 1–13 (captured/confiscated German documents in the British Archives); Hitler, *Monologe im Führerhauptquartier*, fn77, p. 421.

142. This is evident from the spike in publications on various questions appearing in German (but published outside of Germany). See, for example, *Kurze Darstellung der mazedonischen Frage* [Brief presentation of the Macedonian question] (Sofia: Mazedonisches Wissenschaftliches Institut, 1941); Silviu Dragomir, *Die siebenbürgische frage* [The Transylvanian question] (n.p., 1941); Imre Lukinich, *Die siebenbürgische frage; studien aus der vergangenheit und gegenwart Siebenbürgens* [The Transylvanian question: Studies from the past and present of Transylvania] (Budapest: [Verlag des Osteuropa-instituts an der Budapester Péter Pázmány-universität], 1940); George Ioan Brătianu, *Die rumänische Frage 1940* [The Romanian question 1940] (Bucharest: Impr. Nationala, 1940); George Ioan Brătianu, *Zweite Denkschrift über die rumänische Frage 1940: Aufteilung Rumäniens oder Gebiets- und Bevölkerungsclearing im Südosten Europas* [Second memorandum on the Romanian question

1940: The division of Romania, or territory- and population-cleansing in southeastern Europe] (Bucharest: Ed. Dacia, 1941); Italian Library of Information, *The Tunisian Question* (New York: Italian Library of Information, 1939); and Ján Svetoň, *Die Slowaken in Ungarn, Beitrag zur Frage der statistischen Madjarisierung* [The Slovaks in Hungary, contribution to the question of statistical magyarization] (Bratislava: Verlag "Die Slowakische Rundschau," 1943).

143. Pavelić, *Die kroatische Frage*, pp. 11–12. In the concluding paragraph of the memorandum, Pavelić was still more explicit in stating that, in its struggle, "the Croatian people strive for the sympathies of Hitler's Germany." Ibid., p. 40.

144. The examples are far too numerous to allow for an exhaustive list, but see, for example: Croatian diplomatic exchanges on the Medjumurje question, Hrvatski Državni Arhiv, Zagreb, Croatia (hereafter cited as HDA), F. 230, Poslanstvo NDH u Bukureštu, p. 12; Romanian diplomatic exchanges with Bulgaria relating to the Dobruja question, United States Holocaust Memorial Museum Archives (hereafter cited as USHMMA), RG-25.020*12, Fiche 8, Selected Records from Romanian Diplomatic Missions, 1920–1950, Sofia, Bulgaria, Dosar 71/Bulgaria, 1942–1944, vol. 39, Politica internă, f. 508; Slovak diplomatic report relating to the Dobrudja question, Slovenský Národný Archív, Bratislava (hereafter cited as SNA), Ministerstvo Zahraničných Veci (hereafter cited as MZV), K. 192, 2267/1940; Slovak diplomatic report on the Banat question, SNA, MZV, K. 192, 448/1942; Dimitar Peshev speaking on the Macedonian question in 1941, cited in Ножица Желјаножски, *Македонскотоу прашање во бугарскиот парламент 1941–1944, политички и законодавоправни аспекти* [The Macedonian question in Bulgarian parliament, 1941-1944, political and legislative aspects] (Skopje: Скопје Институт за национална историја Матица Македонска, 1966), p. 75; German book to discredit claims of Poland and Czechoslovakia to Teschen/Cieszyn/Těšín, Kurt Witt, *Die Teschener Frage* [The Teschen (Cieszyn/Těšín) question] (Berlin: Volk und Reich Verlag, 1935), see esp. pp. 9–10; D'Agostino Orsini, *A gyarmati kérdés az új rendben*, p. 3; on the history of the Romanian question in Italy, Dimitrie Braharu, *Chestiunea română în Italia în timpul Memorandului* [The Romanian question in Italy in the time of the Memorandum] (Sibiu: Tipografia "Cartea Românească din Cluj, 1942), see esp. p. 112 for hints as to the why this theme was being treated at that time; on the "question algérienne," see "Revindications Musulmanes" [Muslim demands], in *L' Écho de Tiaret: organe hebdomadaire des intérêts généraux et régionaux*, August 1, 1936, p. 2; and "La question d'Indochine" [The Indochina question] in *L'Echo d'Alger: Journal républicain du matin* (August 9, 1941): [cover, pages unnumbered].

145. See, for example, MOL, K63 [Külügyminisztérium, Politikai osztály], 259. csomó. 27. tétel, 1940–27/7/8; Pavelić, *Die kroatische Frage*, pp. 10–11.

146. See, for example, on how the solution to Medjumurje question should be bundled with others at the end of the war, HDA, F. 230, Poslanstvo NDH u

Bukureštu, p. 12; and Hungarian diplomats on Croatia's question bundle of the Medjumurje and the Dalmatian questions, MOL, K64a., 67/a. tétel Muraközi kérdés, 1942, 944/Res. Pol./1942, p. 519v; 2/Res. Pol./1942, p. 551. In 1940, a Hungarian Orientalist Bertalan Hatvany wrote a long pamphlet on the Chinese question, which was part of a series on World Affairs (*Világesemények*). The series was written in a popular style with the aim of "familiarization, in an enjoyable form, of some contemporary questions of world significance." Bertalan Hatvany, *A kínai kérdés története* [History of the Chinese question] ([Budapest]: Pantheon, 1940), (no page no., but approx. p. 62). The series began in 1938 with a treatment of the "most burning" Mediterranean question. Pál Demény, *A Földközi tenger a világpolitika ütközőpontja* [The Mediterranean Sea, crossroads of world politics] ([Budapest]: Pantheon, 1938). They also planned to publish, in addition to the one on the Chinese question, further volumes on the Palestine and the Irish questions. The former actually was published; the latter, it seems, was not. Miklós Horner, *A palesztinai kérdés* [The Palestinian question] ([Budapest?]: Pantheon Kiadás, 1938).

147. HDA, MVP NDH Zagreb, 1941–1945, kut. 1, Tajni spisi MVP-a (T.), 1941, br. 87–625, T. 495/1941, p. 23.

148. MOL, K64a., 67/a. tétel Muraközi kérdés, 1942, 165/Res. Pol./1942, p. 482. See also ibid., 165/Res. Pol./1942, pp. 479v, 481; ibid., 211/Res. Pol./1942, pp. 466.

149. MOL, K64a., 33/a. tétel Ruszinszkói kérdés, 1938–1939, 1358/Res. Pol./1938, pp. 30–30v.

150. MOL, K64a., 7/a. tétel Cseh kérdés, 748/Res. Pol./1938, p. 13. See also ibid., 873/Res. Pol./1938, p. 260v.

151. MOL, K64a., 7/a. tétel Cseh kérdés, 1939, 585/Res. Pol./1938, p. 75v. See also ibid., 1244/Res. Pol./1938, p. 267 (relating to the Ruthenian question).

152. Ferdinand Ďurčanský, *Mitteleuropa in Vergangenheit und Zukunft* (Bratislava: Wissenschaftliche Gesellschaft für das Auslandsslowakentum in Bratislava, 1944), p. 7.

153. Domarus, *Essential Hitler*, p. 636.

154. Ibid., p. 641.

155. Hillgruber, *Staatsmänner und Diplomaten bei Hitler*, vol. 1, p. 315.

156. Ibid., p. 319.

157. In a conversation with Mussolini from October 7, 1942. Hillgruber, *Staatsmänner und Diplomaten bei Hitler*, vol. 2, p. 129.

158. See, for example, closed session of Hitler with German generals from November 5, 1937. Domarus, *Essential Hitler*, p. 614.

159. November 5, 1937. "Das Jahr 1937," in *Hitler*, accessed August 12, 2016, http://www.degruyter.com/view/HITQ/MXD-0015, pp. 751–752.

160. November 22, 1940. Hillgruber, *Staatsmänner und Diplomaten bei Hitler*, vol. 1, p. 356.

161. TsDA, MVRI, f. 176K, op. 7, a.e. 753, January 1938, p. 48; MOL, K64a., 33/a.

tétel Ruszinszkói kérdés, 1938–1939, 1484/Res. Pol./1938, p. 149; 236/Res. Pol./1939, p. 253. See also MOL, K64a., 67/a. tétel Muraközi kérdés, 1942, 136/Res. Pol./1942, p. 490; MOL, K64a., 27/a. tétel Bánáti kérdés, 1941, 202/Res. Pol./1941, p. 1; "Cigánykodás" [Playing Gypsy], in *Ellenzék*, September 11, 1942, p. 2.

162. Meeting on November 5, 1943. Hillgruber, *Staatsmänner und Diplomaten bei Hitler*, vol. 2, p. 341.

163. See Case, *Between States*, pp. 67–96.

164. Horthy Miklós, *Horthy Miklós titkos iratai* [The secret writings of Miklós Horthy] (Budapest: Kossuth Könyvkiadó, 1962), p. 297.

165. Miklós Kállay, *Magyarország miniszterelnöke voltam, 1942–1944* [I was prime minister of Hungary, 1942-1944] (Budapest: Európa História, 1991), p. 91.

166. Cited in Sebastian Balta, *Rumänien und die Grossmächte in der Ära Antonescu, 1940–1944* [Romania and the Great Powers in the Antonescu era, 1940-1944] (Stuttgart: Franz Steiner Verlag, 2005), p. 273. Hungary had attempted to negotiate a withdrawal of its Mobile Corps in September of 1941 in an effort to regroup and prepare for Hungary's "Balkan mission," which was to entail a "showdown with Romania." R. L. DiNardo, *Germany and the Axis powers from Coalition to Collapse* (Lawrence: University Press of Kansas, 2005), pp. 124. Hungary's troop commitment was thus also thought to influence the solution of the Banat question. See SNA, MZV, K. 192, 8.305/1942. Meanwhile, Romanians complained to the German minister of foreign affairs Joachim von Ribbentrop that Germany had done nothing to help solve the Transylvanian question in Romania's favor in spite of Romania's massive commitment of troops to the Axis war effort. See SNA, MZV, K. 192, 8.204/1942, p. 4. Incidentally, the strategy of applying international pressure in the interest of solving a particular regional or domestic question had a long history. Perhaps the most prominent case was in 1878–1879, when the Western Great Powers tied recognition of Romania's independence to its willingness to solve the Jewish question. See, for example, AT-OeStA/HHStA PA XVIII 49, "Judenfrage und Anerkennung Rumäniens," 1879, p. 147v.

167. On November 19, 1940, he told King Leopold of Belgium: "We cannot speak of all these matters because the solution to these questions does not depend on Germany, but rather is more generally conditioned by the question of the ending of the war." On March 17, 1941, he told Turkey's envoy, Hüsrev Gerede: "A solution to certain questions could also be managed for Turkey . . . in the framework of the New Order." Hillgruber, *Staatsmänner und Diplomaten bei Hitler*, vol. 1, p. 336, 480.

168. On January 30, 1939, in his speech to the Reichstag, Hitler declared, "I believe the earlier this problem is resolved, the better. For Europe cannot find peace before it has dealt properly with the Jewish question." On March 27, 1942, Goebbels said, "No other government and no other regime had the strength to resolve this question in its generality. In this respect too the Fuhrer is the constant champion and spokes-

man of a radical solution." Domarus, *Essential Hitler*, p. 399, 404. And on January 25, 1942, Hitler told a small group of Nazi leaders, "I see no other way but absolute extermination if they don't leave of voluntarily." Hitler, *Monologe im Führerhauptquartier*, p. 229.

169. USHMMA, 1998.A.0133, Archives of Macedonia Records, 1915–1961, reel 1, 6.5.1.19/293–294.

170. From the assembly session June 21, 1942, cited in Желјаножски, *Македонското прашање во бугарскиот парламент*, p. 107.

171. Slovenské Národné Múzeum, Múzeum Židovskej Kultúry, *Riešenie židovskej otázky na Slovensku (1939–1945), Dokumenty*, 2. časť [Solution of the Jewish question in Slovakia, 1939-1945, documents, part 2] (Bratislava: Edícia Judaica Slovaca, 1994), doc. 252, pp. 175–6.

172. "4. októbra 1944, Bratislava. Z vystúpenia predsedu vlády dr. Štefana Tisu v sneme, časť týkajúca sa riešenia židovskej otázky" [October 4, 1944, Bratislava. From the speech of prime minister Štefan Tiso in the Diet, the part relating to the solution of the Jewish question], in Slovenské Národné Múzeum, *Riešenie židovskej otázky*, 3. časť, doc. 334, p. 154.

173. On December 20, 1940, during a discussion of the anti-Jewish Law for the Protection of the Nation in the Bulgarian National Assembly, assemblyman Nikola Muschanov protested against the law, expressing his incredulity that Jews were to be placed below even "Turks, Greeks, Armenians, Gypsies." Other Bulgarian politicians were similarly incredulous that the government would expend such energy on such a small and relatively poor population when the state faced heftier threats from other quarters, namely, from hostile neighbors Serbia and Greece, and from the large Greek and Turkish minorities in Bulgaria. See Dieter Ruckhaberle and Christiane Ziesecke, eds., *Rettung der bulgarischen Juden, 1943: eine Dokumentation* [Rescue of the Bulgarian Jews, 1943: A documentation] (Berlin: Publica, 1984), pp. 85, 106, 31–32. National assemblyman Dimo Kazasov observed that the 650,000 Turks and 70,000 Romanians in Bulgaria posed a far greater threat than did the Jews. See discussion of diplomat and publicist Simeon Radev in Nada Kisić Kolanović, ed., *Poslanstvo NDH u Sofiji: diplomatski izvještaji 1941–1945* [Mission of the Independent State of Croatia in Sofia: Diplomatic reports, 1941–1945], vol. 2 (Zagreb: Hrvatski državni arhiv, 2003), pp. 264–65 (doc. 160).

174. Stephen Fischer-Galati, "Fascism, Communism, and the Jewish Question in Romania," in *Jews and Non-Jews in Eastern Europe, 1918–1945*, ed. B. Vago and G. L. Mosse (New York: John Wiley & Sons, 1974), 158.

175. MOL, K63 [Külügyminisztérium, Politikai osztály], 256. csomó, 1940–1942–27/7.I. tétel, pp. 121–122.

176. Horthy, *Horthy Miklós titkos iratai*, p. 306. Werth was replaced by Ferenc Szombathelyi on Horthy's orders on September 6, 1941. Szombathelyi, Horthy

argued, "served the German interest more cautiously, and therefore better" than Werth had. Ibid., p. 307.

177. Krisztián Ungváry, "Kitelepítés, lakosságcsere és a holokauszt egyes összefüggései" [Particular correlations between expulsion, population exchange, and the Holocaust], in *A holokauszt Magyarországon európai perspektívában* [The Holocaust in Hungary in a European perspective], ed. Judit Molnár (Budapest: Balassi kiadó, 2005), pp. 84–100.

178. Andrej Angrick, *Besatzungspolitik und Massenmord: Die Einsatzgruppe D in der südlichen Sowjetunion, 1941–1943* [Occupation policy and mass murder: The Einsatzgruppe D in the southern USSR, 1941-1943] (Hamburg: Hamburger Edition, 2003), pp. 155–158.

179. Ivo Goldstein and Slavko Goldstein, *Holokaust u Zagrebu* [The Holocaust in Zagreb] (Zagreb: Novi liber, 2001), pp. 588–589.

180. Elias Canetti, *Masse und Macht* [Crowds and Power] (Hamburg: Claassen Verlag, 1960), pp. 327–328.

181. In the original: "Întrebare făcută ca să lămurești un lucru. Propunere de examinat, subiect de discutat, afacere: *chestiunea Orientului*. O tortură din evu mediu." Scriban, *Dicționaru limbii românești*, p. 266.

4. The Federative Argument: The Age of Erasing Borders

1. Regnault, *La question européenne*, p. v.

2. Ibid.

3. Hammacher, *Hauptfragen der Modernen Kultur*, p. 6.

4. Richard Coudenhove-Kalergi, *Pan-Europe* (New York: Knopf, 1926), p. xiv.

5. Marx, "On The Jewish Question."

6. Émile de Girardin, *Solutions de la question d'Orient* (Paris: Librairie nouvelle, 1853), p. 94.

7. Herzl, *Jewish State*, p. 56.

8. See Domarus, *Essential Hitler*, p. 410.

9. Coudenhove-Kalergi, *Pan-Europe*, p. xiv.

10. Ibid., p. xiv (italics in the original).

11. Wolfram Fischer writes of this phenomonen in the German context in a brief conceptual history of the "social question" in a 1977 essay, "Der Wandel der sozialen Frage in den fortgeschrittenen Industriegesellschaften" [The transformation of the social question in the more advanced industrial societies], in *Grundtexte zur sozialen Marktwirtschaft* [Fundamental texts of the social market economy], vol. 2, ed. Karl Hohmann and Horst Friedrich Wünsche (Stuttgart: Gustav Fischer Verlag, 1988), pp. 104–105.

12. Rudolf Steiner, for example, even spoke of "*the* social question" as an "eco-

nomic, legal, and spiritual/intellectual question" (Wirtschafts-, Rechts-, und Geistes-frage). Steiner, *Die Kernpunkte der sozialen Frage,* p. 18.

13. *L'Ami de la Religion et du Roi, Journal Ecclésiastique, Politique et Littéraire* (Paris), no. 156 (February 7, 1816): 385–396, see esp. 389.

14. Anne-Henri Cabet Dampmartin, *Lettre à Messieurs de la Chambre des Députés sur l'éducation publique et sur le choix des instituteurs* [Letter to the members of the Chamber of Deputies on public education and selection of teachers] (Paris: impr. de Poulet, 1815). No reference to the "social question" appears in the actual *Letter.*

15. "Paris," *Journal des débats politiques et littéraires* (Paris) (March 20, 1826): 2.

16. See, for example, "Disturbances at Lyons (from the *Moniteur* of Friday, November 25)," in *Courier* (London), November 28, 1831, p. 4. "A social question is more important than a political one." Note this is still a reference to "*a* social question" rather than "*the* social question." There were others, however, wherein references were to "*the* social question," for example, "Events at Lyons," in *Courier* (London), December 20, 1831, p. 2. It has been claimed that the first reference in German did not appear until nearly a decade later, in Heinrich Heine's *Pariser Korrespondenz* [Paris correspondence] from 1840. See Fischer, "Der Wandel der sozialen Frage."

17. Biedermann, *Frauen-Brevier,* p. 334.

18. See https://books.google.com/ngrams/graph?content=polnische+frage& case_insensitive=on&year_start=1750&year_end=2000&corpus=20&smoothing =3&share=&direct_url=t4%3B%2Cpolnische%20frage%3B%2Cc0%3B%2Cs0%3 B%3Bpolnische%20Frage%3B%2Cc0%3B%3BPolnische%20Frage%3B%2Cc0; https://books.google.com/ngrams/graph?content=soziale+frage&case _insensitive=on&year_start=1750&year_end=2000&corpus=20&smoothing=3& share=&direct_url=t4%3B%2Csoziale%20frage%3B%2Cc0%3B%2Cs0%3B%3B soziale%20Frage%3B%2Cc0%3B%3BSoziale%20Frage%3B%2Cc0; https://books .google.com/ngrams/graph?content=orientalische+frage&case_insensitive =on&year_start=1750&year_end=2000&corpus=20&smoothing=3&share =&direct_url=t4%3B%2Corientalische%20frage%3B%2Cc0%3B%2Cs0%3B%3 Borientalische%20Frage%3B%2Cc0%3B%3BOrientalische%20Frage%3B%2Cc0; English—https://books.google.com/ngrams/graph?content=orientalische+frage& case_insensitive=on&year_start=1750&year_end=2000&corpus=20&smoothing =3&share=&direct_url=t4%3B%2Corientalische%20frage%3B%2Cc0%3B%2Cs0 %3B%3Borientalische%20Frage%3B%2Cc0%3B%3BOrientalische%20Frage %3B%2Cc0; https://books.google.com/ngrams/graph?content=eastern+question &case_insensitive=on&year_start=1750&year_end=2000&corpus=15&smoothing =3&share=&direct_url=t4%3B%2Ceastern%20question%3B%2Cc0%3B%2Cs0% 3B%3BEastern%20Question%3B%2Cc0%3B%3BEastern%20question%3B%2Cc0 %3B%3BEASTERN%20QUESTION%3B%2Cc0%3B%3Beastern%20question %3B%2Cc0; https://books.google.com/ngrams/graph?content=social+question

&case_insensitive=on&year_start=1750&year_end=2000&corpus=15&smooth
ing=3&share=&direct_url=t4%3B%2Csocial%20question%3B%2Cc0%3B%2Cs0
%3B%3Bsocial%20question%3B%2Cc0%3B%3BSocial%20Question%3B
%2Cc0%3B%3BSOCIAL%20QUESTION%3B%2Cc0%3B%3BSocial%20
question%3B%2Cc0.

19. See AT-OeStA/HHStA StK Kongressakten 2, Originaux des Protocoles des
huit, September 22, 1814, premier projet du Protocolle de la séance du September 22,
p. 12v (underlining in the original).

20. *Hansard Parliamentary Debates*, 1st series (1803–1820), p. 1197.

21. *Un mot sur la question polonaise en 1829*, p. 13. A similar case was made by a
British MP in the House of Commons, Robert Cutlar Fergusson, before the House
in 1832: "The great question, be it remembered, is not a Russian or a Polish question
merely; it is a European question." Fergusson, *Poland. Speech on the State of Poland;
Delivered in the House of Commons . . . the 18th of April, 1932* (London: Parbury, Allen,
1832), 3.

22. "Europäische Fragen und Probleme," *Augsburger Allgemeine Zeitung*, pp. 362–
363. From a special supplement to the February 27th edition. Hereafter it was not
uncommon for questions to be evaluated as to whether they were "European" questions. See, for example, Klaczko, *Studya dyplomatyczne*, p. 166 (on how the Schleswig-
Holstein question was still an "internal German" question and had not yet become
a "European" one).

23. Jean Czynski, *Question des juifs polonais, envisagée comme question européenne*
[The Polish-Jewish question envisioned as a European question] (Paris: Chez Guil-
laumin, 1833), p. 27.

24. Chaisés, *La question polonaise*, p. 5. See also Regnault, *La question
européenne*.

25. See Regnault, *La question européenne*, pp. vi–vii.

26. Not much is known about Ungár except that he was Hungarian-Jewish, born
in Lipótszentmiklós/Liptovský Mikuláš (in present-day Slovakia) and wrote this
pamphlet. See Péter Ujvári, *Magyar Zsidó Lexikon* [Hungarian Jewish encyclopedia]
(Budapest: A Magyar zsidó lexikon kiadása, 1929), p. 925.

27. Ungár, *Egy szó a maga idejében*, p. 4 (italics in the original). An anonymous
pamphlet on the Hungarian question published the same year appealed to the "sober
mind," promising to clear up misunderstandings and prejudices by examining the
question from the "loftier and higher, which is to say the European and whole-
Empire perspective." *Szózat a magyar kérdés érdemében*, pp. 18, 21, 23, 71. Only if taken
from this perspective could Hungary's position as a *colony* be transformed into that
of an imperial power. Ibid., p. xxi.

28. A Son of the East, *The Eastern Question*, p. 8; see also p. 58: "The Eastern ques-

tion is of such a complicated nature that it cannot be touched in one of its branches without affecting the entire series of problems which compose its entirety."

29. Г. Е., *Восточный вопросъ*, p. 19.

30. BOA, Yıldız Perâkende Evrâkı, Tahrirat-ı Ecnebiye ve Mâbeyn Mütercimliği (Y.PRK.TKM), Dos. 11, Göm. 57, January 20, 1888 (06/C /1305 [Hicrî]).

31. Gusztáv Beksics, *A román kérdés és a fajok harcza Európában és Magyarországon* [The Romanian question and the struggle of the races in Europe and Hungary] (Budapest: Athenaeum, 1895), p. 3. Albert Sorel, *The Eastern Question in the Eighteenth Century: The Partition of Poland and the Treaty of Kainardji* (London: Methuen, 1898), p. 259. In Baron Karl Puttkamer's introduction to a work on *The Polish Question and Europe* from 1913, the baron wrote that "[u]ntil it is properly solved, the Polish question was, is still today, and will remain one of the most important elements of the whole of European politics." In Eugen Starczewski, *Die polnische Frage und Europa* [The Polish question and Europe] (Berlin: Verlag von S. Knaster, 1913), p. 1.

32. See Белић, *Србија и јужнословенско питање*, p. 7. See also Leopold Mandl, *Die Habsburger und die serbische Frage: geschichte des staatlichen Gegensatzes Serbiens zu Österreich-Ungarn* [The Habsburgs and the Serbian question: History of the state opposition between Serbia and Austria-Hungary] (Vienna: M. Perles, 1918), p. 161.

33. Foucault, "What is Enlightenment?," pp. 32–50.

34. Translation in *Courier* (London), December 13, 1830, p. 2. (Also in *Morning Chronicle* (London), December 14, 1830, p. 1; and *London Morning Post*, December 14, 1830, p. 4.) *London Standard*, January 24, 1831, p. 3.

35. Lord William Russell wrote to his brother Lord John Russell (Britain's secretary of state for war and the Colonies) in 1840 that the solution of the Belgian question (à la Palmerston) could lead to the solution of the Eastern question. TNA, PRO 30/22/3D/68, July 10, 1840, p. 343. The Comte de Montalembert, for example, wrote in 1863 that "the Eastern question, the Italian question, and the Mexican question can not permit us to take refuge in indifference and impotence in the face of the Polish question. All three of these issues, despite their extreme gravity, were much less severe and did not take hold of the French heart as much the Polish question." de Montalembert, *L'Insurrection Polonaise*, p. 19. See also Damotte, *Solution mexicaine*, pages unnumbered. Rostislav Fadeeff, *Opinion on the Eastern Question* (London: Edward Stanford, 1871), p. 65. Gusztáv Beksics related the Romanian to the Eastern question; see Beksics, *A román kérdés és a fajok harcza*, p. 3. See also Stanisław Tarnowski in Klaczko, *Studya dyplomatyczne*, p. vii.

36. Dostoievsky, *Diary of a Writer*, p. 430.

37. At around the same time Dostoevsky wrote that "in the solution of the Eastern question all sorts of combinations are being admitted with the exception of the clearest, sanest, simplest, the most natural one." Ibid., p. 435. Furthermore, at one point

earlier in the diary entry, he wrote of the need for "a direct and clear solution—the only one which is possible." Ibid., p. 434; see also p. 428.

38. AT-OeStA/HHStA StK Kongressakten 2, Conférences des Quatre, Séance du December 29, 1814, discussion verbale, p. 1–1v.

39. de Tocqueville, *Oeuvres complètes*, vol. 3, pt. 2, p. 262.

40. *Die Orientalische das ist Russische Frage*, p. 74.

41. Captain Bedford Pim, *The Eastern Question, Past, Present and Future: With Map and Official Documents* (London: Effingham Wilson, Royal Exchange, 1877), pp. 20–21.

42. Campbell, *Blue Books*, p. 50.

43. von Ranke, *Serbien und die Türkei im neunzehnten Jahrhundert*, pp. 369–370.

44. Budge, *The Eastern Question Solved: A Vision of the Future* (London: W. H. Allen, 1881), pp. 10–12, 18.

45. James Lewis Farley, *Turks and Christians, a Solution of the Eastern Question* (London: Simpkin, Marshall, 1876), pp. 181–182.

46. Noel Buxton, *Europe and the Turks* (London: John Murray, 1907), pp. 120–121.

47. Édouard Driault and Michel Lhéritier, *Histoire Diplomatique de la Grèce de 1821 a nos Jours* [Diplomatic history of Greece from 1821 to our time], vol. 1 (Paris: Les Presses Universitaires de France, 1925), p. 5.

48. Czartoryski, *Essai sur la diplomatie, manuscrit d'un philhellène*, pp. 301–303.

49. Emilie Ashurst Venturi, *Joseph Mazzini* (London: H. S. King, 1877), p. 46; Giuseppe Mazzini, "Young Europe," in *Joseph Mazzini: His Life, Writings, and Political Principles* (New York: Hurd and Houghton, 1872), pp. 155–156.

50. Lajos Kossuth, "A balkáni hódítás káros" [The Balkan conquest is damaging], in *Kossuth Lajos Üzenetei* [The messages of Lajos Kossuth] (Budapest: Neumann Kht., 2004), accessed February 21, 2014, http://mek.oszk.hu/04800/04882/html/szabadku0197.html; Leon Trotzky, *The Bolsheviki and World Peace* (New York: Boni and Liveright, 1918), pp. 54–56. "The solution of the Balkan question is unthinkable without the solution of the Austro-Hungarian question, as they are both comprised in one and the same formula—the Democratic Federation of the Danube and Balkan Nations." Ibid., p. 60; on Conrad, see M. B. Biskupski, "Conrad and the International Politics of the Polish Question, 1914–1918: Diplomacy, under Western Eyes, or Almost the Secret Agent," *Conradiana* 32, no. 2 (Summer 1999): 84–98, pp. 87, 90.

51. Coudenhove-Kalergi, *Pan-Europe*, p. xiv.

52. Mikhail Aleksandrovich Bakunin, *The Basic Bakunin: Writings, 1869–1871* (Buffalo, NY: Prometheus, 1992), p. 184. This comes from pieces written between 1869 and 1871.

53. Jehu Mathews, *A Colonist on the Colonial Question* (London: Longmans, Green, 1872), pp. 7, 187.

54. Gustav Adolph Constantin Frantz, *Der Föderalismus als das leitende Princip*

für die sociale, staatliche und internationale Organisation, unter besonderer Bezugnahme auf Deutschland, kritisch nachgewiesen und constructiv dargestellt [Federalism as the guiding principle for social, state, and international organization with particular consideration of Germany, critically proven and constructively presented] (Mainz: F. Kirchheim, 1879), p. 373 (italics and bold in the original).

55. Ibid.

56. Ibid., p. 374.

57. Batchelor, *Social Equilibrium*, p. 6. "Ethics and religion are independent of all sects; and, the questions which relate to them once being settled in accordance with the truth, all sects would soon become superfluous."

58. Regnault, *La question européenne*, p. v.

59. F. Dumons, *Un mot a propos de la question d'Orient*, p. 10. Total reorganization was high on Dumons agenda. See also Dumons, *Situation*.

60. Marx and Engels, *A Few Words on the Eastern Question*, pp. 39, 55–56.

61. Jakobos Georgios Pitzipios, *The Eastern Question Solved, in a Letter to Lord Palmerston* (London: privately printed, 1860), p. 22.

62. Szini, *Magyar irodalom: javaslat a magyar kérdés megoldására*, pp. 36, 39–40, 43–44.

63. Ibid., p. 36.

64. Ibid., p. 44–46.

65. Ibid., pp. 14–15, 58.

66. Edward Jenkins, *The Colonial Question: Being Essays On Imperial Federalism*, 2nd ed. (Montreal: Dawson Bros., 1871), pp. 3–86.

67. Jehu Matthews, *A Colonist on the Colonial Question* (London: Longmans, Green; 1872), p. 142. On emancipation, see also ibid., pp. v–vi. It should be noted that not everyone agreed with Matthews and Jenkins. See, for example, Henry W. Fuller, *The Colonial Question: A Brief Consideration of Colonial Emancipation, Imperial Federalism, and Colonial Conservation* (Kingston, ON, 1875), p. 20. "The project of a British Federacy, while prompted by a lofty motive, cannot reasonably be entertained."

68. See, for example, Gustav Rasch, *Die Völker der unteren Donau und die orientalische Frage* [The peoples of the lower Danube and the Eastern question] (Breslau: J. U. Kern, 1867), p. 94.

69. On Garašanin, see Bogdan Popović, *Istorija Ministarstva Inostranih Dela Srbije* [History of the ministry of foreign affairs of Serbia] (Belgrade: Glasnik, Diplomatska akademija, 2005), p. 108; Victor Roudometof, *Nationalism, Globalization, and Orthodoxy: The Social Origins of Ethnic Conflict in the Balkans* (Westport, CT: Greenwood, 2001), p. 118. On Novaković, see Dennis Deletant and Harry Hanak, *Historians as Nation-Builders: Central and South-East Europe* (Basingstoke: Macmillan and the School of Slavonic and East European Studies, University of London, 1988), p. 64.

70. On von Kállay, see Milojković-Djurić, *Eastern Question*, pp. 49, 55–56.

71. Danilevskii and Woodburn, *Russia and Europe*, pp. 332, 341.

72. Mikhail Bakunin, "Appeal to the Slavs" (1848), in *Bakunin on Anarchy*, trans. and ed. Sam Dolgoff (New York: Vintage, 1971), accessed November 7, 2017, http://www.marxists.org/reference/archive/bakunin/works/1848/pan-slavism.htm. E. H. Carr said of Bakunin's "Appeal": "the Appeal to the Slavs is a landmark in European history. It was the first occasion on which, exactly seventy years before November 1918, the destruction of the Austrian Empire and the building of new Slav states on its ruins was publicly advocated."

73. Gyula Andrássy, *A világháború problémái* [Problems of the world war] (Budapest: "Élet" Irodalomi és Nyomda Rt, 1916), pp. 215, 218–219. The chapter on the Polish question opens with the following assertion: "In our assessment of the great questions that we will have to solve in the course of the present world war, we have to start above all from the common insterests of Central Europe. We must never forget that our own security as well as peace in Europe will depend on how much vital energy can be summoned by the Central European alliance of today." Ibid., p. 210.

74. Mandl, *Die Habsburger und die serbische Frage*, p. 197. Similar plans were put forward during World War II. See, for example, SNA, MZV, K. 192, 1132/1940.

75. Trotzky, *Bolsheviki and World Peace*, p. 60.

76. Thomas Brassey, *The Eastern Question and the Political Situation at Home* (London: Longmans, Green, 1877), p. 41.

77. Cited in Baumgart, "Die 'Orientalische Frage'—redivivus?," pp. 33–55, p. 48. (She cites it from Arthur C. F. Beales, *The History of Peace: A Short Account of the Organized Movements for International Peace* (New York: Dial, 1931), p. 161).

78. Much of their writing seems to borrow from theories in fluid dynamics (or hydrodynamics), and especially of equilibrium as expressed in the work of Blaise Pascal and Jean le Rond d'Alembert. See Blaise Pascal, *Traitez de l'equilibre des liqueurs, et de la pesanteur de la masse de l'air* [Treatises on the equilibrium of liquids and the weight of the mass of the air] (Paris: Chez Guillaume Desprez, 1663); Jean de Rond d'Alembert, *Traité sur l'équilibre et du mouvement des fluides: pour servir de suite au traité de Dynamique* [Treatise on the equilibrium and movement of fluids, as a sequel to the treatise on dynamics] (Paris: J. B. Coignard, 1744).

79. Czartoryski, *Essai sur la diplomatie, manuscrit d'un philhellène*, pp. 23, 418–419, 157, 85.

80. See introduction, "The Science of Questions."

81. On Batchelor, see "Rev. George Batchelor," *Cambridge Tribune* 46, no. 17 (June 23, 1923): 5.

82. Batchelor, *Social Equilibrium*, p. 5.

83. Ibid., p. 9.

84. Ibid., p. 21.

85. Coudenhove-Kalergi, *Pan-Europe*, pp. 168–169.

5. The Argument about Farce: The Farcical Age

1. Dostoyevsky, "Never Has Russia Been as Powerful as Now," pp. 1001–1002. It should be noted that, in the above translation, the phrase "мировые вопросы" is translated as "problems of world importance," whereas the more literal translation is "world questions," so I have changed it here. See https://ru.wikisource.org/wiki /Дневник_писателя._1877_год_(Достоевский)/Май-июнь/ГЛАВА _ВТОРАЯ_III, accessed October 4, 2016.

2. On the "crisis," see Rudolf Schlögl, Philip R. Hoffmann-Rehnitz, and Eva Wiebel, *Die Krise in der Frühen Neuzeit* [Crisis in the early modern period] (Göttingen: Vandenhoeck & Ruprecht, 2016), p. 376.

3. von Ketteler, *Die Arbeiterfrage und das Christentum*, p. 8.

4. For an example of dating the origin of the Jewish question with the emergence of Judaism, see P. Horowitz, *The Jewish Question and Zionism* (London: Ernest Benn, 1927).

5. Toury, " 'The Jewish Question,' " pp. 85–106, 89–90.

6. Ibid., pp. 85–106, 92.

7. Phillips and Görres, "Die Jüdische Frage," pp. 377–397.

8. Toury, " 'The Jewish Question,' " pp. 85–106, p. 100.

9. *Times* (London), April 23, 1830, p. 4.

10. See, for example, Lord Macaulay's speech before the House of Commons from 1830, Israel Abrahams and Solomon Levy, eds., *Essay and Speech on Jewish Disabilities by Lord Macaulay* (Edinburgh: Ballantyne, Hanson, 1910), pp. 22–28.

11. Or more generally with the partitions of Poland (1772, 1793, 1795). See Lempicki, *Grand problème international*, p. 36.

12. The oldest I have found in print is from August 10, 1814, just over a month before the start of the Congress of Vienna (1814–1815). It appears in a letter from the German statesman Ernst Friedrich Herbert von Münster, addressed to his fellow statesman Hans Christoph Ernst von Gagern. Von Gagern himself made another reference, this time in a diplomatic report from November 1814, to the "question polonaise." In Baron Hans Christoph Ernst von Gagern, *Mein Antheil and der Politik, II. Nach Napeons Fall, Der Congreß zu Wien* (Stuttgart: J. G. Cotta'schen Buchhandlung, 1826), pp. 46, 75. The following month, the "question polonaise" appears again in a note from the French Foreign Minister Talleyrand to his Austrian counterpart, Prince Metternich, and a German book from 1816 cites an unnamed "Saxon" who in a supposedly obscure pamphlet made mention of the "sächsisch-polnische Frage." See Poland, *Constitutional Charter of the Kingdom of Poland, in the Year 1815 With Some*

Remarks on the Manner in Which the Charter, and the Stipulations in the Treaties Relating to Poland, Have Been Observed (London: J. Ridgway, 1831), p. 49. The Talleyrand reference is in connection with the views of the plenipotentiaries of Louis XVIII of France at the Vienna Congress, in *Allemannia: für Recht u. Wahrheit*, Volume 5 (1816), p. 146. Two years later, in a history of peace treaties since the peace of Westphalia published in Paris in 1818, there is a section on the "question polonaise et saxonne." Christophe-Guillaume Koch and Frédéric Schoell, eds., *Histoire abrégée des traités de paix, entre les puissances de l'Europe depuis la paix de Westphalie*, vol. 11 (Paris: Gide Fils, 1818), p. 621.

13. For example, Hermann von Boyen, the Prussian field marshal and former Prussian minister of war, published two pamphlets on the Polish question in 1830 and 1831. Reprinted in Hans Rothe, *Hermann von Boyen und die polnische Frage: Denkschriften von 1794 bis 1846* [Hermann von Boyen and the Polish question: Memoranda from 1794 to 1846] (Cologne: Böhlau, 2010), pp. 466–516. In 1831, a chapter on "Die polnische Frage" appeared in a German periodical, as did a pamphlet in English on *The Polish Question Shortly Stated*. See Friedrich Buchholz, ed., *Neue Monatsschrift für Deutschland, historisch-politischen Inhalts* [New monthly for Germany, with historical-political content], vol. 36 (Berlin: Theodor Chr. Fr. Enslin, 1831), pp. 83–101; An Englishman, *The Polish Question Shortly Stated* (London: James Ridgway, 1831). The first mention of the "sprawa polska" (Polish question) in Polish I have found is in a Polish translation of Richard Otto Spazier's history of the 1830–1831 Polish Uprising from 1832 (the translation was published in 1833): Spazier, *Geschichte des Aufstandes des polnischen Volkes in den Jahren 1830 und 1831, Nach authentischen Dokumenten, Reichstagsacten, Memoiren, Tagebüchern, schriftlichen und mündlichen Mittheilungen der vorzüglichsten Theilnehmer* [History of the uprising of the Polish people in the years 1830 and 1831, according to authentic documents, parliamentary records, memoirs, diaries, written and oral accounts of the most prominent participants] (Altenburg: Literatur-Comptoir, 1832); Spazier, *Historja powstania narodu polskiego w roku 1830 i 1831* [History of the uprising of the Polish nation in 1830 and 1831] (Paris: J. Pinard, 1833), p. 339.

14. *Critical review; or, Annals of literature by a Society of Gentlemen*, vol. 44 (London: W. Simpkin and R. Marshall, 1777), p. 414. It may also be worth noting that in the same year (1777) there is mention of the "American question" in *London magazine; or, Gentleman's monthly intelligencer* (1777), p. 75.

15. There is a reference to the "Eastern question" in an article in a London paper from 1829: "French Policy Towards Russia," *London Star*, July 7, 1829, p. 3. See also *Morning Chronicle*, January 21, 1830, p. 6; *Albion and The Star*, April 5, 1833, p. 2. In 1833, a book appeared on the Eastern question by David Urquhart, John McNeill, and David Ross, *Eastern Question* (London, 1833). That same year, a lecture on the "Eastern question" by David Ross of Bladensburg was announced in *Monthly Magazine or*

British Register (of Politics, Literature and the Belles Lettres) (London, 1833), p. 592. Mention in an official source occurs the same year in *The United Service Journal and Naval and Military Magazine, 1833, Part II* (London: Richard Bentley, 1833), p. 401.

16. See, for example, Dr. Richard Roepell, *Die orientalische Frage in ihrer geschichtlichen Entwickelung, 1774–1830* [The Eastern question in its historical development, 1774-1830] (Breslau: Verlag von Trewendt & Granier, 1854), p. 15; Војислав М. Јовановић, *Енглеска библиографија о источном питању у европи* [English bibliography of the Eastern question in Europe] (Belgrade: Државна Штампарија Краљевине Србије, 1908), p. 3; and TNA, FO 373/1/17, "History of the Eastern Question," pp. 3–4.

17. See, for example, Selami Saygın, *Yeni şark meselesi* [The new Eastern question] (Istanbul: Ülke Kitapları, 2003), p. 5. Ludwig Freiherr von Pastor, Goldwin Smith, Frederick Ignatius Antrobus, and Ralph Francis Kerr, *The History of the Popes, from the Close of the Middle Ages: Drawn from the Secret Archives of the Vatican and Other Original Sources*, vol. 3 (London: J. Hodges, 1899), p. 240.

18. Eugen Kvaternik, *Istočno pitanje i Hrvati: Historično-pravna razprava* [The Eastern question and the Croats: Historical-legal debate] (Zagreb: Štamparna Dragutina Albrechta, 1868), p. 1.

19. Cited in J. A. R. Marriott, *The Eastern Question: An Historical Study in European Diplomacy* (Oxford: Clarendon, 1917), p. 1.

20. Şakul, "Eastern Question," pp. 191–192.

21. Alexander Bitis, *Russia and the Eastern Question: Army, Government, and Society, 1815–1833* (Oxford: Oxford University Press for the British Academy, 2006), pp. 15, 21n.

22. Bismarck and the "Polish Question," speech to the Lower House of the Prussian Parliament, January 28, 1886. https://www.h-net.org/~german/gtext/kaiserreich/speech.html.

23. In a confidential handbook on the Eastern question published for internal circulation by the British Foreign Office in 1918, the author introduced the work with a reflection on the origins of the question: "The beginning of the 'Eastern question' is by some dated from the first appearance of the Slavs in the Balkan Peninsula; by others from the entry of the Turks into Macedonia, and subsequently into Constantinople. Its modern phase may be said to begin with the decadence of the Turkish Empire in the eighteenth century. This decadence had as its external result the encroachment of Austria and Russia from the north, and the constantly increasing intervention of Western Powers who felt their vital interests to be affected; while internally the weakening of the central authority admitted a growing consciousness of nationality among the subject races, and a desire, as opporunity offered, to throw off the Turkish yoke and attain independence." TNA, FO 373/1/17, "History of the Eastern Question," pp. 3–4. For the

historian Carl Brown, there were three possible dates: 1774, 1798, and the 1820s (the Treaty of Küçük Kaynarca, Napoleon's invasion of Egypt, and the Greek war of independence). Of the three, only the third appears to have any relation to the emergence of the phrase "the Eastern question." Brown, *International Politics*, pp. 21–30.

24. Jean Ouvrier (pseud.), *Die politische Giftmischerei in der Arbeiter-Frage* [Political poison-brewing in the worker question] (Berlin: Verlag von Eduard Beck, 1863), p. 3. "Man brauchte eine Arbeiter-Bewegung und man schuf eine Arbeiter-Frage."

25. Spengler, *Der Untergang des Abendlandes*, p. 34.

26. See Duane, *Mississippi Question Fairly Stated*; Duane, *Mississippi Question*; Davies Giddy, *A Plain Statement of the Bullion Question in a Letter to a Friend* (London: John Stockdale, 1811); Malthus, "Pamphlets on the Bullion Question," pp. 448–470; Theodor Herzl, *Der Judenstaat: Versuch einer modernen Lösung der Judenfrage* [The Jewish state: Attempt at a modern solution of the Jewish question] (Leipzig, 1896); Coudenhove-Kalergi, *Pan-Europe*.

27. John A. Ryan and R. A. McGowan, *A Catechism of the Social Question* (New York: Paulist Press, 1921).

28. И. А. Гончаро́в, Полное собрание сочинений, Обрыв, Т. 9 [Complete works, vol. 9, The precipice] (Ст-Петербург (St. Petersburg): Изд. А.Ф. Маркса, 1899), p. 18.

29. May, *Von Bagdad nach Stambul*, p. 408.

30. Leo Tolstoy, "The Non-Acting," in *The Complete Works of Count Tolstoy*, vol. 23 (Boston: Dana Estes, 1905), p. 50.

31. This is a reference to something Ludwig Wittgenstein once told a fellow philosopher, Oets Kolk Bouwsma, after crossing a suspension bridge over Cascadilla Gorge in Ithaca, New York. He was talking about faith of the sort Mormons have: "To understand a certain obtuseness is required. One must be obtuse to understand. He likened it to needing big shoes to cross a bridge with cracks in it. One mustn't ask questions." O. K. Bouwsma, *Wittgenstein: Conversations, 1949–1951* (Indianapolis: Hackett, 1986), p. 11. I would like to thank Richard Swedberg and Trevor Pinch for drawing my attention to this exchange in a presentation they gave at Cornell on "Wittgenstein's Visit to Ithaca in 1949: On the Importance of Details" on February 4, 2012, later published as Trevor Pinch and Richard Swedberg, "Wittgenstein's Visit to Ithaca in 1949: On the Importance of Details," in *Distinktion: Journal of Social Theory* 14, no. 1 (2013).

32. MacKenna, *Catholic Question*, p. 2.

33. An Englishman, *Poland*, p. 2.

34. Cited in David Ross of Bladensburg, ed., *Opinions of the European Press on the Eastern Question* (London, 1836), p. xxvii. In 1870, John Dunmore Lang made a similar argument about the Colonial question. "There is no great public question in

which the British nation has so deep an interest, or in regard to which a large proportion of the intelligence of the country is so profoundly and fatally ignorant, as the
Colonial question." Robert Andrew Macfie, *Colonial Questions Pressing for Immmediate Solution, in the Interest of the Nation and the Empire* (London: Longmans, Green,
Reader, and Dyer, 1871), pp. 62–63.

35. Friedrich Engels, "The Frankfurt Assembly Debates the Polish Question,"
Neue Rheinische Zeitung, no. 82, August 22, 1848, http://www.marxists.org/archive
/marx/works/1848/08/09.htm#art.

36. Alexis de Tocqueville, *Œuvres complètes,* vol. 7, *Nouvelle correspondance* (Paris:
Michel Lévy frères, 1866), p. 313. Tocqueville added that Napoleon once said this to
Lafayette.

37. See Rhodes, *History of the United States,* vol. 2, p. 126.

38. Dostoievsky, *Diary of a Writer,* p. 429.

39. Kurt Ehrenreich Floericke, *Spinnen und Spinnenleben* (Stuttgart: Kosmos,
Gesellschaft der Naturfreunde, 1919), p. 51. The work credits this "moody" observation to "Marshall" (otherwise unidentified). "Wie es wohl in der Welt aussähe, wenn
damals keine gefällige Spinne bei der Hand gewesen wäre! Wahrscheinlich gäbe es
keine orientalische Frage, und die Zeitungen würden einen nicht mit bulgarischen
Wirren langweilen."

40. Lipót Thull, *Egyéni nézetek a nemzetiségi kérdés megoldása tárgyában* [Indi-
vidual perspectives on the subject of solving the nationality question] (Pest: Szerző,
Emich Gusztáv Magyar Akademiai Ny., 1867), p. 3.

41. Masaryk, *Die philosophischen und sociologischen Grundlagen des Marxismus,* p. 1.

42. Вышевичъ, *Украинскій вопросъ, Россія и Антанта,* pp. 5–6.

43. William Fraser, *Disraeli and His Day* (London: K. Paul, Trench, Trübner,
1891), pp. 217–218. A character in Marcel Proust's *In Search of Lost Time,* Mme. Leroi,
knew better than to talk about the Eastern question in such settings. "[A]s an agree-
able woman who shunned anything that smacked of the bluestocking, she would as
little have thought of mentioning the eastern Question to a Prime Minister as of
discussing the nature of love with a novelist or a philosopher." Marcel Proust,
Remembrance of Things Past, The Guermantes Way, trans. C. K. Scott-Moncrieff and
Terence Kilmartin (Westminster, MD: Vintage, 1982), p. 199. Special thanks to John
Palattella for drawing my attention to this passage.

44. Heinrich von Treitschke, "A Word about Our Jewry," in *The Jew in the Modern
World: A Documentary History,* ed. Paul R. Mendes-Flohr and Jehuda Reinharz (New
York: Oxford University Press, 1980), p. 281.

45. Cited in Alex Bein, *The Jewish Question: Biography of a World Problem* (New
York: Herzl Press, 1990), p. 20.

46. Cited in Maksim Gorky, Leonid Andreyev, Fyodor Sologub, and Avrahm
Yarmolinsky, *The Shield* (New York: Knopf, 1917), pp. xv–xvi.

47. From John M. Ziman, *Puzzles, Problems, and Enigmas: Occasional Pieces on the Human Aspects of Science* (Cambridge: Cambridge University Press, 1981), p. 34.

48. See http://pl.wikipedia.org/wiki/Słoń_a_sprawa_polska, accessed October 19, 2013.

49. Richard J. Bernstein, *Hannah Arendt and the Jewish Question* (Cambridge, MA: MIT Press, 1996), pp. xi–xii.

50. Theodore R. Weeks, *From Assimilation to Antisemitism: The "Jewish Question" in Poland, 1850–1914* (DeKalb: Northern Illinois University Press, 2006); Geller, "*Atheist* Jew or Atheist *Jew*," pp. 1–14; Ković, *Disraeli and the Eastern Question*; Brown, "Tolerance and/or Equality?," pp. 1–31.

51. Howard Jacobson, *The Finkler Question* (London: Bloomsbury, 2010). Thanks to Vicki Caron for referring me to this work.

52. A book that I checked out from NYU's Bobst Library (Edward Chmielewski, *The Polish Question in the Russian State Duma* [Knoxville: University of Tennessee Press, 1970]) is missing the whole of the introduction and the tear marks are *not* clean. Another book from NYPL (Józef de Lipkowski, *La question polonaise et les Slaves de l'Europe Centrale: avec une carte ethnographique et huit cartes historiques de la Pologne* [The Polish question and the Slavs of Central Europe : With an ethnographic map and eight historical maps of Poland] [Paris: Dépot principal a la redaction de la revue Polonia, 1915])—features the above-mentioned marginalia on pages 86 and 102.

53. Farkas, *A zsidó kérdés Magyarországon*, p. 34. The copy in question is at the Országos Széchenyi Könyvtár in Budapest. To the passage in the pamphlet that reads "[H]e's not going to assimilate into Hungarian society, but on the contrary, by means of his reproductive capacities he will infect society," one reader writes, "That can't happen"; the other writes, "Yes it can, indeed it already has."

54. Réz and Jászi, *A nemzetiségi kérdés a politikai tudomány szempontjából*, p. 18. The copy in question is at the Országos Széchenyi Könyvtár in Budapest [Raktári jelzet: 288.147].

55. "Resurrexi," *Evening Star* of the *Thames Star*, vol. 12, no. 4049, December 20, 1881, p. 2.

56. W. P., "A Lament for Romance," in *Mayfair Magazine*, London, December 1883, p. 29.

57. Heine, *Lutetia*.

58. "Resurrexi," p. 2.

59. Cited in Marriott, *Eastern Question*, p. 1.

60. A. Ubicini and Emile Girardin, *La questione d'oriente innanzi l'europa* [The Eastern question before Europe] (Milan: Cosmorama pittorico, 1854), p. ix.

61. Pim, *Eastern Question*, p. 42.

62. Cited in Musa Gümüş, Namık Kemâl'e Göre 'Şark Meselesi' ve Osmanlı

Devleti'ni Cöküşe Götüren Sorunlar" [The 'Eastern question' and other questions leading to the collapse of the Ottoman state, according to Namık Kemâl], in *History Studies—International Journal of History*, Ortadoğu Özel Sayısı (2010): 145–163, p. 148. Kemâl's characterization is very similar to an observation made by Lord Stratford de Redcliffe in an article in *The Times* in 1875: "Like a volcano, [the Eastern question] has intervals of rest; but its outbreaks are frequent, their occasions uncertain, and their effects destructive." Cited in Stratford Canning, Stratford de Redcliffe, *The Eastern Question* (London: J. Murray, 1881), p. 6.

63. HStA Dresden, Bestand 10722 Sächsische Gesandtschaft für Bayern, Munich, Signatur 054, Hauptfaszikel II: Bundes- und Bundestagsangelegenheiten (Unterfaszikel), 15. Die Orientalische Frage, 1855, B. 86.

64. From a novel by Johannes Scherr, *Michel* (Leipzig: Hesse & Becker Verlag, 1858), accessed November 2, 2013, http://gutenberg.spiegel.de/buch/3546/5.

65. "Nantes Ansicht von England," in Fr. Rabener, *Knallerbsen oder Du sollst und musst lachen: 256 interess. Anekdoten u. 39. Räthsel u. Charaden z. Unterhalt* [Bang snaps, or, you should and must laugh: 256 interesting anecdotes, 39 riddles and charades for amusement] (Quedlinburg: Ernst, 1846), accessed February 22, 2014, http://gutenberg.spiegel.de/buch/7492/19.

66. Robert Cecil, Marquess of Salisbury, *Essays by the late Marquess of Salisbury* (London: J. Murray, 1905), p. 3.

67. Woodrow Wilson, "Socialism and Democracy," in *Woodrow Wilson: The Essential Political Writings*, ed. Ronald J. Pestritto (Lanham, MD: Lexington Books, 2005), p. 77.

68. See, for example, Władysław Kozłowski, *Sprawa Rusko-Ukraińska* [The Russian-Ukrainian question] (Lviv: Drukarna Kornela Pillera, 1867), p. 3. Leon Wasilewski, *Ukraina i sprawa ukraińska* [Ukraine and the Ukrainian question] (Kraków: Spółka nakładowa Książka, [1911]), p. x; Szombatsági, *A nemzetiségi kérdés Magyarországban*, pp. 65–66.

69. Szombatsági, *A nemzetiségi kérdés Magyarországban*, p. 3; *Szózat a magyar kérdés érdemében*, pp. 18, 21, 23, 71.

70. Ibid., pp. 65–66.

71. TNA, WO 33/29, Report on the Eastern question, paper no. 629, 1876, p. 421.

72. In TNA, ZLIB 15/16, pamphlet 11, p. 4. Austin continued, "There is such a thing as being struck dumb with horror. Some men expend their nerves in shouts that awake the neighborhood; while others, equally sensitive, after a half-smothered cry of shame, betake themselves in manly and helpful silence to remedy the scandal and control the ill." Ibid., p. 6.

73. From a satirical piece by the British journalist George Augustus Sala, "The Strange Behaviour of Mr. Apostolo," in *Belgravia Annual* (Christmas, 1877), p. 5.

74. Diary entry from March 21, 1898. Lev Tolstoi, Ludwig Rubiner, and Frieda

Ichak, *Leo Tolstoi Tagebuch 1895–1899* [Leo Tolstoy diaries, 1895-1899] (Zurich: Max Rascher, 1918), p. 167.

75. AT-OeStA/HHStA SB Nl Flotow 3–7/I, "Die 'ukrainische Frage' in ihrer wahren Gestalt" [The 'Ukrainian question' in its true form], pp. 142–142v. The manuscript has no given author, but that the author was Austrian can be gleaned from the final sentences of the text, which refer to "our brothers and neighbors beyond the Leitha" (namely, the Hungarians). A British newspaper similarly declared in 1892 that "there is no Armenian question, in the political sense of the word." Excerpt from the *Morning Advertiser* (London), February 17, 1892; "Reforms in Armenia," in Bilâl N. Şimşir, ed., *Documents Diplomatiques Ottomans, Affaires Arméniennes* [Ottoman diplomatic documents, Armenian affairs], vol. 1, *1886–1893* (Ankara: Impremerie de la Sciete Turque D'Histoire, 1985), doc. 148 (Annexe), p. 163.

76. Julian Marchlewski, "Kwestia polska w okresie rewolucji 1848 r." [The Polish question during the Revolution of 1848], in *Ludzie, czasy, idee* [People, times, ideas] (Warsaw: Książka i Wiedza, 1973), p. 536 (emphasis in the original).

77. Steiner, *Die Kernpunkte der sozialen Frage*, p. 5. See also Karl Heinzen, *Die Helden des teutschen Kommunismus. Dem Herrn Karl Marx gewidmet* [The heroes of German communism, dedicated to Mr. Karl Marx] (Bern: Jenni, Sohn, 1848), p. 74. This has often been the case with the Jewish question, as well. As historian Mary Gluck writes, "It is customary to put quotation marks around the Jewish question, since it was not so much a question as an exclusionary discourse about Jewish citizenship and national identity." Mary Gluck, *The Invisible Jewish Budapest: Metropolitan Culture at the Fin De Siécle* (Madison: University of Wisconsin Press, 2016), p. 40.

78. Julian Klaczko, *Studya dyplomatyczne: Sprawa polska—sprawa duńska (1863–1865), część pierwsza* [Diplomatic Studies: The Polish question—the Danish question, 1863–1865, part one] (Kraków: Spółka Wydawnicza Polska, 1903), p. 51. Klaczko refers to this as "the dual meaning of the phrase 'European question'" (with specific reference to France). Ibid., p. 37.

79. Cited in Allan Cunningham, *Anglo-Ottoman Encounters in the Age of Revolution: Collected Essays* (London: F. Cass, 1993), p. 1. This was also true of the "Ukrainian question" in the aforementioned text. AT-OeStA/HHStA SB Nl Flotow 3–7/I, "Die 'ukrainische Frage' in ihrer wahren Gestalt," pp. 142–142v.

80. Disraeli, *Tancred*, pp. 107, 111.

81. Cited in Heinrich von Treitschke, *Deutsche Geschichte im neunzehnten Jahrhundert*, vol. 4, *Bis zum Tode König Friedrich Wilhelms III* [German history in the nineteenth century, vol. 4, To the death of Friedrich Wilhelm III] (Leipzig: Hirzel, 1927), p. 350. "There is no Eastern question" was also English diplomats' refrain to the Russian government in May of 1860. From August 10, 1860, in *Historisch-Politische Blätter für das Katholische Deutschland des Jahrgangs 1860*, vol. 46 (Munich, 1860), p. 335.

82. "The Eastern Question" from Ambrose Bierce, *The Collected Works*, vol. 4,

Shapes of Clay, Some Ante-mortem Epitaphs, the Scrap Heap (New York: Neale, 1910), p. 367.

83. Dostoyevsky, "Diplomacy Facing World Problems," pp. 995–996. It should be noted that Dostoevsky himself was convinced of its reality.

84. BOA, Yıldız Perâkende Evrâkı Hariciye Nezâreti Maruzâtı (Y.PRK.HR), Dos. 9, Göm. 62, July 18, 1886, (16/L/1303 (Hicrî)), p. 1.

85. Toynbee, *Western Question*, pp. 1–4.

86. "Wie der Dr. Leopold Herbst ausging, die polnische Frage zu studieren, und wie es ihm hiebei ergangen" [How Dr. Leopold Herbst went out to study the Polish question, and how that went for him], in *Der Floh* (Vienna), February 4, 1872, p. 23.

87. George Boole, *An Investigation of the Laws of Thought, on Which Are Founded the Mathematical Theories of Logic and Probabilities* (Cambridge: Macmillan, 1854), p. 20.

88. "Whatever concept one may hold, from a metaphysical point of view, concerning the freedom of the will, certainly its appearances, which are human actions, like every other natural event are determined by universal laws. However obscure their causes, history, which is concerned with narrating these appearances, permits us to hope that if we attend to the play of freedom of the human will in the large, we may be able to discern a regular movement in it, and that what seems complex and chaotic in the single individual may be seen from the standpoint of the human race as a whole to be a steady and progressive though slow evolution of its original endowment. Since the free will of man has obvious influence upon marriages, births, and deaths, they seem to be subject to no rule by which the number of them could be reckoned in advance. Yet the annual tables of them in the major countries prove that they occur according to laws as stable as [those of] the unstable weather, which we likewise cannot determine in advance, but which, in the large, maintain the growth of plants the flow of rivers, and other natural events in an unbroken uniform course. Individuals and even whole peoples think little on this. Each, according to his own inclination, follows his own purpose, often in opposition to others; yet each individual and people, as if following some guiding thread, go toward a natural but to each of them unknown goal; all work toward furthering it, even if they would set little store by it if they did know it." Immanuel Kant, *Idea for a Universal History from a Cosmopolitan Point of View*, accessed April 13, 2017, https://www.marxists.org/reference/subject/ethics/kant/universal-history.htm#n1.

89. See, for example, *Deutsche Allgemeine Zeitung* 95 (April 5, 1846), p. 3; Becher, *Die Arbeiterfrage*, p. 3; Müller, *Die einzig mögliche und wahre Lösung der sozialen Frage*, p. 16; Marriott, *Eastern Question*, p. 3; "Revindications Musulmanes," *L' Écho de Tiaret: Organe hebdomadaire des intérêts généraux et régionaux*, August 1, 1936, p. 2 (on how some call the "question algérienne" the "malaise algérien").

90. See, for example, Steiner, *Die Kernpunkte der sozialen Frage*, p. 42.

91. Barbara Zielke, *Die Orientalische Frage im politischen Denken Europas: vom Ausgang des 17. bis zum Ende des 18. Jahrhunderts* [The Eastern question in the political thought of Europe from the beginning of the seventeenth to the end of the eighteenth century] (Leipzig: Gebr. Gerhardt, 1931), p. 40.

92. The relevant Pascal and d'Alembert texts include Pascal, *Traitez de l'equilibre des liqueurs*; d'Alembert, *Traité sur l'équilibre*.

93. See, for example, Surányi, *A socialis kérdés*, p. 3; Hermann Marggraff, *Fritz Beutel* (Paderborn: Antigonos Verlag, 2012), p. 329; Toynbee, *Western Question*, pp. 26–27; Ferencz Steinberger, *A nőnevelés és a nő-kérdés* [Women's education and the woman question] (Szatmár: Pázmány Ny., 1894), pp. 22–24; Század, *A zsidókérdés Magyarországon*, p. 67; József Ajtay, *A nemzetiségi kérdés: A Magyar Társadalomtudományi Egyesület nemzetiségi értekezlete eredményeinek összefoglalása* [The nationality question: A summary of the results of the Hungarian Social Sciences Association's nationality session] (Budapest: Pesti Könyvnyomda-RészvényTársaság, 1914), p. 26; Gergely Késmárki, *Páneurópa és a kisebbségi kérdés* [Pan-Europe and the minority question] (Lugos: Husvéth—Hoffer Ny., [1930]), p. 3; Béla Mészáros, *A szociális kérdés, sociologikus tanulmány két részben* [The social question, sociological study in two parts] (Szabadka: Szent Antal Ny., 1909), p. 10; and de Tourville, "Preface," p. viii.

94. From Nikolai Danilevsky on the Eastern question. Danilevskii and Woodburn, *Russia and Europe*, p. 332. On the Eastern question as formula, see Dostoievsky, *Diary of a Writer*, p. 428. This automatism will be discussed in more detail and with more examples in subsequent chapters.

95. See, for example, Jászi et al., *A nemzetiségi kérdés a társadalmi és az egyéni fejlődés szempontjából*, p. 9; Katona,´ *Javaslatok a rokkant-kérdés megoldására*, pp. 3–4; Kraus, *A világítási kérdés megítélésére szolgáló új adalékok*, p. 1; Ádám Lázár, *Székely kérdés* [The Szekler question] (Székelyudvarhely: Becsek Ny., 1902), p. 11; Mihalovics, *Mindenki könyve*, p. 5; and Werner Bosch, *Die Saarfrage: Eine wirtschaftliche Analyse* [The Saar question: An economic analysis] (Heidelberg: Quelle & Meyer, 1954), p. 7.

96. To cite just a few: Giuseppe Mazzini writing on the Italian question in 1859, for example, argued that the liberal statesman Camillo Benso, Count of Cavour, had utterly misunderstood and misrepresented the Italian question; see Mazzini, *La questione italiana*, pp. 3, 5. See also von Scheel, *Die Theorie der sozialen Frage*, p. 1; Endre Bosányi, *A"malom-kérdés"* (Budapest: Hornyánszky Viktor Ny., 1894), p. 3; and Steiner, *Die Kernpunkte der sozialen Frage*, p. 22.

97. "Književni Pregled," in *Otadžbina: književnost, nauka, društveni život* [Fatherland: Literature, science, social life], god. 10, knj. 28 (Beograd, 1891), p. 616. Special thanks to Edin Hajdarpašić for sending me this wonderful text.

98. Георги П. Геновъ, *Източниятъ въпросъ: Политическа и дипломатическа история, частъ втора, Отъ Парижския конгресъ (1856 г.) до Ньойския договоръ*

(1919 z.) [The Eastern question: A political and diplomatic history, part 2, from the Paris Congress of 1856 to the Treaty of Neuilly of 1919] (Sofia: Печатница художникъ, 1926), p. 602.

99. Schlett, *A "munkáskérdés" és a szocializmus a magyar politikai gondolkodásban*, p. 193.

100. Strommer, *A női kérdés és korunk*, pp. 17–18.

101. Mészáros, *A szociális kérdés*, p. 3.

102. Réz and Jászi, *A nemzetiségi kérdés a politikai tudomány szempontjából*, p. 1.

103. See, for example, *Szózat a magyar kérdés érdemében*, p. iii; Eötvös, *A nemzetiségi kérdés*, p. 231; Türr, *A keleti kérdés*, p. 17; Jászi et al., *A nemzetiségi kérdés a társadalmi és az egyéni fejlődés szempontjából*, p. 86; and Széchenyi, *A Jelenkorban Megjelent: Adó és Két Garas*, p. 261.

104. Tibor Joó, *A korszellem mint történetfilozófiai kérdés* [The spirit of the time as a philosophy of history question] (Budapest: Egyet. Ny., 1933), p. 20.

105. Hungarian democrat István Bibó, writing on the Jewish question in Hungary in 1948. Bibó, *Válogatott tanulmányok*, p. 795.

106. See, for example, Holly Case, "The Media and State Power in Southeastern Europe up to 1945" in *Ottomans into Europeans: The Limits of Institutional Transfer*, ed. Alina Mungiu-Pippidi and Wim van Meurs (London: Hurst; Boulder, CO: Columbia University Press, 2010), pp. 279–305; David Mitch, "Education and Skill of the British Labour Force," in *The Cambridge Economic History of Modern Britain*, vol. 1, *Industrialisation, 1700–1860*, ed. Roderick Floud and Paul Johnson (Cambridge: Cambridge University Press, 2004), p. 344.

107. TNA, PRO 30/22/3E/100, Lord John Russell: Papers. Correspondence and Papers, vol. 3E, October 22, 1840, p. 237. "[A]bout the Press . . . I do not see when you are told that the articles in the newspapers form part of the conduct of the negociations, how you can avoid giving your opinion to those who direct their insertion."

108. Disraeli, *Tancred*, pp. 175–176.

109. Dr. Karl Lemayer, "Populärer Jurisprudenz" [Popular jurisprudence], in *Allgemeine Österreichische Gerichtszeitung*, April 15, 1870, p. 3.

110. Ibid., p. 119.

111. Е., *Восточный вопросъ и условия мира съ Турцıей*, pp. 5–6.

112. See, for example, Bosányi, *A"malom-kérdés,"* p. 3; Dávid Löwy, *Az ínség és nyomor vége vagy, A szociális kérdés végleges megoldása, írta Egy emberbarát* [The end of want and misery, or the definitive solution of the social question, written by a friend of humanity] ([Budapest]: Robicsek Zs., [1897]), p. 13; and Müller, *Die einzig mögliche und wahre Lösung der sozialen Frage*, p. 6.

113. Антон Павлович Чехов, "Новогодняя пытка," *Рассказы* ["The New Year's drink," short stories], accessed September 26, 2016, http://ostrovok.de/p/chekhov/novogodnyaya-pytka.html.

114. Eduard von Keyserling, *Die dritte Stiege* [The third staircase] (Heidelberg: Carl Winter, 1985), p. 217.

115. Bosányi, *A"malom-kérdés,"* p. 3.

116. Singer, *Briefe berühmter christlicher Zeitgenossen über die Judenfrage*, p. xviii.

117. Ibid., p. ix.

118. Század, *A zsidókérdés Magyarországon*, p. 77. Mentioned by the respondent Győző Concha.

119. Weydmann, *Die Fragen*, pp. 1–2.

120. Század, *A zsidókérdés Magyarországon*, p. 159. See also Vasile M. Kogâlniceanu, *Chestiunea țărănească* [The peasant question] (Bucharest: Tipografia Gutenberg Joseph Göbl, 1906), pp. 3–4.

121. See Jászi et al., *A nemzetiségi kérdés a társadalmi és az egyéni fejlődés szempontjából*.

122. Hans Poeschel, *Die Kolonialfrage im Frieden von Versailles: Dokumente zu ihrer Behandlung* [The colonial question in the Treaty of Versailles: Documents on its treatment] (Berlin: E. S. Mittler & Sohn, 1920), p. iv. See also Moritz Julius Bonn, ed., *Die Balkanfrage* [The Balkan question] (Munich: Verlag von Duncker und Humblot, 1914), Vorwort, page unnumbered.

123. Joseph Jacobs, *The Jewish Question, 1875–1884: Bibliographical Hand-List* (London: Trübner, 1885), pp. v, x–xi, 1.

124. See, for example, TNA, CUST 155/19, Sugar duty: "The Sugar Question," includes a brief retrospect from 1864–1903; Rudolph Meyer, *Die neueste Literatur zur Socialen Frage* [The latest literature on the social question] (Berlin: A. Schindler, 1873); Alfred Russel Wallace, *Land Nationalisation, Etc.: A Short Bibliography of the Land Question* (London: Swan Sonnenschein, 1892); Јовановић, *Енглеска библиографија о источном питању у европи*; Robert Ernest Cowan and Boutwell Dunlap, *Bibliography of the Chinese Question in the United States* (San Francisco: A. M. Robertson, 1909); Fővárosi Könyvtár, *Balkán kérdés* [The Balkan question] ([Budapest]: Székesfőv. Ny., [1912]); Th. Savtchenko, *L'Ukraine et la question ukrainienne: Suivi d'une esquisse d'une bibliographie ukrainienne*. [Ukraine and the Ukrainian question: Followed by a sketch of a Ukrainian bibliography] (Paris: Imprimerie slave, 1918); Horváth, *The Hungarian Question*; Bibliothek für Zeitgeschichte, *Bibliographie zur Geschichte der polnischen Frage bis 1919* [Bibliography on the history of the Polish question to 1919] (Stuttgart: Weltkriegsbücherei, Institut für Weltpolitik, 1940).

125. Milos Popovich, *A nemzetiségi kérdés Magyarországban szerb szempontból* [The nationality question in Hungary from a Serbian perspective] (Subotica: Bittermann Ny., 1865), pp. 149–150.

126. Robert Musil, "Politik in Österreich" [Politics in Austria] in *Der deutsche Mensch als Symptom: Reden und Aufsätze zur Politik* [The German person as symptom: Speeches and essays on politics] (Vienna: Karolinger Verlag, 2014), p. 7.

127. Toynbee, *Western Question*, p. 3.

128. Tolstoï, *Anna Karenina*, p. 386, see also pp. 340–341, 344–347, 384–388. See Milojković-Djurić, *Eastern Question*, pp. 32–47, 36–37.

129. See Quataert, *Ottoman Empire*, p. 56; Caroline Finkel, *Osman's Dream: The History of the Ottoman Empire* (New York: Basic Books, 2006), pp. 323, 445, 489. See also "Not only does a historian of the Ottoman Empire work against the stereotypes of decline embodied in the 'Eastern Question' historiography . . ." Virginia H. Aksan, *Ottoman Wars, 1700–1870* (Harlow, UK: Longman/Pearson, 2007), p. 1. See also ibid., p. 88.

130. Selim Deringil, *The Well-protected Domains: Ideology and the Legitimation of Power in the Ottoman Empire, 1876–1909* (London: I. B. Tauris, 2011), p. 6

131. See, for example, Nahid, *Üç muamma*; Şakul, "Eastern Question," p. 191.

132. See, for example, Deringil, *Well-Protected Domains*, p. 6; Aksan, *Ottoman Wars*, p. 88.

133. See, for example, Brown, *International Politics*, p. 21.

134. Tuncer, *Osmanlı Devleti ve Büyük Güçler, 1815–1878*, p. 12.

135. Edmund Jan Osmańczyk, *Rzeczpospolita Polaków* [Polish commonwealth] (Warsaw: Państ. Instytut Wydawniczy, 1977), p. 5.

136. Norman Davies, *God's Playground: 1795 to the Present* (New York: Columbia University Press, 2005), p. 11.

6. The Temporal Argument: The Age of Spin

1. Hungarian publicist and writer Károly Szini, writing on the Hungarian question in 1866. Szini, *Magyar irodalom: javaslat a magyar kérdés megoldására*, p. 6.

2. Charles Baudelaire, "The Painter of Modern Life," in *The Painter of Modern Life and Other Essays*, ed. Jonathan Mayne (London: Phaidon Press, 1964), pp. 27–29.

3. Émile de Girardin, *Solutions de la question d'Orient* (Paris: Librairie nouvelle, 1853), p. 7.

4. The German question was understood by the author to relate to the unification of German states. HStA Dresden, Bestand 10717, Ministerium der auswärtigen Angelegenheiten, Signatur 1034, Die deutsche Frage, Abschrift: Geheimes Actenstück, die deutsche Frage betr., 1870, Bl. 14.

5. Emil Reich, *History of Civilization, Being a Course of Lectures on the Origin and Development of the Main Institutions of Mankind, with Illustrations* (Cincinnati, OH: Emil Reich, 1887), p. 191.

6. A further example is provided by Hitler, who said on June 14, 1943: "When Metternich was at the helm, the time was simply not ripe for a definitive solution of the [German] unification question." Hitler, *Monologe im Führerhauptquartier*, p. 401.

7. Frederick Douglass, *The Anti-slavery Movement: A Lecture by Frederick Douglass*

Before the Rochester Ladies' Anti-Slavery Society (Rochester: Press of Lee, Mann & Company, 1855), pp. 39, 43.

8. Marx and Engels, *A Few Words on the Eastern Question*, pp. 39, 55–56.

9. Campbell, *Blue Books*, p. 27.

10. Herzl, *Jewish State, p.* 6. For another, earlier example of urgency and necessity relating to the Jewish question, see AT-OeStA/HHStA PA XVIII 49, "Judenfrage und Anerkennung Rumäniens," 1879, p. 68.

11. AS, MID-PP, 6M, red. 229, 1895, "Македония и Европа" [Macedonia and Europe], in *Гласъ Македонски*, vol. 2, no. 31 (Sofia), July 9, 1895, p. 1.

12. *Kurze Darstellung der mazedonischen Frage*, first of four unnumbered pages.

13. Pownall, *Administration of the Colonies*, p. vii.

14. Ibid., p. x (emphasis in the original).

15. Reprinted in *Debates of the House of Commons Containing an Account of the Most Interesting Speeches and Motions, Accurate Copies of the Most Remarkable Letters and Papers, of the Most Material Evidence, Petitions, &C. Laid Before and Offered to the House*, vol. 1 (London: Reprinted for John Stockdale, Piccadilly, 1802), p. 245.

16. Watson's own reference to it was in the past tense. See also *Gentleman's Magazine* (London), May 1783, p. 383; *The Parliamentary Register; or, History of the Proceedings and Debates of the House of Commons ... during the Third Session of the Fifteenth Parliament of Great Britain*, vol. 26 (vol. IX) (London: J. Debrett, 1883), pp. 39, 283; John Jebb and John Disney, *The Works Theological, Medical, Political, and Miscellaneous of John Jebb* (London: Sold by T. Cadell, 1787), p. 552; John Wilde, *An Address to the Lately Formed Society of the Friends of the People* (Edinburgh: Printed for P. Hill, 1793), p. 512.

17. *Critical Review; or, Annals of Literature, Series the Third*, vol. 13 (London: Printed for J. Mawman, 1808), p. 536. The "subject" of the question was delineated in a review of three pamphlets as "the discussions which have for about two years existed in form between this country and the United States, which have in reality, however, been growing up with the increase of the American commerce since the beginning of last war, and which have now come to the point of being speedily terminated, either by mutual concessions, or by an appeal to arms." (The expected termination was to come with the War of 1812). See *Edinburgh Review*, no. 21 (October 1807): 1.

18. See, for example, "On the American Question," in *Tradesman; or, Commercial Magazine* 8, no. 48 (June 1, 1812), pp. 470–475; *Hansard Parliamentary Debates*, 1st series (1803–1820), p. 439; and Conciliator, *Why Are We Still at War?; or, The American Question Considered In a Series of Essays Rejected by the Journalists As Unpopular: Recommended to a Candid Perusal* (London: Printed by A. J. Valpy, 1814).

19. *The American Question: Secession, Tariff, Slavery* (Brighton: H. Taylor, 1862), p. 45.

20. See, for example, *A magyar kérdés rövid vázlatban* [A brief sketch of the Hun-

garian question] (Vienna: Eurich S. Ny., 1863), pp. 3–6; Rőnyi, *Indokolt programm a magyar kérdés törvényes és praktikus megoldását illetőleg*, p. 1; László Varga, *The Unsolved Hungarian Question* (New York: Federation of Free Hungarian Jurists, 1969), preface, pages unnumbered; and Gáspár Miklós Tamás, "A magyar kérdés" [The Hungarian question], in *A magyar kérdés: Kelet-Európa jövője [The Hungarian question: Eastern Europe's future]*, Magyar Füzetek, 11. Szám (Paris: Dialogues européens, 1982), p. 66.

21. See, for example, Lajos Hajnald, *Felsöházi Beszéde az Erdélyi Unio Tárgyában: (Junius 17-kén) [Speech in the upper chamber on the subject of union with Transylvania, June 17th]* (Pest: Lampel R., 1861), p. 4; Emil Horváth, *Erdély és az oláh kérdés* [Transylvania and the Vlach/Romanian question] (Dej: Horgos és Medgyesi Könyvnyomdája, 1912), pp. 17–19; and József Ajtay, Benedek Jancsó, and Alois Kovács, *The Transylvanian Question* (London: Low, W. Dawson & Sons, 1921).

22. See, for example, MOL, K64a., 33/a. tétel Ruszinszkói kérdés, 1938–1939, 1358/Res. Pol./1938, pp. 30–30v; SNA, MZV, K. 192, 8.204/1942, p. 4; Kállay, *Magyarország miniszterelnöke voltam*, p. 91. The Jewish question similarly took many forms in Hungary, as it related to Jewish emancipation, to the split between reform and Orthodox Jews in Hungary, or to the problem of anti-Semitism and Jews' relationship to non-Jews, or to Christianity and the possibility of conversion. See, for example, [Mór Grosz], *Kol meged: Külföldi hang a jelenlegi magyar-zsidó kérdés ügyéről* [Kol meged: A foreign voice on the matter of the current Hungarian-Jewish question] (Vácz: Katzburg Ny., 1908), pp. 44–45; Század, *A zsidókérdés Magyarországon*; Kmoskó, *Zsidó-keresztény kérdés*, p. 16.

23. Examples are far too numerous to list, but for a sampling, see Duane, *Mississippi Question Fairly Stated*, p. 1. Duane refers to "forged pamphlets, rescripts, and fictitious correspondence [that] have been seconded by the exaggeration and mutilation of facts ... [T]ruth has been disregarded or concealed by those who are determined to deceive, and to inflame the public mind; and every artifice is employed to irritate and to wound the feelings and the pride of those who could not be assailed on the side of their understandings, if correctly and fairly informed." See also Charles Maclean, *Abstract of the East India Question: Illustrating in a Concise Manner the Contraversy between the East India Company and His Majesty's Ministers* (London: Printed for J. Mawman, 1813), p. 1; "This Question has been so frequently, and perhaps designedly misstated, that it becomes necessary to set out by establishing what it really is." M. J. Brunet, *La question algérienne* [The Algerian question] (Paris: Librairie Militaire, 1847), pp. v–vi; George, *The Irish Land Question*, p. 12; and Wasilewski, *Ukraina i sprawa ukraińska*, p. x.

24. MacKenna, *Catholic Question*, p. 2.

25. Ibid., p. 3.

26. Ibid., p. 3.

27. See, for example, *Courier* (London), December 13, 1830, p. 2 (also in *Morning Chronicle* (London), December 14, 1830, p. 1, and *London Morning Post*, December 14, 1830, p. 4.); *London Standard*, January 24, 1831, p. 3; and de Montalembert, *L'Insurrection Polonaise*, p. 19. It is telling that in 1878, the Ottoman administration gathered information on the (unsuccessful) efforts of Poles in the Austrian parliament to tie the Polish to the Eastern questions at the Congress of Berlin negotiations. BOA, Hariciye Siyasi (HR.SYS), Dos. 160, Göm. 41, March 15, 1878.

28. Most notably the Greek uprising in the Ottoman Empire (1821–1832), resulting in the independence of Greece; the Polish November Uprising in tsarist Russia (1830–1831), crushed by tsarist troops; the Belgian Revolution (1830–1839), resulting in Belgium's independence; the French invasion and conquest of Ottoman Algiers (1830); the Mehmet Ali crisis in the Ottoman Empire (1831–1833), which resulted in the Great Powers coming together to prevent Ottoman collapse; and the June rebellion in France (1832). The claim of hypocrisy in international intervention played a role in how discussion of the Polish question relates to the events in France, for it was the Bonapartist general Lamarque's funeral that was the occasion for the outbreak of the June rebellion in Paris, not least of all because the general had been a vocal critic of the French state's failure to mobilize in support of the Polish November uprising.

29. In 1878 a handkerchief trick featuring the Eastern Question was made in Britain. Fiammetta Rocco, "A Fine Collection of Handkerchiefs," *The Economist, Intelligent Life,* March 2, 2008 http://moreintelligentlife.com/story/beautiful-blowhards.

30. TNA, PRO 30/22/3D/68, September 1839, p. 33.

31. de Redcliffe, *Eastern Question*, p. 22.

32. Е., *Восточный вопросъ и условия мира съ Турціей*, p. 5.

33. In being cast as of "vital" importance for this or that state or group, the Eastern question was in no way unique. There are countless examples of other questions being discussed in the same key. In 1911, the sewer question was framed as "a matter of 'life'" in a Polish pamphlet. Angerman, *Sprawa kanałowa*, pp. 43–44. In 1915, the Ukrainian nationalist Dmytro Dontsov wrote of the Ukrainian question that it had become a "vital question of all Russiandom" and "an international question." See Dontsov, *Die ukrainische Staatsidee*, p. 53. Speaking in the Hungarian parliament in June of 1916, for example, the Hungarian statesman and former interior minister of Hungary Gyula Andrássy (the younger) said of the Polish question that he considered it "one of the most important questions for world politics and for our own interest." Andrássy, *A világháború problémái*, pp. 215, 218–219. In 1899, a pamphlet of the Catholic People's Party in Hungary argued that "[t]he settlement and resolution of the Jewish question has become a virtual life and death issue in Hungary, because something has to happen." Cited in Gluck, *Georg Lukács*, p. 58.

34. Franz Grillparzer and August Sauer, *Grillparzers sämtliche Werke in zwanzig Bänden*, Band XIV, *Studien zur Philosophie und Religion; Historische und politische Studien* [The complete works of Grillparzer in twenty volumes, vol. 14, Studies on philosophy and religion; historical and political studies] (Stuttgart: J. G. Cotta Nachf., [1892]), accessed February 22, 2014, http://gutenberg.spiegel.de/buch /1530/7. The above was stated in the context of a critique of Metternich's policies; see William Henry Trescot, *An American View of the Eastern Question* (Charleston, SC: John Russell, 1854), esp. pp. 62–63.

35. Manjiro Inagaki, *Japan and the Pacific, and a Japanese View of the Eastern Question* (New York: Scribner and Welford, 1890), pp. 9–10.

36. On reopening, see, for example, "Vzhodno vprašanje" [The Eastern question], in *Slovenski Gospodar, poduč̌ivan list za slovensko ljudstvo* [Maribor], vol. 4, no. 46, November 17, 1870, p. 1; Laurence Oliphant and Charles A. Dana, *Haifa; or, Life In Modern Palestine.*(New York: Harper & Bros., 1887), p. 289. From charts generated by Google Ngram Viewer, certain trends become evident. See, for example, https://books.google.com/ngrams/graph?content=Eastern+question&case _insensitive=on&year_start=1800&year_end=1930&corpus=15&smoothing=0& share=&direct_url=t4%3B%2CEastern%20question%3B%2Cc0%3B%2Cs0%3B% 3BEastern%20Question%3B%2Cc0%3B3BEastern%20question%3B%2Cc0%3B %3BEASTERN%20QUESTION%3B%2Cc0%3B%3Beastern%20question %3B%2Cc0; https://books.google.com/ngrams/graph?content=question+d+' +orient&case_insensitive=on&year_start=1800&year_end=1930&corpus=19& smoothing=0&share=&direct_url=t4%3B%2Cquestion%20d%20%27%20orient% 3B%2Cc0%3B%2Cs0%3B%3Bquestion%20d%20%27%20Orient%3B%2Cc0%3B %3BQUESTION%20D%20%27%20ORIENT%3B%2Cc0%3B%3BQuestion %20d%20%27%20Orient%3B%2Cc0; https://books.google.com/ngrams/graph? content=Восточный+вопрос&case_insensitive=on&year_start=1800&year_end =1930&corpus=25&smoothing=0&share=&direct_url=t4%3B%2CВосточный %20вопрос%3B%2Cc0%3B%2Cs0%3B%3Bвосточный%20вопрос%3B%2Cc0 %3B%3BВосточный%20вопрос%3B%2Cc0%3B%3BВОСТОЧНЫЙ %20ВОПРОС%3B%2Cc0; and https://books.google.com/ngrams/graph?content =orientalische+frage&case_insensitive=on&year_start=1800&year_end=1930& corpus=20&smoothing=0&share=&direct_url=t4%3B%2Corientalische%20frage %3B%2Cc0%3B%2Cs0%3B%3Borientalische%20Frage%3B%2Cc0 %3B%3BOrientalische%20Frage%3B%2Cc0. There are many problems with these charts, so I caution the reader about taking them for anything more than very general trends. For one thing, the language reveals nothing about the place where sources were printed (many of the Russian pamphlets, for example, were published abroad due to censorship). And the viewer can only run searches in particular languages. Ngram also makes a distinction between "English," "American English," and "British

English" (with all the concomitant confusions that entails). And because of the qual- ity—or lack thereof—of many of the scans, and therefore also the meta-data on many books, the program turns up false positives with some regularity. For example, where you see peaks prior to the 1830s, if you examine the actual sources to which they refer, they are generally scan errors (where "1899" will be read as "1800," etc.). And German Fraktur script—commonly used in nineteenth-century publications— cannot be properly read by the OCR software for German (for example, the s often is mistaken for an f or a "/"), which makes references to the "orientalische Frage" largely undetectable if they are found in texts written in Fraktur. Still, some trends are visible from these charts, namely, that different languages (and therefore to some extent states) had differing levels of interest in the Eastern question over time, with noteworthy spikes in interest across the board during the Oriental Crisis (1840), the Crimean War (1853–1856), the Eastern Crisis (1875–1878), and the Balkan Wars through the declaration of the Turkish Republic (1911–1923).

37. https://books.google.com/ngrams/interactive_chart?content=%22polnisch e+Frage%22&case_insensitive=on&year_start=1770&year_end=2008&corpus =20&smoothing=3&share=&direct_url=t4%3B%2C%22%20polnische%20Frage %20%22%3B%2Cc0%3B%2Cs0%3B%3B%22%20polnische%20Frage%20 %22%3B%2Cc0%3B%3B%22%20Polnische%20Frage%20%22%3B%2Cc0" width=900 height=500 marginwidth=0 marginheight=0 hspace=0 vspace=0 frame border=0 scrolling=no.

38. References to the Polish question after World War II are mostly historio- graphical treatments of the period preceding, rather than revivals of the question per se. See, for example, Chmielewski, *Polish Question*; R. F. Leslie, *The Polish Question: Poland's Place in Modern History* (London: Historical Association, 1964). Nonethe- less, there were some exceptions (commentators who cast the communist period as similar to Poland's situation in the nineteenth century, for example).

39. Şimşir, *Documents Diplomatiques*, vol. 1, p. xii.

40. See HStA Dresden, Bestand 10730, Sächsische Gesandtschaft für Österreich, Vienna, Signatur 428, Türkei, Orient-Frage, Kreta-Frage, Bosnische Frage, Tripolis- Frage, Bl. 91–92, 113–114, 161, 165, 185. Includes also the Adriatic, Albanian, Skutari, and Bulgarian-Romanian questions.

41. Cited in Patricia Jalland and John Stubbs, "The Irish Question after the Out- break of War in 1914: Some Unfinished Party Business," in *English Historical Review* 96, no. 381 (1981): pp. 778–807, 781.

42. AT-OeStA/HHStA SB Nl Flotow 3–7/I, "Die 'ukrainische Frage' in ihrer wahren Gestalt," p. 143. In 1915, the Ukrainian nationalist Dmytro Dontsov went so far as to declare that "[e]very time a critical moment for Russia approaches, the Ukrainian question regularly appears like a comet in the political heavens over Eu- rope." Dontsov, *Die ukrainische Staatsidee*, p. 67. With the war, wrote Longin Ce- helskyj in 1915, "the Ukrainian question—as a component of the great war aims—

also pushed itself more to the fore and became relevant." See Cehelskyj, *Die grossen politischen aufgaben des krieges im Osten und die ukrainische Frage* (Berlin: Zentralstelle des Bundes z. Befreiung der Ukraine, 1915), p. 6.

43. In the single archival folder containing the above reference to the Ukrainian question (from the collection of Ludwig von Flotow spanning the years 1913–1920), for example, one can also find correspondence and manuscripts relating to the Serbian and Danube questions. AT-OeStA/HHStA SB Nl Flotow 3–7/I, pp. 28–29, 60–64, 142–145, 167–168. See also, on the sugar question, AT-OeStA/HHStA MdÄ AR F36–188–1, Krieg 1914–1918, Dep. 9, Abt. 6, Mappe 23, Zuckerfrage, esp. Dok. 11, Z. 83.286/1914 and Dok. 12, Z. 85512/1914; and Nachum Goldmann, "Das polnisch-jüdische Problem" [The Polish-Jewish problem], in *Frankfurter Zeitung*, no. 244, September 3, 1915, p. 1 (relates the Polish to the Polish-Jewish question as soluble only together), in HStA Dresden, Bestand 10717, Ministerium der auswärtigen Angelegenheiten, Signatur 2167, Zukunft Polens betr. Judenfrage, 1915–1916, Bl. 16.

44. Поточњак, *Југословенско питање*, unnumbered back of title page.

45. See chapter 3, "Hitler as Question Bundler."

46. See, for example, the Croatian fascist Ante Pavelić's speech on the Croatian question from October 28, 1936 (translated and reprinted in Germany on the eve of the invasion of Yugoslavia in April of 1941). Pavelić, *Die kroatische Frage*, p. 10.

47. Cited in Желјаножски, *Македонското прашање во бугарскиот парламент*, p. 75.

48. *Kurze Darstellung der mazedonischen Frage*, first of four unnumbered pages.

49. See, for example, Paper Prepared by the Ambassador to Vietnam (Taylor) and the Deputy Ambassador to Vietnam (Johnson), Department of State, Central Files, POL 27–14 VIET S., https://history.state.gov/historicaldocuments/frus1964 -68v02/d309; Telegram from the Embassy in Poland to the Department of State (China), Department of State, Central Files, POL CHICOM-US, https://history .state.gov/historicaldocuments/frus1964-68v30/d101; Memorandum of Conversation, Beijing, October 26, 1971, 5:30–8:10 p.m., National Archives, Nixon Presidential Materials, NSC Files, Box 1035, Files for the President-China Material, HAK visit to PRC, October 1971, Memcons-originals, accessed August 17, 2017, https://history .state.gov/historicaldocuments/frus1969-76ve13/d55; "Algerian Question Drives France from U. N.," in *Africa Today* 2, no. 4 (September–October, 1955): p. 3, http:// www.jstor.org/stable/4183730; "Solving Algerian Question: Talks by U.N. Group," in *Times of India*, March 31, 1957, p. 4; India, *Twelve Months of War in Kashmir* (Washington, DC: Govt. of India Information Services, 1948); Pakistan, *The India-Pakistan Question, Kashmir: A Brief Study* (New York: Permanent Mission of Pakistan to the United Nations, 1962); *The Kashmir Question* (Lucknow: The Research Institute of India, 1950); and Abdul Gafoor Abdul Majeed Noorani, *The Kashmir Question* (Bombay: Manaktalas, 1964).

50. See https://books.google.com/ngrams/interactive_chart?content=Question

+alg%C3%A9rienne&case_insensitive=on&year_start=1800&year_end=2000&
corpus=19&smoothing=3&share=&direct_url=t4%3B%2CQuestion%20alg%C3
%A9rienne%3B%2Cc0%3B%2Cs0%3B%3Bquestion%20alg%C3%A9rienne%3B
%2Cc0%3B%3BQuestion%20alg%C3%A9rienne%3B%2Cc0%3B%3BQuestion
%20Alg%C3%A9rienne%3B%2Cc0%3B%3BQUESTION%20ALG%C3
%89RIENNE%3B%2Cc0" width=900 height=500 marginwidth=0 marginheight
=0 hspace=0 vspace=0 frameborder=0 scrolling=no, accessed August 17, 2017.

51. Н. С. Хрущев, "Свободу и независимость всем колониальным народам решить проблему Всеобщего Народам, решить проблему всеобщего разоружения!" [Freedom and independence to all colonized nations solves the problem of the United Nations, solves the problem of general disarmament] *Правда*, 24 сентября 1960 г. (268): 1–4, p. 4. It is interesting to note that the English translation renders Khrushchev's "вопросы" as "problems." "It could be said that these are complicated problems . . . ," etc. "Speech by Mr. Khrushchev, Chairman of the Council of Ministers of the Union of Soviet Socialist Republics, at the 869th Plenary Meeting of the 15th Session of the United Nations General Assembly," September 23, 1960, History and Public Policy Program Digital Archive, United Nations Document A/PV.869: 65–84, p. 84, http://digitalarchive.wilsoncenter.org/document/155185. The slippage between "question" and "problem," which seems to appear with particular frequency in translations from various languages into English, is discussed in greater detail in the Prologue. See, for example, pp. 17 and 231n31.

52. Giuseppe Mazzini, "Alcune parole sulla questione polacca: 30 gennaio 1836" [A few words on the Polish question: January 30, 1836], in *Scritti editi e inediti di Giuseppe Mazzini [The published and unpublished writings of Giuseppe Mazzini]*, vol. 12 (Milan [Rome]: Daelli, 1883), p. 231.

53. This was especially true in France, one of the hothouses of popular and political support for Polish independence. "The Polish question," wrote Edwin de Leon to the rebel secretary of state, Judah Benjamin, in September of 1863, has "entirely obscured ours." FRUS, US Department of State, *Message of the president of the United States, and accompanying documents, to the two houses of Congress, at the commencement of the first session of the thirty-eighth congress*(1863), Supplement, p. cxiv. But that attention to the Polish question was as quick to disappear when the rebellion was put down, as a member of the US legation in Vienna wrote to Union secretary of state William Seward in November of 1863. Ibid., *Papers relating to foreign affairs, accompanying the annual message of the president to the second session thirty-eighth congress*(1864), Austria, p. 122.

54. Roman Dmowski, *Niemcy, Rosja i kwestia polska* [The Germans, Russia, and the Polish question] (Warsaw: Instytut Wydawniczy Pax, 1991), pp. 32, 105.

55. W. A. Arendt, *Des intérêts de l'Allemagne dans la question belge avec des documents sur l'état et l'importance de l'industrie et des chemins de fer en Belgique* [German

interests in the Belgian question, with documents on the state and the importance of industry and railways in Belgium] (Brussels, 1839), p. 1.

56. *Der Humorist*, November 30, 1856, vol. 20, no. 324, p. 1. The passage in question is presented as a quote from a British paper.

57. "Poland," in *Saturday Review of Politics, Literature, Science, and Art* (London), April 27, 1861, p. 2.

58. In 1871, the Scottish MP Robert Macfie argued, along with the Scottish Presbyterian minister and statesman John Dunmore Lang, that the "*Status quo* of the Colonial Question [relating to Australia] was not sustainable" and warned of the "evil" that deferring its consideration would entail. Robert Andrew Macfie, *Colonial Questions Pressing for Immmediate Solution, in the Interest of the Nation and the Empire* (London: Longmans, Green, Reader, and Dyer, 1871), pp. xiii–xiv, 57.

59. Farkas, *A zsidó kérdés Magyarországon*, p. 4; Löwy, *Az ínség és nyomor vége*, p. 4; Század, *A zsidókérdés Magyarországon*, pp. 62, 159.

60. [Wienbibliothekin Rathhaus] Karl Lueger, speech draft, Ca. 1886, Nachlass Karl Lueger, St. Slg. zl. 1257/12, Box II, Mappe: Redekonzepte.

61. See, for example, Deschamps, *Histoire de la question coloniale en France*; TNA, CUST 155/19, Sugar duty: "The Sugar Question" includes a brief retrospect from 1864–1903 (also contains a bibliography, see below on bibliographies); TNA, FO 373/1/17, "History of the Eastern Question"; and TsDA, MVRI, f. 176K, op. 8, a.e. 1071, n.d., "България и беломорскиятъ вопросъ" [Bulgaria and the Aegean question], pp. 17–26.

62. Budge, *Eastern Question Solved*, pp. 8, 12.

63. Ibid., pp. 10–12, 18, 23–24.

64. Cited in Mary Gluck, "The Budapest Flâneur: Urban Modernity, Popular Culture, and the 'Jewish Question' in Fin-de-Siècle Hungary," in *Jewish Social Studies*, n.s., 10, no. 3 (Spring–Summer, 2004), pp. 19–20.

65. *Un mot sur la question polonaise en 1829*, pp. 17, 23.

66. Löwy, *Az ínség és nyomor vége* , p. 13.

67. Sándor Giesswein, *Társadalmi problémák és keresztény világnézet* [Social problems and the Christian world view] (Budapest: A Szent-István-Társulat Kiadása, 1907), pp. 3–4.

68. Budge, *Eastern Question Solved*, p. 82.

69. Tolstoï, *Anna Karenina*, p. 386, see also pp. 340–341, 344–347, 384–388. See Milojković-Djurić, *Eastern Question*, pp. 32–47, 36–37.

70. Sala, "Strange Behaviour," p. 5.

71. See Southey, "The Poor," pp. 187–235, 235.

72. A few book-length works on questions that fit the above description include Masaryk, *Otázka sociální*; Jászi, *A nemzetiségi kérdés és Magyarország jövője*; and Steiner, *Die Kernpunkte der sozialen Frage*. It was also the case that some querists who

might have written pamphlets on a given question chose to write longer works instead since pamphlets were more likely to be subject to censorship. See *Deutsche Allgemeine Zeitung*, no. 95 (April 5, 1846), p. 3.

73. The poem is "To Russia's Detractors" by Alexander Pushkin from 1831, and mentions merely "a dispute between the Slavs / A domestic, age-old argument, too laden with fate / A question that is not for you [Europeans] to solve." Пушкин, "Клеветникам России," pp. 200–202. Sincerest thanks to Joachim von Puttkamer for drawing my attention to this poem.

74. See, for example, Mickiewicz, *La tribune des peuples*; Disraeli, *Tancred*; Dostoievsky, *Diary of a Writer*; Joseph Conrad, *The Polish Question: A Note on the Joint Protectorate of the Western Powers and Russia* (London: privately printed by C. Shorter, 1919); and Léon Deschamps, *Histoire de la question coloniale en France* (Paris: E. Plon, Nouritt et cie, 1891).

75. M. Nault, "J. Fenimore Cooper," in *Mémoires de l'Académie des sciences, arts et belles-lettres de Dijon* (Dijon, 1832), p. 129.

76. To name just a few of the 1848 pamphlets and other publications on "the social question": A. L. Trenn, *Die soziale Frage und ihre Lösung* [The social question and its solution] (Berlin: Reichardt, 1848); *Die soziale Frage im Vordergrunde oder die drei Hauptforderungen der Arbeiter an den Staat . . . : in ihrer Ausführbarkeit nachgewiesen von einem Tuchfabrikanten* [The social question in the foreground, or, the three main demands of the workers on the state, their feasibility proven by a cloth manufacturer] ([s.l.]: Grünberg, 1848); Stella [pseud.], *Studien über die soziale Frage* [Studies on the social question] (Vienna: Gerold, 1848); *An die Urwähler: die soziale Frage* [To the delegate-voters: The social question] (Cologne: DuMont-Schauberg, 1849), accessed July 27, 2014, http://nbn-resolving.de/urn:nbn:de:hbz:061:1-172096.

77. Sand, "La question sociale," pp. 75–78.

78. On drunkenness and sobriety, see Szombatsági, *A nemzetiségi kérdés Magyarországban*, pp. 65–66; Rönyi, *Indokolt programm*, pp. 5, 7–8; and Schlett, *A "munkáskérdés" és a szocializmus a magyar politikai gondolkodásban*, p. 153. On the Gordian knots and vicious circles, see Pitzipios, *Eastern Question Solved*, p. 12; *Szózat a magyar kérdés érdemében*, p. iii; Türr, *A keleti kérdés*, p. 17; Jászi et al., *A nemzetiségi kérdés a társadalmi és az egyéni fejlődés szempontjából*, p. 86; and Széchenyi, *A Jelenkorban Megjelent: Adó és Két Garas*, p. 261. On volcanoes, see Gümüş, Namık Kemâl'e Göre 'Şark Meselesi' ve Osmanlı Devleti'ni Cöküşe Götüren Sorunlar," p. 148; and de Redcliffe, *Eastern Question*, p. 6. On little beasties and spiders, see Dostoievsky, *Diary of a Writer*, p. 429; and Kurt Ehrenreich Floericke, *Spinnen und Spinnenleben* [Spiders and spider life] (Stuttgart: Kosmos, Gesellschaft der Naturfreunde; Geschäftstelle: Franckhl, 1919), p. 51. On ostriches, see Farkas, *A zsidó kérdés Magyarországon*, p. 4; and Löwy, *Az ínség és nyomor vége*, p. 4; Század, *A zsidókérdés Mag-*

yarországon, pp. 62, 159. On magical potions and miracle cures, see Strommer, *A női kérdés és korunk*, pp. 17–18; Bibó, *Válogatott tanulmányok*, p. 795; Schlett, *A "munkáskérdés" és a szocializmus a magyar politikai gondolkodásban*, p. 193.

79. Biedermann, *Frauen-Brevier*, pp. 334–335.

80. *Russell's Magazine* (Charleston), vol. 6, no. 4, January 1860, p. 371.

81. See, for example, Henry Wadsworth Longfellow, *Poems On Slavery*, 2nd ed. (Cambridge: J. Owen, 1842). Whittier wrote an abolitionist pamphlet, but it did not contain mention of the "slavery question." See John Greenleaf Whittier, *Justice and Expediency; or, Slavery Considered with a View to Its Tightful and Effectual Remedy, Abolition* (New York, 1933). For mentions of the "slavery question" in Lowell's publicistic works, see, for example, James Russell Lowell, *The Anti-slavery Papers of James Russell Lowell*, vol. 2 (Boston: Houghton Mifflin, 1902), pp. 54, 168.

82. See Theodor Fontane and Friedrich Eggers, *Theodor Fontane und Friedrich Eggers: Der Briefwechsel: mit Fontanes Briefen an Karl Eggers und der Korrespondenz von Friedrich Eggers mit Emilie Fontane* [The correspondence of Theodor Fontane and Friedrich Eggers, with Fontane's letters to Karl Eggers and the correspondence of Friedrich Eggers with Emilie Fontane], ed. Roland Berbig (Berlin: W. de Gruyter, 1997), p. 251n.

83. Conrad's memorandum was written in 1916. Conrad, *Polish Question*. On the authorship of the memorandum, see Biskupski, "Conrad," pp. 84–98, 90.

84. Fischer, "Der Wandel der sozialen Frage in den fortgeschrittenen Industriegesellschaften."

85. The poem was likely written after 1875. Hugo, "XIV: La question sociale," pp. 321–323.

86. On June 20, 1848, he addressed the constituent assembly on the subject of the "social question" as "the general question which now troubles all spirits and poisons all events . . . stands before us today with threats according to some, with promises according to others." Victor Hugo, "Assemblée Constituante 1848, Ateliers nationaux, 20. Juin 1848" [Constituent Assembly 1848, national workshops, June 20, 1848], in *Oeuvres complètes de Victor Hugo, Actes et Paroles, T. 1* [The complete works of Victor Hugo, documents and speeches, vol. 1] (Paris: Michel Albin, 1937), pp. 124–125. And in June of 1849, as the revolution was living out a long and inglorious reversal, Hugo addressed the assembly again, saying, "[M]isery hangs over the people . . . This misery, this immense public suffering is today the whole social question." Hugo, "Assemblée législative, 1849–1851, Note 9, Proposition Melun, Enquête sur la Misére, Bureaux, Juin 1849," in ibid., p. 346.

87. In a recent biography of Mickiewicz by Roman Koropeckyj, the author writes that "Mickiewicz avoided touching on the Polish question often or in any great detail." Roman Robert Koropeckyj, *Adam Mickiewicz: The Life of a Romantic* (Ithaca,

NY: Cornell University Press, 2008), p. 413. There are some notable exceptions, namely, in some articles he published in his own weekly magazine, *La tribune des peuples*; see Mickiewicz, *La tribune des peuples*, pp. 54, 105, 407.

88. Dostoevsky, for example, addressed several period "questions," among them the "Jewish question" and the "Eastern question," in the pages of his *Diary of a Writer*; see Dostoievsky, *Diary of a Writer*, pp. 428–430, 434–435. See also Grabowsky, *Die polnische Frage*, p. 107.

89. Tolstoï, *Anna Karenina*, p. 386, see also pp. 340–341, 344–347, 384–388.

90. On the discussion in Anna Karenina, and Fyodor Dostoevsky's vehement response to it, see Milojković-Djurić, *Eastern Question*, pp. 32–47, see esp. p. 37.

91. See Fyodor Dostoevsky, *Crime and Punishment*, accessed July 27, 2014, http://www.gutenberg.org/files/2554/2554-h/2554-h.htm.

92. See, for example, Fyodor Dostoyevsky, *A Writer's Diary*, vol. 1, trans. K. A. Lantz, with introduction by Gary Saul Morson (Evanston, IL: Northwestern University Press, 1994), pp. 515–516, 519, 522, 531, 541, 546, 550, 554, 595, 606, 611, 618, 750.

93. As Gary Saul Morson writes in an introductory study to the *Diary*, "Dostoevsky's solution [to the simultaneous emergence of various questions, among them the Eastern and the Catholic questions] is that history manifests a well-plotted story; when Dostoevsky refers to a 'denouement' he is not speaking merely metaphorically. History is shaped like a novel, which is presumably why only a novelist, not a diplomat, could discover its hidden plot." Ibid., p. 36.

94. Algernon Charles Swinburne, "The Question" (1887) in *The Poems of Algernon Charles Swinburne*, vol. 6 (London: Chatto & Windus, 1904), pp. 359–362 (see also W. Robertson Nicoll and Thomas James Wise, *Literary Anecdotes of the Nineteenth Century: Contributions towards a Literary History of the Period* (New York: AMS, 1967) pp. 339–41); Bierce, "Eastern Question," p. 367.

95. Southey, "The Poor," pp. 187–235, 235; Malthus, *Principles of Political Economy*, pp. 9–10.

96. Amicis, "Úvahy o socialné otázce," pp. 8–13, 10–12.

97. Other umbrella questions include the European, Eastern, nationality, and colonial questions, all of which were claimed by commentators as questions of the century, encompassing many others. See, for example, BOA, Yıldız Perâkende Evrâkı, Tahrirat-ı Ecnebiye ve Mâbeyn Mütercimliği (Y.PRK.TKM), Dos. 44, Göm. 33, February 25, 1901 (06/Za/1318 [Hicrî]); de Tocqueville, *Oeuvres complètes*, vol. 3, pt. 2, p. 282 (who called the Eastern question "la grande affaire du siècle"); and Deschamps, *Histoire de la question coloniale en France*, p. 291; see also p. 260. At the European Nationalities Congress in Geneva in 1931, the Baltic German jurist and politician Werner Hasselblatt said of the nationality question that it "belongs among the legal, cultural, and economic questions." TsDA, MVRI, f. 176K, op. 6, a.e. 1843,

p. 83. Ungár, *Egy szó a maga idejében*, p. 4: "[T]here is really only one question, the *great European question* [*az európai összes kérdés*]" (italics in the original).

98. See, for example, de Amicis, "Úvahy o socialné otázce," pp. 8–13, p. 13

99. von Scheel, *Die Theorie der sozialen Frage*, p. 2. See also Giesswein, *Társadalmi problémák és keresztény világnézet*, pp. 79, 128.

100. Biederlack, *Die sociale Frage*, pp. 2–3.

101. These included the agrarian question, craftsman question [*Handwerkerfrage*], worker question, and the woman question.

102. Biederlack, *Die sociale Frage*, pp. 7–9.

103. Ibid., p. 10.

104. Charles Antoine and J. Gonzalez Alonso, *Curso de economía social, por Ch. Antoine* [The trajectory of social economy, by Ch. Antoine] (Madrid: La España Moderna, 1898), p. 1.

105. Louis Garriguet, *Introduction à l'étude de la sociologie: question sociale et écoles sociales* [Introduction to the study of sociology: The social question and social schools] (Paris: Bloud et Barral, 1909), p. 9 (cited from the 8th edition; original edition from 1901).

106. BOA, Yıldız Perâkende Evrâkı, Tahrirat-ı Ecnebiye ve Mâbeyn Mütercimliği (Y.PRK.TKM), Dos. 28, Göm. 37, pp. 1–32.

107. See "An Answering Being" in chapter 2.

108. See, for example, the German Mennonite preacher Leonhard Weydmann from 1834 on *The Questions of Our Tumultuous Time* (cited above); the words of a German member of the Conservative Party from 1883, on using anti-Semitism to "lay the ethical foundation for the solution of the social question"; and a memorandum to the Catholic hierarchy from 1886, noted the "spiritual and moral anarchy" of the time, and that "[i]n the first place the social question is the question of the possibility of, and the means towards, the living re-Christianization of society." Cited in Peter G. J. Pulzer, *The Rise of Political Anti-Semitism in Germany and Austria.* (Cambridge, MA: Harvard University Press, 1988), pp. 113, 158.

109. de Tourville, "Preface," p. vi.

110. Johann Wolfgang von Goethe, *Faust: Eine Tragödie*, "Der Tragödie Erster Teil, Nacht" [The tragedy, part 1, Night] (Stuttgart: Reclam Verlag, 1971), p. 19.

111. Georg Wilhelm Friedrich Hegel, *Grundlinien der Philosophie des Rechts* [Elements of the philosophy of right] (Leipzig: F. Meiner, 1911), p. 272.

112. Karl Marx and Friedrich Engels, *The German Ideology*, accessed July 27, 2014, https://www.uni-due.de/einladung/Vorlesungen/hermeneutik/marxid.htm.

113. Ibid.

114. Eötvös, *A XIX. század uralkodó eszméinek befolyása az álladalomra*, pp. 574–574. This volume was published in German already in 1851. See József Eötvös, *Der Einfluß der herrschenden Ideen des 19. Jahrhunderts auf den Staat* (Vienna: Manz, 1851).

115. Eötvös, *A nemzetiségi kérdés*, p. 9.

116. Ibid., pp. 7, 158.

117. Count László Szápáry in "Országos ülés 1894. október 17-én, szerdán" [National session, October 17, 1894, Wednesday]," in *Az 1892–97. évi országgyűlés képviselőházának naplója*, vol. 20, p. 36.

118. Giesswein, *Társadalmi problémák és keresztény világnézet*, p. vii.

119. Ibid., pp. 3–4.

120. Dostoyevsky, "Never Has Russia Been as Powerful as Now," p. 998.

121. *Revue Politique* (Paris), May 20, 1831, p. 240.

122. See, for example, Becher, *Die Arbeiterfrage*, p. 3; Danilevskii and Woodburn, *Russia and Europe*, pp. 225, 256; Elek Szathmáry, *A szociális munkás kérdés* [The social worker question] (Hód-Mező-Vásárhely: Lepage Ny., 1895), p. 16; X. Y., *Bunyevác kérdés és az 1868-iki XXXVIII. és XLIV. törvényczikkek végrehajtása* [The Bunjevac question and the implementation of laws XXXVIII and XLIV from 1868] (Budapest: Athenaeum, 1895), p. 18; Hobson, *The Social Problem*, p. 91; Steiner, *Die Kernpunkte der sozialen Frage*, p. 10; and Laudyn, *World Problem*, pp. 5–6. "To heal a malady, it is necessary to examine it carefully, analyze it thoroughly and expose its nature fearlessly, before applying the necessary remedies."

123. Stein, *Die soziale Frage*, p. 10.

124. Regarding critiques of day-to-day politics, see, for example, Hobson, *The Social Problem*, pp. 298–299. "The Social Question finds, perhaps, its clearest unity in that common education of the intelligence and goodwill of the citizen ... Society as an organism must be animated by a common moral and intellectual life, vested in individuals who are working in conscious cooperation for a common end." This could not be achieved by politics, Hobson felt, for "[t]urning to concrete politics, [t]he problem drives back into the region of individual character and motive." See also Southey's critique of Malthus on the bullion question.

125. Stein, *Die soziale Frage*, p. 28.

126. Erich Adickes, "Ethische Prinzipienfragen" [Ethical principles questions], in *Zeitschrift für Philosophie und philosophische Kritik*, vol. 177 (Leipzig: Verlag von C. E. M. Pfeffer, 1900): 38–70, p. 39.

127. Stein, *Die soziale Frage*, p. vi.

128. Adickes, "Ethische Prinzipienfragen," p. 39.

129. Ibid., p. 41 (italics in original).

130. Ibid., p. 44.

131. Ibid., p. 69.

132. Ibid., p. 48.

133. Masaryk, *Die philosophischen und sociologischen Grundlagen des Marxismus*, p. 79.

134. Garriguet, *Introduction à l'étude de la sociologie*, p. 9.

135. Weydmann, *Die Fragen*, pp. 1–2.

136. Hobson, *Social Problem*, p. 6.

137. Hannah Arendt, "Ideology and Terror," p. 464.

138. Szombatsági, *A nemzetiségi kérdés Magyarországban*, p. 4.

139. Becher, *Die Arbeiterfrage*, p. 2.

140. Edward Jenkins, *The Colonial Question: Being Essays On Imperial Federalism*, 2nd ed. (Montreal: Dawson Bros., 1871), p. 3.

141. Gregor Samarow [Oskar Meding], *Europäische Minen und Gegenminen: Zeitroman* [European mines and counter-mines: A period novel] (Stuttgart: E. Hallberger, 1874), p. 355. The original reads: "wir dürfen weder Rußland feindlich gegenübertreten, noch auf der anderen Seite dulden, daß die orientalische Frage irgendwie einer endgültigen Lösung oder auch nur einem vorläufigen Abkommen entgegengeführt werde.—Wir müssen Österreich überbieten! . . . Wir müssen es so weit überbieten, daß—alles beim alten bleibt!"

142. Robert Musil, *Der Mann ohne Eigenschaften* [Man without qualities] (Berlin: Rowohlt Verlag, 1957), pp. 1359–1360.

7. The Suspension-Bridge Argument: The Age of Spanning Contradictions

1. Bouwsma, *Wittgenstein*, p. 11.

2. Georg Lukacs, "What is Orthodox Marxism?" in *History and Class Consciousness*, accessed August 16, 2017, https://www.marxists.org/archive/lukacs/works/history/orthodox.htm.

3. See Czartoryski, *Essai sur la diplomatie, par le prince*, pp. iv, 83, 86, 87, 89, 94.

4. Ibid., p. 235.

5. Czartoryski, *Essai sur la diplomatie, manuscrit d'un philhellène*, p. 418.

6. Alfred Briosne, *Remaniement de l'Europe, reflexions sur la question polonaise* [The remolding of Europe, reflections on the Polish question] (Paris: E. Dentu, 1865), p. 19.

7. Batchelor, *Social Equilibrium*, pp. 24–25.

8. TNA, FO 139/44, Austria, Prussia, Russia. Aix-la-Chapelle, September–November 1818, pp. 62, 63v.

9. It was significantly this phrase ("casus foederis et belli") that resurfaced in reference to the automatism of defensive alliances in the years preceding the Great War. See, for example, German secretary of state Alfred von Kiderlen-Waechter cited in John C. G. Röhl, *Wilhelm II: Into the Abyss of War and Exile* (2013), p. 811, http://dx.doi.org/10.1017/CBO9781139046275.

10. *Die Orientalische das ist Russische Frage*, pp. 84–85.

11. Dumons, *Situation*, p. 3.

12. Dostoyevsky, "Never Has Russia Been as Powerful as Now," p. 1000.

13. Ibid., p. 1002.

14. Herzl, "Preface," in *Jewish State*, accessed April 17, 2017, https://www.guten berg.org/files/25282/25282-h/25282-h.htm.

15. Coudenhove-Kalergi, *Pan-Europe*, p. xv.

16. Mickiewicz, *Księgi narodu polskiego*, p. 93.

17. This was evident already with the first pamphlet on the Polish question from 1829, which drew attention to "the dangers that threaten the political balance of Europe, the independence and nationality of peoples." *Un mot sur la question polonaise en 1829*, pp. 17, 23.

18. See Mandl, Danilevsky, and others cited above in "The Federation Consensus" section. See also Holly Case, "The Strange Politics of Federative Ideas in East-Central Europe," in *The Journal of Modern History* 85, no. 4 (December 2013): 833–866.

19. See Biskupski, "Conrad," pp. 84–98, 87, 90.

20. Nor was Conrad unique in this respect. With regard to the Ukrainian question, the Ukrainian nationalist Dmytro Dontstov made a similar claim at roughly the same time. "Were Russia to be defeated," he wrote, then the Central European empires could finally solve the Ukrainian question, but until then "no lasting peace can be expected." Dontsov, *Die ukrainische Staatsidee*, p. 67.

21. Conrad, *Polish Question*, p. 10.

22. Ibid., p. 12.

23. Hillgruber, *Staatsmänner und Diplomaten bei Hitler*, vol. 1, p. 315. Hitler to Molotov, November 13, 1940.

24. *Akten zur Deutschen Auswärtigen Politik, 1918–1945*, Serie E: 1941–1945, Band V (Göttingen: VandenHoeck & Ruprecht, 19[?]), doc. 229, p. 440.

25. I have written about this elsewhere. See Case, "Strange Politics," pp. 833–866.

26. Г. П. Генов, *Рухна последната постройка на Версайлската система. Реч, произнесена на 9 май 1941 година в столичния Военен клуб* [The collapse of the last structure of the Versailles system: Speech delivered to the Sofia Military Club, May 9, 1941] (София: Всебългарският съюз „Отец Паисий," 1941), pp. 7-8.

27. This emerged from a 1935 draft of the Arrow Cross platform titled *Cél és követelések* (Goal and demands) in which Szálasi laid out plans for the undoing of Trianon and the creation of the "United Lands of Hungary" (Hungária egyesült földek). USHMMA, RG-30.003, Reel 10, Collection of Hungarian political and military records, 1909–1945, frame 8.

28. Dostoyevsky, "Diplomacy Facing World Problems," p. 995.

29. Herzl, *Jewish State*, p. 56.

30. Trotzky, *Bolsheviki and World Peace*, p. 58.

31. Domarus, *Essential Hitler*, p. 399, 404.

32. Tourville, "Preface," p. vi.

33. Coudenhove-Kalergi, *Pan-Europe*, p. 16.

34. Ernest Germain, *Jewish Question since World War II* (July 1946), accessed April 16, 2017, https://www.ernestmandel.org/en/works/txt/1946/jewish_question_since_world_war.htm.

35. Carl Schmitt, *The Concept of the Political* (Chicago: University of Chicago Press, 2007), p. 48. "It is manifest fraud to condemn war as homicide and then demand of men that they wage war, kill and be killed, so that there will never again be war."

36. Danilevskii and Woodburn, *Russia and Europe*, pp. 225, 256.

37. Ibid., p. 332.

38. Karl Kraus, *Pro domo et mundo* (Munich: A Langen, 1912), p. 6.

39. Grabowsky, *Die polnische Frage*, p. 3.

40. Ibid., pp. 3–4.

41. Adolf Hitler, *Hitler's Table Talk, 1941-1944: His Private Conversations* (New York: Enigma Books, 2000), p. 540. It should be noted that this edition of Hitler's conversations is generally not considered to be as reliable as the one cited elsewhere (namely, the version based on Heinrich Hein's notes: Hitler, *Monologe im Führerhauptquartier*). For a partial inventory of the mistakes in *Hitler's Table Talk*, see Hitler, *Monologe im Führerhauptquartier*, pp. 16-18. But since the Hein volume does not include any of the conversations from March 12 to August 1, 1942, *Table Talk* is the only source we have for this conversation, so I have cited it here. Although this is not one of the records with known errors, the reader should nonetheless view it with caution.

42. Miklós, *Eötvös József könyvei és eszméi*, pp. 5, 9, accessed June 27, 2014, http://mek.oszk.hu/03100/03176/03176.pdf. Bényei does not cite Szécsen's as one of the books that influenced Eötvös. Though the two likely knew each other, Eötvös had early on been a minister in the Hungarian revolutionary government of 1848 but spent much of the period in Munich.

43. Eötvös, *A XIX. század uralkodó eszméinek befolyása az álladalomra*, pp. 574–574.

44. Eötvös, *A nemzetiségi kérdés*, p. 9.

45. Ibid., pp. 7, 158.

46. Ibid., p. 157.

47. Pulszky, *Töredékes észrevételek a Dunaszbályozás s keleti kérdés iránt*, p. 65.

48. Szécsen, *Politische Fragen der Gegenwart*, p. 150.

49. Eötvös, *A nemzetiségi kérdés*, pp. vi–vii.

50. Ibid., p. 157.

51. Szécsen, *Politische Fragen der Gegenwart*, p. 13; Eötvös, *A nemzetiségi kérdés*, p. 79.

52. Hitler, *Monologe im Führerhauptquartier*, p. 122; Musil, *Der Mann ohne Eigenschaften*, p. 270.

cotton question, 73
Coudenhove-Kalergi, Richard, 136,
    138, 146, 152, 157, 213, 215–217
Crimean War, 7, 48, 107, 110–111
Croatian question, 53, 94, 126–127,
    275n123
Czartoryski, Adam, 82–83, 98, 107, 109,
    112, 136, 145, 151, 209–211, 257n13,
    266n32; Polish question and, 74–75,
    102, 112, 257n12, 270n55
Czech question, 9, 44, 127, 128, 132
Czermak, Emmerich, 96
Czyński, Jan, 140

Dalmatian question, 127
Dampmartin, Anne-Henri Cabet, 139
Danilevsky, Nikolai, 103, 107, 149–150,
    217–218
Danubian question, 55, 127, 218, 247n75
Danzig question, 126, 129
Davies, Norman, 18, 179
Defoe, Daniel, 27
dentist question, 73
Deringil, Selim, 178
Deschamps, Léon, 83
diplomacy, 41, 43, 45, 210; press and
    public opinion as, 47, 48, 172; rein-
    vention of, 6, 74, 151
disarmament question, 188
Disraeli, Benjamin, 9, 109–110, 112, 160;
    Tancred, 47, 110, 166, 167, 172
Dmowski, Roman, 189
Dobrudja question, 127, 132
Dontsov, Dmytro, 69, 304n33, 306n42,
    316n20
Dostoevsky, Fyodor, vii, 5, 9, 17, 161,
    196, 202, 204, 213, 312n93. *See also*
    Eastern question: Dostoevsky on
Douglass, Frederick, 9, 182
Dragomanov, Mikhail Petrovich, 13
Driault, Édouard, 145
Duane, William, 157
Dumons, François, 105, 147, 212–213

Ďurčanský, Ferdinand, 128

Eastern Crisis, 144, 190, 306n37
Eastern question, 6, 10, 11, 12, 13, 18,
    49–50, 53–55, 76, 80, 92, 99, 103,
    105–114, 116, 137, 139, 141–151, 169,
    176, 182, 185–186, 212; definitions of,
    4, 17, 70–71, 110, 112, 157, 158, 179,
    208, 218; Dostoevsky on, 13, 96,
    107–108, 112, 120, 142, 159, 166–167,
    196, 213, 215–216, 270n59, 285n37;
    doubts about, 158–160, 162–167,
    170–171, 174, 177–179, 192–193,
    293n43, 296n81; Gladstone and, 48,
    144, 164–165, 190; Marx on, 99, 111–
    112, 150; origins of, 156, 260n42,
    290n15, 291n23; Tocqueville on, 9,
    81, 143, 159; Tolstoy on, 8–9, 177,
    192, 196
East India question, 36, 38, 239n14
East-West dynamic, 105–115, 151, 169
education question, 83–88
Eggers, Friedrich, 195
emancipation, 2, 12, 72, 75–80, 92, 97,
    117, 118, 123, 137, 154, 165, 172, 179,
    255n5; arguments against, 93–94,
    101–104, 146, 149
Engels, Friedrich, 99, 159, 200–201
English question, 71
Eötvös, József, 56–57, 68, 99, 201–202,
    218–220, 317n42
European question, 41, 50, 78, 104, 136,
    138, 140–144, 146, 166, 213, 216,
    284nn21–22

Fadeev, Rostislav, 120, 274n105
Faluhelyi, Ferenc, 68
Farley, J. Lewis, 144
federalism, 135–136, 140, 144–151,
    214–218
Fergusson, Robert Cutler, 284n21
Final Solution. *See under* solutions
Finnish question, 129

A NOTE ON THE TYPE

This book has been composed in Arno, an Old-style serif typeface in the classic Venetian tradition, designed by Robert Slimbach at Adobe.